Information Security Governance Simplified

From the Boardroom to the Keyboard

OTHER INFORMATION SECURITY BOOKS FROM AUERBACH

Information Security Governance Simplified

From the Boardroom to the Keyboard

TODD FITZGERALD, CISSP, CISA, CISM

Foreword by Tom Peltier

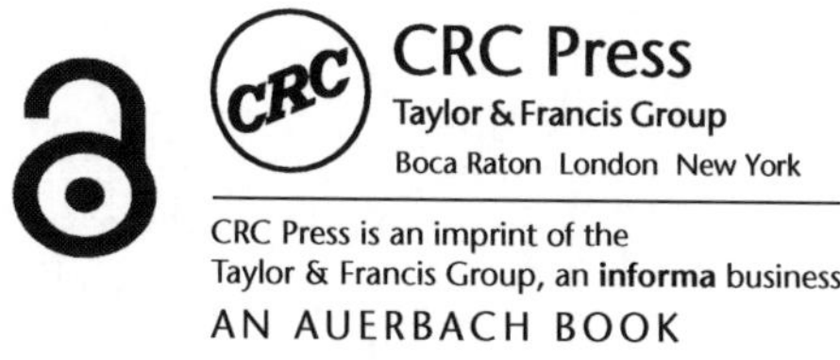

CRC Press
Taylor & Francis Group
6000 Broken Sound Parkway NW, Suite 300
Boca Raton, FL 33487-2742

First issued in paperback 2020

ISBN-13: 978-1-4398-1163-4 (hbk)
ISBN-13: 978-0-367-65922-6 (pbk)

Visit the Taylor & Francis Web site at
http://www.taylorandfrancis.com

and the CRC Press Web site at
http://www.crcpress.com

To my wife Char, for without her endless love, daily caring, understanding, support, and positive outlook on living this life, this book would still be an idea waiting to happen and life would still be waiting to be lived.

Contents

Foreword

For nearly 35 years I have been closely involved in information security and the development and implementation of supporting policies, standards, and procedures. This has often been an overlooked and undersupported portion of implementing an effective information security program. What was missing in the early years was an authoritative examination of the processes needed to manage the implementation of such a program from executive row to entry-level personnel.

Todd Fitzgerald's new book, *Information Security Governance Simplified: From the Boardroom to the Keyboard*, presents 15 chapters of advice and real-world experience on how to handle the roll out of an effective program.

Corporate governance addresses the foundation upon which an organization will build its information security program. The foundation of a successful information security program begins with strong upper-level management support. This support establishes a focus on security within the highest levels of the organization. Without a solid foundation (i.e., proactive support of those persons in positions that control information technology [IT] resources), the effectiveness of the security program can fail when pressured by politics and budget limitations. Chapter 2, "Developing Information Security Strategy," provides insight into what is needed to establish the foundation upon which a security program can be built.

Any information security program must get its direction from executive management. The requirements of today's laws and regulations have identified either the organization's board of directors or an executive management steering committee as responsible for instituting an effective program. To be effective, the typical security professional will need to learn how to interact with the "C-suite" of executives. Chapter 4 addresses this key issue and provides valuable tips on how to sell the program to management.

The responsibilities for each group of management and employees must be established. Typically the roles and responsibilities are established in mission statement, and Chapter 3, "Defining the Security Management Organization," will give the reader the tools needed to establish a workable information security charter. Once this is established, the need to establish the formal job descriptions will help complete the security organization's infrastructure.

An effective security program needs practical security policies and procedures backed by the authority necessary to enforce compliance. Practical security policies and procedures are defined as those that are attainable and provide meaningful security through appropriate controls. The ability to determine the effectiveness of the security program is not easily obtainable if there are no procedures in place. Chapter 6, "Creating Effective Information Security Policies," will provide the keys to success in this endeavor.

Developing and establishing an effective security program requires the ability to capture and provide meaningful information on program effectiveness. To provide meaningful data, quantifiable security metrics must be based on IT security performance goals and objectives, and be easily obtainable and feasible to measure. They must also be repeatable, provide relevant performance trends over time, and be useful for tracking performance and directing resources. Chapter 7, "Security Compliance Using Control Frameworks," addresses some of these elements.

The security program itself must emphasize consistent periodic analysis of the program. The results of this analysis are used to apply lessons learned, improve the effectiveness of existing security controls, and plan future controls to meet new security requirements as they occur. Accurate data collection must be a priority with stakeholders and users if the collected data is to be meaningful to the management and improvement of the overall security program. The chapter to really look forward to is Chapter 11, "The Auditors Have Arrived, Now What?"

Todd has taken the time to include for the reader some practical security considerations for managerial, technical, and operational controls. This is followed up with a discussion on how legal issues are impacting the information security program.

I have known Todd for a number of years, and I asked his peers and colleagues to give their impressions of him and as a consensus we came up with the following: Todd is outgoing, ambitious, social, appears to love what he does, and is very passionate about helping those he works with. He seems to especially enjoy doing training activities for information security topics, in particular how they relate to Health Insurance Portability and Accountability Act (HIPAA). One more adjective for Todd would be enthusiastic; he uses more exclamation points in his writing than any other person I know!

Finally, Todd provides some thought-provoking insights in the final chapter, "17 Ways to Dismantle Information Security Governance Efforts." I know I've been guilty of at least a couple of them. The only thing more enjoyable than reading Todd's book on information security governance simplified would be to be part of one of his sessions where you get to see and hear his enthusiasm.

Tom Peltier, CISSP

Acknowledgments

One of the secrets of speakers at security conferences is that we learn much from the process of preparing the material and from the individuals who chose to attend the session. This book represents the culmination of the interaction of many conference attendees from San Francisco to Vienna, sharing their knowledge, as well as from my own experience in leading or advising information security program development for several companies. I am forever grateful to all those who speak up during the sessions with their ideas, whether in agreement or not with what I may be selling. I want to thank Madeline Parisi, Robert Richardson, Jean Hey, David Lynas, and Marci McCarthy from Information Systems Audit and Control Association (ISACA), Computer Security Institute (CSI), Management Information Systems Training Institute (MISTI), Computer Security Audit and Control (COSAC) Symposium, and Information Security Executive (ISE)/ Tech Exec Networks (T.E.N.), respectively, for providing me with the opportunity to share ideas through speaking engagements at international and national conferences over the past decade. It has provided me with the opportunity to meet so many wonderful people with different perspectives from different places.

Thanks to Tom Peltier for his relentless contribution for advancing the information security field to the profession it is today and for graciously writing the foreword to this book.

Thanks to the many people who asked me along the way, "How is the book coming?" You know who you are but may not realize the positive impact that had on me. It may been just the energy I needed to make it through one more late night, early morning, or weekend afternoon writing (I do have a day job!). Thanks for the positive encouragement to keep on writing.

I save the biggest thanks for two people last, first Hal Tipton. Hal has been reviewing my writings for almost a decade, and stretched my knowledge and writing ability by having me contribute to the articles to the *Information Security Handbook* about varying subjects. And finally, Rich O'Hanley, who suggested that I write my first article years ago and has shown unwavering support for my efforts ever since. Rich's ideas, confidence, and patience are truly admirable qualities.

Introduction

He that would govern others, first should be the master of himself.

Phillip Massinger, 1583–1640

Information security as a *technical practice* has been around long enough that some individuals have retired from an entire career focused on information security. As a career path with multiple disciplines as part of a *profession*, information security has only gained real traction over the past 10 to 15 years. In fact, many of the laws, regulations, standards, and control frameworks driving how information security controls are implemented have been promulgated in the new millennium.

Security incidents have prompted companies to implement controls in a reactive nature, without the benefit of a planned governance framework to guide the security investments. New laws have mandated compliance dates where organizations work steadfastly toward the dates by placing a check in the completed box to demonstrate compliance. Security activities are occurring as threats exploit vulnerabilities within organizations and require attention to information security governance (doing the right thing) and information security management (doing things right). The following are key actions that need to be addressed to provide effective information security governance to protect the information assets:

- Align the security program with business needs
- Develop an information security strategy
- Create the information security management structure
- Communicate effectively with the CEOs (chief executive officers), CIOs (chief information officers), and CFOs (chief financial officers)
- Determine and manage acceptable risk
- Create security policies with organizational participation
- Select a governing control or standards framework
- Select the appropriate, risk-based controls that align to the laws and frameworks
- Prepare for and leverage internal and external audits to enhance processes
- Create a security-aware culture
- Understand the existing and emerging laws and regulations impacting the organization
- Learn from the security incidents of others
- Recognize pitfalls to information security governance

The body of knowledge for information security is extensive, including the managerial, operational, and technical issues represented by the various control requirements. So how does an organization effectively manage the information security practices to ensure compliance with the laws, increase the predictability of business processes, establish a structure to optimize the use of security resources, provide a process for effective risk management, and ensure that the appropriate organizational stakeholders are sufficiently involved? There is no silver bullet, however, the information security governance guidance provided in this book provides insights as to what actions will increase the certainty that the information security program will be effective and reduce the likelihood that internal and external threats will damage the information security program.

The information security officer role has been emerging and was initially viewed primarily as a technical role. However, today the function must combine leadership, managerial, and technical abilities, with the emphasis on the leadership and managerial abilities to provide the critical policy and business guidance to support the enterprise. This book provides guidance to build an information security program that incorporates the policies, standards, communications, relationships, organizational structures, and controls necessary to be effective not just for this week or this month, but as part of a long-term information security strategy addressing the appropriate laws and business operations.

This book is written for

- Information security officers (including chief information security officers, directors, and managers of information security)
- Technical information security professionals
- Internal and external auditors
- Risk managers
- Board of directors
- Information technology (IT) leadership/steering committees
- CEOs, CFOs, CIOs
- Technical specialists
- Compliance officers, privacy officers
- Legal staff, general counsel
- Executive/senior/middle/first-line management
- End users

Chapters 1 to 4 lay the information security governance foundation by focusing on getting the right strategy, security management organization, and relationships with the executives and middle management in place. Chapters 5 and 6 begin with insights on risk management and ensuring the appropriate security policies, standards, guidelines, and procedures are developed to enable the organization to formalize management's intent for the specific controls addressed in Chapters 7 through 10. Chapter 7 provides discussion of the various control frameworks and standards, with Chapters 8 through 10 providing practical security considerations for implementation of the controls. Chapter 11 discusses how to prepare for and leverage external audits, followed by Chapter 12 that provides insight to the "soft skills" and security awareness communication skills needed to deliver the security message effectively. Chapters 13 and 14 provide a survey of some of the current laws impacting information security as well as recent incidents of others, which can provide lessons learned for our organizations. And finally, Chapter 15 provides 17 ways to dismantle the efforts that have been set forth in the previous 14 chapters, as well as some final thoughts.

The chapters are structured in a way that this book may also be used as a textbook for a semester course. Each of the 15 chapters can be used as the basis for discussion of the different key topics that make up the foundation of a great information security governance program.

This book shares insights about what works and what does not work when building the information security program to protect a company's information assets. The chapters that follow are based upon practical experience versus a theoretical concept pulled from a documented framework. As you read these chapters, ask yourself, "How would this work in my organization?" or "What do we have in place to mitigate that issue?" Your experience and resulting solutions may be very similar or vastly different depending upon the company culture and constraints. The important point is that the questions raised in these chapters are asked and action plans to address how the organization should manage information security are *consciously decided.*

I hope that you will enjoy reading this book as much as I enjoyed writing it. If, as you are reading through this book, you have some "aha, that's a great idea" moments, or "yes, we are doing that too," or it spurs some new thought altogether that helps you, then I am glad to have helped make a difference.

About the Author

Todd Fitzgerald, CISSP, CISA, CISM, ISO27000, CGEIT, PMP, HITRUST, and ITILV3 certified, is responsible for external audit technical compliance for National Government Services (NGS), Milwaukee, WI, one of the largest processors of Medicare claims and a subsidiary of WellPoint, Inc., the nation's leading health benefits company, serving 1 out of 9 Americans. Fitzgerald has initiated, developed, and led information security programs as the Information Security Officer for several companies. Fitzgerald served as the chair/co-chair for the 2011/2010 ISACA North America and Europe Information Security & Risk Management conferences.

Fitzgerald coauthored, with Micki Krause, the 2008 (ISC)² Press book titled *CISO Leadership: Essential Principles for Success.* Fitzgerald has authored articles on information security for the *2007 Official (ISC)² Guide to the CISSP Exam*, *The Information Security*

Handbook Series (2003–2012), *The HIPAA Program Reference Book*, *Managing an Information Security and Privacy Awareness and Training Program*, *CISM Review Manual*, and several other security-related publications. He is also a member of the editorial board for *(ISC)² Journal/Information Systems Security Magazine.* Fitzgerald is frequently called upon to present at international, national, and local conferences for Information Systems Audit and Control Association (ISACA), Computer Security Institute (CSI), Information Systems Security Association (ISSA), Management Information Systems Training Institute (MISTI), COSAC, and the Centers for Medicare & Medicaid Services (CMS) systems security officer community. He also serves on the board of directors for the HIPAA Collaborative of Wisconsin and several other industry groups. Fitzgerald has received several awards including a Midwest Information Security Executive of the Year Award Finalist award and Health Ethics Trust HIPAA Implementation Award.

Fitzgerald has 32 years of information technology experience, including 20 years of management and the past 13 years focused solely on information security. Prior to joining NGS, he held various broad-based senior information technology management positions for Fortune 500 organizations, including American Airlines, IMS Health, Zeneca (subsidiary of AstraZeneca Pharmaceuticals), and Syngenta, as well as prior positions with Blue Cross Blue Shield of Wisconsin.

Fitzgerald holds a BS in business administration from the University of Wisconsin-Lacrosse and serves as an advisor to the College of Business Administration, as well as an advisor to the Milwaukee Area Technical College information security program. He also earned an MBA with highest honors from Oklahoma State University.

1

Getting Information Security Right

Top to Bottom

Our chief want in life is somebody who shall make us do what we can.

Ralph Waldo Emerson, 1803–1882

The Rocky Mountains are an amazing display of nature that stretch across the western states. The mountains have been viewed many times in travels to the West Coast, but the real beauty of the mountain tops and the depths of the canyons can be appreciated best by taking a long train ride from Chicago to San Francisco. It becomes clear that the majestic tops of the mountain cannot exist without the canyons down below; rocks of all sizes grace the mountain, with little rocks sometimes holding up the big rocks, and sometimes vice versa; vegetation is sometimes very sparse, yet it seems to have a role there; and finally, as strong as the mountains are, man has sometimes blasted their way through, with tunnels like the Moffat Tunnel, which is 6.2 miles long and cut the distance between Denver and the Pacific Coast by 176 miles in 1928.

We like to think of our organizations as solid fortresses built on solid rock foundations that cannot be blasted through. We like to believe that all of the little rocks at the bottom in our organizations are being led to a greater vision by the top, massive rocks that often sit at the top of the mountain. We like to believe that our organizations are strong enough to endure any headwinds or storms that will come our way. We want to believe that what may have taken many years to build will endure and fend off competitors. Yes, we want to believe we have built a solid foundation just like those shown in Figure 1.1. As we all know, large rocks once at the top of the organization sometimes

Figure 1.1 Building a security rock foundation.

crumble, or are subject to attacks by avalanches, acting as external forces that serve to threaten the stability of the organization.

What does this have to do with information security? Plenty and the answer is twofold. First, without building within the organization an adequate security foundation that can withstand external and internal threats from the environment, our organizations will become reactionary to protect the information assets. Second, the security organization must be adopted within the context of a larger whole—involving the board of directors, senior management, middle management, frontline supervisors, and the end user in order to have sustained success over time. Engaging individuals in a constructive security commitment to the organization does not happen by accident but rather must be intentional. Individuals must know what their responsibilities are at all levels to protect the confidentiality, integrity and availability of the assets. We call this knowledge *information security governance.*

Information Security Governance

Governance comes from the Latin origins to define "steering" or to "have power over." Information security governance defines the roles and expectations of the management levels and nonmanagement levels alike so that each party understands what it is responsible for. Without taking the time to define these expectations, organizations will still operate with a set of practices, but they may not achieve the desired result. Failure to define a set of security policies leads individuals to make up their own rules and methods of operating, which may not be in the best interest to the organization. Information security governance grants the power to the appropriate individuals to carry out the security mission.

Performance expectations in the form of qualitative and quantitative metrics should be set to ensure that the security program is being fulfilled. For example, if it is expected that everyone in the organization receive security awareness training, including the executives, then this information should be tracked and evaluated against a standard, just as market share, increases in revenue, and hitting cost targets are measured within the organization.

Undesirable outcomes are avoided with a strong information security governance program. Since expectations of each management level are articulated and communicated according to their role, the likelihood is reduced that activities are not performed correctly. For example, if the organization sets a policy of shredding sensitive documents at the end of the day, and the vice president of the claims area decides to dedicate an employee to shred the many claims that need to be disposed of quickly, he or she may choose to hire an external contractor to come onsite to shred the documents. If the vice president chooses this action, he or she then needs to make sure that this is permissible under the information security policy, even though intentions are consistent with the policy. There may be retention requirements or background policies for the contractor that could be violated. The decision-making process followed by the executive must follow the thought process for the information security program. In other words, can the executive make this decision on his or her own? Or does the executive need to obtain approval from the information security officer? If an external vendor is chosen, how does the executive ensure that the information will be properly protected in transit and destruction? Are there existing contracts in place? How will the documents be stored securely onsite until they can be shredded?

This example illustrates why it must be clear within the organization who has what authority and role with respect to information security. The individuals within the organization need to be able to perform their roles within the policies and procedures that have been agreed upon, as well as have the ability to recognize when an exception to a policy needs to be considered and then subsequently seek appropriate approval prior to implementation.

A security governance framework controls and coordinates the security activities within the company. For example, knowing that an end user department must have all access requests for its local applications processed by security administration increases the likelihood that the appropriate segregation of duties principles are being enforced. It also indicates the organization's desire to control all access through centralized management and not permit individual departments to set up their own administration activities, where the organization may have decided that there was a likelihood that the access approvals would be granted by someone who was also a user of the system having the access capability but not the proper management authority. The proper logging mechanisms of the request, approval, and granting of the access request may also not be in place in the end-user department. Just as the organization controls who enters individuals into payroll (human resources) and who approves salary increases (managers and the manager's supervisor), it needs to establish clear control over the information security activities.

Information security governance also defines processes to control the activities. Standard operating procedures should include documented processes to carry out the security mission as well as indicating who has the authority to approve the processes.

The policies, processes, and decision rights for a specific area of responsibility must be maintained to provide consistent management of the enterprise. The IT Governance Institute's (ITGI) definition of information security governance reads, "Information Security Governance is a subset of enterprise governance that provides strategic direction, ensures objectives are achieved, manages risk appropriately, uses organizational resources responsibly, and monitors the success or failure of the information security programme" (ITGI, n.d.).

Tone at the Top

Why is it at a third-grade concert, you hear the squeaky flute or the strings on the violin that went astray? The entire saxophone section could be sounding in perfect harmony, but if one, and just one was playing with a bad reed, the efforts of the rest of the saxophone section will not even be heard or recognized for its good work. If we like to think of our organizations as orchestras, then the conductors leading the instruments of all types need to also ensure that they are contributing to excellence by walking the walk. People in companies are very smart and look for cues that the senior management is advocating and following the rules that it is expected to follow. If it is not, then associates at the lower organizational level in the company fail to see the credibility in the rule and feel that they can also bypass the security policy.

Tone at the Bottom

Some legislation, such as the Health Insurance Portability and Accountability Act (HIPAA) final security rule mandated that all people within the organization receive security awareness training (DHHS, 2003). The senior executives were not exempt from attending the training. Subsequent audits could reveal that the senior management was not participating. In practice, when the senior management would attend security awareness training along with their staffs, it had the side effect of showing the staff, "Hey, this must be important." The words and actions from senior management should not be underestimated in their impact. Alternatively, if a manager is discounting the need for a policy and decides not to follow it, he cannot expect others on his team to take the policy seriously. If, for example, he comes to work one day and forgets his physical ID access badge and asks a staff member to "just let me in," the manager should not be surprised when a staff member holds the door open for another person at another time.

Organizations have traditionally been managed with a hierarchical command and control structure, whereby the individuals at the top of the organization define the policies that must be adhered to by the rest of the organization. As long as management is demonstrating consistent application of the rules and these rules make sense to them, these rules are likely to be followed. If the manager encourages the associate to cut corners to meet deadlines on a regular basis, this may carry over into the end users attitude toward sidestepping information security policies to meet their deadlines.

Nonmanagement associates tend to discuss what is going on in their departments and their leadership, and even if an individual's own leader is a stickler for following the rules, failure to follow the rules by other department leaders can have a negative impact on the performance of the individual, questioning why the other department does not have to follow the same security rules.

Governance, Risk, and Compliance (GRC)

A variety of laws and regulations have surfaced over the past decade in an attempt to strengthen the security of information stored within the companies to which the information assets are entrusted. As a result of the laws that have been enacted, various security control "standards" and "frameworks" have evolved and become popular means to meet the requirements of the laws. Since laws and regulations are intentionally developed at a higher "what needs to happen" level versus the "how to secure the information" level, the standards and control frameworks become valuable tools to ensure that security is planned, organized, implemented, tested, and monitored.

Governance, risk, and compliance (*GRC*) is a term that has been embraced primarily by the vendor community in recent years in recognition of the fact that companies are struggling with the plethora of controls which must be implemented to meet the extensive requirements of the laws and regulations. Governance is simply the structure, policies, and practices that are put in place by the organization to ensure that the controls are adequately communicated, carried out, and enforced by engaging direction and support at the appropriate organizational level. Risk is the act of making informed decisions about the losses that the company is willing to accept given a breach of security and building the appropriate mitigating risk strategies to reduce the risk to acceptable levels defined by the business. Compliance is ensuring that the controls are being adhered to on an ongoing basis, thereby increasing the likelihood of a reduction of risk and increased adherence to the governance intended by the organization (Fitzgerald, 2008).

The three components of governance, risk, and compliance are necessary for adequate security controls; however, implementing them does not ensure that a security program is adequate. Compliance is a necessary control that has been recognized by governments for centuries. Criminal acts, by their very nature, are forms of noncompliance with the laws that are in place. Take driving a car for example. As a teenager obtains his or her driver's license, the diligent parent warns about the downside of not following the laws, reckless driving, speeding, and paying attention to parking and vehicle regulations. The teenager says, "Sure Dad, no problem" and forgets 5 minutes later as they morph into their busy teenage social network of friends and peer pressure, away from the constant reminders of Mom and Dad. Teenagers do not realize at the time the consequences of their actions. Or, maybe they do subconsciously, but it is not the most important thought in their daily "work life." Time goes on, piling up speeding tickets, tickets for excessive window tinting, unpaid parking tickets, and so on until one day they have the opportunity to pay their own car insurance! The parent at that point transfers the risk to the child, and then the learning of true cost of noncompliance begins. The risk is ultimately acknowledged and accepted, and new mitigating strategies are put in place, such as better driving. Organizations are made up of many busy "teenagers," each of which are influenced by their peer work groups and need to be educated as to the future costs of noncompliance to the security controls. Adopting a control framework is a good start. However, compliance must be addressed as an ongoing, deliberate strategy.

The Compliance Dilemma

Answers.com provides a definition for compliance as "the act of complying with a wish, request, or demand; acquiescence." It further provides a definition that may resonate with how many companies feel about the plethora of government regulations: "a disposition or tendency to yield to the will of others." Compliance with security regulations is no trivial task; in fact, in a survey conducted by the Security Compliance Council, as much as 34% of information technology resources were being consumed to demonstrate compliance

(Hurley, 2006). These are valuable, technical resources that could be deployed to other high-value, new development efforts or to improving the efficiency of operations, but rather are being utilized to ensure that the regulations are being followed. This is a significant burden for large businesses. However, in smaller businesses the resources dedicated may be smaller in numbers, except that the hidden costs must be considered, such as burnout of the one or two information technology (IT) people who are working many hours of overtime to comply.

Compliance ensures that due diligence has been exercised within the organization to meet the government regulations for security practices. Compliance can be achieved in many ways, as many of these regulations provide a higher-level definition of the requirement of what must be done; however, the lower-level, platform-specific details of how the solution is implemented are typically not stated in the regulation itself. The regulation's primary task is to ensure that the appropriate processes are in place, people are aware of their responsibilities, and technical issues are appropriately managed. The regulations are drafted at a policy level and, as such, it would be difficult to mandate the selection of a specific platform from a particular vendor, as this would provide an undue advantage for that vendor. Furthermore, because technology changes at a pace faster than the policy-making process, by the time new legislation was enacted, the legislation would most likely be out of date. This approach would also stifle innovation by mandating the use of specific, currently present technology to address security challenges.

The landscape of government regulations and security control frameworks covered in the subsequent sections is shown in Figure 1.2. These laws, regulations, and security control standards and frameworks are covered in more detail in subsequent chapters. These provide the structure for what must be complied with to protect the particular vertical industry security protection and assurance needs, as well as some potential frameworks for selecting and managing the controls within those frameworks. There is value in reviewing the security laws and standards outside of the mandates within a particular industry (for example, reviewing the Federal Financial Institutions Examination Council [FFIEC] handbook while being subject to HIPAA security requirements), as this may provide security control thought leadership to strengthen the security program.

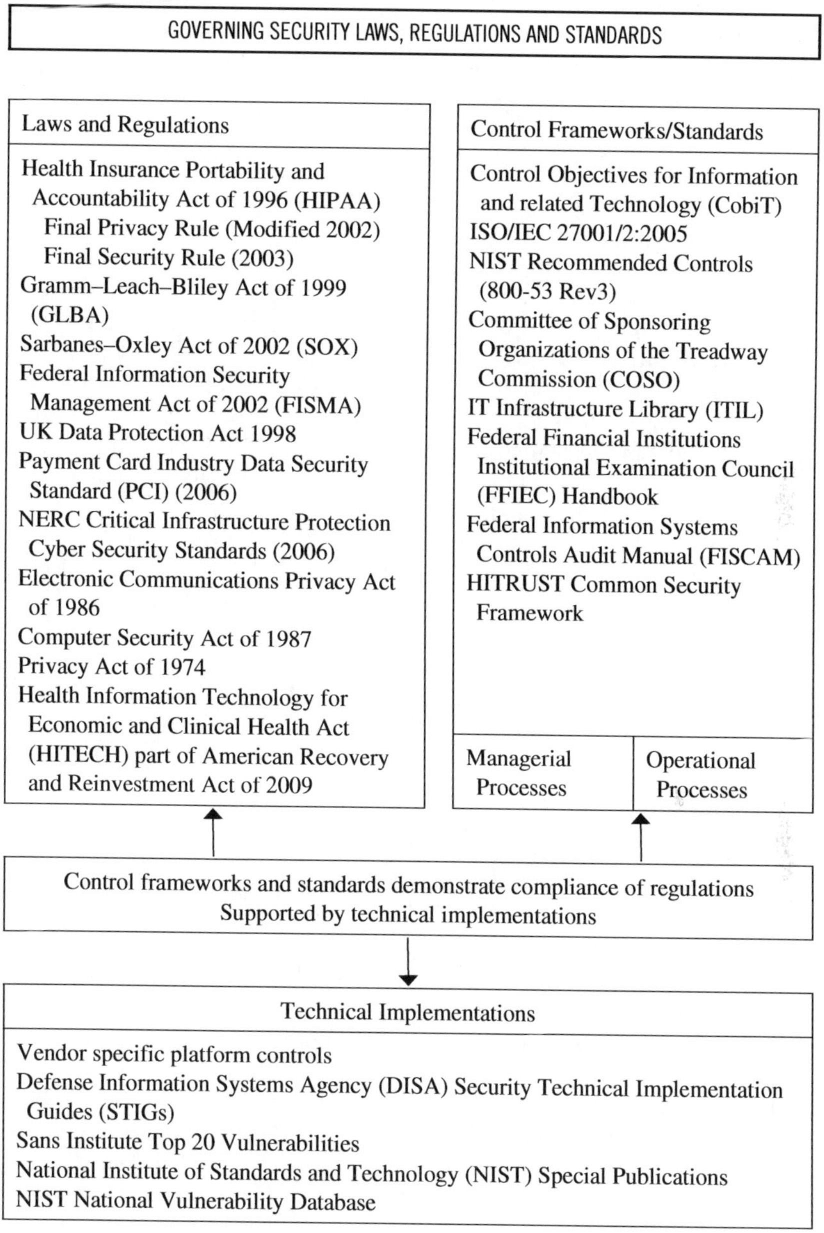

GOVERNING SECURITY LAWS, REGULATIONS AND STANDARDS

Laws and Regulations	Control Frameworks/Standards	
Health Insurance Portability and Accountability Act of 1996 (HIPAA) Final Privacy Rule (Modified 2002) Final Security Rule (2003) Gramm–Leach–Bliley Act of 1999 (GLBA) Sarbanes–Oxley Act of 2002 (SOX) Federal Information Security Management Act of 2002 (FISMA) UK Data Protection Act 1998 Payment Card Industry Data Security Standard (PCI) (2006) NERC Critical Infrastructure Protection Cyber Security Standards (2006) Electronic Communications Privacy Act of 1986 Computer Security Act of 1987 Privacy Act of 1974 Health Information Technology for Economic and Clinical Health Act (HITECH) part of American Recovery and Reinvestment Act of 2009	Control Objectives for Information and related Technology (CobiT) ISO/IEC 27001/2:2005 NIST Recommended Controls (800-53 Rev3) Committee of Sponsoring Organizations of the Treadway Commission (COSO) IT Infrastructure Library (ITIL) Federal Financial Institutions Institutional Examination Council (FFIEC) Handbook Federal Information Systems Controls Audit Manual (FISCAM) HITRUST Common Security Framework	
	Managerial Processes	Operational Processes

Control frameworks and standards demonstrate compliance of regulations
Supported by technical implementations

Technical Implementations
Vendor specific platform controls Defense Information Systems Agency (DISA) Security Technical Implementation Guides (STIGs) Sans Institute Top 20 Vulnerabilities National Institute of Standards and Technology (NIST) Special Publications NIST National Vulnerability Database

Figure 1.2 Landscape of governing security laws, regulations, and standards.

It is important to recognize at this point that the information security governance program leverages the laws, regulations, frameworks, and standards from multiple places and may have to simultaneously be compliant with multiple laws and regulations. The chapters that follow provide the necessary "security rocks" for laying the information security governance foundation.

Suggested Reading

1. National Institute of Standards and Technology (NIST). August 2009. Special Publication 800-53 Rev3: Recommended security controls for federal information systems and organizations. http://csrc.nist.gov/publications/nistpubs/800-53-Rev3/sp800-53-rev3-final_updated-errata_05-01-2010.pdf
2. Government Accountability Office. January 1999. Federal Information Systems Controls Audit Manual (GAO/AIMB-12.19.6). http://gao.gov/special.pubs/ai12.19.6.pdf
3. Cobit 4.1, IT Governance Institute, http://www.itgi.org, n.d.
4. Hurley, J. 2006. The CSO's security compliance agenda: Benchmark research report. *CSI Computer Security Journal* 22: 37–44.
5. Wikipedia, http://www.en.wikipedia.org/wiki/information_security_governance, n.d.
6. Defense Information Systems Agency (DISA). Security Technical Implementation Guides (STIGS), http://iase.disa.mil/stigs/stig
7. International Organization for Standardization (ISO). ISO/IEC 17799:2005 Information technology security techniques—Code of practice for information security management. http://www.iso.org/iso/en/prods-services/popstds/informationsecurity.html
8. SANS Institute Top 20, www.sans.org/top20
9. NIST National Vulnerability Database, http://nvd.nist.gov
10. Department of Health and Human Services, Office of the Secretary. February 20, 2003. 45 CFR Parts 160, 162, and 164 Health insurance reform: Security standards; Final rule. Federal Register 68(24). http://www.hhs.gov/ocr/privacy/hipaa/administrative/securityrule/securityrulepdf.pdf
11. Department of Health and Human Services, Office of the Secretary. August 14, 2002. 45 CFR Parts 160 and 164 Standards for privacy of individually identifiable health information; Final rule. *Federal Register* 67(157). http://www.hhs.gov/ocr/privacy/hipaa/administrative/privacyrule/privruletxt.txt
12. Fitzgerald, T. 2008. Compliance assurance: Taming the beast. In *Information Security Handbook*, H. Tipton and M. Krause, eds., chap. 28. Boca Raton, FL: Auerbach.

2

Developing Information Security Strategy

Mirrors should reflect a little before throwing back images.

Jean Cocteau, 1889–1963

Most organizations today have a vision statement to direct the company employees to conduct business in a way that meets the overall goals of the organization. Vision statements are generally very short so that employees can easily grasp the essence of the strategy and behave in a manner that is consistent with the strategy. This is helpful to determine the right course of action in absence of a documented policy. Just as the overall business needs to have a vision, mission statement, goals, and action plans, so does the information security program if it is to sustain long-term viability and be effective in meeting the needs of the business.

What happens more often than not is that a need for information security appears one day as the result of an incident, public disclosure of information, a new law or regulation that must be complied with, or an inquiry from a member of senior management that was reading about a security incident that was experienced by a competitor in the news. This scenario is depicted in Figure 2.1. What follows is that someone is assigned to resolve the incident or come up with what needs to be done for information security. The individual assigned is usually within the information technology (IT) department, as security is usually seen as an information technology problem to be solved. The person then takes this assignment on, in addition with his or her other responsibilities, and starts fixing the problem at hand. After a series of small successes and a further understanding of the scope of information security, the person charged with addressing information security requests more resources and is initially met with resistance.

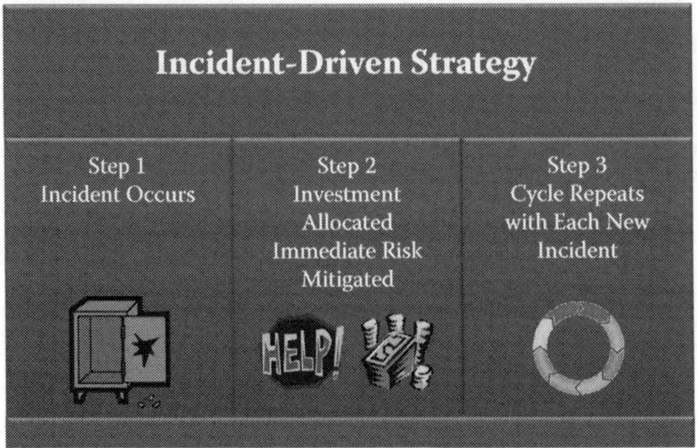

Figure 2.1 Incident-driven security strategy approach.

A few more projects are taken on, and problems tackled, increasing the visibility of the security function. In this scenario, the strategy is the result of looking in the rear-view mirror and articulating the accomplishments of what has been completed in an attempt to gain more funds to further more initiatives. Thus, the strategy emerges, so to speak, and is generated from a bottom-up approach.

An alternative approach is to perform an assessment of the information security practices that are in place by hiring an external firm to conduct an objective review, and then creating short and long-term multiyear plans for addressing the problem areas, concentrating on the areas of highest risk first as depicted in Figure 2.2. This top-down approach is beneficial in that it provides broad coverage for all of the domains and can be established without focusing on an immediate trigger, as in the bottom-up approach. The top-down approach also takes into consideration the risks of the security areas evaluated, whereas the immediate, bottom-up approach starts by focusing on the issue that is getting the most visibility at the time.

One could argue that using an immediate security incident to spur the organization into action is not developing a strategy at all and is more akin to running by the seat of your pants. The reality is that organizations do not always have the foresight or the knowledge within the organization to recognize the role that information security should play within the business. They may not have an advocate for information security that can articulate how implementing information security can be good for the business by reducing costs,

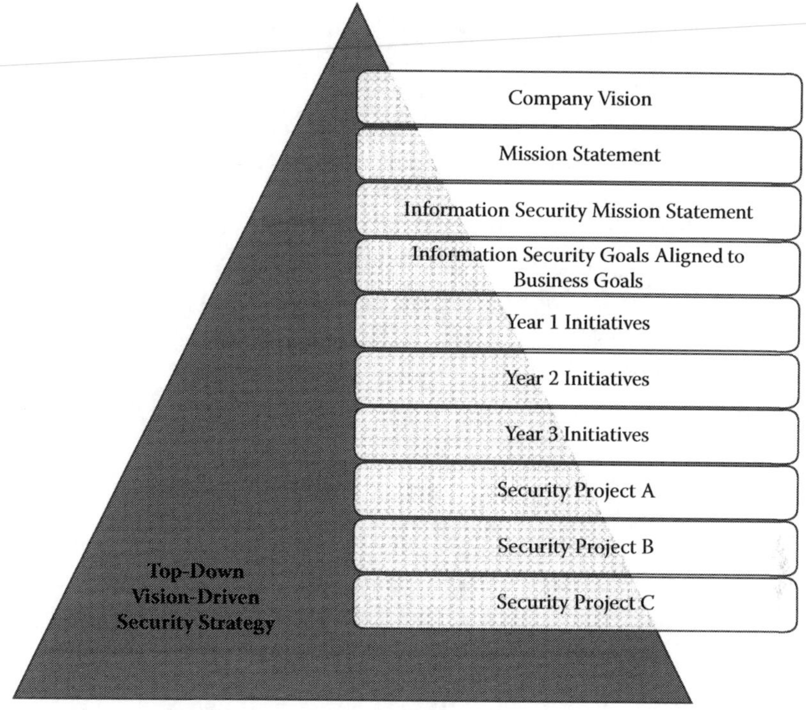

Figure 2.2 Top-down vision-driven security strategy.

increasing market share, creating a competitive advantage, and so on. Imagine also that a security incident is occurring and the person assigned says, "We should create a strategy to develop and implement an information security program to deal with this." Using the nomenclature put so well within the book *Good to Great* (Collins, 2001), there may not be a seat on the next bus for that individual! When there are urgent business problems to solve, the first order of action is to put out the fire, and then work on the fire suppression equipment and safety procedures, buy fire extinguishers, and so forth. The same principle applies to security incidents; although they may spur us into action and get the ball rolling, we must address the immediate issue at hand first.

A third type of strategy development is by not consciously creating a strategy at all, as shown by Figure 2.3. Organizations that could be classified as security unaware fall into this category. They are the organizations that have individuals performing security functions, however, not in a premediated manner. Security "happens" within

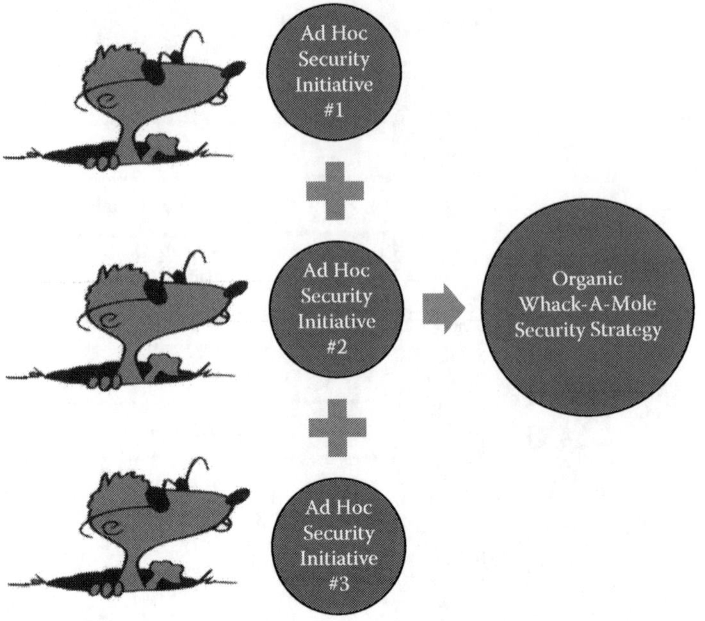

Figure 2.3 Organically driven whack-a-mole security strategy.

these organizations as different individuals are assigned the various functions of information security, whether or not it is called that. For example, the systems administrator may receive requests for access via e-mail and she provides the access requested. An individual is responsible for moving source code to production status within the version control software. The help desk administers password resets upon request. Security functions are distributed across different individuals within the organization without a master plan of what should be performed. Risk assessments and reviews of the latest threats are usually nonexistent in this type of organization. Plans for upcoming initiatives are sparse and new initiatives are generated by the next large incident that impacts availability or an unintended public disclosure.

So whatever method has been used to initiate the development of an information security strategy, whether leveraging the security incident in the bottom-up strategy or via the preplanned, systematic top-down strategy assessment, or by not consciously creating a strategy, it should be recognized that all organizations have one. The more planned the strategy is, the more likely that the strategy will be one that meets the needs of the business and is properly aligned with the business strategy. The unconscious strategy has a relatively slim chance of meeting the needs of the business, as security events tend to drive what the security response will be versus a thought-out plan for the future. Few companies can afford to take risks without knowing the risk that they are assuming by doing nothing (more about information security risk assessment is covered in Chapter 5 about risk management). The chance that an unconscious effort will address each of the information security domains prior to when they are needed in a proactive manner is like spinning the roulette wheel to determine what the next business strategy would be.

The rest of this chapter will focus on the top-down or bottom-up strategy development approach as viable alternatives for developing an information security strategy. Although each organization will vary in the areas that are of most importance, the subsequent sections provide some areas that need to be considered when developing the strategy. Failure to do so can cause the information security program to be out of touch with the needs of the business and not in alignment.

Evolution of Information Security

No security book would be complete without recognizing how the computing environment has changed from the early days of the mainframe to distributing computing to personal computers to laptops to smart phones. Rather than exploring the laborious details of the challenges that each of these environments provided, suffice it to say that the number of platforms have increased and the data has moved further away from the data center "glass house." We are having to protect information that is more accessible in more ways by more people than ever before. The quantities of information desired are also staggering.

Even with the proliferation of information and the complexity of the environments that house this information, information security as a whole is still regarded as an IT issue that involves the creation of user IDs or accounts, and issuance of passwords. That's it. Although it is important to get the security administration, identity management, or access management correct, that is only one piece of the information security program. The various functions that must make up an information security program are explained in detail in the security management chapter (Chapter 3). When developing any information security strategy, it is important to understand that the common view of individuals within the organization may be that the security staff's role is limited to the issuance of user IDs and granting access. There may be an education process necessary prior to engaging individuals in the development of an information security strategy or the focus may center on the traditional security administration functions.

Organization Historical Perspective

Before developing the security strategy, the person responsible for developing the strategy needs to understand the organization's past experiences with information security. Organizations tend to have long memories with projects that failed and relatively short-term memories with projects that were successes and had little visibility. If the previous security officer implemented a strategy that failed, possibly evidenced by their short tenure or abrupt departure, then it would behoove the new security officer to informally obtain what some of the issues were and the approaches attempted to solve them. This does not mean that the same approach would not work by a new person with additional management support or attempted under a different set of new circumstances, but the reasons should be uncovered as quickly as possible. Failure may have been due to not enough resources applied, lack of available technical expertise, failure to communicate project vision, lack of management support, and so forth. Alternatively, it may have had more to do with clashes of personality of the individual responsible for the implementation utilizing an autocratic approach versus a collaborative approach.

Fear, Uncertainty, Doubt, Fear, Uncertainty, Doubt

One reason that the predecessor's information security strategy may not have been well received by the organization was that the security officer utilized the fear–uncertainty–doubt cycle. It works like this:

Step 1—A security incident occurs that gets (unwanted) management attention.

Step 2—The security officer indicates what a large problem this is and requests a large amount of funding to implement new controls, hire more resources, and so forth to fix the problem. This is usually the response to a senior executive's question of, "How can we prevent this and ensure it does not happen again?"

Step 3—The security officer implements the solution and all is well … until the next time the same event happens.

Step 4—Repeat steps 1 through 3. The security officer indicates that there is new technology that will reduce the risk even further.

Step 5—A new incident occurs, and the same process is followed again.

What is wrong with this model? Many security officers will echo the sentiment, "There is nothing like a good incident." Although it is true that the first incident raises the level of awareness and importance that adequate controls be in place and many times does provide the necessary funding, the problem is the second, third, and fourth time the "sky is falling" message is given, Chicken Little tends to get little additional funding. The response from senior management is more likely to be to find a way to prevent the issue from reoccurring with the resources that have already been provided. The reality is that the fear, uncertainty, and doubt message tends to dissipate over time and is not effective. It is much more effective to have a security strategy roadmap that provides concrete enhancements to the business to deal with the threats facing the organization.

Understand the External Environment

Companies work within the context of a much larger environment and are subject to external circumstances beyond what is created by them. These include the regulatory environment, strategies of the competitors, being aware of the emerging threats, knowing the cost structures, and leveraging the external independent research that is available.

Regulatory

Each organization should understand the regulatory environment within which it participates. Is it a publicly traded company subject to the Sarbanes–Oxley rules? Does it maintain protected health information (PHI) and subject to the Health Insurance Portability and Accountability Act (HIPAA)? Does it serve customers in one of the 40-plus states that have enacted security incident notification laws? Are they processing credit cards and subject to the Payment Card Industry Data Security Standards (PCI DSS)? The regulatory environment will drive security rules that have been mandated for the particular public or private sector.

Competition

Most boards of directors want to know how the security strategy and investment compares with the strategy of their competitors. The objective in many companies is to spend no more and no less than that of their competitors, unless security is seen to provide a competitive advantage that is worth the additional investment. It can be very difficult in practice to ascertain what the competitors are actually spending on information security, as this information is not generally shared. Companies may discretely obtain information from social media websites (e.g., job profiles on LinkedIn articulating current function and activities for individuals in security roles) or from attendees at conferences. They may also have information from other employees that were hired away from competitors. Intelligence, whether formal or informal, is obtained at some level by an organization, hopefully through ethical means, to enable the organization to differentiate their products and services to obtain a competitive advantage.

The reason organizations prefer to spend the same amount on information security as their competitor is that an organization must allocate funds across the different business units in a way that maximizes profitability. Spending more on a function such as information security, which is traditionally viewed as an overhead cost (i.e., does not increase revenue), would normally be viewed as money that is not available to grow the business. This assumption makes security investment a hard sell in most organizations; however, being able to articulate competitor investments in developing the strategy is one way to garner support for the strategy. This is especially true if the competitor will be using this knowledge to bid on or obtain new business that the company is also pursuing. Spending the same amount in this context provides the board of directors the comfort that it are not overspending, while at the same time, providing the comfort that it is exercising due diligence in funding the security efforts. If a security breach occurs in the future and the company is subject to external governmental review or a lawsuit, the board can provide justification that it spent an appropriate amount on information security given the business climate in which the company operates.

Emerging Threats

Many information security threats are common across industries in that they represent vulnerabilities to generally available software. Vulnerabilities in Microsoft Office or the latest vulnerability found within Adobe Reader represent opportunities for the hacker to exploit the code, irrespective of the industry in which the company resides. The ability to exploit the opportunity has more to do with how widespread the technology is used within the organization and the manner by which defense-in-depth strategies have been deployed to protect the information assets.

The strategy needs to consider the emerging threats in building the security strategy. As discussed further in Chapter 5, certain types of information will need more protection focus than others and will need further protection strategies. For example, an organization that processes credit card information or handles social security numbers, will want to know where that information is located via the data classification activities. This information is more likely to be the subject of a targeted attack and will need to be protected appropriately.

Technology Cost Changes

When developing an information security strategy it may appear that the costs for a particular solution may be cost prohibitive when the strategy is initially developed. Since technology costs are continually dropping due to competition, increasing technology advances, impact of mergers and acquisitions, and by companies trying to increase market share, once a security strategy is put in place, the initial cost assumptions should be revisited. For example, it was not uncommon for database administrators to be reluctant to implement logging of the database servers due to the perceived impacts to performance and the requirement that large amounts of disk space be used. As recently as the mid-1990s, the cost for this disk space could easily run into the millions of dollars for a few terabytes of storage. Today, we know that the local electronics or office supply store can provide the same storage capacity for less than $50. Thus, the cost of implementing a logging and monitoring solution today involving terabytes of information would not be nearly as expensive and should be part of the strategy for an organization with the appropriate resources.

External Independent Research

Organizations such as Gartner, Forrester, The Burton Group, and others are valuable sources for product evaluations, emerging strategies, and emerging trends. These organizations provide predictions, typically 2 to 3 years out, of what vendors and products are leaders in their field. They also provide a vast amount of information on the products themselves and how they may fit into the security solution. Organizations do not have the funds to research all of these products themselves, even through a request for proposal (RFP) process. RFPs can yield a great deal of information for a given security business need, but at the same time require significant resource time to adequately send out the requests, evaluate the responses, score the responses, hold vendor presentations, and make a final selection. RFPs are good vehicles if the organization has the time and resources, or is narrowing the selection of an expensive long-term solution. The external independent reports can serve as input into jump-starting the RFP process, or in less expensive solutions, quickly provide a cost-effective path toward product selection.

The Internal Company Culture

The company external environment is clearly important to information security strategies, as they represent how the world is interacting with our organizations. The internal company culture has a great impact on how successfully our security programs will be received. Although it would be nice to be able to copy another organization's security strategy, implement the strategy in ours and call it a day, unfortunately no two organizations have the same "norm of operation" and a security strategy that may work for one company may not work for another.

The following are areas to give some thought to. It may not even be readily apparent how the organization is operating and may need the perspective of several individuals at different management and end user levels to achieve an accurate assessment.

Risk Appetite

A community banking organization may have a low risk appetite and will tend to make very risk-averse decisions. A small credit union, for example, may wait until the technology is well developed or many other companies have embraced the technology before committing to its use. Establishing an Internet banking presence in the early days, for example, was only embraced by the large banks with sufficient resources to commit to the technology, thus minimizing the risk. Today, even small organizations have embraced the online banking technology as a business imperative. The risk is perceived to be less when the application has been installed by several hundred banks and supported by a software vendor with the ability to spread the security development costs over multiple customers versus building the application with the limited resources of a single small credit union.

Risk-averse organizations will tend to have more rigid rules for information security and less likelihood to grant exceptions. On the other hand, innovative organizations promoting creativity or research will tend to allow more creatively. Users may be allowed to purchase and download designer or specialized software on their machines that a more structured environment would not allow. For example, a company such as Apple that is very innovative would be more permissive internally to promote creative expression than a pharmaceutical manufacturer would be with those engaged in tracking product shipments. This is not to say that one organization cares about security and the other does not, as both are concerned about the protection surrounding intellectual property within their companies. What differs is the internal approach to information security and securing the information in a way that provides security that is consistent with the culture, business operations, and management direction, and at the same time provides an adequate level of protection from unauthorized users.

Some organizations view new technology like oil wells and are willing to invest the money in multiple initiatives knowing that several will fail, understanding there will be one that is successful and will make up for the others. These organizations have the ability to invest larger amounts because they can spread their costs across many more users, systems, or products and services. If the solution does not turn out to be effective within a few years, the same organization will invest funds to replace it with a better solution. The smaller organization is more likely to select a product that will last for a longer period of time, and live with or incrementally enhance the usage of the product.

Speed

Organizations move at different speeds, some acquiring one business and then acquiring another before the first acquisition is fully implemented. A major airline published its new innovative sales promotions in the newspaper about 3 weeks prior to when the IT department needed to have the systems available for processing the new promotion. Several programmers made sure they read the ads in the newspaper each day so they could be aware of what the marketing department was selling. This strategy was done to ensure that the promotion was kept under wraps until absolutely necessary so that the competition did not find out. This is an example of an organization working with lightning speed. How long do projects typically take? Weeks? Months? Years? An 18-month implementation will not be very well received in an organization that typically implements initiatives in a 3-month timeframe. The security strategy needs to mirror the speed culture of the organization.

Collaborative versus Authoritative

Organizations structured in a command-control-type organization where the subordinates are expected to follow the directives of their immediate supervisors tend to operate in an authoritative manner. Individuals may be encouraged within the organizations to suggest improvements to existing practices or suggest new processes; however the decision-making authority resides within the superior manager and is pushed down through the organization. Security policies and procedures are introduced via directives and established at higher levels within the company. Alternatively, collaborative organizations tend to request input and more discussion prior to the decisions made. Decisions are made collectively by a team or steering committee to achieve consensus on a particular direction. Security councils are very well received within this type of organization, and security policies are less likely to emerge solely as directives from one department.

Knowing who are the individuals in an authoritative structure whose opinions shape most of the company actions and plans would be beneficial. Time would be well spent with these individuals early in the strategy planning process to get them behind the strategy. In the collaborative organization, the senior executive may be looking for clues that opinions were solicited from others within their organization before they will agree to the strategy.

Trust Level

An organization with low trust levels is a very difficult organization to work within, as it is unclear as to whom the message needs to be communicated to for it to be effective and who is ultimately in control. In this type of organization, it may be necessary to increase the number of stakeholders that need to accept the security strategy. By garnering broader support it will be harder for a single individual acting on his own to undermine the security strategy. Trust level can be evaluated by matching the statements made and the actions observed. Two-way trust is obviously preferred to exist at the beginning of strategy development. However, the security officer may have to take the first step by implementing projects within the committed timelines and functionality promised to build the trust over time.

Individuals may also have hidden agendas related to their own advancement that the security officer should be conscious of. If a security strategy is viewed as adding time to a project that the individual is responsible for implementing, or it is perceived that the project may not meet the deadline as a result of a new security policy, the individual may not fully support the implementation. The worst case may come when the manager appears to support the security initiative publicly, meanwhile does little to advance the effort. The manager could also not like the constraints that security places on operations, not like structure, or may have been dissatisfied with the length of time it takes the security department to onboard a new employee. Whatever the reason, it is important to understand which individuals are advocates for the security program and which individuals will serve as detractors.

Growth Seeker or Cost Cutter

Stocks can be classified in many different ways, such as large capitalization stocks (greater than $1.5 billion revenue), small capitalization stocks, domestic, international, or by the sector or industry in which they operate. Stocks are also classified as to whether they are considered a growth stock or a value stock. A growth stock is one in which there appears to be significant opportunities for the stock to grow in the future. These stocks typically represent either new start-ups or innovative established companies with product ideas that have not reached their full potential. Value stocks are those stocks where companies are perceived to be worth more than their book asset value, but for some reason, have been beaten down by the market and are now out of favor. These stocks are purchased in the hopes that someday the negative events pushing down the stock price are changed and the stock will rise in value.

All companies want to increase revenues and cut costs. The distinction that is important here is that growth companies tend to invest more money than value companies in future product development and are more likely to embrace a growth security strategy that projects initiatives into the future that may not have immediate payback. Value companies, on the other hand, may be out of favor and are looking for significant cost reductions to increase the stock value. Projects may be cut and layoffs may be the norm to regain financial viability. If an organization is in cost-cutting mode, and the security officer suggests a project with a large financial commitment with a payoff several years into the future, this may be embraced by a growth-oriented company that is willing to take the risk, but not by the value-oriented company that is searching for new ways to cut costs. There needs to be an immediate or short-term payback to gain the support of leadership with the cost-cutting company.

Company Size

Large companies tend to be more willing to invest in more initiatives as noted earlier, in large part because the total impact to the budget of the organization will be less when initiatives do not work out as anticipated. In other words, larger organizations have the ability to hedge their bets. On the flip side, larger organizations are sometimes more bureaucratic, with more buy-in and management approval necessary before the initiative can move forward. Security strategies need to take this into account when establishing timeframes for implementation. Whereas a smaller organization may readily accept a contract from a vendor without challenging it due to the lack of legal support or leverage with the large vendor, a large organization may require a couple of months to move the contract through the legal process. Similarly, a small organization may not need the level of documentation that a large organization may need to conduct business. For example, a small doctor's office with an office staff of two people may not need as formal of a termination process ensuring that the keys to the office are changed versus a large organization of 100,000 employees that would need card access systems and documented proximity badge collection policies, recertification policies, and new badge issuance policies. The small organization still needs to address each of the security domains within the security strategy. However, the degree of definition, documentation, and approach to satisfying the domain will be vastly different.

Outsourcing Posture

The security strategy should consider the company's inclination to outsource functions or processing. What has been the history of the company? Is someone else currently providing the IT services for the organization? Is processing occurring outside of the United States? The outsourcing posture has implications not only for how the security organization should be managed as a function (employees, contractors, or outsourcing of pieces of the security function), but also for the controls that must be put in place for information assets being processed by another company or beyond our borders. If the cost savings are significant or if the quality of work is viewed to be superior to the work that could be done internally, the security strategy must be written to incorporate controls that make the processing feasible. Quite often, the outsourcing decisions are made at a very high company level with limited detailed input of costs at the time of agreement, as they tend to be kept very confidential. Few individuals are in the loop at this juncture.

The security strategy needs to ensure that contractual obligations are established and it is clear how the external functions will be managed. Take the case of outsourcing the server support to an external company. The question that should be addressed by the security strategy is who is responsible for the disaster recovery of the information if it is lost. Is the outsourcer responsible for maintaining and testing backup tapes on a regular basis? Is there a hot site in the strategy or is there redundant hardware supported by the outsourcer? There is nothing inherently wrong with outsourcing functions, where it typically goes wrong is when expectations are not clear. Finding out that the outsourcer only retains backup tapes for 1 month when the security strategy indicates that the organizations servers are recoverable for a period up to one year could cause an unwanted issue for the organization. Without the proper strategy and agreements in place, such as service level agreements, the lack of backups beyond 1 month may not be discovered until there is a need for recovery of critical information, a point that would be too late and could have been prevented by creating the appropriate security outsourcing strategy.

Prior Security Incidents, Audits

Evaluation of the prior security incidents can be of great value in developing an information security strategy. Did an end user leave a box of confidential information in his car with the engine running, only to have it stolen? Did an executive share her password with her administrative assistant so she could access her e-mail? Was the business strategy sent unencrypted across the Internet? Was a misconfigured firewall responsible for an external party using the mail server to send spam? Did a review of external background checks by the contracting company reveal that only 5 out of 25 background checks occurred? Incidents provide a wealth of information as to what actions are not being performed within the company. Security incidents are like mice—where you see one, you must have many more that are not seen. The question to ask when building the security strategy is, Do I have a stated control in place, as evidenced by the existence of a policy, procedure and implemented activity which serves to mitigate or reduce the likelihood or impact of this event occurring? If the answer is no, then this item needs to be included in the security strategy. The tendency to evaluate how important an incident is by the number of occurrences should be avoided, as there may only be one incident, but the potential impact may be large.

Internal and external audits also provide significant knowledge as to the process breakdowns within an organization. For instance, companies may do a very good job in documenting the policies and procedures, but may do a very poor job of executing them. Is the problem one of communication (awareness)? Is the problem due to shortcuts taken to implement a new system or change a system by the weekend? Is the problem one of misinterpretation? Or is there a personal disagreement with the standard or lack of supporting technical controls to support the policy? Audits should be reviewed and unresolved findings should be used to enhance the security strategy. Previously resolved findings can also provide input, as an issue may have been resolved by a quick fix to remove the finding, but a better long-term solution may be warranted and should be reflected within the security strategy.

External audits may or may not provide recommendations to mitigate the audit issue depending upon the nature of the audit (some firms will not provide recommendations in the post-Enron era as this may be viewed as a conflict of interest as it could possibly be viewed as providing consulting services). If they are providing an attestation of the controls, they are not supposed to provide advice. However, many auditors will informally be willing to provide their opinions outside of the formal written report as to what types of actions would have made the situation be a nonissue and not result in a finding. This information can be very valuable in constructing the strategy, as the auditors are exposed to many different solutions across industries and companies.

If the organization is in the business of contracting work to other organizations, the government, or a parent company, other formal reviews of past performance should be reviewed. Reviews of past performance may include metrics such as quality, timeliness, meeting project deadlines, and so forth. These reviews can highlight areas where information security may be able to help. For instance, if there are delays in the early morning call center availability due to virus scans starting at undesirable times, the information security strategy could examine methods to shift the running of the scans, reduce the time of the scans by allocating more hardware or faster desktops, or examine alternative products for deployment.

Security Strategy Development Techniques

Specific information security strategy considerations for each of the information security domains are noted in the appropriate security control determination chapter for the primary managerial (Chapter 8), technical (Chapter 9), and operational (Chapter 10) controls. These provide some insight into the questions that should be asked to formulate the information security strategy. Following are some of the techniques that can be used to develop the strategy specific to the company.

Mind Mapping

Mind mapping (Buzan, 1996) is a very powerful technique to extract thoughts out of different individuals and subsequently organize those thoughts. Mind mapping encourages the free flow of thought and organizes these thoughts together. The greatly simplified process works according to the following steps:

1. The topic is drawn in a circle in the center of a flip chart for a group or on a piece of paper if done individually.
2. Lines are drawn outward from the circle in a spider-like fashion to represent the main thoughts. These lines are labeled with the thought.
3. Thoughts come to people's minds from the main spokes drawn in step 2 and are added as smaller perpendicular lines from the main spokes and labeled.
4. This process is repeated, drawing more perpendicular lines or branches from the prior lines until the majority of the thoughts around the subject noted in the circle are expressed.

For example, if the circle in the middle was labeled "Develop an Information Security Program" some of the thoughts that may come to mind are policies, procedures, staffing, vulnerability testing, access control, business continuity planning, and strategy development. These could form the spokes coming from the circle and then as the brainstorming continued, more thoughts could be added. The word "staffing" may cause expression of the words experience, certifications, education, years in the industry, security tool knowledge, budgets, number of staff, and training. Then the training spoke could be explored and the concepts of cost, training organization, type, prerequisites, tracking, and so forth could be added to the training branch. A sample mind map is shown in Figure 2.4.

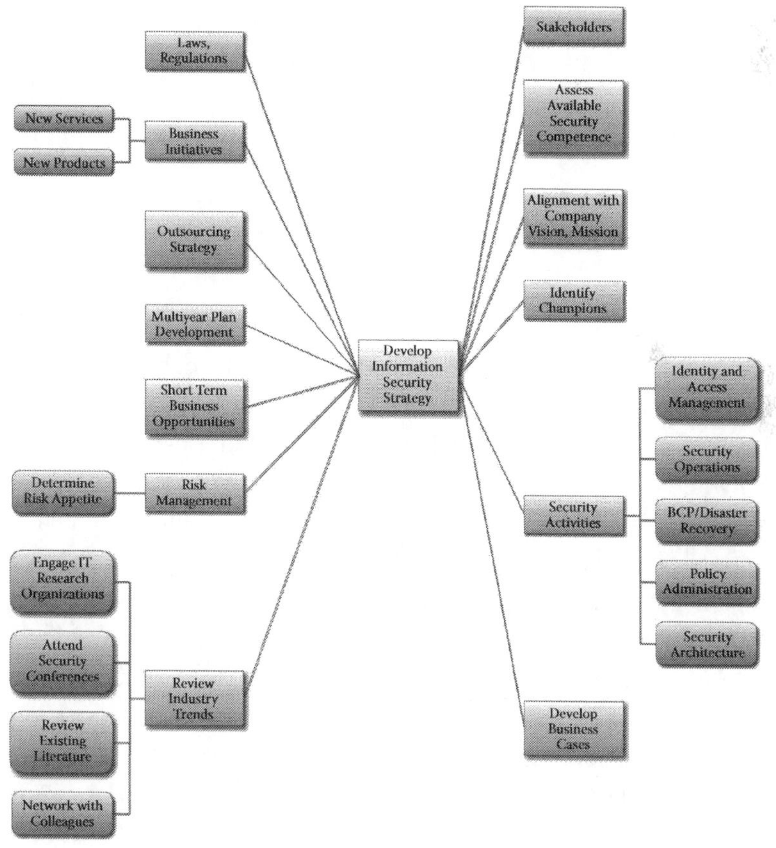

Figure 2.4 Strategy Mind Map example. (Created with Mind Mapping software, www.smartdraw.com.)

The power comes from obtaining multiple thoughts from different people with different perspectives or vantage points of the issue being discussed. Many ideas can be captured in quick succession. As an experiment, at a conference of IT auditors, each person was given 1 minute to draw a mind map with at least 10 thoughts coming from the word "happiness." As one can imagine, happiness means many different things to many different people. Amazingly, out of about 150 people in the room, there were only a handful of matches, on concepts such as travel and children. While some people matched on these commonalities, it was even more alarming to see that few people even matched on those. The key takeaway here is that even as experienced as the security officer may be, he or she should recognize that the organizational knowledge, experience, and ideas contained in others needs to be understood. The mind mapping tool is an excellent method of capturing the components that should be addressed in an information security strategy. As a side note, each chapter of this book started with the creation of a mind map to capture the starting point for the chapter.

SWOT Analysis

When businesses are embarking on a new business venture a SWOT (strengths, weaknesses, opportunities, threats) analysis is typically used to determine the organization's current ability to compete in that marketplace. The process involves a facilitated brainstorming discussion whereby a box is drawn divided into four quadrants (each representing one of four dimensions of the SWOT acronym) and each of the quadrants are then evaluated by the team. An example SWOT analysis for a security program is shown in Figure 2.5. In practice much time is usually spent on defining the strengths and weaknesses as these appear to be easier to grasp as they tend to be based upon past observations of performance within the organization. Opportunities require an understanding of items that are more abstract, such as possibilities of the future without necessarily being currently equipped to develop the product or service. Threats are those actions that may serve to derail future plans or disrupt the existing environment.

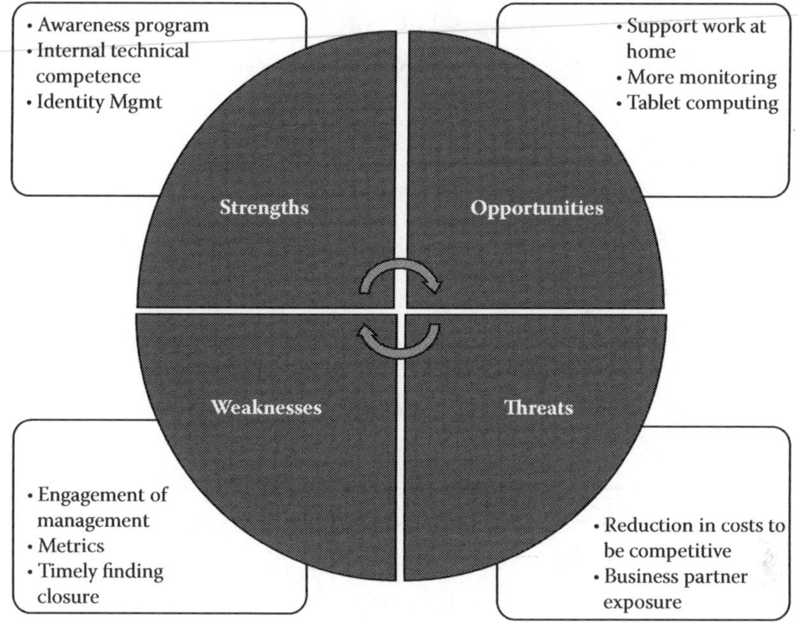

Figure 2.5 Security program SWOT analysis example.

Applied to information security strategy development, the SWOT process can illuminate areas where security could make a positive, proactive impact to the organization (opportunity), but to date has not acted. For example, creating and deploying an identity management system that would ease the manual burden of submitting paper forms while providing faster access to the needed systems would benefit the business process by making it more efficient. Other benefits could be added into the security strategy such as the integration with the corporate help desk ticketing system, enabling password resets, and reducing the number of profiles by implementing role-based access. Each of these would represent an opportunity to the business.

In the aforementioned example, through the SWOT analysis it may be determined that the skills are not available in-house to implement a complex identity management product and resources from outside need to be obtained. It may also be identified that it is not well understood what access should be granted to what job function, making the construction of accurate profiles difficult or that a role-discovery tool is needed to jump-start the effort. Strengths may include project management expertise in-house, knowledge of the existing processes, or the ability to receive excellent pricing on the security software.

Balanced Scorecard

The balanced scorecard was developed by Kaplan and Norton and gained popularity after the idea was published in the *Harvard Business Review* (Kaplan and Norton, 1996). Essentially the balanced scorecard approach encourages organizations to not only examine the financial measures of profitability, but rather to also continuously examine the measurements of how well the customer, process (quality), and learning perspectives are being attained. Each of these processes eventually contribute to the financial measures and by focusing upon these other measures as well as the financial measures, the overall financial profitability of the organization will be improved.

Some organizations identify a few key measures such as growth in the number of customers, nonconformance to processes, or the percentage of staff that have acquired a new skill. Other organizations drive the balanced scorecard concept to an individual employee level, whereby goals are created for each employee and rolled up into higher-level goals (or vice versa). In either case, the balanced scorecard provides a mechanism to review the progress of the organization in meeting their goals. As management guru Peter Drucker noted, “If you can’t measure it, you can’t manage it” (Drucker, 1993).

Security strategies can be developed using the balanced scorecard approach and building appropriate measures to track whether the customer, quality, learning, or financial perspectives are being enhanced by the security strategy.

Face-to-Face Interviews

Face-to-face interviews are not as formal as the other techniques, albeit it can be very effective in understanding what is really important to the management and technical staff in the organization. The security officer schedules a 1-hour meeting with each senior management member, middle management, front-line supervisors, and a cross-section of end users and key technical staff. In the first 20 minutes, the security officer discusses at a high level some of the information security concerns today facing companies with respect to the confidentiality, integrity, and availability of information. It may be helpful to provide some statistical information, new stories of events within similar industries, and some specifics of events that have occurred with the company. This is then followed with a brief 10-minute discussion of the functions of the information security department and ways that the security department can help. The next 30 minutes is then devoted to listening to the challenges of the business area and identifying where the security area may be able to help. Through this process, a champion or two for the security strategy may emerge in addition to learning what the issues are. For example, it may be learned that an executive is trying to reduce the costs per transaction and that the facility costs are a major expense. He also indicated that he does not want to incur the expense of maintaining another machine for each individual. As a possible solution, he was thinking about a work-at-home solution and did not know if this would increase the likelihood that information would become exposed. As the security officer, this should ring a bell that maybe a secure virtual private network (VPN) solution coupled with virtualization of the desktop may be a feasible alternative.

Face-to-face interviews also serve to build rapport with key people within the business. By just taking the step of demonstrating that the security department cares about their needs, concerns, and issues begins to build the relationship. These are the same individuals that may be called upon later to support the implementation of the strategy by the departmental projects that are initiated.

Key to each of these techniques is to not try to determine the security strategy without the input of the business leaders and appropriate technical staff. What may appear as an important security concern heard at a security conference may not be the largest security concern facing the business. The CEO may have some real concerns concerning brand image at the moment, and an opportunity would be missed by not connecting the security strategy to the needs of the CEO. Demonstrating how applying the proper security controls can protect the brand, for example, would enable maturity of the security program.

Security Planning

Strategic, tactical, and operational plans are interrelated and each provides a different focus towards enhancing the security of the organization. Planning reduces the likelihood that the organization will be reactionary towards the security needs. With appropriate planning, decisions on projects can be made with respect as to whether they are supporting the long-term or short-term goals and have the priority that warrants the allocation of more security resources.

Strategic

Strategic plans are aligned with the strategic business and information technology goals. These plans have a longer-term horizon (3 to 5 years or more) to guide the long-term view of the security activities. The process of developing a strategic plan emphasizes thinking of the company environment and the technical environment a few years into the future. High-level goals are stated to provide the vision for projects to achieve the business objectives. This type of plan is the outcome from the top-down, vision-driven approach to security strategy previously discussed and shown in Figure 2.2. These plans should be reviewed minimally on an annual basis or whenever major changes to the business occur, such as a merger, acquisition, establishment of outsourcing relationships, major changes in the business climate, or introductions of new competitors. Technological changes will be frequent during a 5-year time period, so the plan should be adjusted. The high-level plan provides organizational guidance to ensure that lower-level decisions are consistent with executive management's intentions for the future of the company. For example, strategic goals may consist of

- Establish security policies and procedures
- Effectively deploy servers, workstations, and network devices to reduce downtime
- Ensure all users understand the security responsibilities and reward excellent performance
- Establish a security organization to manage security entity-wide
- Ensure that risks are effectively understood and controlled

Tactical

Tactical plans provide the broad initiatives to support and achieve the goals specified in the strategic plan. These initiatives may include deployments such as the establishing an electronic policy development and distribution process, implementing robust change control for the server environment, reducing the likelihood of vulnerabilities residing on the servers, implementing a "hot site" disaster recovery program, or implementing an identity management solution. These plans are more specific and may contain multiple projects to complete the effort. Tactical plans are shorter in length, such as from 6 to 18 months to achieve a specific security goal of the company.

Operational/Project Plans

Specific plans with milestones, dates, and accountabilities provide the communication and direction to ensure that the individual projects are being completed. For example, establishing a policy development and communication process may involve multiple projects with many tasks:

- Conduct security risk assessment
- Develop security policies and approval processes
- Develop technical infrastructure to deploy policies and track compliance
- Train end users on policies
- Monitor compliance

Depending upon the size and scope of the efforts, these initiatives may be steps of tasks as part of a single plan or they may be multiple plans managed through several projects. The duration of these efforts are short term to provide discrete functionality at the completion of the effort. Traditional waterfall methods of implementing projects spent a large amount of time detailing the specific steps required to implement the complete project. Executives today are more focused on achieving some short-term or at least interim results to demonstrate the value of the investment along the way (Fitzgerald, 2007). Demonstration of value along the way maintains organizational interest and visibility to the effort, increasing the chances of sustaining longer-term funding. The executive management may grow impatient without realizing these early benefits.

Suggested Reading

1. Collins, J. 2001. *Good to great: Why some companies make the leap and others don't*. New York: HarperCollins.
2. National Conference of State Legistlatures. State Security Breach Notification Laws. http://www.ncsl.org/IssuesResearch/Telecommunications InformationTechnology/SecurityBreachNotificationLaws/tabid/13489/Default.aspx
3. Fitzgerald, T., Goins, B., and Herold, R. 2007. Information security and risk management. In *Official ISC²® Guide to the CISSP CBK*, H. A. Tipton and K. Henry, eds., 9–17. Boca Raton, FL: Auerbach.
4. Kaplan, R. S., and Norton, D. P. 1996. *The balanced scorecard: Translating strategy into action*. Boston: Harvard Business School Press.
5. Buzan, T., and Buzan, B. 1996. *The Mind Map® book: How to use radiant thinking to maximize your brain's untapped potential*. New York: Plume.
6. Drucker, P. 1993. *The practice of management* (reissue edition). New York: Harper Business.

3

Defining the Security Management Organization

Sow a thought, and you reap an act;
Sow an act, and you reap a habit;
Sow a habit, and you reap a character;
Sow a character, and you reap a destiny.

Samuel Smiles, 1812–1904

The role of the information security leader has been being changing quite dramatically over the past few decades. Even as recently as 10 years ago, the position of chief information security officer was largely unheard of except for in the largest banking institutions. Emerging laws and regulations have pushed the need for information security to the forefront of business and are seen as strategic and tactical issues that require an appropriate investment. The role of the information security officer has also received attention from multiple organizations providing awards for "Executive Security Officer of The Year" or "Chief Information Security Officer of the Year," further providing visibility to the profession.

History of the Security Leadership Role Is Relevant

Prior to the start of the new millennium, information security departments were buried deep within the information technology (IT) departments, typically within an infrastructure team or operations area focused on the deployment of servers, networks, and applications. The primary focus was on what was known as security administration, or in today's nomenclature, identity management or access management. The primarily functions involved (1) setting up accounts, (2) providing access to resources after proper approval was obtained, and (3) monitoring. The scope was primarily centered on ensuring that users were provisioned the access needed to perform their jobs when they needed access. This is not to say that other functions were not provided, however, the predominant focus was on logon ID administration.

Disaster recovery was typically thought of as a data center operation and not really well-coordinated with the concept of business continuity, whereby the organization recognizes the complete process that is required to maintain operations in the event of a disaster. Disaster recovery terminology has been largely associated with bringing the organization's computing resources back to an operational level to conduct business. More important, disaster recovery was typically managed outside of the information security department and while seen as important to those performing the function, it was usually seen as an added cost that was one of the first to be trimmed back during staff reductions. Business leaders rationed that if nothing had happened in the last several years, it was unlikely to happen and the resources could be redeployed to work on revenue-producing or cost-reducing efforts. This sentiment shifted in the new millennium after the tragic terrorist attack at the World Trade Center in New York City on September 11, 2001, and damage caused by Hurricane Katrina in August 2005. Audit firms were very busy following these events constructing business continuity and disaster recovery plans.

The passage of regulations such as the Health Insurance Portability and Accountability Act (HIPAA) Final Security Rule (February 2003) requiring that responsibility for information security must be assigned; Sarbanes–Oxley Act of 2002 (SOX) Section 404 bringing attention to the need for information security controls to ensure accurate financial statements; Gramm–Leach–Bliley Act (GLBA), also known as the Financial Services Modernization Act of 1999, whereby the Safeguards Rule required that at least one employee be denoted as having responsibility for information security; and the Federal Information Security Management Act of 2002 (FISMA), also known as the E-Government Act of 2002, does not specifically require that a security officer be named, however, it does require that the National Institute of Standards and Technology (NIST) guidance be used, which promotes the designation of an information security leader role in Special Publication 800-12, "An Introduction to

Computer Security: A NIST Handbook," and Special Publication 800-53, "Recommended Security Controls for Federal Information Systems and Organizations." Each of these regulations has an underlying theme: someone must be designated to manage the information security program.

These actions were deliberate in the laws, as it was clear that organizations were not providing the proper investment toward information security and designating someone to the role. The impact of these changes in the law are very significant, as it was the real beginning for organizations to commit the resources necessary to secure their information assets. Without this legislation, it is doubtful that organizations below the Fortune 100 would have designated someone at a high enough level to make a significant impact in properly securing the resources. The net result of the regulations was to squarely send a message to financial, healthcare, publically listed, government, and contracting organizations that information security was important and that the commitment to the function needed to be evidenced by an individual charged with the responsibility for the organization's security. None of these regulations made mention as to the time commitment (i.e., full or part time) that would be required to permit scalability with the size of the organization, however, it needed to be appropriate with the size and resources available to the organization. In other words, a large organization with $50 billion in annual revenues having one person dedicated to information security would be judged woefully insufficient when stacked up against its peers, whereas another organization with 50 employees may be judged adequate to designate part of one person's job as being responsible for leading the information security efforts.

The period from 2001 to 2005 was predominantly characterized by organizations scurrying to meet the demands on SOX, HIPAA, GLBA, and so forth ahead of the compliance mandates, which were typically two years out. Security assessments or gap analyses were the norm, as many organizations were unclear as to where they stood with respect to the broad spectrum of information security and not clear as to where they stood with respect to the new legislation. Large- and medium-tier audit firms were extremely busy during this period helping organizations to beef up security. The Payment Card Industry (PCI) Security Standards Council issued version 1.0 in 2006 and added more security requirements that had to be complied with in subsequent updates. The impact of these regulations was to bring an auditable focus to the security programs of these companies. As various audit and consulting organizations developed standardized approaches to assess the security posture of the organization, these services would be increasingly utilized by security officers as one of "the first steps in office" to understand the challenges that were before them.

The New Security Officer Mandate

So why is the past decade of information security so important with respect to the emergence of the information security officer? The importance lies in the recognition that the security officer position, as we know it today, is in its infancy. With the data processing profession being very young itself, dating to the 1950s, and becoming more mainstream in the 1960s for back-office-type operations, the leader of information security of today for most organizations has been in place for less than a decade. Factoring in that prior to the year 2000 many IT organizations spent the preceding years leading up to Y2K engaged in retiring old, nonconforming applications and upgrading the infrastructure, the focus on security was not prevalent until the early years of the new millennium with the passage of the aforementioned laws and regulations. Considering that these laws passed in the 2002 to 2003 timeframe, with mandates for compliance extending two years, this suggests that most organizations had established information security roles for leaders by 2004–2005, midway into the new decade. Relatively speaking, 5 to 10 years puts the information security officer role as we know it today as being low on the maturity curve. This means that the industry is continually shaping and defining what the role is, how the individual should operate, in what capacity and level the role should be placed, to whom the role should report to, how the individual relates to the rest of the organization, and the roles of others in participating in the protection of the information assets.

Although this ambiguity may be unnerving to some, it can be invigorating to others that are shaping the information security industry. The following sections contain the components which need to be considered to construct an effective security management organization. Security organizations will vary across organizations due to the resources available and the specific needs of the organization. However, each of the functions indicated need to be managed by someone within the organization, or this presents an information security management risk that may be unacceptable to the organization. Regulations will continue to increase and competitors will continue to get smarter about information security, and failure to keep up will leave the company at a disadvantage.

Day 1: Hey, I Got the Job!

Congratulations, Mr. or Ms. Security Officer, you now have the job. This may be welcome news or not, depending upon whether you (1) chose this career path and interviewed extensively for the position, (2) raised your hand at the wrong time during the meeting, (3) didn't attend the selection meeting, or (4) were the last guy in the IT shop and now "you're it!" Hopefully, the honor of being the security officer was something that was chosen and aligns with a passion to protect the information assets for the customers of your company.

Leading information security today is hard work, surrounded by audits that seem to come one right after another, the continual threat of the impact breaches will have on the reputation of the company, separating the hype from the reality of information security products, and the increasing pressure to do more with less resources. Whereas information security departments of the past were primarily internally focused to ensure that the only the right users had access to the information, today's external connectivity has given rise to an increased focused at protecting the perimeter and the evaporating perimeter characterized by the mobile workforce, Internet connectivity, distributed company locations, and increased external threats. This does not suggest that the internal threats have dissipated but rather that organizations must now deal with another set of problems that become added to the mix. One minute the security officer is in the hot seat trying to determine if the USB stick that was lost by Ashley contained personally identifiable information on it, and the next minute was preparing for a 15-minute presentation for the board of directors to explain the progress made toward attaining compliance in one of the many government regulations, to the next minute developing an information security program for the end users aimed at minimizing the susceptibility of the end users being "phished." The security officer is then wondering what the next day, Tuesday, will bring.

The security officer must be astute enough to not get bogged down in the day-to-day issues or the crisis of the moment, such that a long-term strategy is not laid out. Methods for achieving the long-term strategy were noted in the Developing Information Security Strategy chapter (Chapter 2). Time must be set aside daily, if not at least once a week, to review the information security strategy and the progress made toward it. Senior management needs to have a comfort level that progress is being made toward increasing security of the information assets to an acceptable level, which also serves to lessen the culpability in the event that a breach does occur. For example, if the executives are aware that patching is done on a regular basis on the company's externally facing databases, monitoring through vulnerability scans is occurring, the latest penetration tests found minimal problems, and the information was breached through the use of a very new exploit, management may be more forgiving given that industry-accepted practices were followed and procedures were regularly followed. If on the other hand there were no long-term strategy and no understanding or communication of the database protection processes in place, it may be difficult for the security officer to survive the breach.

Security Leader Titles

Mark Sanborn (2006), in his book *You Don't Need a Title to Be a Leader*, says "People who lead—whether or not they have a title—strive to make things better." Again, as evidence of a security leader profession in its earlier stages, titles of the person leading information security programs may be one of chief information security officer (CISO), chief security officer (CSO), security director, security manager, security practice leader, or other. A recent survey by PricewaterhouseCoopers indicated that 43% of consumer products/retail companies had someone in the role of CISO, whereas 83% of the financial services companies had someone in a similar position. A Computer Security Institute survey indicated that their respondents, primarily of the information security field, were composed of 23% holding the security officer title, 13% CISO, 12% systems administrator, 6% CSO, 8% CIO, 7% CEO, and a full 32% in the "other" category. This is representative of the security profession as a whole, where the CISO/CSO/Vice President title is often used in very large organizations, with the security director and manager or security administrator titles appearing in small- to medium-sized organizations.

The actual title is less important than the fact that there is someone designated to drive and lead the information security program to a level that did not exist previously and one that the executive management would be pleased with in terms of cost and benefit.

Techie versus Leader

Why would anyone want a job in the first place where a really bad day could be your last? Why would anyone sign up to deal with the plethora of government regulations, auditors, and users that have to comply with extra controls to get their work done? The answer is simple: Security officer is a very cool and rewarding job and profession. No matter what level of the organization the security officer is starting out, given the appropriate skills, experience, and relationships, the opportunities are endless.

In the not too distant past, people were moved into the role of information security leader due to their success as a technician. Maybe the individual was a firewall administrator, system administrator, network administrator, security administrator, or jack-of-all-trades. The individual was promoted to the role of information security officer because of his or her technical knowledge and because information security was primarily thought of as an IT function. Although the technical skills are still valued, they are not valued as much as the leadership skills necessary to hold the position in the long term.

Leadership skills separate the technical analyst from becoming an effective information security leader that provides added value to the business. This is not an issue that is new to IT, as organizations have dealt with the promotion issue for years within IT organizations. Many organizations promoted individuals who were very successful in their technical jobs, understanding standards, applying solutions to problems, fighting fires, developing new technology products based on emerging technologies, and so forth, and not based on their leadership and people competency skills. These individuals, while technically sound, have to develop the same competencies that they are missing, just as a new programming language must be learned. This is not to say that technical individuals are not successful in these roles, but rather to be successful requires recognition that these additional competencies must now be developed in the role of the security officer.

Left-brain thinking is necessary to bring the logical and analytical competencies to technical projects and is much different than the right-brain competencies necessary to manage relationships and the feelings of individuals involved in projects. The selection of the security officer that is able to influence the organization to adopt secure practices, inspire a staff to go the extra mile, and maintain credibility within the organization over a long period of time, requires a good look into the "soft skill" side of the individual. Granted, the security officer must understand the technology well enough to communicate with the technical staff, vendors, and be able to discern where the technologies will provide benefit to the business. As much as the technical security language is viewed as a baseline competency for security officers, the language of leadership must also be viewed as a baseline skill. Understanding the layers of TCP/IP are useful when designing security architectures, but have little relevance when trying to explain to the board of directors why continuing investments need to be made in the information security program.

The Security Leaders Library

Just as the technical specialist has learned his trade through attending technical conferences and seminars and reading targeted technical books on the technology, so must the information security leader invest in books on leadership skills to continue the education in the skills that are important. Earlier in my career, I managed two groups of totaling forty-five Database Modelers and Database Analysts, including seven technical project managers for a major airline. During each monthly staff meeting, I created a 25-question multiple-choice quiz based upon one of the database development magazines at the time and offered a prize for answering 100% of the questions. I also challenged the team members to invest $1,000 of their own money annually on books and training materials. Some members took up the challenge; others disagreed that they should have to do this. This exercise and the suggestion that they invest their own money in their careers served two purposes: (1) since I had to write the questions, I had to understand the content as well, which increased my learning and also showed the team members that I was committed to their work, and (2) each person has a responsibility to invest in his or her education, whether or not it is employer sponsored. The commitment to learning about leadership principles must be just as strong for the information security officer as learning how to optimize SQL and as database performance is to the database analyst.

Many books have been written on leadership skills over the years. Leadership books tend to be a favorite staple at airport newsstands, as business people seem to be on the constant search for understanding the answers to the questions such as: What is leadership? What makes successful companies more successful than their competitors? Are leaders born or made? Is there a secret formula? The books are presented as short stories such as *The Present* (Johnson, 2003) providing parables on learning from the past, living in the present, and planning for the future; how-to books like *The Effective Executive* (Drucker, 2004) providing insights on managing knowledge workers from great leadership analysts such as the late management guru Peter Drucker; or the slicing and dicing of companies in the same industries to discern the differences in books such as *Good to Great*. Alternatively there are the abridged versions of leadership available through small paperbacks such as Tom Peter's *Leadership Essentials* (2005) series, or books packed full of time-management-type tips such as *Never Check E-Mail in the Morning* (Morgenstern, 2004). Otto Kroeger and Janet M. Thuesen leverage individual personality differences in the work environment in psychology titles such as *Type Talk at Work* (1992). Of course there is the staple leadership series by Stephen R. Covey on the *Seven Habits of Highly Effective People* (2004). Each of these books contributes in their own way to some facet of leadership, helping to recognize the leadership capacity of individuals and companies.

Security Leadership Defined

Definitions are useful to provide the context and create a common language. Security leadership is about the application of the soft skill competencies to the business of information security. Many of the leadership books focus on the growth of their organizations through product innovation, increasing market share, cost containment and reduction, engaging the workforce in the company's vision, expanding services and markets, leveraging information technology, and developing appropriate strategies and action plans. Information security should be regarded as a business within a business, whereby the leadership strategies presented in the leadership literature are adopted to create a successful, sustaining, long-term business that supports the mission of the parent business. In other words, the information security department must lead in such a way that enables the core business function to depend upon their supporting services to meet the overall vision of the company. Effective security leadership blends the technical, business, and soft skill knowledge to support the business needs.

Security Leader Soft Skills

Security officers today now find themselves interacting with many different levels across the organization, from the board of directors, C-suite, senior and middle management, peers, and end users. They are no longer communicating with just the IT staff and those front-line managers end users needing logon IDs and access to systems. Security officers are being increasingly involved in determining strategy, engaging in new product releases, and providing input to solutions that reduce the bottom-line costs to the organization (e.g., outsourcing, off shoring, usage of personal mobile devices) without increasing risk beyond an acceptable level. The interaction with individuals from multiple levels and different disciplines in a team environment require a new set of skills, primarily soft or nontechnical skills to advance the security agenda. Figure 3.1 from a survey of 100 security leaders shows the relative importance of the different skill areas (Fitzgerald and Krause, 2008). Notice that technical knowledge was not the most important, but rather those skills such as oral and written communication, influence, teamwork, collaboration, and self-confidence were.

Seven Competencies for Effective Security Leadership

There are seven key areas that information security officers should honestly evaluate themselves as to where they stand. Why seven?

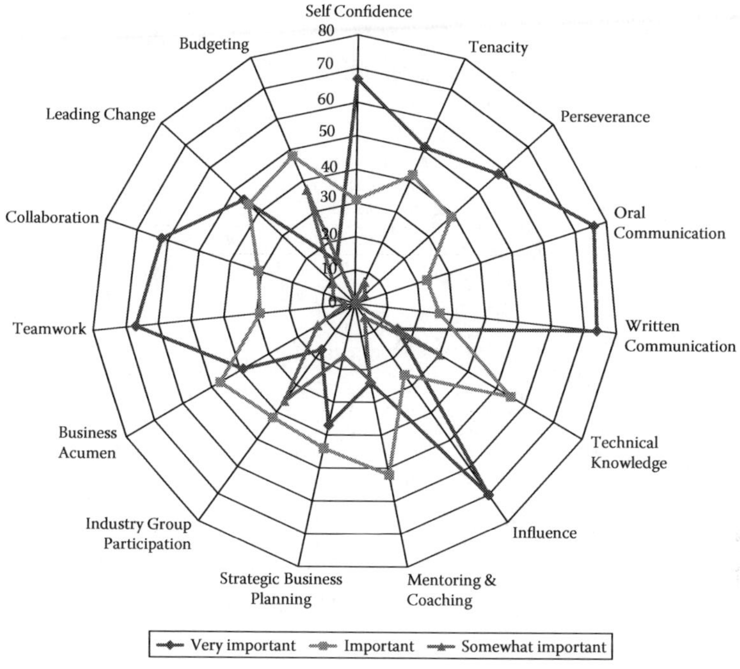

Figure 3.1 Security management competencies/skills. (Fitzgerald, T., and Krause, M, 2008, *CISO Leadership Essential Principles for Success*, New York, Auerbach.)

The reason is that the human mind has difficulty juggling more than seven things at once. Too many goals lead to frustration, confusion, hopelessness, and procrastination to start any of them. Narrowing the focus to a number of key areas and developing an action plan to build upon the strengths and enhance the areas needing improvement will contribute greatly to a security leader's career. When a technical security analyst is faced with a situation where something does not work, the approach is to go to the documentation, manuals, and test; seek advice from colleagues; and try, try again until a solution is found. The same approach applies to enhancing leadership skills; it is an iterative process of trial and error, and focus on the discipline of leadership. Stephen Covey's landmark book, *The Seven Habits of Highly Effective People* (2004), first explored the value of providing a seven-step, easy to comprehend method to achieve greater results. These competencies are not the soft skills noted in the earlier section, but rather represent the higher-level application of the soft skills toward organizational effectiveness. In other words, once the soft skills have been developed,

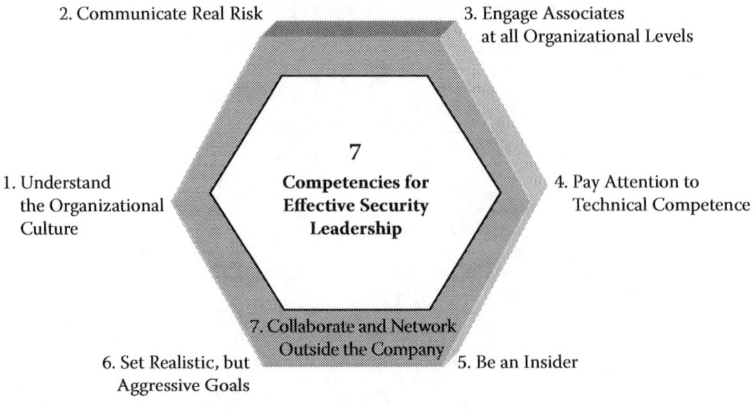

Figure 3.2 Seven competencies of effective security leadership.

the security leader should be able to use that knowledge to achieve greater results by practicing the seven competencies. The seven competencies for effective security leadership are shown in Figure 3.2.

1. Understand the Organizational Culture

Organizations establish a culture or "the way things are done around here" that is unique to the organization. Culture is created over time based upon the past and present leadership, history, geographic dispersion, collaborative versus hierarchical decision making, profitability, industry regulations, and each individual person within the organization. Every individual brings their own unique set of values, backgrounds, experiences, and capabilities into the workplace every day, in other words their own individual "culture."

The effective security officer understands how the organization works, what is accepted and what is not. Do people normally bend the rules to get the job done? Does the organization reward taking chances for innovation or does it view those activities as violating the prescribed rules? Does a strong individual in a position of formal authority make decisions unilaterally, or is consensus building and collaboration expected? Are individuals regularly working 60 to 70 hours a week with high energy and commitment, or is there stress and burnouts evidenced by continuous turnovers and new-hire recruiting? Are individuals recognized or is there an effort to recognize the contributions of the entire team? Is customer service the key driver of the organization at all costs or is the focus on engineering the best new product, in other words, where is the organization placing its investment dollars? Spending time to understand this focus will help the security officer position the programs effectively and learn how to get the deliverables accomplished.

2. Communicate Real Risk

The sky is falling! The sky is falling! Security is not either (1) in place or (2) not in place. As security professionals, there is obviously the desire to secure the environment through managerial, technical, and operational controls to the highest degree possible; however, there are degrees of protection between no security and absolute 100% security that are acceptable for the business. Executives are used to dealing with risk, every single day. Business risk is accepted by underwriting new insurance policies, entering new markets, adding new services, outsourcing business lines, merging with or acquiring other companies, making technology investments, and so forth.

To be adept in communicating with the business executives about risk, the security officer must be able to capture metrics, meaningful metrics, by which the value of security can be seen by the business. This is not an easy task, as it depends very much on first understanding what is important to the business. Companies mired in government regulations may want metrics related to the compliance efforts. It may be useful in product- or service-focused companies to relate the security metrics of availability and loss prevention to the individual product lines and services that are produced by the company, demonstrating the business value, or contribution, of security to the key products. Executives also want to know what their competitors are doing, with the goal being to match the security practices of the competitor. Why match? Matching ensures that the organization is spending enough on security, while not spending an excessive amount. The only exception may be in an environment where security can be promoted as a competitive advantage to gain the trust of the consumer. In today's environment, these competitive advantages for security appear to be evaporating and have become expected as the norm.

Lengthy, risk-analysis-by-the-pound documents should be a thing of the past. Although these analyses may be very detailed, thorough, and accurate in describing the risk, in practice, these documents become shelfware and as such offer limited value. Qualitative approaches permit faster analysis and getting the results in front of the executives in a way that the issues can be discussed. Even if a detailed quantitative approach is the chosen method, the pragmatic security officer will reduce the voluminous data into clear, manageable, summarized proposals that relate the risk to the business product or service that will be impacted if the risk is not mitigated or reduced.

3. Engage Associates at All Organizational Levels

Security happens at all levels within the organization, from the board of directors to the end users to the middle management and front-line supervisors in between. The security officer must be visible, accessible, and approachable to all associates. The security awareness programs provide an excellent opportunity for the security officer to develop relationships with all associates. Establishing these relationships are very important for the security officer to discern what is really going on within the organization, beyond the documented policies and procedures. When the rapport is established, individuals are much more likely to seek out the security officer for security advice, concerns, or to report security incidents.

Security councils with management representation for each of the primary business units, human resources, information technology, legal, compliance, risk management, internal audit, physical security, and so forth are effective tools for establishing the buy-in of developed policies. These councils also establish a linkage between the security department and the business where the business concerns and impediments to the business can be discussed. Security departments these days want to be viewed as enablers of the business; however, without the existence of a council, the departments may still be viewed as the controllers of getting the work done, or "some techie department within information technology" that does not understand the business needs. Whether this would be a fair representation depends upon the actions of the security department. An added advantage of the security council is that the mere existence of such a body promotes the perception that the security department is there to support the business.

4. Pay Attention to Technical Competence; It Is Still Needed

Understanding the business and developing the business acumen is undoubtedly a key element to the security officer's success. Continuing to stay abreast of technology developments is also important so that the security officer is aware of the technical capabilities, which may benefit the business. The security leader must have a broad understanding of the technologies available, leaving the deep technical understanding to the information security analysts and other IT professionals. The security officer must be able to converse with business people in nontechnical terms and with information technology people in technical terms. With access to the Internet, free newsletters, webinars, and security conferences, there is no reason that the security officer cannot dedicate one hour per day to maintaining the technical discipline.

This is different than the technical skills that were referred to earlier as being less important. The difference here is that the security officer is not engaging in the mastery of the technical skills, but rather is maintaining (1) a sufficient awareness of the technology that exists, and (2) the ability to obtain information through self-study and leveraging the knowledge of the technical staff to provide strategic and tactical security direction in support of the company initiatives.

5. Be an Insider

Does it seem like you are the last one to know what is going on in the organization? Do you wait for the org chart to come out to see if you have a seat on the bus? Build internal relationships and support colleagues with their projects. They need to also know who you are and what value you bring to the organization. Organizations are designed to get work done to accomplish the organizational goal. Taking accountability for individual actions, delivering the services when promised, and being a good team player working to contribute to other individual's projects, as well as the security initiatives, builds trust within those relationships.

6. Set Realistic But Aggressive Goals

Goals need to be set around a vision, strategy, and concrete action plans. These plans should be multiyear created through a realistic, but aggressive mind-set. The first question should be, What does the business need from information security to be successful? Visions and strategies that are not connected with specific action plans with deliverables and discrete completion dates do not move the security program forward. Success also needs to be delivered within the first three to four months of a security officer's arrival to build the confidence for future endeavors. It is better to miss a goal that was established than to never set one and use hope as a strategy. Action plans are essential to establishing accountability, responsibility, and ensuring that the appropriate resources are dedicated to security.

7. Collaborate and Network Outside of the Company

The security field is very complex and has many areas of specialization. Some individuals have focused their activities on security awareness, computer forensics, disaster recovery, physical security, access control across multiple platforms, identity management, remote access, vulnerability, penetrating testing, and the list goes on. One must understand the vertical industry, how market share is achieved, competitor profiles, marketing strategies, product development, and the specific language of the business. It is unreasonable to expect that one individual has all they need to know about any of these topics. There are many opportunities for networking through security conferences, participation in industry advisory groups, attending external business meetings with business partners, and establishing relationships with individuals met at the various forums. In today's e-mail, text messaging, Xbox–PlayStation-paced, "iPhone, iPad, Android, BlackBerry person at the click of a button" world, answers to questions from peers are invaluable. Many people are more than willing to share their expertise with someone that is passionate about their work. These collaborations reveal many other people that are struggling with the same issues. Collaboration is a two-way street, where deposits need to be made (sharing own expertise) before substantial withdrawals can be taken (obtaining expertise).

Security Functions

Learning from Leading Organizations

In an effort to understand what leading organizations were doing to meet the information security challenges, the General Accounting

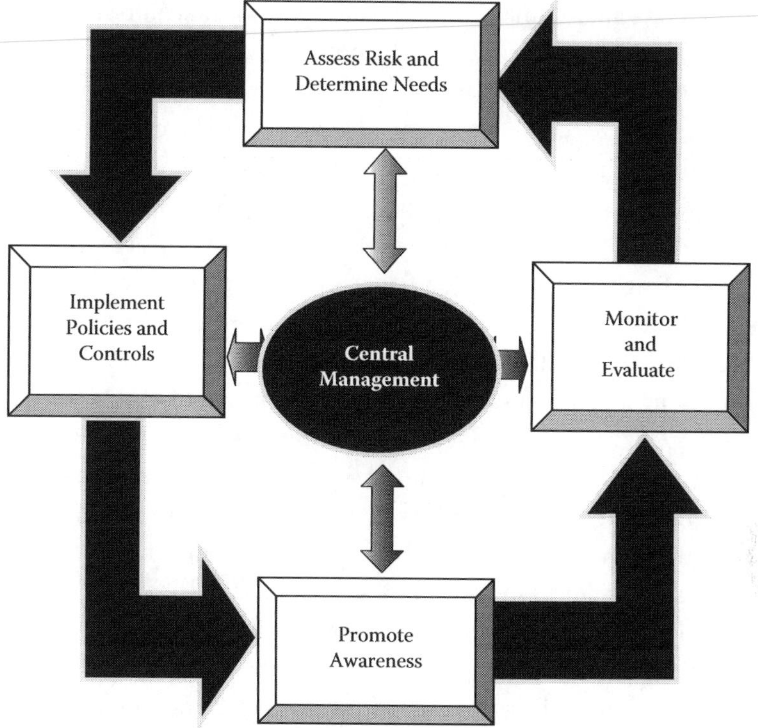

Figure 3.3 Security leadership, learning from leading organizations. (United States General Accounting Office. 1998. *Executive guide: Information security management; Learning from leading organizations.* http://www.gao.gov/archive/1998/ai98068.pdf)

Office (GAO) studied several leading organizations in 1998 to determine what activities we performed by organizations that were leaders in information security. It found that five critical functions were consistently applied as shown in Figure 3.3.

Assess Risk and Determine Needs To many security practitioners assessing the risk and determining needs would appear as a logical, if not obvious, first step. However, how many times have we have seen a knee-jerk reaction to implement a new policy or procedure, or buy a technical product without first understanding what the real business risk is to the organization? Assessing risk, which is provided in more detail in Chapter 5, weighs the cost of implementing the control against the losses that would be experienced by the organization if the risk is not mitigated. The analysis may bear out the fact that it is more costly to implement sufficient security controls than accept the risk.

For example, an organization sponsoring the annual auto show of new cars could perceive that there is the potential threat of someone angry with a car manufacturer from a personal bad experience (e.g., they may have purchased a "lemon" in the past or had a car's brakes malfunction at a critical time) and may want to retaliate against the car company by keying or vandalizing the display vehicle. The auto show could implement controls such as roped-off areas around the cars or by requesting that each person deposit their keys in a container before approaching the car. Most of us would find either of these controls as silly or unwarranted, as most people would be well-behaved and not present a risk. Implementation of a control of this type would be unnecessary and would be viewed by many as an overreaction. Conversely, many times cars in the $100,000 and up range will typically have their doors locked, as they do not want to risk damage to the shifting mechanisms on the cars. People appear to understand why these vehicles have additional security controls. Cameras are also installed in the convention center, so any damage that would result would be detected versus prevented.

The car example illustrates what can happen in organizations if the security department does not take into account the business needs of the operation and unilaterally implements security controls. The purpose of the risk assessment is to determine what the adequate level of controls needs to be. Organizations that best manage security view the risk assessment as a critical first step in the process.

Implement Policies and Controls Once the risk is determined, the appropriate policies and controls to support the policies are implemented. Policies are specific to the organization and take into account the needs of the organization and support the business operations. Controls are selected that match the risk profile of the organization and reduce the likelihood and impact of a security breach. In the care example, the implementation of cameras may be a sufficient control, while still permitting individuals to experience the auto show and be able to sit in the vehicles they may be interested in. Policies that govern the implementation of cameras and salesperson monitoring of the customers need to be written to ensure that those individuals coordinating the show know what is expected of them. The NIST has produced an excellent special publication (800-53) for federal information systems for control selection titled "Recommended Controls for Federal Information Systems and Organizations." This reference contains controls for low-, medium-, and high-risk systems and can be applied to nongovernment environments as well. The publication ISO/IEC 27002: Security Techniques—Code of Practice for Information Security Management is also an excellent resource for the types of control that should be implemented, albeit this framework does not go to the level of detail as that of NIST publication 800-53.

Traditionally, laws have not been very prescriptive in defining the information security controls needed, as this must be governed by the risk of the system, the technology that is available, scalability, and the resources that are available to the organization. Hence, the assessment of adequate controls is somewhat subjective and depends upon the exposure of the individual performing the assessment to different alternatives that have been successfully implemented in organizations with similar size and similar issues. Guidance is starting to emerge from the experiences within vertical industries to create best practices, good practices, essential practices, and so forth to deal with some of the issues. One organization may determine that it is willing to accept the risk of smartphone protection by requiring a password be implemented on the phone. Other organizations may view this control as insufficient and require that the password also be made a strong password by company policy, requiring that the password be eight characters, include at least one upper and one lower case character, along with at least one special character (@, &, $, %, etc.). Another organization may require even stronger controls and require that the password be technically enforced and that the device is remotely wiped after three invalid attempts, and the user attest to a smartphone security training if a reset is required. Another organization may decide that the technology of the Android or iPhone is not appropriate for business usage and are not allowed, while another may yet encourage the use the use of a non-company-owned device and provide complete support with the addition of a third-party security product. The choices may seem endless for each decision that must be made, which further illustrates the importance of performing an adequate risk analysis and then implementing the appropriate controls to mitigate or reduce the risk to an acceptable level. Just as new risks are continually emerging, so are the methods with which to mitigate the risk.

Promote Awareness Most people want to do the right thing in life; they just need to be aware of what the right thing is. If policies and controls are not properly communicated, this step becomes very difficult. Security departments often will draft voluminous policy documents and then wonder why they are not being followed (techniques for increasing the success of security policy development are noted in Chapter 6 about security policy development). People cannot be held responsible for policies that they have not seen or understand. As much effort that went into determining the risk and deciding what controls were appropriate, should also be placed in ensuring that the individuals responsible for executing the policies and procedures understand and are able to implement the controls. Otherwise, nice documents exist, but the security controls are not protecting the information assets as desired.

Monitor and Evaluate If everything worked well the first time around, monitoring would be unnecessary. Unfortunately, security controls may be effective at the time they are first implemented; however, due to changing circumstances, they must be re-evaluated periodically to remain effective. Threat levels may increase, technology changes, procedures are found to be implemented differently than designed, business requirements change, and so forth. Organizations may change and the person that once was very diligent in performing the control has now left and the new person has not been executing the control as frequently or, worse yet, not at all. Or the policy changes such that all employees visiting another office outside of their home office is considered a visitor and must sign out at the end of the day. Without proper monitoring to ensure the policy and control are being executed, it may never be discovered that employees were not made aware of the policy change and it was not being practiced consistently. Monitoring would also discover if all of the security guards themselves were appropriately notified of the change in policy.

Central Management Leading organizations also recognized that someone needed to be focused on ensuring that the aforementioned four activities were occurring. Organizations are busy, dynamic institutions that have many competing demands for expenditures and resources. Just as other parts of the organization need management to set direction and ensure that resources are being appropriately used to meet the mission of the business, management is also needed to be focused on managing information security. While there will be components that may be decentralized, typically due to business unit differences or geographic differences, the overall security program should be unified to provide the sharing of practices across the multiple business units and locations.

This model while appearing simple can be a very powerful way to address information security management by guiding an information security program to perform the right activities. Every organization is constrained by the resources available to it, whether time, cost, materials, or labor, and by starting with the risk assessment to determine the real needs and implementing the appropriate controls, communicating those controls, and following up to ensure that the controls are still adequate and properly implemented, the organization will continually enhance the security of the environment it operates within.

What Functions Should the Security Officer Be Responsible For?

If we accept the proposition that leading organizations address each of the five critical functions in the model previously described and depicted in Figure 3.4, then a useful approach would be to identify the related security activities that must be performed to achieve the due diligence suggested by the model. Organizations may have all of these functions reporting to the information security officer or may decide to segregate the functions between multiple departments, such as a chief security officer maintaining responsibility for policy development, while an IT security manager retains responsibility for security violation monitoring. Before delving into the discussion as to what functions should report where, let's describe the core security functions that must be addressed somewhere within the organization as shown in Figure 3.4.

CRITICAL FUNCTION	RELATED ACTIVITY
Assess risk and determine needs	Risk assessment/analysis System security plan development External penetration testing
Implement policies and controls	Security policy development Security architecture Security control assessment Identity and access management Business continuity and disaster recovery
Promote awareness	End user security awareness training Intranet site and policy publication Targeted awareness
Monitor and evaluate	Security baseline configuration review Logging and monitoring Vulnerability assessment Internet monitoring Management of managed services Incident response Forensic investigations
Central management	Audit liaison Plan of action and milestones

Figure 3.4 Security critical functions and related security activities.

Assessing Risk and Determining Needs Functions

The three security functions that support the assessing risk and determining needs activity in the model are risk assessment/analysis, systems security plan development, and external penetration testing. In other words, performing these three activities will satisfy this activity within the model. These should be considered functions that need to be performed somewhere within the company. Larger organizations may have whole departments performing risk assessments, whereas smaller organizations may assign one person to complete the risk assessment and systems security plan development and may outsource external penetration testing. What is important is that someone performs each of these functions, otherwise an important component of information security will be missed and the controls chosen may not be sufficient to protect the information assets.

Risk Assessment/Analysis Risk assessment, or also known as risk analysis, is the formal process of reviewing the threats facing the organization, reviewing the likelihood or probability that vulnerability could be exploited, and the impact of the event should it occur. This is a key function of the information security department and performing the risk assessment as accurately as possible is the key to ensuring that money is spent in the more productive manner to reduce the security risk. This is also one of the most difficult functions to perform for the information security department, as it can be very challenging to obtain information on what the real risk may be. At the end of the day, risk assessments become subjective in nature. For example, what is the risk that a newly drafted first-round National Football League quarterback will face a career-ending injury during the first 5 years after the draft? Or the likelihood that the quarterback will take the team to the Super Bowl within 5 years? Past statistics may be used; however, as noted in many investment recommendations, past performance does not guarantee future results. Sometimes it is very difficult to determine the risk by not having a particular security control in place. Organizations many times do not have the broad perspective to determine what the risk would be and will hire an external consultant to provide an assessment or gap analysis of the security controls. External consulting organizations, whether they are large Big Four accounting firms or smaller security firms, can bring the experience gained from multiple assessments at multiple clients into the organization. This is not to suggest that adequate risk analysis cannot be done solely from staff within the organization. However, to leverage the external experience from other organizations, this is one area where external firms are typically engaged as a first step. Once the organization has more experience performing risk assessments and has a clearer understanding of the threats, vulnerabilities, and controls in place, it may decide to perform the risk assessment solely in-house.

Systems Security Plan Development The name "systems security plan" is somewhat misleading, as a systems security plan (SSP) is not really a plan at all but rather a document that provides a snapshot of the security controls at a point in time. The SSP contains the contact information for the system; documents the criticality/sensitivity level of the system; describes the business use of the system; defines the system boundaries and system interconnections; and describes the managerial, operational and technical controls that are in place to protect the information assets contained within the system. Systems may be general support systems, whereby they represent interconnected sets of information resources under the same direct management control that shares common functionality, or they may be major applications that are defined because they require special attention due to risk and magnitude of harm resulting from loss, misuse, or unauthorized access or modification of information in the application.

Developing an SSP is much more than just a documentation exercise, as the process of creating the plan brings clarity to the information system, the boundaries, and how it is protected. In medium to large organizations, a common answer when asking people about specifics of the computing environment or security controls is, "I don't know." The larger the organization and the more specialized the knowledge is across knowledge workers (e.g., information security, midrange infrastructure, network, and application development), the more this type of response should be expected. Individuals in different areas know their piece of the puzzle and are not necessarily expected to know what is going on in the rest of the organization. For example, the firewall administrator on the network team may know what firewalls are in place, what ports are open, and what baselines are applied, but might not know how often the firewall logs are reviewed by the security network monitoring team reporting to the IT security operations manager or what types of events are being monitored. So, depending upon whether the organization views the development of the SSP as purely a documentation exercise or if it is viewed as an opportunity to obtain clarity around the security controls will determine the ultimate value to the risk assessment process.

External Penetration Testing External penetration testing provides some comfort, or discomfort, that the security controls intended to block external entry into the systems are functional and working as designed. These are typically performed minimally on an annual basis, usually in conjunction with an overall risk assessment. Penetration testing is also typically done by an external organization, as most organizations do not have the resources available to keep up with the latest tools and attacks that may be used to gain unauthorized access from an external source. The value of external penetration tests is subject for debate, as it shows at one point in time the controls that a skilled attacker may be able to circumvent. Since organizations do not have the resources to spend to be 100% secure, it is likely with the budgets of more security departments that the attacker will find some way to infiltrate the organization. Technical means through the use of a step-by-step procedure to locate weaknesses through the running of foot printing and reconnaissance tools, as well as the use of social engineering (e.g., pretending to be someone from the help desk to obtain information or entering the building and plugging into an open LAN jack in a conference room), are both used to attempt entry. Odds are that the penetration test will reveal one or more vulnerabilities within the environment. Security managers are often required to have penetration testing performed at least once a year to meet a compliance regulation, or may use penetration testing as a method to raise visibility to security vulnerabilities to obtain more resources or funding to reduce the risk.

Implement Policies and Control Functions

Security Policy Development Security policy development is covered extensively in another chapter, but suffice it to say that without a formal, documented information security policy, the organization has no assurance that there is a common set of rules or practices that can be depended upon. The information security policy is the most visible document that the information security department creates. The document is necessary to guide the actions of everyone with respect to information security and need to be easily available and read by everyone.

Security Architecture Security architecture provides the security research and technical review of information security products to ensure that the appropriate security tools are purchased to solve the right problems. There are different methods to protect the environment, such as deciding between one vulnerability scanner over another. One may have more robust reporting features, whereas the other may be more accurate, delivering fewer false positives and representing more value to the organization. Likewise security architecture needs to be considered when purchasing products to ensure that they are compatible with existing products that are already in use. The purchase of an identity management system running on a Unix platform may not have interfaces with the Windows-based help desk ticketing system and require custom coding to make the system operational. Alternatively, the product may come bundled with an internal ticketing system that may not be as robust. The purchaser of the potential system would typically issue request for proposals (RFPs); talk with industry analysts such as Gartner Group, Burton, or Forrester and perform independent research; have vendors provide presentations; and talk with existing customers of the product. The goal of security architecture is to define a set of compatible products and processes to support the security controls that are necessary to mitigate the risks discovered in the risk assessment.

Security Control Assessment If the risk assessment is the brain of the security program, the security controls are the heart. Keeping the security controls flowing through the organizational veins on a continuous basis provides the protection needed. Security controls can be divided into three primary classifications—managerial, operational, and technical. Because the implementation of the security controls is core to the creation of a good security program, the controls are covered in detail in Chapters 8 through 10. Controls should be assessed on an annual basis at a minimum, and in practice are examined more often by internal and external auditors. A good practice is to review all controls annually and further test one-third of the controls each year. Processes and technologies rarely stay static year after year and should be tested when changed.

Identity and Access Management Identity and access management is typically a department on its own due to the size of the staff required to administer the function and the focus being primarily operational in nature. This area ensures that logon IDs are created and access is appropriately authorized by management and provisioned to the end user. Organizations that are more mature have embraced automation of the ID creation, whereby access is then requested based upon a profile (set of predefined accesses for a particular job function or role versus an individual need) and access is automatically provisioned. The benefit of this approach is the speed by which requests can be filled, as once the electronic approvals are received from the manager, the system is performing the provisioning work. These products are still in their infancy and applications typically require custom coding to provide the automation, which can be very expensive. These implementations can cost well into the millions, placing them out of reach for small- to medium-sized companies. Short of purchasing a product, simplified solutions using electronic forms and e-mail can be created at a relatively low cost to reduce the workflow time to manage the access administration. This function is the function that most people think of when they think of information security. Increasingly, this function is being challenged with finding ways to lower costs and perform the same work with fewer resources, as this area represents an operational, nonstrategic overhead cost to the business.

Business Continuity and Disaster Recovery Business continuity provides the analysis as to whether the business can sustain operations in the event of a disaster, whereas disaster recovery is largely thought of as bringing the information technology resources back online in the event of a disaster. As seen in recent years, the world has no shortage of disasters, whether it is an East Coast power grid blackout, flooding in North Dakota, earthquakes in Japan, oil spills in the Gulf of Mexico, closing of European airports due to volcanic ash, or the collapse of a major bridge in Minnesota. Each disaster brings new attention to business continuity and disaster recovery practices. The business continuity and disaster recovery teams need to exercise tests each year to ensure that the computer systems can be brought up in a remote location. They also conduct mock tests with different departments to ensure their business continuity plans are still accurate, and also lead emergency crisis management teams, made up of senior management, to ensure that the organization can react to a crisis or unexpected event. For example, if there are blizzard conditions near the call center, should the call center close? Will call center employees be able to work from home and provide the same level of service? Should the work shift to another, geographically different location to handle the calls? How will people get to work if the offices remain open? Who makes the decision and based upon what information? All of these questions would be answered by the business continuity and disaster recovery function. This function would also create business impact assessments (BIAs) to determine the amount of time the company could afford to be without the information. They would also, with business participation, prioritize the systems in the order they needed to be brought back online.

Each of these functions contributes toward defining the requisite controls to protect the information system. Due to the different skills required in each of the control areas, as well as the diverse interest areas, it is also likely in medium- to large-sized organizations that different individuals are performing each of these functions. For example, security policy development requires the ability to translate technical jargon into communications that the nontechnical end user can understand. Likewise, the business continuity and disaster recovery areas require the ability to work with management and understand where business needs may not be met in the event of a disaster, as well as manage the technical ability to bring up the system operating environment and coordinate end user testing to ensure the functionality is present. Identify and Access management requires the ability to be customer service oriented and manage multiple "gotta have it now" requests and complete the access requests in a timely basis.

Promote Awareness Functions

The goal of promoting awareness is to ensure that the security policies and procedures are available to those beyond the information security department. Everyone in the organization should be able to locate them. A random test asking questions about the security policy across the organization would reveal how effective the communications are. Many organizations put much effort into the development of information security policies, only to see them not followed because of a lack of communication. Timely security incidents or currents news items can be leveraged in a subtle way to highlight the existence of internal security policies.

End User Security Awareness Training End users need to be able to do two basic actions with respect to information security: (1) recognize when an incident occurs or what could cause an incident to occur, and (2) where to report the incident when the incident does happen. The end users are the eyes and ears of information security and a crucial piece in ensuring that security is being administered. Security "awareness" is just that—not the in-depth technical understanding that a security analyst may need for their jobs, but rather an understanding of how they are to handle and protect information entrusted to them. This function ensures that this training is provided prior to any systems access, refreshed and administered at least annually, and supplemented with interim e-mails, newsletters, awareness campaigns, and so forth.

Intranet Site and Policy Publication The security policies need to be readily accessible by all associates and contractors within the organization. The policies can be posted on the intranet site, or made available through policy management software that can track user acknowledgement that they have read, understood, and accepted the security policies. Providing the end users with a Google-type search engine is also very useful in delivering security policy content to enable end users to quickly locate information.

Targeted Awareness Delivering the information security message should not be limited to the training sessions and posting of the policies, as the message needs to be continually communicated at all levels. The security department should establish a formal communication plan, whereby different audiences are made aware of the information security requirements. Information can be distributed through participation by a standing agenda item in the managers' meetings, IT steering committees, or by monthly attending a different departmental staff meeting to communicate plans and listen to their issues. Specific technical training should also be provided to those areas in need, such as the server engineer that needs to understand the security settings in the active directory, or the network administrator that learns about the audit capabilities for the network firewalls and routers. Although all users can benefit from the generalized end-user security awareness training, others will need training adapted to their specific needs.

Monitor and Evaluate Functions

The following functions are excellent candidates for the creation of a security operations center or SOC team within the information security department. This group provides the oversight for the other areas outside information security to ensure that security is given the appropriate attention. Separating the function provides stronger control through the separation of duties.

Security Baseline Configuration Review Each computing platform should have a defined security baseline to limit the exposure of exploits. The Defense Information Systems Agency (DISA) has developed a series of checklists known as Security Technical Implementation Guides (STIGs) that contain the security settings that should be in place to protect the environment. For example, parameters such as password lockout attempts, revision history, or what services should be enabled are set. The security department should ensure that the security configurations are reviewed and monitored on a frequent basis, preferably quarterly at a minimum.

Maintenance of the security baselines typically resides in the operational, infrastructure areas that are responsible for those platforms. It is important that baselines be developed for each platform and are frequently reviewed when new releases of the standards are available. This can be a time-consuming task to ensure (1) baselines are developed for each operational platform (e.g., Windows, Unix, Mainframe, RACF, Oracle, SQL databases, virtualization servers, network devices, desktops), (2) baselines are kept up to date, (3) baselines are properly documented, (4) exceptions to the baselines are approved by management and documented, (5) baselines are tested prior to rolling out to production, (6) all devices are monitored and compared to the baseline, (7) a corrective action plan process exists to upgrade to the current baseline if necessary, and (8) quarterly reviews of compliance are conducted. The information security department is in the best position to provide leadership to ensure that the baselines are being kept up to date and applied to the devices within the environment.

The security department can coordinate weekly meetings with the operational areas to review the compliance with the baselines and track the process that is being made. The additional oversight increases the likelihood that security baselines will receive the proper attention. The security department can also play a role in ensuring that changes to the standards the baselines are built upon (i.e., DISA, Federal Desktop Core Configuration [FDCC]) are communicated to the operational areas in a timely manner.

Logging and Monitoring An organization cannot be really sure what attempts are being made to exploit vulnerabilities to access information unless there is an active monitoring program in place. Some organizations do a great job of collecting logs, however, there is no formal log review process in place and the logs are merely saved in the event an investigation is initiated. This can cause undesired events to go undetected, as the reliance then becomes dependent upon some other external stimulus to kick off an investigation. Log monitoring should be a daily event to be effective, even if a subset of the information is reviewed (e.g., administrator privilege access).

Since log data can be voluminous, security departments will often use a security information and event management (SIEM) product to aggregate and correlate the log information, a reporting tool, or create scripts to reduce the amount of data that must be reviewed. Logs are reviewed for external infiltration events and administrator access attempts, as well as the review of internal users and excessive login attempts. A threshold of the number of violations should be established, after while follow-up is required. Training can then be provided to the habitual user that is not following information security access policy. Due to the time-consuming efforts in reviewing the log, automation has a large payoff in this area. Many times the reports produced for the platforms are rudimentary and can be difficult to use unless some automation of the output is created to determine the exceptions.

Vulnerability Assessment Vulnerability assessments are frequently confused with penetration testing, and they represent two different activities. Penetration testing is the practice of attempting to gain entry to the system and typically obtaining higher-level privileges to demonstrate that the information assumed to be protected by the organization could be disclosed, modified, corrupted, or deleted by an unauthorized user outside of the organization. Vulnerability assessments on the other hand test for flaws in the system, mainly software and hardware, to determine where the exposures are that could be potentially exploited. The vulnerabilities are usually determined by running software tools (e.g., Tenable's Nessus, nCircle's IP360, Application Security's DbProtect) against the computing platform. Individual identifiers are associated with each vulnerability for tracking and remediation purposes. The risk level is also reported by the tools so that those of the highest risk can be acted on immediately. Most tools also provide the links to the patch or release level that should be applied to fix the issue.

The vulnerability scans should be run on a frequent basis, at least quarterly at a minimum. A good process is for information security to administer the scans and feed the information into a tracking document for the high and medium risk items, such as an access database or Excel spreadsheet, and establish owners and commitment dates for mitigation of the issues found in the scans. Weekly meetings to resolve the issues can be held, and the expectation to complete all issues within 90 days of the scan, or a senior executive (e.g., chief information officer [CIO]) justification and approval is needed. There will always be some issues that the operational areas will not be able to complete within 90 days; however, these should be the exceptions due to a lengthy process to resolve or a major system implementation or upgrade that is preventing progress. For example, a vendor product may require a version of Java that is five versions back that contains known exploits, however, the product is not scheduled for update/new release until 6 months from now. The organization may decide to temporarily accept the risk until the new release is available.

Vulnerability scans are necessary to ensuring that holes have not been inadvertently created within the computing infrastructure.

Internet Monitoring/Management of Managed Services Companies that do not have the staff to provide 24/7 monitoring of the externally facing devices may consider the use of managed security services to provide the monitoring. These organizations can achieve economies of scale by monitoring multiple clients in different shifts. Outsourcing to an external company does not dismiss the need of internal staff to respond to the security incidents. It typically requires an on-call person on the company security team that will be able to respond if there is a critical theat. Service level agreements should be put in place as to the services that will be provided and the timeframes expected to respond to issues.

Incident Response The ability to respond quickly to incidents depends largely on how well the process is thought out in advance. Valuable time can be lost during an incident if there is not a process in place, and the result may be following a very chaotic, unorganized process of determining what has happened, containing the security incident, and eradicating the damage that was caused. Mistakes can be made without a well-defined process. The security department's role should be to facilitate the resolution of the incident to ensure that all of the right departments are engaged and the computer security incident response team (CSIRT) process defined by the organization is generally followed. Not all incidents will require the enactment of the CSIRT, so it should be understood under what conditions the team will be invoked. Other departments, such as the business owners, infrastructure teams (server, desktop), and network teams are also engaged, either as a responsible party or an informed party.

Forensic Investigations Forensic investigations have not received much attention within information security departments and tend to receive little investment. If the number of investigations is low, outsourcing this function may be a viable alternative. The time required to build a level of forensic expertise can be very extensive. Performing this function in-house can also be risky if the evidence is to be presented in court, primarily because the opposing counsel will ask, "How many forensic investigations have you performed?" "What training have you had that ensures you have the sufficient level of knowledge?" or "Demonstrate that the appropriate chain of custody was followed completely throughout the process." Still, this is valuable expertise to develop within the organization at a basic level, as the act of going through forensic investigations will highlight gaps in the current logging, monitoring, or configuration processes, as well as creating further learning opportunities for the information security staff.

Central Management Functions Along with providing the general management of the information security program, the security department must also provide the following two functions to interface with the audit requirements and ensure that issues are formally tracked to closure.

Audit Liaison The security controls may be audited frequently depending upon the type of industry in which the company is participating. The security area is well advised to have someone designated to coordinate these audits that understands information security controls. Although the internal audit department may lead the overall audit with the audit firm, they may not have the technical expertise to understand what is being requested, or the potential alternative, compensating or mitigating controls within the environment that can be provided. Information security can provide the expertise and contribute to a smoother running audit, which is explained in more detail in Chapter 11.

Plan of Action and Milestones Security deficiencies need to be tracked and corresponding plan of actions and milestones (POA&Ms) are developed to establish interim steps and dates for completion. Care should be taken in setting realistic dates, or these POA&Ms are recorded as delayed. A formal approval process for the submission of evidence, to whom, and who will review and approve the items for closure should be established. The security operations center team would be an excellent organizational position to close company-generated issues. Issues surfaced by an external audit firm on behalf of another agency (e.g., government contractor–government agency relationship, Office of Inspector General, PCI Assessor) would need to be reviewed by the assessor and closed during his process, which may be during the next onsite audit.

Reporting Model

The security officer and the information security organization should report as high in the organization as position to (1) maintain visibility of the importance of information security and (2) limit the distortion or inaccurate translation of messages that can occur due to hierarchical, deep organizations. The higher up in the organization, the greater the ability to gain other senior management's attention to security and the greater the capability to compete for the appropriate budget and resources. Where the information security officer reports in the organization has been the subject of debate for several years and depends upon the culture of the organization. There is no one best model that fits all organizations, but rather pros and cons associated with each placement choice. Whatever the chosen reporting model, there should be an individual chosen with the responsibility for ensuring information security at the enterprise-wide level to establish accountability for resolving security issues. The discussion in the next few sections should provide the perspective for making the appropriate choice for the target organization.

Business Relationships

Wherever the information security officer reports, it is imperative that he or she establishes credible and good working relationships with executive management, middle management, and the end users that will be following the security policy. Information gathered and acted upon by executive management is obtained through its daily interactions with many individuals, not just executive management. Winning its support may be the result of influencing a respected individual within the organization, possibly several management layers below the executive. Similarly, the relationship between the senior executives and the information security officer is important if the security strategies are to carry through to implementation. Establishing a track record of delivery and demonstrating the value of the protection to the business will build this relationship. If done properly, the security function becomes viewed as an enabler of the business versus a control point, which slows innovation, provides roadblocks to implementation, and represents an overhead cost function. Reporting to an executive that understands the need for information security and is willing to work to obtain funding is preferable.

Reporting to the CEO

Reporting directly to the CEO greatly reduces the message filtering of reporting further down the hierarchy and improves the communication, as well as demonstrating to the organization the importance of information security. Firms that have high security needs, such as credit card companies, technology companies, and companies whose revenue stream depends highly upon website purchases, such as eBay or Amazon, might utilize such a model. The downside to this model is that the CEO may be preoccupied with many other business issues and may not have the interest, time, or enough technical understanding to devote to information security issues.

Reporting to the Information Systems Department

In this model, the information security officer reports directly to the CIO, director of information systems, the vice president of systems, or whatever the title of the head of the IT department is. Most organizations are utilizing this relationship, as this was historically where the data security function was placed in many companies. This is due to the history of security being viewed as only an information technology problem, which it is not. The advantage of this model is that the individual to which the security officer is reporting has the understanding of the technical issues and typically has the clout with senior management to make the desired changes. It is also beneficial because the information security officer and his department must spend a good deal of time interacting with the rest of the information systems department, which builds the appropriate awareness of project activities and issues and builds business relationships. The downside of the reporting structure is the conflict of interest. When the CIO must make decisions with respect to time to market, resource allocations, cost minimization, application usability, and project priorities, the ability exists to slight the information security function. The typical CIO's goals are more oriented toward delivery of application products to support the business in a timely manner. If the perception is that implementation of the security controls may take more time or money to implement, the security considerations may not be provided equal weight. Reporting to a lower level within the CIO organization should be avoided, as noted earlier; the more levels between the CEO and the information security officer, the more challenges that must be overcome. Levels further down in the organization also have their own domains of expertise they are focusing on, such as computer operations, applications programming, or computing infrastructure.

Reporting to Corporate Security

Corporate security is focused on the physical security of the enterprise, and most often the individuals in this environment have backgrounds as former police officers, military, or were associated in some other manner with the criminal justice system. This alternative may appear logical; however, the individuals from these organizations come from two different backgrounds. Physical security is focused on criminal justice, protection, and investigation services, whereas information security professionals usually have different training in business and information technology. The language of these disciplines intersects in some areas but is vastly different in others. Another downside may be the association with the physical security group may evoke a police-type mentality, making it difficult to build business relationships with business users. Establishing relationships with the end users increases their willingness to listen and comply with the security controls, as well as to provide knowledge to the security department of potential violations.

Reporting to the Administrative Services Department

The information security officer may report to the vice president of administrative services, which may also include the physical security, employee safety, and human resources departments. As in reporting to the CIO, there is only one level between the CEO and the information security department. The model may also be viewed as an enterprise function due to the association with the human resources department. It is attractive because of the focus on security for all forms of information (paper, oral, electronic) versus residing in the technology department, where the focus may tend to be more on electronic information. The downside is that the leaders of this area may be limited in their knowledge of information technology and the ability to communicate with the CEO on technical issues.

Reporting to the Insurance and Risk Management Department

Information-intensive organizations such as banks, stock brokerages, and research companies may benefit from this model. The chief risk officer is already concerned with the risks to the organization and the methods to control those risks through mitigation, acceptance, insurance, and so forth. The downside is that the risk officer may not be conversant in the information systems technology, and the strategic focus of this function may give less attention to day-to-day operational security projects.

Reporting to the Internal Audit Department

This reporting relationship can create a conflict of interest, as the internal audit department is responsible for evaluating the effectiveness and implementation of the organization's control structure, including those of the information security department. It would be difficult for the internal audit to provide an independent viewpoint, if the attainment of meeting the security department's objectives is also viewed as part of its responsibility. The internal audit department may have adversarial relationships with other portions of the company due to the nature of its role (to uncover deficiencies in departmental processes), and through association the security department may develop similar relationships. It is advisable that the security department establishes close working relationships with the internal audit department to facilitate the control environment. The internal audit manager most likely has a background in financial, operational, and general controls, and may have difficulty understanding the technical activities of the information security department. On the positive side, both areas are focused on improving the controls of the company. The internal audit department does have a preferable reporting relationship for audit issues through a dotted-line relationship with the company's audit committee on the board of directors. It is advisable for the information security function to have a path to report security issues to the board of directors as well, either in conjunction with the internal audit department or through its own.

Reporting to the Legal Department

Attorneys are concerned with compliance with regulations, laws, and ethical standards, performing due diligence, and establishing policies and procedures that are consistent with many of the information security objectives. The company's general counsel also typically has the respect or ear of the CEO. In regulated industries, this may be a very good fit. On the downside, due to the emphasis on compliance activities, the information security department may end up performing more compliance-checking activities (versus security consulting and support), which are typically the domain of internal audit. An advantage is that the distance between the CEO and the information security officer is one level.

Determining the Best Fit

As indicated earlier, each organization must view the pros and cons of each of these types of relationships and develop the appropriate relationship based upon the company culture, type of industry, and what will provide the greatest benefit to the company. Conflicts of interest should be minimized, visibility increased, funding appropriately allocated, and communication effective when the optimal reporting relationship is decided for the placement of the information security department.

Suggested Reading

1. National Institute of Standards and Technology (NIST). August 2009. Special Publication 800-53 Rev3: Recommended security controls for federal information systems and organizations. http://csrc.nist.gov/publications/nistpubs/800-53-Rev3/sp800-53-rev3-final_updated-errata_05-01-2010.pdf
2. Fitzgerald, T., and Krause, M. 2008. *CISO leadership: Essential principles for success*. Boca Raton, FL: Auerbach.
3. United States General Accounting Office. 1998. *Executive guide: Information security management; Learning from leading organizations*. http://www.gao.gov/archive/1998/ai98068.pdf
4. Information Security Executive of the Year Awards, http://www.iseprograms.com/
5. SC Magazine, Chief Security Officer of the Year Award, http://www.scmagazineus.com
6. Sanborn, M. 2006. *You don't need a title to be a leader: How anyone, anywhere, can make a positive difference*. New York: Crown Business.
7. Drucker, P. F. 2004. *The Effective Executive*. Collins, New York.
8. Johnson, S. 2003. *The present: The gift that make you happier and more successful at work and in life, today!* New York: Doubleday.
9. Covey, S. 2004. *The 7 habits of highly effective people* (Rev. ed.). New York: Free Press.
10. Peters, T. 2005. *Tom Peters essentials series* (Leadership). New York: DK Publishing.
11. Collins, J. 2001. *Good to great: Why some companies make the leap and others don't*. New York: HarperBusiness.
12. Morgenstern, J. 2004. *Never check e-mail in the morning*. New York: Simon & Schuster.
13. Kroeger, O., and Thuesen, J. M. 1992. *Type talk at work: How the 16 personality types determine your success on the job*. New York: Delacorte Press.

4

Interacting with the C-Suite

> Politics are almost as exciting as war, and quite as dangerous. In war, you can only be killed once, but in politics many times.
>
> **Sir Winston Spencer Churchill, 1874–1965**

Along with the rapid rise in visibility of information security within medium- to large-sized organizations has also emerged the desire to gain a seat at the table with the members of the C-suite. Obtaining the ear of the chief executive officer (CEO), chief information officer (CIO), chief financial officer (CFO), and the vice presidents of the business areas often becomes a mission for the individual managing the information security program. Security officers attending the information security conferences frequently ask the questions, "How do I get the attention of the executive management? How do I obtain their support for the information security program?" What these questions are really trying to ask is, "How do I ensure that information security becomes one of the critical priorities for the organization and is sustained on a long-term basis?"

Organizations are much like people, where thoughts and activities are compartmentalized and prioritized so that they do not overwhelm us. Information security is not different in this regard, as it is typically categorized as an IT function, so it becomes the responsibility of the CIO. The activities surrounding this are often placed, in the eyes of the CEO, in the hands of the CIO, so that the CEO can focus on the items that are in his or her box that require attention, such as defining the vision, mission, and strategy for the organization to grow the business; developing new products and services; and increasing market share and revenues. The CEO does not depend upon the CIO to perform these functions, albeit information technology can serve as a large enabler of the growth strategy, so this becomes an area that the CEO has to keep inside his own box. Information security can be delegated from the CEO's perspective, and thus ends up in someone else's box to ensure that it is appropriately taken care of.

There is nothing inherently wrong with the CEO designating ownership of the information security function to another executive, and the process works well as long as the assets are protected adequately and the organization is not experiencing any major incidents. However, when the organization faces a major incident, and the CEO has not been aware of the true security posture of the organization, then the incident takes over the CEO's valuable time to question how the incident happened, who is accountable, and what steps are being taken to prevent the incident from reoccurring in the future.

No one likes surprises, especially Wall Street, where earnings surprises are routinely punished. A better model is that the CEO is informed as to the security posture of the organization on a periodic basis, so he or she can become an advocate in the advancing the security program. The more the CEO and the rest of the executive suite understand about why the lack of adequate controls places undue risk upon the business operations, the more likely funding support for future investments will be made available. No department within an organization is truly independent, although many organizations operate in a silo manner, because financially and programmatically they are interdependent upon each other. Funding made available to the marketing department for a new ad campaign, for example, is less funding that can be made available to the information security area and vice versa. Every decision, whether characterized that way in conversation or not, is subtly asking the question, "What is the risk to the organization if we don't invest the money in this activity?"

Communication between the CEO, CIO, Other Executives, and CISO

The chief information security officer's effectiveness in large part depends upon the support of the executive management, as it is this relationship that provides the necessary funding and support for the security initiatives to move forward to implementation. Communicating with the C-suite requires a different language from what is normally used with the end users or technical staff. Descriptions of security initiatives using technical jargon is analogous to a financial analyst providing a presentation to the organization on internal rates of return, present value, or the interest rate yield curve to the marketing staff. The language that must be used must speak in terms of the business value that the security initiatives will provide to the organization. In many ways, the chief information security officer and the other executives have very complimentary goals, and the security officer should make the connection between the organization's goals and the goals of information security. For example, the organization may have a goal to increase revenue by 10% in the coming year. The security officer has a goal to protect information assets from loss, destruction, and unavailability. Both of these goals are very related, as it would be very difficult to increase revenue if the brand is tarnished by the public disclosure of a breach. A bank seeking to gain new customers to increase the revenue and market share would have a difficult time expanding the customer base if the new smartphone application that was deployed disclosed sensitive information to unauthorized users. Or the mishandling of protected health information (PHI) by a hospital may make people change their hospital of preference if they felt that the privacy of their operation would be disclosed.

Several of these shared goals between the company executives and the chief information security officer (CISO) are shown in Table 4.1. A good exercise for information security is to run through the list of management objectives and understand what the company's position

Table 4.1 Management and Information Security Goals

MANAGEMENT OBJECTIVE	SECURITY OBJECTIVE
Increase shareholder value	Protect information from loss, destruction, unavailability
Increase revenue/market share	Enable secure development of new products
Reduce administrative costs	Ensure efficient service
Accept reasonable business risk	Implement effective and appropriate risk-based controls
Increase worker productivity	Develop secure remote-worker access strategies
Attract and retain talented workforce	Provide assurance through continuous control practices

is on these strategies before communicating with the CEO, CIO, CFO, and so forth. The connections should then be drawn between these objectives and the information security objectives. The stronger the relationship and the more developed this bridge is made between information security program and the management objectives, the stronger the support will be for the initiatives needed to protect the information assets.

13 "Lucky" Questions to Ask One Another

As children we are told to raise our hand and speak up in class. In prior generations, the mantra was children should be seen and not heard. Today's Generation Y has grown up with technology and are used to communicating in a somewhat virtual world. The question is not so much the medium that we are communicating, but rather what we are communicating and are we asking the right questions? Most of us communicate by stating our opinions, desires, concerns, and spend less time actually asking questions and listening to what other individuals think is important. Each of us feels that our job is the most important job at hand, as we have invested years of training into our professions, so it becomes the center from where our conversations start. However, to be an effective communicator, we have to move away from our own center and enter the uncomfortable area of understanding the needs of others first. Our effectiveness is greatly enhanced if the security initiatives that are desired by information security can meet the needs of the executives. The only way to really determine this is by asking the right questions, listening to the answers, and then determining the strategy to meet and exceed those needs. Similarly, the chief information security officer needs to be prepared for the questions that may be asked of them, so that answers can be readily available. When we go on a job interview it is common practice to think through the questions that might be asked. Each interaction with a company executive should be regarded as a job interview, where small incremental judgments are continually made about the information security program and the value to the organization.

The following sections provide thirteen questions that the CISO should be prepared to answer from the CEO, thirteen questions from the CIO, and 13 questions that the CISO should ask of both the

CEO and CIO (Fitzgerald, 2007). Being prepared for and asking these questions will increase the credibility for information security.

The CEO, Ultimate Decision Maker

The CEO is faced with challenges and opportunities on a daily basis. The CEO may be oriented toward improving efficiency by reducing administrative costs as one of the management objectives in the previous discussion, or may be confronted with challenges of merging with another organization, increasing revenues by X%, improving market share, or introducing new innovative products for the company. A CEO's role is to create an inspiring vision and mission for the organization and to ensure that the actions of the culture match this vision. Consider the difference in culture between a processor of health care claims and that of a company such as Apple that produces the popular iPad. The former may be very focused on providing excellent customer service at the lowest possible administrative cost, whereas the later may be focused on creating an environment where creativity and innovation can flourish. This does not mean that the health insurer does not care about innovation or that the iPad manufacturer does not care about costs, but rather that the emphasis in priorities and the subsequent decision making is likely to be consistent with the most important values.

CEOs are the big picture people. So what should be their role with respect to security? Equal support. Equal support means that CEOs should be expected to (1) support the security department's initiatives as they relate to the mission of the business, (2) ensure responsible funding is provided for ongoing security operations, and (3) hold the components of the business accountable for achieving their objectives in a secure manner. In other words, the responsibility of the CEO to security is no different that their responsibility to any other part of the business or any other executive. Consider that you are the CEO in charge of manufacturing an automobile. Although you may be responsible for meeting quarterly sales and production goals at a tactical level, the key role is to ensure that over time, the company continues to produce automobiles demanded by consumers over the long term at a reasonable profit to attract investors and create sustainable shareholder value. Although a great design could take many years and multiple focus groups, and could be built with the highest quality imaginable by spending more in production and time, the reality is that the car may never make it to market in time or may cost too much if these parameters are ignored.

Since CEOs are dealing with financial, operational, and business risk decisions on a continuing basis, they need to have enough information to make a fact-based decision that will not expose the organization to regulatory compliance issues, risk to the business reputation, or decrease the efficiency and effectiveness of the organization's capability to produce. When launching a new product or service, if there is not a clear understanding of the security risks, the organization could end up closing its doors due to the lack of controls.

Many CEOs today are aware of the security risks that have created financial and public relations nightmares related to the loss of information. Astute CEOs take the time to understand this risk and ensure that appropriate responsibility is designated for reducing the risk. The stories of data loss that have been in the news are endless: Card Systems is out of business after 40 million customers were potentially exposed, TJX stores incurred a large financial impact after 45 to 90-plus million customers had their credit card accounts exposed, Bank of America had 1.3 million people exposed due to a missing backup tape, and Eli Lilly disclosed confidential information in an e-mail to 669 people on Prozac, which ended up costing millions in fines and oversight by the Federal Trade Commission for 20 years (FTC, 2002). The key takeaway from these stories is not so much in the exposure themselves, but rather that these are events that have set up the *potential* for real loses by the consumers. A much smaller fraction of actual personal damages really occurs. The message for the CEO is that once the breach happens, the possibility of a loss by a customer sets off a chain reaction of events that involve costly public relations; incident response; increased audits; implementation of additional processes, people, and technology; offer of free credit monitoring; and so forth. This does not include the intangible costs that much management and technical staff attention is focused away from the core business issues to respond to the security event. Money is also diverted from projects or projects are delayed to enable the mitigation of the incident.

Funds are a finite resource within any organization. The CEO must weigh the costs of a breach, the costs of other initiatives, and decide the appropriate amount to be spent on information security. Typically, after an incident, the checkbook seems to be open. When nothing is going wrong, the concern might if we have too much staff. Could we do this for less? This makes providing the appropriate amount of information by the security officer to influence the CEO a challenging task. Security is a typically viewed as a cost to the business. There is nothing sexy about a security project, because in and of itself, it does not produce increased revenues or reduce costs for the organization. Revenues that are produced are a result of the products and services that are created, and administrative costs are a result of the assets, people, or processes that can be eliminated or reduced. Security investments are a choice for the CEO, not an absolute. Just as other departments may implement technology or create efficient manual processes, there are trade-offs. The CEO should be asking the following questions of the security officer when security investments are being solicited.

Question 1: How Will This Level of Funding Ensure That I Have an Adequate Control Environment That Ensures I Am Performing the Documented Activities on a Consistent Basis? Notice the question is not "How will this level of funding ensure that we have the best security across all of our peers?" Although this may be a strategic initiative depending upon the industry of the company, most CEOs was to ensure that they are spending just enough to get the job done. If the marginal benefit does not outweigh the marginal cost, then it would most likely not be considered a wise investment. The question also expects consistency within the security department. In other words, if the person in charge of security is handed X dollars, the expectation is that they can run their program primarily on X dollars without frequently returning for more funds.

Question 2: Will Our Security Controls Meet the Regulatory Compliance Requirements We Are Exposed to (GLBA, SOX, HIPAA, FISMA, PCI Standard, etc.)? Executives are concerned with regulatory compliance, as some of the regulations have large financial impacts to the organization, as well as to them personally. Failing to meet regulatory compliance can also result in criminal prosecution, albeit it is rare that this would occur for failure to meet security controls. Nonetheless, failure to meet regulatory compliance can have negative consequences for the company and may require additional oversight. For example, several organizations have been found by the Federal Trade Commission to have violated their published privacy practices and were required to pay fines of as much as $15 million and subject themselves to 10 to 20 years of additional oversight.

Question 3: What Level of Funding Are Our Competitors Doing? Related to question number 1, companies want to spend the appropriate amount and not overspend on security, as this represents resources that can be deployed elsewhere.

Question 4: How Will This Security Investment Reduce My Business Reputation Risk (i.e., Keeping Us out of the Headlines)? In some ways the security incidents are not shocking news anymore, as they seem to occur much more frequently. However, no organization wants to be associated with bad news, especially if the implication is that the organization is not capable of protecting the business relationship and the information that consumers and other businesses are entrusting to the company's care. People have too many choices today and have much less loyalty to a particular brand. Not only is the brand damaged when an incident occurs, the time that must be invested from a public relations viewpoint can be very costly. Instead of focusing on the daily business and the next business acquisition, the CEO has to spend time receiving updates on the situation, ensuring that the problem is being properly addressed, and ensuring the appropriate media message is being communicated by the organization.

Question 5: How Will This Investment Support a Key Product or Service That Supports Our Corporate Vision? Security is much more valuable if it can be linked to a product or service offering versus seen as an overhead function. Most security activities fall under the category of overhead, but there may be cases where security can be directly tied to the enablement of a product. For example, developing the security controls to ensure a secure virtual desktop environment would permit the company to promote a work-at-home policy due to the secure controls being designed and developed within the infrastructure. Without this investment, the confidentiality of information or the reliability of the network would not be attainable. The more that the information security department can articulate this value, the more in-tune with the business the security department will be perceived.

Question 6: Will These Investments Have an Impact on the Reduction of Ongoing Audit Issues? Audit issues are viewed negatively in most organizations (versus viewed as quality self-checking of the controls within the enterprise), and as such, the CEOs want to be sure that these are addressed in a timely manner. The expectation of the CEOs is that given an adequate level of funding, there should be minimal audit issues, and no issues should persist or be repeated that would represent a high risk to the company.

Question 7: Is There Support from the Other Executives for This Investment? The other executives in the company should be regarded as the trusted advisors to the CEO, just as the U.S. president has a cabinet of senior leaders that help shape the president's decisions. Failure to engage these executives and garner their support is a mistake, especially if one of the executives has a larger ear of the CEO than the others and has the ability to turn the security initiatives into a success or sabotage their implementation.

Question 8: Can This Investment Be Performed at a Lower Cost by an External Consultant or Outsourcing the Process? As the CEO is always looking for lower costs, if becomes very important to remain competitive with outside services. The security officer must be sure that they are spending the appropriate time on the right areas to remain competitive. If the security officer spends 70% of his or her budget drafting the security policies, there is little left over to implement the technical controls that may be necessary.

Question 9: Does This Investment Require a Multiyear Commitment? Security investments are typically within a 3- to 6-month timeframe, however, sometimes the commitment for a large initiative (e.g., identity and access management) may need to be spread across multiple years. When this is done, the security officer should be prepared to defend the remaining expenditures during each budget cycle and to continue to gain support from other (new) executives to the work effort.

Question 10: Are There Short-Term Paybacks That Can Be Realized through a Phased Project Implementation? Where multiyear commitments are required it is important to show incremental deliverables along the way. A multiyear project with no substantial deliverables is likely to get cut before the end of the project.

Question 11: What Other Resources within the Organization Are Required? Security implementations are rarely conducted by just the information security department to the exclusion of the business areas, infrastructure, applications development, computer operations, facilities, human resources, and so forth. The costs of these resources are often hidden costs as they may not charge specifically to a security project to support the security initiatives.

Question 12: Where Is This Type of Security Investment on the Adoption Curve? In Other Words, Are We an Early Adopter (Higher Risk, Such as an Identity Management Effort), or Is This a More Mature Practice (Lower Risk, Such as Implementing Antivirus/IDS Technologies)? The risk appetite of the organization often determines the type of adopter the organization is. Companies that view themselves as highly innovative are likely to invest in multiple technologies and understand that some of the projects will fail. Others are happy to wait until the products have matured and are generally accepted in the marketplace, where the pricing is typically lower, before deciding to commit to the technology. As little as 15 years ago some leading-edge companies were deciding on how to use the Internet for business and if this made sense. Today, that would be a silly question for a business to ask (if it should have a Web presence). The barriers to entry and cost are much less today than they were during this prior period, making more sense for many more companies. CEOs need to understand if the proposals are bleeding edge (interpreted as high risk) or have been mainstream for some time (perceived as low risk).

Question 13: Do We Have the Skills within Our Organization to Adequately Execute This Investment or Is Additional Expertise Needed to Lower the Risk? The answer to this question is many times yes to both parts. Security technology implementations can be very complex and require an individual that has intimate knowledge of the product to help with the initial implementation. Security policy development and compliance assessments may require additional manpower than what is in-house, or may require the services of an auditor to accurately capture the correct documentation. Obtaining external resources may be due to a skill issue or a lack of resource issue. To meet the time-to-market demands it may be necessary to bring in additional resources.

The CEO Needs to Know Why

The security officer needs to be able to provide the CEO with the answer to the most important question: Why? Even after an incident occurs at a competitor company within the same industry, the why is still not necessarily a given. The CEO should challenge the current control infrastructure, soliciting input from the security officer, CIO, and the business executives to ascertain whether the event could happen within their organization. It may be that the current level of security investment is still appropriate and additional funding is not needed. It may be that the security area is not spending money in the highest risk areas and funds need to be reallocated.

The CIO, Where Technology Meets the Business

The role of the CIO has evolved over the past 15 to 20 years to the point where in medium and large organizations the existence of the role is expected. In some respects, the evolution of the chief information security officer (CISO) is following a similar path of (1) an understanding that the role is needed, followed by (2) role ambiguity, (3) maturation of the role to be the intersection between the business and the technology versus being the most knowledgeable technology person in the organization, and eventually (4) obtaining an executive presence on par with the business executives and being invited to the table so to speak. Much of this evolution in today's world can be attributed to the significant role that technology plays in business effectiveness and efficiency.

Although the earlier staffing of the CIO came predominantly from the information technology ranks and, more specifically, from those individuals responsible for running the data center or in charge of development of the mission-critical applications for the business. These areas were chosen for their knowledge of how technology supported the business (applications) or how to run the IT business (data center operations). In today's environment, the CIO is just as likely to be chosen from the business side of the house, as they bring with them the knowledge of what needs to be accomplished through information technology. In the end, the how is figured out by the middle and first-line management and their technical staffs.

Some organizations still run with an IT focus at the CIO level versus a business focus. In either case, CIO is usually under pressure to (1) deliver the projects on time and within budget to the business, and (2) to ensure availability. Most IT projects involve a high degree of variability and interdependencies, and rarely meet time and budget estimates. To manage the variability, project goals must be developed to constrain the deliverables. The security implications are that in order to meet the deadlines, security investments must be pragmatic and be introduced at the appropriate time during the project life cycle. For example, if the security department first reviews the implementation of access controls during the testing phase, the project team will not be excited about having to go back and rewrite code to meet the new security requirements. As an alternative, if security is represented on the project team during the initial analysis and design phases, the project can proceed without these roadblocks. The CIO needs to ensure that a system development life cycle is followed and the appropriate parties and deliverables are identified to avoid this situation. Attention to security should be on a risk-adjusted basis, with the higher priority projects receiving increased, formalized attention, while the smaller efforts could be accomplished by the development team through the use of internal peer reviews of the security requirements.

Since availability is critical to the organization, the CIO must ensure through a business impact analysis (BIA) that critical applications are identified, along with their recovery time objectives (RTO) to ensure that there is minimal impact to the business in case there is an outage or disaster. This will involve working with the business to determine its priorities. The CIO must also ensure that servers are configured according to documented baselines, applications are coded using secure coding techniques, access to the networks by third parties are controlled, and audit issues (internal and external) are followed up promptly by IT management. Each of these items not only supports the confidentiality and integrity security requirements, but also reduces the risk of unexpected unavailability. It is a given these days that proper investments must be made in firewalls, antivirus software, spam filtering, and spyware. Many of the security vulnerabilities identified through penetration testing or vulnerability assessments are typically the result of failure to analyze what settings were appropriate or failure to consistently adhere to a defined process, not that more technology was necessary. Purchasing an elaborate aggregation tool for logs is of little value if the most important events have not been identified or no one is reviewing the logs on a consistent basis. The informed CIO understands the impact of not performing all of these tasks and the impact it can have in causing unexpected downtime.

Just as the CEO must be aware of the external environment, the CIO needs to be able to depend upon the CISO to provide accurate information as to the risk of doing nothing and what issues the competitors are facing. When the Veterans Administration (VA) lost a laptop containing personal information on 26.5 million individuals, and subsequently required that all of its laptops be encrypted, many organizations took notice. The VA ultimately also ended up paying $20 million to the active duty troops and veterans impacted by the incident (CNN, 2009). Although security programs should not be run by the "incident of the week," due to the widespread media coverage, such major incidents put the CIO in the position of having to answer the question of could this happen to us. Savvy CIOs will not want to accept the risk of this type of situation and will require their IT management and systems security to develop a proposal with several different cost alternatives that would mitigate the problem.

Question 1: What Is the Minimum Necessary Effort Required to Produce Code That Is Secure? The CIO will want input from the CISO to ensure that the developers are creating code that minimizes the possibility of exploit. Over the past few years, the Web applications that are Internet facing have become great opportunities for external hackers. Secure coding guidelines need to be developed by the organization, along with code reviews to ensure that the standards are being followed.

Question 2: What Do We Need to Do to Avoid Audit Issues in the Application Development Process without Adding Significant Expense or Delays to Our Projects? The CIO has committed to deliver products to the business to meet the business needs in a timely manner and is driven by the time tables such as new product launches, a sales promotion, or to meet a contractual obligation of a bid. Rarely does information security have the ability to hold up an implementation at the last minute, so it is vitally important that the requirements are communicated during the development process.

Question 3: Do You See Your Role as an After-the-Fact Reviewer of Security Controls or Engaged in the Implementation of the Controls? This question is getting to the heart of the involvement of the CISO and his or her team. Are they hands-on advisors, consultants, partners in the process, or are they reviewers and approvers after the fact? This will depend upon the organizational culture, as the collaborative organization may lean toward inclusion of information security professionals upfront, whereas the more bureaucratic organization may see the role of security as the final approver (more likely rejecter) of the security controls.

Question 4: What Technologies Are Available to Reduce the Labor-Intensive Process of Keeping Up with the Latest Patches, System Vulnerabilities, Configuration Management and Compliance Monitoring? The more manual the process, the more time consuming it will be, and the possibility that key resources that could be performing other work will be tied up in security activities. If it takes 70 to 80 hours a month for a server engineer to determine whether the virtualization servers are in compliance with the latest Defense Information Systems Agency (DISA) Security Technical Implementation Guides (STIGs) versus 5 hours per month with an automated tool, then the tool may be more cost effective. The hidden costs are the projects that are delayed because the key resource is now unavailable.

Question 5: Can You Provide Information on the "Real Risks" That Are Present in Our Specific Industry and the Appropriate Implementation Alternatives That Companies Use to Mitigate These Risks? The CIO wants to cut through the sky is falling hype with this question to enable his team to appropriately focus on the areas that have the largest payback. This requires networking with other companies to have a broad view of solutions that other companies have implemented.

Question 6: How Can We Ensure That We Have Reduced Our Exposure to an Acceptable Risk? How do we make this determination? Through risk analysis (as described in Chapter 5) a systematic process of determining and documenting risk should be implemented to be able to articulate the risk level of the organization. What is an acceptable level? The executives and not the security officer must determine this.

Question 7: What Tangible Benefit Will We Receive from the Security Investments That Will Enable the Business? Information security practitioners understand the vulnerabilities that may be exploited if a particular security control is not implemented. It may also be able to communicate in general terms what will happen to a business if a breach occurs. However, it is very important that the security officer examine the security investments in the context of what will it do for the business, beyond the basic statement that "we will be more secure." This is an assumed outcome, and the stronger the security officer can tie the investment to how it will ease business operations, enable more business opportunities, reduce the time needed to gain access (increase productivity), or benefit the systems development process, the greater the acceptance of the initiatives will be.

Question 8: Which Internal and External Audit Issues Will These Investments Eliminate? Just as the CEO is concerned over the audit issues, so is the CIO, as these represent areas of work to fix existing problems that are not nearly as exciting as developing new applications. In many cases the CIOs rely on the information security department that still reports to the CIO in many organizations, to lead the charge for the IT department to reduce the number of findings under the CIOs control.

Question 9: What Other Information Technology Resources Are Required, in Addition to Systems Security Staff, to Implement the Security Solution Presented? What Support Is Required from the Business? These hidden costs need to be understood to enable appropriate resource allocation of the remaining IT resources. If a network engineer is spending 40% of his or her time reviewing the baseline configurations, monitoring the network devices, and upgrading to the latest versions/patch levels, then only 60% of his or her time will be available for project work and other maintenance. There will always be constant pressure of the information security area to reduce these expenditures.

Question 10: How Do the Security Requirements Integrate with the Systems Development Life Cycle? Are We Performing These Tasks Already? Organizations may develop a systems development life cycle in response to an audit finding, desire to be certified as being compliant with a standard, such as the Capability Maturity Model Integration (CMMI) from the Carnegie Mellon Software Engineering Institute or the International Organization for Standardization (ISO), to demonstrate that a consistent process for developing software has been implemented. Organizations that do not have a periodic review process in place tend to find that the documented system develop life cycle becomes shelfware after a while, as there is not enforcement mechanism. Developers, like most people, given the choice to follow their own process with less documentation, may opt to do so. As system develop life cycles have emerged, security controls are added at a greater frequency. A few years ago, the Information International Systems Security Certification Consortium Inc. (ISC^2) recognized the need for recognizing the knowledge and experience in this area and created the Certified Secure Software Lifecycle Professional designation. Security must be added into all phases of the life cycle and include areas such as planning, costing, research of potential controls, control design, security testing, implementation, and follow-up and ongoing maintenance of these controls. Applications and platforms also need to have planned technology reviews and upgrades as technology advances, as the existing controls may no longer be sufficient to protect the information assets. For examples, Windows servers running version 2000 or 2003 may no longer be able to be adequately patched and would also no longer be on support, necessitating an upgrade in the infrastructure. The applications running on these software versions may in turn break and need to be upgraded to a more current version. Therefore a holistic view must be taken with developing software and the subsequent upgrades necessary.

Question 11: Do We Have the Necessary Experience In-House to Implement These Solutions? Should We Consider Outsourcing Some of the Functions? To outsource or not is a question that swings as often as the pendulum on a grandfather clock. Companies should periodically examine the possibility of outsourcing, as this may represent an opportunity to acquire a skill set that has not been available within the organization and deliver cost savings. Outsourcing also forces an organization to look more closely at its information security processes and eliminate those processes that are no longer necessary. This occurs because activities that used to be considered as "free" within the organization, in other words there was no billing or chargeback for the activity, is now identified as an activity by the outsourcer and typically charged on a per-request basis (i.e., a security password reset is charged a $25 to $35 help desk call for every reset). Outsourcing of entire functions can also be beneficial, such as the case where there is a lack of in-house staff that is able to staff a 24/7 security operations team. Outsourcing the function to a managed systems security provider (MSSP) would enable the in-house staff to remain more focused on projects and be alerted when there are significant events that must be dealt with.

Question 12: What Are the Critical Success Factors for Achieving Success in Our Security Efforts? How Much Security Is Enough? Security can always be enhanced, the question is should it. Just as the CEO must answer the question for the organization, the CIO will want to determine what percentage of resources should be allocated to information security. Is 4% of the IT budget sufficient? 5%? 10%? The range, depending upon the industry and the organization performing the study, seems to be somewhere in the 3% to 9% range of the IT budget. These numbers need to be evaluated with caution, as different organizations include different items into what constitutes the overall IT budget, different industries have different information security needs, and the larger the organization, the larger the budget and the smaller expenditure that should be expected to implement similar controls due to advantages in pricing, implementation of more cost-effective tools, and the economies of scale.

Question 13: How Can You Help Reduce the Time I Spend on Compliance-Related Efforts in Gathering Documentation and Audit Samples? Compliance activities require taking IT professionals away from their normal work to collect and produce the standard operating procedures, evidence, participate in interviews, and so forth in support of an audit. The security department should be an enabler, provisioning information with minimal distraction for these resources, as this becomes very costly not only in the hourly cost but in the potential delays in other work that may not be getting done.

CIO's Commitment to Security Is Important

The CIO may find himself from time to time serving in the role of arbitrator between the IT management and systems security for security issues. IT projects are driven by deadlines to produce the required functionality. As a result, shortcuts may be taken in the testing, change control, documentation, peer review, or training processes in preference to spending more time and resources in the code development process. Shortcuts in these areas can lead to segregation of duties issues, lack of appropriate documentation, and lack of evidence that the correct processes were being followed. For example, live production data may have been used in the testing environment, potentially disclosing more information than needed to be known by the developers. Additionally, change control procedures may not have been followed by the server engineers, thus increasing the possibility that the baselines are not matching the intended configuration. This also increases the risk that external auditors will not have the documented evidence necessary for their review.

CIOs have a responsibility for sustaining the information technology investment on behalf of the business and to ensure that the information is being made only available to those who are authorized in a secure manner. It is a continuous balancing act of allocating the appropriate resources to systems security, while ensuring that ample resources are available to operate the infrastructure and create new functionality through innovative business applications for the business.

The Security Officer, Protecting the Business

The security officer must have a sense of what the real risks are to the business and not feel that every event has the ability to cripple the business. True, budgets do get cut, performing more with less money than was provided the prior year is oftentimes expected in business, and security is no exception. It is only logical, as increasing numbers of security investments are made, that a point is reached where the cost of maintaining a service should be less than the cost to build the service. Imagine building a complex interstate highway interchange with supporting bridges over a period of several years. The costs are typically very large for engineering, moving the soil, removing the old infrastructure, moving the new beams in place, constructing the bridge, and managing traffic flow during the process. To support the bridge in an ongoing manner, periodic road surfacing, bridge inspections, and repainting of the lines are necessary; however, the original investment is not. Security works the same way, and security officers must be able to separate (1) new investments that provide increased functionally and (2) support for the ongoing security operation. After the initial "we better fix our security program and do something" dies down, the CIO and CEO will be expecting that costs are managed efficiently and either more work is being performed at a level cost or the costs are reduced. Implications for the new security officer are that this life cycle of spending should not be unexpected. Since security departments are typically considered overhead, a cost center, or a non-revenue-producing department, pressures to cut any unnecessary costs will be continuous. As the old adage is applied here, that a good day for the security officer is when nothing happens, it is a challenge to be rewarded with increased investments for "nothing happening" when other departments are investing to make things happen.

Security officers have the opportunity to talk about the technical controls in place in the organization with technical detail to the CIO and CEO, or they have the opportunity to communicate how their department's activities contribute to enabling the delivery of the latest new company product. Savvy security officers provide information related to the latter or show how they are reducing ongoing costs, reducing the wait time necessary for business user access to systems, or reducing the lost productivity that happens as a result of a virus. The CEO may be interested in how the government regulatory compliance requirements are being satisfied or how the audit issues are being reduced year to year. The CIO may have the same desires for information as well as how well the security area is working with the other IT management areas.

Security has become a broad discipline with the security officer responsible for facilitating the implementation and ongoing compliance with the multiple domains of the common body of knowledge, such as risk management, operations security, physical security, business continuity, laws and ethics, network security, and so forth. Obviously, detailed expertise for these domains resides in many different individuals. The security officer is expected to have broad security knowledge and why each of these areas is important to the business. The ability to work up and down the organization translating technical jargon into a language appropriate for the CEO, CIO, business executives, middle management, end users, and external parties is an essential skill. Leadership involves influencing, written and oral communication skills, and building relationships with business partners for the bigger picture (of supporting the vision and mission of the business).

Question 1: What Are the Top Three Business Priorities within the Next 12 to 18 Months? When the security officer asks this question, this creates the perception that information security is concerned not only with protecting the information assets but it also cares about how the information security activities can contribute to the success of the business. The question needs to be framed with a short-term horizon, so that investments in information security can be viewed as supporting the business today and not through a theoretical point in the future.

Question 2: If We Could Develop and Implement Solutions for Two Security Issues Tomorrow, What Would They Be? In Other Words, What Are Your Biggest Pain Points? Each CEO and CIO is wrestling with many issues each day, and 80% of the issues reside in 20% of the projects.

Understanding these pain points will help the security department to direct activities to these visible areas to help solve their most nagging problems. Information security may not be able to help solve these issues, but if we assume that we know what they are, the real issues may never be known to us, thereby passing up opportunities.

Question 3: What Would Be the Best Way to Engage You to Ensure That You Get What You Expect out of the Information Security Program? The CIO may be the type of person that wants to know all the detail and have cost–benefit calculations before making a decision, or he may be the type that responds to a reasonable proposal and thinks it will move the organization in the right direction. He may also want to approve each step or be notified when the initiative is finished. She may want a weekly detailed status report of the process along with a weekly meeting or may be satisfied with a monthly two-slide PowerPoint presentation during a staff meeting on the progress. Simply asking this question will avoid wasting time by the security department to prepare detailed analysis or be embarrassed when presenting a two-slide presentation and being grilled for the detail. The business often relies upon the CIO's judgment as to the adequacy of the technical infrastructure and in this role the CIO needs the assessment of the information security officer. The information must be delivered in a manner that is expected by the CIO.

Question 4: What Level and Frequency of Reporting Would You Like to See? What Metrics Would Be the Most Meaningful to You? As put so well in the old adage "You can't improve what you don't measure," security improvement is the same way. Consider how well our students would function if there were no tests and no grades published? Aside from some students rejoicing, probably the ones on the lower end of the grading scale, and some students being upset, most likely those being on the top-end of the grading scale, it would be very difficult to know how the school's students were performing. CIOs want to know how well the investments are performing, just as the Dow Jones or S&P500 Index tracks stocks, to enable them to make future decisions about the worthiness of investing more money in that area. For example, investing in an e-mail filtering product to reduce the amount of spam should result in a reduction of the number of unwanted e-mails that end up in employees' inboxes. This is a metric that can be measured by the number of e-mails that are blocked at the perimeter. Initially, the CIO may want frequent monitoring of the metric before and after implementation, and as time goes on may only want to see a trending graph on a less frequent basic (e.g., quarterly).

Question 5: What is the Period of Time That You Expect Medium- and High-Risk Issues Identified by the Internal or External Auditors to be Resolved by the Organization? Audits typically occur on an annual cycle, with the auditors closing off the prior year's findings on their next visit or sooner with the appropriate documentation. Letting these issues remain open for an extended period of time places management in a precarious situation, as its now know about an issue but has failed to take prompt action. Resolving most issues within 90 days or less would be a good standard and could be proposed to the CIO, whereby any issues requiring longer than this period would require written authorization by the CIO. Gaining these agreements up front is important for the rest of the organization to follow the process.

Question 6: How Involved Would You and Your Management Like to Be in the Development of the Information Security Policies? Engaged in the Development? Formal Approval? Informed? Additionally, What Resources Are You Willing to Commit and at What Organizational Level? The CIO or his team may want to be engaged in policy development from the start or may be satisfied with the information security department taking the lead and providing them with the draft for discussion.

Question 7: What Have You Read in the News That You Would Not Want Associated with Our Company? CEOs have read the stories from technology magazines, mainstream magazines and newspapers, and online articles. Understanding their hot button issues can be very useful in constructing the appropriate security program that plays to the CIO's needs. Is the CIO more concerned about the unauthorized disclosure of information or the backup of the data center in the event of a disaster?

Question 8: Would You Characterize Our Organization as an Early Adopter, Innovator, or Follower Utilizing Mature Technologies? Organizations that are early adopters generally have funds that are allocated to new technology projects that take the form of pilots, proof concepts, prototypes, and so forth. They are willing to experiment, knowing that all projects do not see production implementation. The security officer must be careful in interpreting the stance of the organization, as it may include "innovation" in the mission/vision statements, but fail to provide funds outside the normal business operations to truly be innovative or may show a track record of terminating individuals that lead failed projects. Most organizations by definition are followers and implement mature technologies where there are more resources with experience to carry out the implementation, thus reducing the risk. An organization may be a hybrid organization, implementing new, unproven technologies such as a foray into cloud computing for their e-mail services, but operating in mature security technologies with the implementation of secure token identification devices.

Question 9: Would You Characterize Our Organization as a Risk Taker or Risk Averse? Security is all about managing risks to the company, so it is important that the security officer ensure that the risk appetite that is taken by information security is consistent with the risk appetite of the C-suite executives, or the security officer risks losing his audience when discussing the risks determined through the risk analysis or assessment process.

Question 10: What Are Your Expectations for How Information Security Can Support the Organizational Goals within the Next 12 Months? 18–24 Months? Beyond 3 Years? As an extension to question 1, security needs to plan for those initiatives that are longer in the making. The company may be planning to relocate to a new office building or data center under construction and waiting 2 to 3 years would miss the window of opportunity to prepare for the eventual move.

Question 11: What Products or Services Would You Like to be Able to Provide Right Now, But Are Apprehensive Due to the Perceived Security Exposures? The company may be considering the development of an e-commerce site that could have issues with the handling of credit card information, or it could want to deploy reports to its hospital providers on the Internet versus mailing the weekly reports, but are concerned that only the appropriate individuals should be able to access the information. The security department may not have the complete solutions to these issues, as they may be new to the department as well, but they can serve as the catalyst to partner with another company to provide the necessary expertise if this is the case.

Question 12: If We Were to Have a Significant Incident Happen to Us, What Are Your Expectations of My Area? Other Business Areas? Where Does the Responsibility Lie? The security officer needs to understand what is the existing protocol for incident reporting and response, and when the information security department should become engaged and lead the resolution of the incident. The security officer will need to determine where the CIO or CEO will need to be engaged in the computer security incident response team (CSIRT) plan.

Question 13: How Else Can I Help You? This final question is a very simple, albeit powerful question to ask the CIO or CEO. The open-endedness of the question serves two purposes: (1) it again establishes that information exists to support the business and not the other way around, and (2) it reveals any needs that were not provided by asking the questions.

The CEO, CIO, and CISO Are Business Partners

In a sense, the CEO, CIO, and CISO are each running a business with a vision, mission, and a set of operating principles, policies, and procedures for effective and efficient operation. There is conflict when the norms of the three individuals and their supporting organizations are not aligned with each other. Information technology and security provide support to the business and only exist because of that relationship. The business vision and mission must drive the projects, the risk profile, and the investments required. Each individual is responsible for different facets of information security, from establishing and maintaining an organizational culture that supports the activities and the implementation of secure technology projects to the ensuring that ongoing security operations are appropriately managed. Although the CEO and CIO roles are more clearly defined due to the maturity of the job description, the CISO role continues to evolve.

Building Grassroots Support through an Information Security Council

Individuals that have been unable to secure the attention or financial commitment from the senior leadership of their respective organizations typically voice concerns that management is not involved or committed to the security program. The statement is usually accompanied with frustration as a result of multiple attempts to obtain funding, only to be faced with flat budgets, cuts to the current expenditure levels, or the elimination of separate information security budgets. Although each organization has different values, principles, and strategies to move the business forward in a secure manner, the following section explores some techniques for building management commitment through the implementation of a successful information security council. Experience indicates that security councils are excellent mechanisms for establishing buy-in across middle management, senior management, and the end users of the organization.

Establishing the Security Council

The information security council forms the backbone for sustaining organizational support for comprehensive information security programs. Additionally, the security council serves as the governance or oversight function for the information security program. The vision of the security council must be clearly defined and understood by all members of the council. Before the appropriate representation of the council can be decided, the purpose of the council must be decided. Although the primary purpose is to provide governance and oversight for the security program and provide a mechanism to sustain the organizational security initiatives, the purpose that will be most meaningful to the specific organization will depend upon the current organizational culture and the maturity of information security practices, as discussed in other sections of this book.

A clear vision statement should be in alignment with and support the organizational vision. Typically, the statement would draw upon the security concepts of confidentiality, integrity, and availability to support the business objectives. The vision statement is not technical and should focus on the advantages to the business. People will be involved in the council from management and technical areas and have limited time to participate, so the vision statement must be something that is viewed as contributing to the business. The vision statement should be short, to the point, and achievable.

Mission statements are objectives that support the overall vision. These become the roadmap to achieving the vision and help the council clearly view the purpose for their involvement. Some individuals may choose nomenclature such as goals, objectives, and initiatives. A sample mission statement is shown in Figure 4.1. Effective mission statements do not need to be lengthy, as the primary objective is to communicate the goals so technical and nontechnical individuals readily understand them. The primary mission of the security council

The information security council provides management direction and a sounding board for the SocialBook Company's information security efforts to ensure that these efforts are

- Appropriately prioritized
- Supported by each organizational unit
- Appropriately funded
- Realistic given SocialBook's information security needs
- Balanced with business needs with respect to cost, response time, ease of use, flexibility, and time to market

The information security council takes an active role in enhancing our security profile and increasing the protection of our assets through

- Approval of organization-wide information security initiatives
- Coordination of various workgroups so that security goals can be achieved
- Promoting awareness of initiatives within their organizations
- Discussion of security ideas, policies, and procedures and their impact on the organization
- Recommendation of policies to the SocialBook Company IT steering committee
- Increased understanding of the threats, vulnerabilities, and safeguards facing our organization
- Active participation in policy, procedure, and standard review

The SocialBook Company information technology steering committee supports the information security council by

- Developing the strategic vision for the deployment of information technology
- Establishing priorities, arranging resources in concert with the vision
- Approval of the recommended policies, standards, and guidelines
- Approval of major capital expenditures

Figure 4.1 Sample security council mission statement.

will vary by organization but should include statements that address the following.

Oversight of Security Program By establishing the goal of security program oversight in the beginning, the members of the council begin to feel that they have some input and influence over the direction of the security program. This is key, as many security decisions will impact their areas of operation. This also is the beginning of management commitment at the committee level, as the deliverables produced through the information security program now become recommended or approved by the security council versus the information security department.

Decide on Project Initiatives Each organization has limited resources, that is, time, money, and people to allocate across projects to advance the business. The primary objective of information security projects is to reduce the organizational business risk through the implementation of reasonable controls. The council should take an active role in understanding the initiatives and the resulting "business" impact.

Prioritize Information Security Efforts Once the security council understands the proposed project initiatives and the associated positive impact to the business, it can be involved with the prioritization of the projects. This may be in the form of a formal annual process or may be through the discussion and expressed support for individual initiatives.

Review and Recommend Security Policies Review of the security policies should occur through a line-by-line review of the policy, a cursory review of the procedures to support the policies, and a review of the implementation and subsequent enforcement of the policies. Through this activity, three key concepts are implemented that are important to sustaining commitment:

1. Understanding of the policy is enhanced.
2. Practical ability of the organization to support the policy is discussed.
3. Buy-in is established to subsequent support of implementation activities.

Champion Organizational Security Efforts Once the council understands and accepts the policies, it serves as the organization's champion behind the policies. Why? Because the council members were involved in the *creation* of the policies. They may have started reviewing a draft of the policy created by the information systems security department, but the resulting product was only accomplished through their review, input, and participation in the process. The security leader must involve the business areas in the creation of policies to create ownership of the deliverable, which generates a desire to see the security policy or project succeed within the company.

Recommend Areas Requiring Investment Members of the council have the opportunity to provide input from the perspective of their individual business units. The council serves as a mechanism for establishing broad support for security investments from this perspective. Resources within any organization are limited and allocated to the business units with the greatest need and the greatest perceived return on investment. Establishing this support enhances the budgetary understanding of the other business managers, as well as the chief financial officer, which is essential when obtaining the appropriate funding.

A mission statement that incorporates the previous concepts will help focus the council and also provide the sustaining purpose for their involvement. The vision and mission statements should also be reviewed on an annual basis to ensure that the council is still functioning according to the values expressed in the mission statement, as well as to ensure that new and replacement members are in alignment with the objectives of the council.

Appropriate Security Council Representation

The Security Council should be made up of representatives from multiple organizational units that are necessary to support the policies in the long term. Possible participants shown in Figure 4.2 include

Human resources—The human resources department is essential to provide knowledge of the existing code of conduct, employment and labor relations, termination, and disciplinary action policies and practices that are in place.

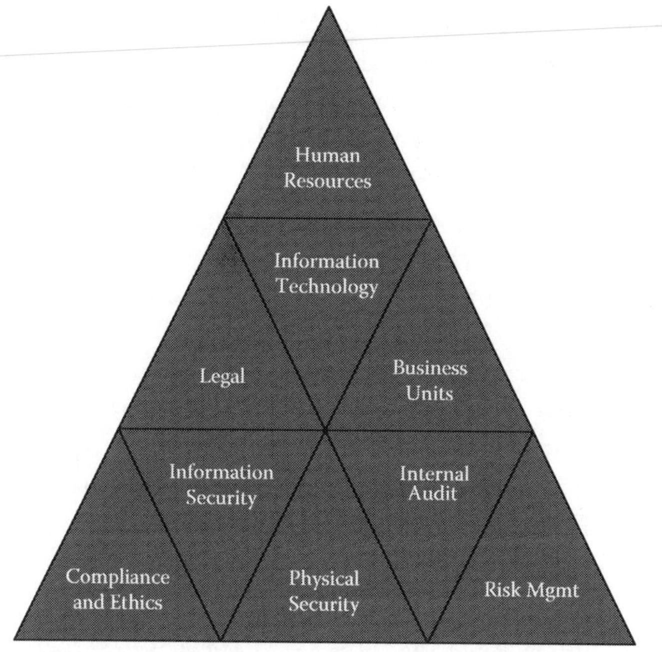

Figure 4.2 Security council representation.

Legal—The legal department is needed to ensure that the language of the policies is stating what is intended, and that applicable local, state, and federal laws are appropriately followed.

Information technology—The information technology department provides technical input and information on current initiatives, and the development of procedures and technical implementations to support the policies.

Business unit representation—The individual business unit representation is essential to understand how practical the policies may be in carrying out the mission of the business.

Compliance and ethics—Compliance department representation provides insight on ethics, contractual obligations, and investigations that may require policy creation.

Information security—The security officer should represent the information security department and members of the security team for specialized technical expertise.

The security council should be comprised primarily of management-level employees, preferably middle management. It is difficult to obtain the time commitment required to review policies at a detailed level by senior management. Reviewing the policies at this level is a necessary step to achieve buy-in within management; however, it would not be a good use of the senior management level in the early stages of development. Line managers are very focused on their individual areas and may not have the organizational perspective necessary (beyond their individual departments) to evaluate security policies and project initiatives. Middle managers appear to be in the best position to appropriately evaluate what is best for the organization, as well as possessing the ability to influence senior and line management to accept the policies. Where middle management does not exist, then it is appropriate to include line managers, as they are typically filling both of these roles (middle and line functions) when operating in these positions.

The information security officer (ISO) or the CISO should chair the security council. The ISO is in a better position knowledge-wise to chair the council, however, politically it may be advantageous for the CIO to chair the council, where he may be able to better communicate support through the information technology department. It is my experience that the stronger argument is for the council to be chaired by the ISO, as it provides for better separation of duties and avoids the "rooster in the hen house" perception if the CIO chairs the council. This is true even if the ISO does not report through the information technology organization. In addition to the ISO, the council should also have one to two members of the systems security department available to (1) provide technical security expertise and (2) understand the business concerns so that solutions can be appropriately designed.

Many issues may be addressed in a single security council meeting, which necessitates having someone record the minutes of the meeting. Since the chairperson's role in the meeting is to facilitate the discussion, ensure that all viewpoints are heard, and drive the discussions to decisions where necessary, another participant should record the proceedings. Recording the meeting is also helpful to capture key points that may have been missed in the notes, so that accurate minutes are produced.

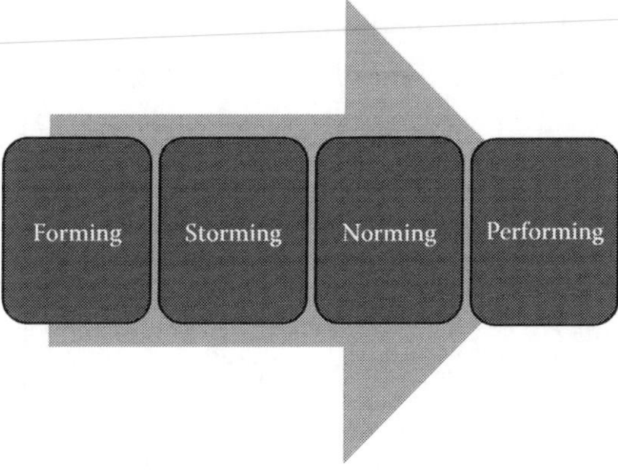

Figure 4.3 Four stages of Tuckman's group development model.

"-Inging" the Council: Forming, Storming, Norming, and Performing

Every now and then, an organization will recognize that collaboration is not taking place between the functional departments and it is time to talk about enhancing the team development process. This is usually the result of poor or no communication between the departments. Why wait for the problems to occur? When committees are formed, they are not magically functional the moment they are formed, but rather must go through a series of necessary steps to become an operational team. The classic four phases of team development are shown in Figure 4.3 (Tuckman, 1965). Let's visit each of the concepts briefly and how they apply to the security council.

Forming Forming is the stage where the efforts are moving from an individual to a team effort. Individuals may be excited about belonging to something new that will make a positive change. The tasks at hand and role of the council are decided (as described earlier). Teams should be communicating openly and honestly about their likes and dislikes, deciding what information needs to be gathered to carry out their mission, and should be engaging in activities that build trust and communication with each other. It is critical to draw out the responses of those that may appear to be silent in the meetings, as they may be thinking some very valuable thoughts, but may be afraid at this stage that their ideas may be rejected. It is important to have patience at this stage and let the team form and not rush the discussion. The leader must serve as a facilitator for bringing the parties together, but not be overly authoritative, as that can jeopardize or slow the buy-in process.

Storming Now that the objectives are understood and the team has had the chance to discuss some of the challenges that it is tasked to resolve, doubt may settle in. Some members may become resistant to the tasks and return to their old comfort zones. Communication between members starts to erode and different sections of the team form alliances to counterpositions. The team becomes divided and there is minimal collaboration between the individuals. At this stage, it may be necessary to reestablish or change the rules of behavior for the council, negotiate the roles and responsibilities between the council members, and possibly return to the forming stage and answer any open questions about the purpose and clarity of the council. And finally, listen to the concerns of the council members and let them vent any frustrations. They may have some very valid concerns that need to be addressed in order to be successful. The leader must continue to reemphasize the importance of the security council and the importance of gaining alignment with objectives that everyone can live with. Specific frustrations of members should be explored and brainstorming sessions should be held with the entire council to resolve the frustrations. The leader must recognize that this dissention is a critical step for individuals to feel that their individual concerns will be heard and reacted to during the long-term operation of the council.

Norming At the norming stage the members of the council begin to accept their roles, the rules of behavior, their role on the team, and respect the individual contributions that others on the team can provide. Now wouldn't it be nice if the storming stage could be skipped and the security council just moved to the norming stage? Think of a child learning to ice skate. The concept of ice skating is explained in vague terms such as, "Put these skates on your feet, then stand up, and skate around the rink." The child has an idea of how this works because she has seen others skating and it looks pretty easy. However, when the child stands up, she is in for a big surprise … boom! The same applies for teams, as much as individuals have seen other teams' success, worked on other teams until the issues are worked out, the team cannot feel how bad the fall will hurt until this particular team falls down. As the norming stage progresses, competitive relationships may become more cooperative, more sharing is present, the sense of "we are a team" evolves, and the team members feel more comfortable working together. This stage of development should focus on detailed planning, creation of criteria for completion of goals, and continuing to encourage the team and build upon the positive behaviors demonstrated within the team and to change the unhealthy ones. The leader must seize the opportunity provided during the team norming stage to focus on meaningful work. The council will lose patience if there are still discussions in this stage about what the vision statement should be, as the council has limited time and needs to now see progress toward the objectives.

Performing The team is now functioning as a unit focused upon the objectives of the security council. The team has the best opportunity at this stage to meet deadlines, utilize each member's unique talents, and produce quality deliverables. The members of the team have gained insight into the unique contributions to everyone on the team and recognize that the team can accomplish much more than any one individual on the team. The leader must recognize in this stage that the council can slip back into earlier stages if individual concerns are ignored. Council members also may change over time and new council members need to be assimilated into the process.

The security council may be formed in a day but does not become a team in a day. Understanding the path that every team traverses can be helpful in knowing where the team is currently functioning, as well as to permit the application of strategies to move the team to the next stage. Depending upon the organizational culture and the individuals involved, the Security Council may become a functioning team within weeks or months. What is important is that the commitment to getting to the team stage has a level of persistence and perseverance equal to the passion to build a successful security program within the organization.

Integration with Other Committees

As indicated earlier, management has limited time to be involved in efforts that may not seem to be directly related to their department. Examine the performance objectives and performance reviews of the management of most organizations, and it becomes readily apparent that the majority of the performance rewards are based upon the objectives of the individual department goals. There is typically little incentive for participating to "enhance the corporate good" even though that may be communicated by the organization's vision, mission, goals, and objective statements. Therefore, committees where there is not a direct benefit or their involvement is not seen as critical will be met with a lukewarm reception.

So when the information security department decides to "add a few more committees," this is likely to be met with resistance. A practical approach is to leverage the committees that are already established, such as an information technology steering committee, electronic commerce committee, standards committee, a senior management leadership committee, or other committee that has a history of holding regularly scheduled (and attended!) meetings. Tapping into these committees and getting 30 minutes on the agenda reserved specifically for security will provide ample airtime for security issues and the appropriate linkage to the company decision makers. In committees such as the information technology steering committee, many of the issues discussed have information security issues embedded within them and being present provides the mechanism to be at the table for these issues.

Since the time allocated for discussing information security issues tends to decrease as the management chain is traversed to higher levels of management, it is important to ensure that the security council is well established and performing in the norming or performing stages. Participation at the higher levels should be limited to review, discussion, communication of initiatives, and primarily decision making (approval of policies and projects). The senior management stamp of approval is necessary to win broad organizational support and is a key component for successful implementation. If the security council does not perceive that the recommendations are important to the senior leadership, it will lose interest. If the senior leadership does not approve the security policies, organizational management and staff support will also dissipate. Therefore, it is important to get on the agenda and stay on the agenda for every meeting. This also creates the (desired) perception that security is an ongoing business process necessary to implement the business objectives.

Once it is decided which committees would be the best candidates for integration, then a decision needs to be made as to how the committees will function together. Is the IT steering committee the mechanism for policy and project approval? Is there a dollar threshold required for it approval? How are changes to the security policies made at this level? Do they go back to the security council for re-review, or are they changed and considered final at this point? Much of this will depend upon each individual cultural norm of how teams and committees function.

Establish Early, Incremental Success

Organizations tend to get behind individuals and departments that have demonstrated success in their initiatives because they believe that the next initiative will also be successful. Organizations lose patience for 15- to 18-month initiatives (these tend to be labeled as long-term strategies these days). Projects should be divided into smaller discrete deliverables versus trying to implement the entire effort. This allows the organization to reap the benefits of the earlier implementation while waiting for the results of the longer-term initiative. The early initiative may also help shape or redefine the longer-term initiative through the early lessons learned.

The early initiatives should provide some benefit to the organization by making their processes easier, enabling new business functionality, providing faster turnaround, reducing paper handling, making more efficient or effective processes. The primary objective should not be something that benefits the information security department but rather provides benefit to the business (although it most likely will provide information security benefit even though this is not the "sell"). Management may be skeptical that the investment in information security will produce an equal amount of benefits. Nothing helps future funding opportunities more than through establishing a track record of (1) developing projects that contribute to the business objectives, (2) establishing cost-effective aggressive implementation schedules, and (3) delivering on time, (4) delivering within budget, and (5) delivering what was promised (at a minimum).

Let Go of Perfectionism

Imagine being a dancer of 15 years, dancing since you were 2½ years old, practicing a couple of nights a week learning jazz and ballet. Imagine the hours of commitment to a discipline, which makes movements that would be difficult for most of us, appear to be purposeful, graceful, and flow with ease. Imagine that it is the big night for showcasing this enormous talent, the recital, and the dancer is rightfully filled with excitement in anticipation of performing in front of friends and family. As the curtain rises, and the dancers are set to begin the performance, a dancer's hairpiece falls off as the dance begins. Oh no, what to do? Does she stop to pick up the hairpiece? Does the dancer look at the floor to avoid stepping on the hairpiece? Does the dancer break into tears, stop and say, "I messed up?" No, none of the above. While it is preferred that dancers firmly attach their hairpieces, and that is what was planned for and practiced, in the scope of the dance, it is not a big deal. In fact, few people in the audience would actually notice it unless the dancer pointed it out. The dancer dances on, smiling with great pride, demonstrating the skill that she has possessed to the audience's delight.

We should all strive to perform to the best of our ability. The argument could be made that the security profession is made up of many individuals that are control oriented, primarily detail oriented, and analytical and logical decision makers. These personality preferences suit the profession very well, as these attributes are many times necessary to master the information security skills. However, one of the traits also represented by the profession is that of perfectionism, the need to get it right, do the right thing. Security professionals often speak in terms of musts and wills versus shoulds and mights. For example, imagine a policy written that would state, "As an employee, you may choose to create an eight-character password made up of a combination of the alphabet, numbers, special characters, or you may choose something less if you have a hard time remembering it. If KATE123 or your dog's name is easier to remember, then just use that." That would be absurd. We tell users not only the rules, but how to implement them and that they *must* do that action.

Carrying the perfectionist standard forward into every project is a recipe for failure. First, resulting project costs will be higher trying to get everything right. Second, the time to implement will be longer and opportunities to create the business benefit when needed may be missed.

When other individuals across the business units are asked to participate in security initiatives, they may not have a complete understanding of what is expected of them, and some tolerance for this gap in understanding should be accounted for. It may be that they believe that they are supplying the right level of support or are completing the deliverables accurately given their knowledge of what was communicated to them. The minimum expected deliverable for security initiatives should be that if 80% of the goal is completed, then the risk absorbed by the company is considered as reasonable. Achieving the remaining 20% should be viewed as the component that, if implemented, would return increased benefits and opportunities, but not necessary to achieve the minimum level of risk desired. Taking this posture permits the information security initiatives to drive toward perfection but not require attainment of complete perfection to maintain a reasonable risk level. This approach keeps the costs of security implementations in balance with the reduction of risk objectives.

Sustaining the Security Council

Humpty Dumpty sat on the wall, Humpty Dumpty had a great … well we know the rest of this story. Putting the pieces back together again is much more difficult than “planning for the fall.” As mentioned in the section titled “‘-*Ing*ing’ the Council,” the team will go through various stages. Frustration, boredom, impatience, and inertia may set in as the sizes of the efforts are realized or their roles in the process become blurred. When we know that something is likely to occur, it is much easier to deal with. Understanding that these events will occur can be helpful to the leader of the security council to continue the mission and not give up hope. Members of the organization may view the security council as a vehicle to deposit their security issues for resolution. Alternatively, the council may be viewed as a committee that produces no tangible benefits and consumes the most valuable resource—time. The truth is that both views will exist simultaneously within the organization based upon how the council personally affects each person’s individual role. There will be periods where individuals will become disinterested and it may be necessary to bring in some new blood into the council, thereby expanding the knowledge of the council. It is also a good practice to periodically bring new individuals into the council to inject new ideas and skills to the team. As this is done, it is important to revisit the mission and vision steps as this person and the rest of the team (with respect to the new individual) is repeating the forming, storming, norming, and performing process.

End User Awareness

The existence of the security council and the relationships with the other committees should be embedded in the security awareness training for every end user within the organization. By establishing the message that the security policies are business decisions (versus information technology decisions emanating from the information systems security department), there is likely to be greater acceptance for their implementation. If the message is constructed in such a way that it is clear that middle management and senior management have reviewed and agree with all of the policies line by line, this can be a very powerful message. Line managers and supervisors are less likely to ignore the policies, as they understand that the directives are coming from management and not another functional unit, which they consider to be their peers. This assumes that the organization is following the necessary practice of training all management with the security training as well as the end users.

If there are multiple organizational units participating in the policy development and review process in addition to the security council (e.g., IT steering committees, executive leadership team reviews, focused business and or technical workgroups), then the relationships between these committees and their associated functions should be explained in concise terms at a high level. For example, if the role of the security council is to review and recommend policies to the IT steering committee, which approves the policies, then state these basic functions so that the end users understand the role. If the role of the security council is to establish the security strategy for the organization, prioritize projects, and implement the mission through these initiatives, then state that as well. The advantage to having the end users understand the role of the security council is threefold by (1) helping them to understand how these policies are created, (2) conveying that their management is involved in the direction of information security (versus security mandates), and (3) providing individual understanding to keep their own management in line with the security policies.

Is end user awareness of the security council's existence really a critical success factor? To answer that question, we need to look no further than what the ultimate goal of a security program should be: to have every user of an organization's information protect it with the same diligence as if it was the purse around their shoulder or the wallet in their back pocket. The answer is, you bet! Although they may not need to understand the working dynamics of the Security Council, they do need to understand that the organizational structure exists, is operating, and is effective at balancing the needs of security and the need to operate the business.

Establishing the security council may be seen as threatening to some managers at first, as it means that now some decisions will not be made by the security manager, director, or officer, but rather by the security council. Some security leaders may not want that sort of insight into or control of their activities. However, to be truly effective and truly maintain management commitment, the continued participation by business unit managers is essential. This can also be established informally without a security council, but the time commitment is much greater and the collaboration between the business unit managers is less likely to occur.

The security council is not the answer to resolving all of the management commitment issues, as there will always be other business drivers impacting the decisions. Mergers and acquisitions may put security efforts on hold. Debates over the constraints of the technology on the business operations may stall projects. Budget constraints due to a drop in sales volume or public sector funding may preclude security investments. Acceptance of risk by insurance or outsourcing initiatives may change the company's security posture. Other company high-priority projects may consume the needed internal resources for security projects. Each of these can serve to limit the information security focus and related investments. These are normal events in the course of business. However, consider the individual responsible for information security having to address these issues alone (lack of management commitment) versus acting on these issues with the collaboration of the security council (supportive management commitment), and the advantages of the security council can be readily appreciated.

Security Council Commitment

The word *commitment* according to the *Merriam-Webster's Dictionary of Law* is defined as "an agreement or promise to do something in the future." According to the *Merriam-Webster's Medical Dictionary*, *commitment* is defined as "a consignment to a penal or mental institution." As security practitioners, hopefully we would agree that the former definition is much preferred over the later. Alternatively, if we fail to get the lawyer's definition of commitment, we might end up with the medical definition of commitment.

Management commitment is not something that can be held, touched, or seen, but rather it is a state of being. It is also a current state, subject to change at any moment. The level of commitment is arrived at by management's memory of historical events that led up to the present and paves the path for the future. If these experiences have not been good, then their commitment to spending large investments on future security initiatives will also not be good. Therefore, appropriate care must be taken to deliver upon the promises made through the security council by the security team, information technology departments, and the business unit representatives, or the next project will not be met with enthusiasm. Security councils are an essential element to building management commitment, and continued delivery provides the necessary oxygen to keep the council functioning.

Commitment is the two-way street; if commitment is expected from management, once it is obtained, the security program must also be committed to deliver on the expectations agreed upon. Doing less makes withdrawals from the goodwill that has been established, doing more creates increased satisfaction and confirmation that the investment choices supported by management were, in fact, the right choices. This also increases their trust in their own ability to make decisions supporting the security program.

Finally, each security officer should evaluate their own commitment to enhancing the security of the organization and the current cultural view toward security. Where does the organization stand? It will feel uncomfortable at first to establish the council, but it is well worth the effort. So assemble the security champions from legal, information technology, human resources, the individual business units, and begin.

Suggested Reading

1. Fitzgerald, T., and Krause, M. 2008. Building management commitment through security councils. In *CISO leadership: Essential principles for success*, chap. 14. New York: Auerbach.
2. Fitzgerald, T. 2007. Clarifying the roles of information security: 13 questions the CEO, CIO, and CISO must ask each other. *Information Systems Security* 16 (5): 257–263.
3. Federal Trade Commission. 2002. Eli Lilly settles FTC charges concerning security breach (January 18). http://www.ftc.gov/opa/2002/01/elililly.shtm
4. Frieden, T. 2009. VA will pay $20 million to settle lawsuit over stolen laptop's data. CNN (January 27). http://articles.cnn.com/2009-01-27/politics/va.data.theft_1_laptop-personal-data-single-veteran?_s=PM:POLITICS.
5. Tuckman, B. 1965. Developmental sequence in small groups. *Psychological Bulletin* 63 (6): 384–399.

5

Managing Risk to an Acceptable Level

> Attachment is the great fabricator of illusions; reality can be attained only by someone who is detached.
>
> **Simone Weil, 1909–1943**

Risk analysis is a much discussed area in the information security field for several reasons. First, risk analysis is core to understanding the state of information security that exists within the company. The process of risk analysis uncovers how well the control environment is protecting the information assets. Second, risk analysis helps organizations target the information security expenditures where they are most needed and are used to allocate funds to the appropriate security controls. Finally, risk analysis and management is very subjective in nature and tends to be more art than science. Even though the process may be more art than science, there are still processes that can be followed to increase the likelihood that the risk analysis will be useful to the organization and provide visibility into the risks that the organization is exposed to. Artists are very creative in nature and can look at an object and see something different that a normal person may see. He then paints that object using techniques, or the science, that he has learned to create the appropriate texture, shading, design, symmetry, and so forth to express the image he is feeling. Many times the artist explores with different substances and types of painting, drawing, sculpturing, and so on to provide the desired end state through trial and error. The security officer or risk manager creates a risk assessment in a similar manner, starting with a methodology, concepts, and experiences, and formulating the best depiction of the organization. Just as the finished painting is an expression of a snapshot in time, so is the risk assessment.

Risk in Our Daily Lives

Everyday we are subject to threats and are vulnerable to some event happening that is not desired and not within our control. We cannot stop the threat from occurring, however, we can minimize the impact of the event by the steps that we have taken or will take when the event happens. Consider the protection we implement daily to protect our automobiles from theft. Most of us lock the car doors when we park our car at the mall. The car manufacturers have decided that on more expensive cars that the risk of being stolen is perceived to be greater and therefore have implemented alarms and flashing lights inside the cars to act as a deterrent. Some consumers feel an alarm is not enough and have equipped their vehicles with a tracking device, such as one made by LoJack, to notify the police of vehicles' whereabouts if stolen. Other consumers have felt that a lock over the steering wheel, known as the "club" would provide the adequate level of protection. And then there is the limousine driver that would not leave his vehicle unattended under any conditions.

In the automobile example, each of us may make a different decision when it comes to the security that we would place on our car. We arrive at our decisions based upon our past experiences, the value we place on our cars, the likelihood that we believe it will be stolen, will be reimbursed for the car if it is stolen through insurance, or our general feeling that society is either a good place with primarily good people or an inherently bad place with many ill-intentioned people. Some individuals may feel it is perfectly normal to leave the engine running while running into the mall for "just a second."

We take risks unconsciously every day whether or not we recognize it at the time. We may cross the street 30 times a day and it never enters our mind of the risks we are taking. Then one day, you receive a phone call that your 17-year-old son has been hit by a car going 25 miles per hour through a crosswalk protected by a school crossing guard. Is the solution to keep him home from school in the future? Erect a bridge over the street to cross? Put up additional signs advising cars to slow down more in the school zone? Each of these could be implemented, albeit at different costs. So we accept the risk, and after an event happens, we are typically more cautious and aware of the potential dangers. Our goal should be to identify as many threats up front so that we do not have to incur the damage of each event to learn from it. We should not need to be hit by a car to understand the risks of crossing the street or have our car stolen before we lock our car doors.

Accepting Organizational Risk

Just as we accept a certain amount of risk in our daily lives, organizations accept daily risk also, whether or not they have completed a formal risk analysis. Risk in inherent in everything that we do and there is no such thing as a risk-free activity. Why do banks offer an interest rate to hold your money in the form of a certificate of deposit (CD)? Because there is a risk that the money will be worth less in the future due to inflation and we need to be compensated for that risk that our money will be worth less in the future. The stock market compensates traditionally at 11% over time for stocks. Why? Because of the risk we are taking in investing in these companies that their products or services may not produce the expected income. Whether investors recognize this or not, whether investing in CDs or stocks, they are taking on risk and are being compensated for the risk.

The danger for an organization occurs when risks are being accepted implicitly without providing the visibility that the risk is being accepted. In this scenario, the company may be taking on more risk than they can afford to take on. For example, say that a small office space is available at a great price on the second floor of a building occupied by other tenants. The company could proceed on the basis that the office space is the perfect size and very cost competitive. However, if the buildings surroundings were not evaluated properly, they may be taking on too much risk. If, for example, there was a restaurant directly below them, they would be taking on the risk of business disruption or permanent loss should the restaurant have a fire. A risk analysis would reveal the threat, and while the threat could still be accepted (e.g., off-site backups or paperless scanning put in place to minimize the impact of the damage should a fire occur), the acceptance would be a conscious decision based upon review of the facts. This approach is much better than waiting until the event happens and being unaware of the risks that are being implicitly accepted.

Just Another Set of Risks

Executives face risk-based decisions every day. Should the new product be launched? Should we open 100 more stores? Does it make sense to merge with this other organization? Should we close this factory and move the jobs to another state? Should we compete for this business? And so on. The risks related to protecting the information assets of the organization represent just another set of risks.

The security officer needs to be cognizant of this fact when delivering the risk message. Just as the executive must accept a certain amount of risk to proceed with any plan, the security officer must be willing to facilitate the risk discussion without an all-or-nothing approach to risk. Security departments traditionally have been criticized for their first reaction to a new idea being similar to "No, we can't do that, it would not be secure." This posturing has earned many security departments of the distinction of being the "'no' department." What does this say about the level of risk acceptance that the security officers feel the organization should accept? The answer is none. A better approach is to examine what the desired end state the executive is trying to achieve and work toward a solution to enable the use of the technology or process in a secure manner.

Management Owns the Risk Decision

The security officer acts as the facilitator for the risk decisions and should not be the one making them. Risk is owned by the management of the company, as it is through their operational areas that the risk is present and through their areas with which the risk must be controlled. The security officer must manage risk within his or her own departments as well, and they are the owners ensuring that agreed upon policies and procedures are followed to mitigate the risk.

Security officers and their teams bring security expertise to the discussion, which will assist in management making informed decisions. Alternatives can be presented and recommendations made, however, the level of risk accepted is decided by management after the information has been presented. One useful technique to ensure that risk is appropriately understood and accepted is to formally require that the person accepting the risk sign a document accepting the risk. When some people have to apply their signature to a document, they tend to review what is being agreed upon more closely.

A risk acceptance agreement could include the following key items:

- Description of the threat/vulnerability
- Description of the mitigating controls currently implemented
- Residual (remaining) risk to the organization
- Controls evaluated but not implemented and reason why
- Justification for accepting risk
- Level of risk (high, medium, low)
- Timeframe of the acceptance (typically no more than 1 year)
- Future plans to mitigate risk
- Departments impacted
- Approximate dollar impact expected should the vulnerability be exploited
- Signature(s)/title(s)

By including these variables, it should be clear that the risk must have a business justification, is not approved for an indefinite period, and must have a plan for mitigating the risk now as well as providing for a future scenario where the acceptance form is not needed.

Qualitative versus Quantitative Risk Analysis

One of the difficulties with performing risk analysis is the availability of objective risk information from past experiences. Companies do not typically share information of the risks they have accepted or the occurrence of unfavorable events. Consulting firms typically establish a practice for risk consulting and leverage their firm's internal knowledge across clients, or databases that have been accumulated by the government of other software companies producing risk management products.

Quantitative risk analysis attempts to place a dollar value on the cost of accepting risk versus the cost of implementing controls to reduce the risk level. These analysis can be very voluminous as each risk is measured using statistical information or historical dollar values and probabilities of the event occurring.

Qualitative risk analysis is widely used due to the relative each of understanding and speed of the analysis. This analysis estimates the potential loss or impact and the likelihood that the events would occur in a manner similar to the quantitative analysis, with the exception of using values such as Low, Medium, and High for probabilities and impacts. This is in contrast to attempting to use dollar values for the impacts, which is very difficult to obtain agreement, and probability factors for the likelihood. Since there is no universally accepted master accurate "probability database," the quantitative method tends to try to apply precision to an assessment that is inherently subjective. For this reason, the quantitative method has limited use and the qualitative method is easier for management to quickly grasp the risks of terms of Low, Medium, and High values.

Risk Management Process

The quantitative risk analysis process has the ability to provide a great deal of information, however, for many organizations, a qualitative risk analysis can arrive at similar conclusions in less time with less cost. Quantitative analyses give the appearance of providing precise measurements or dollar amounts related to the risk; however, these calculations are also many times based upon the same subjective probability measures that the qualitative measures are based upon. In practice, management seems to grasp the more simplistic high, medium, and low assignments to risk coming out of the qualitative analysis. For this reason, the subsequent sections outline a very pragmatic step-by-step approach to risk analysis that can be used for almost any size organization. Those familiar with the NIST 800-30 risk management process will recognize the approach, as this is consistent with the concepts articulated there (NIST, 2002).

Risk Analysis Involvement

To properly conduct a security risk analysis, the right technical and management staff need to be included. The resulting analysis is only as good as the accurate picture that can be painted of the current environment. The list of involved participants should include

- Chief information officer
- Chief security officer/security director/security manager
- Senior management
- Middle management
- Internal audit
- System and information owners
- Business and functional management owners
- IT security practitioners
- Infrastructure personnel

There will be others that may need to be called into the process to participate in the interviews, such as facilities, data center manager, human resources, and physical security.

Step 1: Categorize the System

Documenting the business application of the system ensures that the system or area being assessed is clear to those involved in the interviews and the person analyzing the system. The business description should include only the business specifics of the system. What is the system being used for? Who will be the users? What is the primary functionality? The definition establishes the scope and boundaries under review.

Once the business functions have been written, the technical description of the infrastructure, at a high level, is documented. This provides the basis for review of the technical components of the system that is supporting the business function.

The controls that are implemented to protect a system and its information ultimately depend upon the criticality and sensitivity categorization of the system. For low criticality systems, it would be unnecessary to spend the same amount for controls as what is spent to protect systems that have been categorized as high criticality or sensitivity. This is analogous to building a 15-foot-high fence around your house to keep the neighbors from looking into your yard.

The Federal Information Processing Standard (FIPS) 199 provides guidance for categorizing systems according to their attributes of confidentiality, integrity, and availability (NIST, 2004). As shown in Table 5.1, a system is categorized as high for confidentiality if the loss of confidentiality could be expected to have a severe or catastrophic

Table 5.1 System Categorization

FIPS PUBLICATION 199	LOW	MODERATE	HIGH
Confidentiality	The loss of confidentiality could be expected to have a limited adverse effect on organizational operations, organizational assets, or individuals.	The loss of confidentiality could be expected to have a serious adverse effect on organizational operations, organizational assets, or individuals.	The loss of confidentiality could be expected to have a severe or catastrophic adverse effect on organizational operations, organizational assets, or individuals.
Integrity	The loss of integrity could be expected to have a limited adverse effect on organizational operations, organizational assets, or individuals.	The loss of integrity could be expected to have a serious adverse effect on organizational operations, organizational assets, or individuals.	The loss of integrity could be expected to have a severe or catastrophic adverse effect on organizational operations, organizational assets, or individuals.
Availability	The loss of availability could be expected to have a limited adverse effect on organizational operations, organizational assets, or individuals.	The loss of availability could be expected to have a serious adverse effect on organizational operations, organizational assets, or individuals.	The loss of availability could be expected to have a severe or catastrophic adverse effect on organizational operations, organizational assets, or individuals.

Source: National Institute of Standards and Technology (NIST). 2004. Standards for security categorization of federal information and information systems, FIPS PUB 199. http://csrc.nist.gov/publications/fips/fips199/FIPS-PUB-199-final.pdf

adverse effect on organizational operations, organizational assets, or individuals. If the loss of confidentiality was deemed to have a serious effect, then the system would be categorized as medium with respect to confidentiality. Likewise, if the effect is determined to be limited, then categorization would be low for confidentiality.

The categorization continues by looking at the dimensions of integrity and availability using similar criteria. If the loss of integrity could be expected to have a severe or catastrophic effect on organizational operations, assets, or individuals, this would cause the categorization with respect to integrity to be categorized as high, serious would cause the categorization to be medium, and if limited it would be low. Similarly, the availability dimension is categorized as high, medium, and low depending upon the severe or catastrophic, serious, or limited effects of a loss of availability.

The final categorization of the system is done by reviewing each of the categorizations for confidentiality, integrity, and availability, and selecting the categorization that best protects the system. For example, if both confidentiality and availability are considered high, and integrity is considered a medium concern, then an appropriate response would be to select those controls that would provide a high level of assurance. For example, the Centers for Medicare and Medicaid Services (CMS) determined that the health records of the Medicare population should be rated as high, primarily due to the high confidentiality requirement and the damage that would be caused if the records were inadvertently disclosed to the wrong parties (CMS, 2009). This would undermine the trust in the government's (and their contractors) ability to protect the health insurance information. Availability is important, but a lesser concern, as the information is not needed on an immediate, real-time basis for the payment of claims. This would contrast with a provider of ATM services, where although confidentiality would be very important, availability would be very important as well.

By now the question that may be coming to mind is, "How do I accurately decide between severe, catastrophic, serious, or limited?" This assessment, as with much of risk analysis as previously stated, is of a subjective nature. The best way to answer this is to evaluate what the impact would be in terms of shutting down the business for a few days, or causing a high public relations nightmare, or causing an unrecoverable situation. The higher the categorization of the system, the more stringent and more expense will have to be incurred to protect the system. Google and Yahoo Internet-facing search engines would assuredly garner a high availability rating and require security controls of high redundancy hardware to ensure the availability. They would also need extensive monitoring for attacks and proactive measures to detect denial of service attacks. In other words, classifying the system is an important step as all other controls that are selected flow from the categorization. The NIST 800-53 controls (shown in

Chapters 8 to 10) provide a set of controls and enhancements to the controls based upon the categorization of the system (high, medium, or low).

Step 2: Identify Potential Dangers (Threats)

Threats are those dangers that have the potential to cause harm to our business and the systems that we support. Threats are not necessarily what have happened in the past but rather those dangers that our organizations face that we should have a response in place for. A threat may or may not be exploited, as we may not be vulnerable to that threat because of other control measures that have been implemented.

Each organization should brainstorm the specific threats specific to their industry, which may include human, environmental/physical, or technical threats.

Human Threats As long as we have people working in our organizations, they will be our most valuable asset and also at the same time considered a threat. Through acts of carelessness, inadvertent compromises of security or malicious intent, the human factor must be considered as a threat source. A listing of potential human threats are shown in Figure 5.1

Environmental/Physical Threats Environmental risks typically are focused on the environmental systems protecting the computing environments in data centers and server rooms where temperature and humidity control is important to protect the associated equipment.

Human

Data Entry Errors	Inadvertent Acts or Carelessness	Impersonation
Shoulder Surfing	User Abuse/Fraud	Theft/Vandalism
Espionage	Physical Intrusions	Sensitive Data Disclosure
Phishing/ Website Access	Terrorism	Disgruntled Employees
Social Media Exploits	Sabotage	Fraud

Figure 5.1 Human threats.

Environmental Physical

Hazardous Material	Power Fluctuation	Sensitive Media Disposal
Server Rooms	Physical Security	Theft/Vandalism
Pollution	Chemical Spillage	Cable Cuts
Broken Water Pipes	Air Conditioning Failure	Electromagnetic Interference
Animals	Office Cleaning Products	Poor Ventilation/ Humidity

Figure 5.2 Environmental/physical threats.

Technical

Misrepresentation of Identity	Intrusion/Advanced Persistent Threats	Unauthorized Access
Data/System Destruction	Malicious Code/ Malware/Spyware	Authorized Session Takeover
Lack of Logging	Installation Errors	Mobile Media
Hardware/Software Failure	Eavesdropping	Misuse of Known Software Weaknesses

Figure 5.3 Technical threats.

Other threats such as fires, lack of power, and so forth are noted in Figure 5.2.

Technical Threats Technical threats such as authorized access, infrastructure intrusion, or inadvertent configuration errors can permit an intruder to exploit the vulnerabilities of the system and compromise or gain access to information. Technical threats are shown in Figure 5.3.

Step 3: Identify Vulnerabilities That Could Be Exploited

Once the threat has been defined, the next step is to identify the vulnerabilities that can be exploited by the threat. The threat may be thought of as the source of the attack, and the vulnerability is that which is exploited to cause harm. A burglar standing outside a warehouse may be considered a threat, and the degree that he will be able to break into the warehouse depends upon the level of vulnerabilities that exist within the warehouse. Vulnerability may be that the windows could be broken, the doorjamb could possibly be opened with a credit card, or the lock could be picked. The burglar could also pose as a warehouse worker and gain entry during the daytime hours.

Vulnerabilities may exist within our computing environments if we have not applied the most current patch levels or applied a consistent, current baseline configuration to our systems. The intruder decides to gain unauthorized access (the threat) and exploit one or more vulnerabilities, such as a vulnerability found within the Windows 7 operating system, application software, in-house developed software, or a customized vendor product.

A good question to ask when determining vulnerabilities that may be exploited is to ask the question: What could go wrong? A technique that may have been invented by 3-year-olds worldwide is to ask why five times to get to the real root cause of the issue, while along the way this will also identify the vulnerabilities and the controls that could be implemented. After the vulnerabilities are determined, the risk analysis can proceed forward with examining the existing controls.

Step 4: Identify Existing Controls

Since our organizations are not starting at day one when the risk analysis is conducted, odds are that we have implemented controls to manage some of the risk. In the warehouse burglar example noted earlier, we may have implemented bars over the windows, cameras scanning the parking lot, visitor badge control, and a night-duty guard to protect the premises. We may have also placed steel plates over the doorjambs to prevent tampering with the door. The controls that we believe are mitigating some of the risk of exploitation of the vulnerability should be listed.

The chapters on managerial, technical, and operational controls (Chapters 8, 9, and 10) provide a good starting reference to determine what types of controls should be considered. There tends to be a preference to provide automated controls to replace manual controls, however, there are instances where the manual controls may still be more effective. For example, few organizations have done away completely with security guards, as they still provide an effective deterrent when used in addition to technical controls such as mounted cameras, proximity readers, and alarm systems.

LIKELIHOOD	DESCRIPTION
Negligible	Unlikely to occur
Very Low	Likely to occur two to three times every 5 years
Low	Likely to occur once every year or less
Moderate	Likely to occur once every 6 months or less
High	Likely to occur once per month or less
Very High	Likely to occur multiple times per month
Extreme	Likely to occur multiple times per day

Figure 5.4 Likelihood of occurrence.

Step 5: Determine Exploitation Likelihood Given Existing Controls

Step 5 is where the rubber starts to meet the road, where an assessment of the first factor in determining risk, likelihood, or probability is determined. This is not a mathematical calculation based upon statistical probabilities as may be the case in the quantitative method. This value is an expression of the likelihood that the vulnerability is likely to be exploited given the existing control environment. A qualitative description is assigned to the likelihood starting from a low of negligible likelihood (unlikely to occur) to extreme (likely to occur multiple times per day) as shown in Figure 5.4.

This assessment should be made by individuals responsible for the business and facilitated by the security officer. Ownership of the likelihood determination cannot occur if the security officer is determining how often an event may occur, unless it is related to vulnerability within his domain that he has knowledge of. Let's say for example that there is a policy in place that users are not to share user accounts, but there is no control in place that would prevent concurrent logins other than a formal policy instructing the users not to share an account. The security officer may learn through the incident reporting process that individuals are sharing an account at least several times a month. In the absence of a technical control to prevent this access, this would be assigned a likelihood of very high based upon the frequency of the event.

An important point to note is that likelihood is one component of risk, and at this point the "risk level" has not been determined. It is advisable to keep the conversation about the likelihood of occurrence and not about risk, or managers will immediately jump to discussing high, medium, or low risk level without having the complete foundation (likelihood and impact) to determine risk. A "hold off, we're getting to that next" stance is warranted here.

The warehouse burglar in the earlier example may have had a low likelihood of exploiting the vulnerability given the existing controls that were in place, as it appears that most of the known areas of vulnerability were already implemented (since this company was broken into frequently in the past, last year it upgraded its control environment as a result of the prior risk analysis).

As with the rest of the risk analysis, the likelihood should be examined with a fresh set of eyes, meaning that what was decided as the likelihood last year is irrelevant. New controls may have been put in place, existing controls may have been removed, and the intensity of the threat may have changed. For example, tracks may have been laid for a new high-speed train going past the data center or a fuel storage plant may be constructed, both creating potential vulnerabilities that did not previously exist. Alternatively, an office may have closed and the vulnerabilities that were identified with the office are no longer relevant. A prudent approach is to review and update the risk assessment annually and perform a ground-up risk assessment every 3 years.

Step 6: Determine Impact Severity

This step assumes that the vulnerability has been exploited and now the organization must deal with the harm that was done by the action. An impact designed as minor, according to Figure 5.5, would require minimal effort to repair the system. If the impact was large, designated as critical, then the impact would be expected to result in an extended outage. Figure 5.5 provides a quick means to assign an impact to the event.

Management and technical staff are in the best position to explain what would happen if the system was lost for a day or a shipment was not delivered. Finance areas are also excellent sources of information when calculating the loss of productivity per hour when a system is down. E-commerce websites can calculate the approximate lost dollar volume when their sites become unavailable. Depending upon the time of year, the severity may increase, such as online retailers

IMPACT SEVERITY	DESCRIPTION
Insignificant	• Will have almost no impact if the threat occurs or vulnerability is exploited • Will result in minimal loss of functional integrity • Requires little or no recovery cost
Minor	• Will have some minor effect on the business function or system • May cause minor financial loss, but will not result in negative publicity or political damage • Will require only minimal effort to complete corrective actions and continue or resume operations • Will require minimal effort to repair or reconfigure the system
Significant	• Will result in some tangible harm, albeit negligible, and perhaps only realized by a few individuals or agencies • May cause political embarrassment, negative publicity, and moderate financial loss • Will require a moderate expenditure of resources to repair
Damaging	• May cause damage to the reputation of system management, CMS, and/or notable loss of confidence in the ability for CMS to complete its stated business mission, system resources, and services • May result in legal liability, and will require significant expenditure of resources to repair or to complete corrective actions and restore operations
Serious	• May cause considerable disruption in the business function, system outage, and/or loss of customer or business partner confidence • May result in compromise of large amount of government information or services, a substantial financial loss, and the failure to deliver CMS public programs and services
Critical	• May cause an extended disruption in the business function, system extended outage • May require recovery in an alternate site environment or hot site environment • May result in full compromise of CMS' ability to provide public programs and services, and ability to complete the stated business mission

Figure 5.5 Severity of impact.

during the holiday season. A recently quoted statistic indicated that 13% of Black Friday sales came from Cyber Monday (the Monday following Black Friday).

If the burglar was able to break into the warehouse in our example, this would have caused considerable damage, as the warehouse was full of shipments to a key manufacturer that needed the goods shipped tomorrow. If those goods were damaged or stolen, we could have lost a client. According to Figure 5.5, this may be assessed as damaging, or damage to reputation, loss of public confidence.

Step 7: Determine Risk Level

Step 7 is where the risk level is determined based upon the likelihood and the impact level. Using the table shown in Figure 5.6, the likelihood of occurrence is located in the first column, and the impact severity is located in the row across the top. These are then used to find where the likelihood and impact intersect in the table, indicating a risk level of low, moderate (or medium), or high. For example, in our burglar example, the likelihood was low and the impact severity was damaging, resulting in a risk level of moderate.

This process is repeated for each of the threat and vulnerability pairs until each has been addressed and assigned a risk level. The risks are then prioritized from high to medium to low. The low risks should be worked on only after the high and medium risks have been addressed, unless they are simple changes that will not divert substantial resources from addressing the higher risk items.

The best part about this method is that the risk was determined by focusing the discussion on (1) likelihood of occurrence and (2) impact severity. Nowhere in the discussion was risk mentioned up until this step. This step still does not debate risk but merely establishes the risk based upon the matrix. Management can always decide to raise or lower the risk level at this point; however, it should be cautioned that

LIKELIHOOD OF OCCURRENCE	IMPACT SEVERITY INSIGNIFICANT	IMPACT SEVERITY MINOR	IMPACT SEVERITY SIGNIFICANT	IMPACT SEVERITY DAMAGING	IMPACT SEVERITY SERIOUS	IMPACT SEVERITY CRITICAL
Negligible	Low	Low	Low	Low	Low	Low
Very Low	Low	Low	Low	Low	Moderate	Moderate
Low	Low	Low	Moderate	Moderate	High	High
Moderate	Low	Low	Moderate	High	High	High
High	Low	Moderate	High	High	High	High
Very High	Low	Moderate	High	High	High	High
Extreme	Low	Moderate	High	High	High	High

Figure 5.6 Risk determination.

this should be based upon a reevaluation of the likelihood or the severity. Sometime management may have good reason to increase the risk rating to ensure that it receives some attention within the organization.

Step 8: Determine Additional Controls

Now that the risks have been identified, it is necessary to identify controls to mitigate or reduce the risk level to an acceptable level. Typically the focus is on the high risks that should be remediated as soon as is feasible. Moderate or medium risks should also be handled urgently and plans created to address their implementation. It may not be clear at the moment precisely what solutions will be implemented at this juncture, but plans of action to investigate the alternatives can be created until it is clear what solutions will be implemented.

Once the control has been identified that will reduce the risk, the residual likelihood, residual severity impact, and the resulting residual risk is recalculated. Controls should at least bring the high risks to medium, the mediums to lows, and if the lows are addressed at this time, they should be eliminated. Some organizations will retain all risks as a low risk, because even though the vulnerability has been addressed by a control, there is always a risk (albeit low) that the vulnerability may be exploited. Other organizations take the viewpoint that they do not want to see any mitigated vulnerabilities on the report, as it gives the wrong impression. The security officer needs to be aware of the culture of the organization and how the risk level will be perceived.

Risk Mitigation Options

The preceding overview of the risk analysis process provides a framework for conducting a risk analysis. The most likely outcome is that new risks will be uncovered through the analysis and the company can focus resources toward mitigating the vulnerabilities and reducing the risk levels. In addition to implementing their own controls to resolve the issue, there are other additional options for managing the risk.

Risk Assumption

The organization may decide that the risk does not represent an unacceptable risk outside the company's risk appetite and chooses to accept the risk. The organization may continue to operate, or plan to implement additional controls in the future. This strategy is perfectly acceptable provided that the risk being assumed has been analyzed and the financial implications have been accepted by the appropriate parties. As indicated in an earlier section, formalizing this process with a risk acceptance letter is preferable.

Risk Avoidance

Risk can be avoided by eliminating the cause of the risk or the consequence. A server may have an old version of the operating system, such as Windows 2000, which has much vulnerability that can be exploited due to the aging of the system. Instead of upgrading the system to a new operating system, the system itself may be retired, thus eliminating the vulnerability.

Risk Limitation

Adding other preventative or detective controls to the process might reduce the adverse impact of the risk. In the earlier example of shared logins, software may be purchased to prevent the concurrent login on those systems (such as windows) that do not have the native capability and configuration settings made on other systems that do. Monitoring of logs could also be implemented.

Risk Planning

All vulnerabilities may not be able to be addressed at the present time and the construction of a plan for mitigating the current and future vulnerabilities would be put in place.

Risk Research

If the vulnerability cannot be immediately remediated, the fact that the vulnerability exists may be acknowledged with plans to research viable alternatives.

Risk Transference

Losses are compensated for by purchasing insurance or transferring risk via contract. Rates are many times dependent upon the level of security controls that exist or external evaluations of the controls.

Conclusion

Risk analysis must be done for each organization to address the unique circumstances and risks they face. The process described in this chapter provides a very logical, systematic process for determining the risks that are specific to the company. If these processes are followed consistently, over time the review process of the existing threats becomes easier and more time can be spent addressing the new threats to the organization.

The process does not have to be a lengthy one either. The facilitated risk analysis process (FRAP), for example, may be completed in days versus weeks or months (Peltier, 2001). Having personally been involved in the FRAP for an electronic commerce site, whereby a group of individuals get together for a couple of days in a conference room to analyze and come to consensus on the risks, there are clearly approaches such as this that can gather information quickly and provide an assessment of the risk that can be very effective. The risks determined from these approaches can then be managed according to their risk level and be managed as part on an ongoing risk management program.

Suggested Reading

1. National Institute of Standards and Technology (NIST). July 2002. Risk management guide for information technology systems. http://csrc.nist.gov/publications/nistpubs/800-30/sp800-30.pdf
2. Centers for Medicare and Medicaid Services. March 19, 2009. CMS information security risk assessment (IS RA) procedure. Version 1.0-Final. http://www.cms.gov/informationsecurity/downloads/IS_RA_Procedure
3. Peltier, T. R. 2001. *Information security risk analysis*. New York: Auerbach.
4. National Institute of Standards and Technology (NIST). 2004. Standards for security categorization of federal information and information systems, FIPS PUB 199. http://csrc.nist.gov/publications/fips/fips199/FIPS-PUB-199-final.pdf

6

Creating Effective Information Security Policies

We haven't the time to take our time.

Eugène Ionesco, 1912–1994

When organizations first recognize that they need to ensure that the information assets of the organization are adequately protected, this usually results in asking the question, "What applicable policies are in place?" There may be some human resource policies that might apply or corporate policies noted in the ethics and compliance code of conduct, however, these are normally insufficient to address the breadth of the information security needs. The next step is for the organization to embark upon the time-consuming task of developing information security policies.

Why Information Security Policies Are Important

To the seasoned information security practitioner, asking why information security policies are important may seem like a question with an obvious answer. The question is not so obvious to the end users of the organization, as many of them may feel that if everyone applies common sense, there is no need for them to read and sign off on voluminous sets of policies. The reality is that each person has a different interpretation of what is common sense. For example, leaving a scruffy old backpack containing books in a car may seem like a reasonable act to one employee who wonders why would anyone want to steal a bag full of books. Another employee might think that because of the condition of the backpack, no one would want to steal it. Another might think that their car is parked in broad daylight in a heavily traveled area, which would make the risk of stealing it quite low. Another employee may think that the car alarm would be a sufficient deterrent from anyone wanting to go through the trouble of stealing the backpack.

Then along comes the information security officer, whose job it is to evaluate the course of action that will provide reasonable security. The security officer knows the stories of break-ins all too well, and knows that criminals do not know for sure what is in the backpack. The criminal might assume that there is a laptop, money, or credit cards that could be sold for a nominal amount to buy drugs, alcohol, or support rudimentary living expenses. Thus, the opportunity and motivation presents an unacceptable risk that must be mitigated. The organization cannot afford to leave these individual decisions up to the common sense internal barometer of thousands of employees. The organization must set forth advice or a baseline of what behavior is expected for each employee, and not leave this up to individual discretion. This advice, and expected behavior, is manifested through a set of information security policies. The policies form the cornerstone of the information security program and are representations of management's intention that are needed to control the information security assets.

Avoiding Shelfware

Although information security policies are very important, they can easily become shelfware if their development, management, and distribution are not handled appropriately. Countless security departments have filled binders full of policies over the years that remain unread and require frequent dusting. As the Intranet-based environments started to take hold in the mid-'90s, these environments moved from paper-based shelfware to electronic-based shelfware. The security department may have had a large project to develop the information security policies, place them on the Intranet, and then they were "done." Lengthy, technical documents with all the technical jargon may have sounded impressive to the security department, but fail when end users are required to read them because they are not understandable. Who would read these lengthy documents? The same individuals that would read the complete car owners manual after purchasing a new car before they put the key into the ignition—in other words, a very small segment of the population. The security policies should be written in a language from the user and be brief enough to get the point across without overwhelming the end user. More detailed descriptions can be placed in standards documents that the users can read if they need additional information. An organization security policy beyond 30 to 60 pages is normally much more than would be required by any medium- to large-sized organization. Beyond that level, the policies are likely to go unread.

Electronic Policy Distribution

To avoid shelfware in electronic policies, they need to be kept (1) brief, (2) updated, and (3) relevant. Web-based policies should each be no more than two online pages to get the point across as to what is expected (Fitzgerald, 2004). Resumes are kept to two pages for a reason—people stop reading them if they have not received what is needed within the first two pages. Daily online articles on sites such as Yahoo and USA Today are no more than two pages, as the reader may lose interest after that.

The policies need to be updated at least annually to ensure that the management direction is still desired. As employees comes across a policy that was last updated 4 years ago, they may make the conclusion on their own that the policy no longer applies. The organization may have gone through a merger, and the conflicting policies may exist for the two organizations or worse yet, if the policies have never been integrated, the employees of the acquired company may make the erroneous assumption that they should still follow their old company policies and may not be aware of the new acquiring company policies.

Policies need to maintain their relevancy to remain effective. For example, if an organization has not addressed the use of social media in their policies, the management and end users will have to rely on the existing policies to determine whether social media is acceptable. Or, suppose an employee just purchased an iPad tablet computer, but the policy indicates that no personal desktop or laptop computers may be used within the company. Should the iPad be allowed? Technically, according to the policy, the iPad "tablet" computer has not been addressed, and the associate may leave it to an interpretation more favorable to the employee as to whether to use the device.

Policies posted online should always ensure that the revision history is provided as well, so that users can see what changes were made to the documents and also determine if they are looking at the correct version. Even with many companies moving toward green, environmental-friendly initiatives to reduce wasteful printing and disposal costs, many end users still prefer to have a paper document that can be referenced when needed. The revision update date and history help ensure that the correct document is being utilized.

Several security vendors have products that will provide an electronic distribution of security policies and also provide a mechanism for end users to confirm that they have read, accepted, and understood the policy contents. The results are then recorded in a database that can be queried as needed. This information becomes very useful during incident investigations, terminations, and lawsuits where the company wants to demonstrate that the employee had clear knowledge of the policy and chose to violate it against the corporate policy.

Canned Security Policies

Consulting organizations have sets of policy templates that are used to jumpstart a client's need for information security policies. These are then tailored to the needs of the organization. This process may be more effective than writing the information security policies from scratch, as long as the policies meet the compliance, laws, regulations, and desires of the organization. It is not unusual to see where an organization has implemented a copied policy verbatim, sometimes even forgetting to change the company name on the template. During the 2010 BP oil spill, it was revealed that the business continuity/disaster recovery documents from several major oil companies appeared to have used the same templates for their disaster recovery plans (Gupta, 2010).

Although developing the complete information security policy is beyond the scope of this book, there are several information security books available with sample polices that can be used to jumpstart the development. Two very good sources are *Information Security Policies and Procedures—A Practitioner's Reference* (Peltier, 2007) and *Information Security Policies Made Easy by Information Shield* (Wood, 2009). Both of these sources contain valuable information at a fraction of the cost of a security consultant for one day.

Policies, Standards, Guidelines Definitions

Organizations typically do not have a consistent understanding as to what a "policy" is. This seems like such a simple concept, so why the difficulty? The reason is not the lack of understanding that a policy is meant to govern the behavior within the organization. The reason for the confusion has more to do with the fact that in the interest of saving time, organizations will combine policies, procedures, guidelines, and standards into one document and call it the policy. This is not really a time saver because it makes it more difficult by introducing inflexibility into the policy each time the policy needs to change. This is similar to denormalizing a database structure to make the performance more efficient, when in fact it becomes harder to add new data elements to a particular table without redesigning the table. The policies and procedures end up getting fused together, and so when the procedure changes, the policy document by default is changing as well when the policy does not need to change. Or, the employees begin to think that the procedure is the only way the policy can be implemented, when there may be multiple procedures across the organization that are implemented to comply with the policy. For example, an organization might have a policy that all systems need a full backup weekly and they need to be maintained off site. The data center may have a procedure that ensures that tape backups are taken weekly and the tapes are picked up by a vendor and transported to the secure off-site storage. The midrange server infrastructure team may have a procedure to ensure that full backups are taken weekly through the online data vaulting process, in addition to the daily incremental backups at the remote site. The desktop support department may have a procedure that ensures that company critical information is stored on network drives, also subject to the weekly online backup process. In this case, each area has designated local procedures that ensure that they are in compliance with the higher-level corporate policy.

Policies Are Written at a High Level

Policies should be written at the highest level possible to still be able to communicate the intentions of the company. The higher the level of the policy, the more likely the policy is able to stand the test of time. Companies do not want to be reissuing policies on a frequent basis unless they have to. This involves resources for development and, more important, the time and expense of each person to reread the complete policy. Whereas changes in technology, company structure, laws and regulations, emerging trends, and so forth warrant changes to the security policy, frequent changes due to minor technology changes are not desired. The reaction of most users will be, didn't we just do this? For example, if password standards are written into the password policy for a primarily Windows-based environment, what happens when a Unix server for the SQL server data warehouse project is introduced? Will the password policy need to be redistributed and attested to by thousands of users, when the change impacted only a small number of users?

Security officers and their teams are charged with the responsibility of creating the security policies. The policies must be written and communicated at a level that is understood by the end users of the organization if there is to be any chance of compliance. If the policies are poorly written or written at too high of an education level (common industry practice is to focus the content for general users at the sixth- to eighth-grade reading level), the policies will not be understood.

Whereas security officers may be charged with the development of the policies, the effort is normally a collaborative effort to ensure that the business issues are addressed. Utilization of an security council, executive oversight committee, or a subgroup of that committee, depending upon the policy being drafted, is an approach that considers the business impacts of a security policy decision. Developing the policies solely within the information technology department and then distributing the policies without business input is likely to miss important business considerations. As always, deciding on the appropriate security controls is a decision of risk by the organization, which ultimately should be decided by the business leaders. The organization is also more likely to accept security policies that have been approved and endorsed by the business leaders versus the security officer or the information technology department.

Once these different documents have been created, the basis for ensuring compliance is established. These deliverables form the basis for organizational compliance with the security policies. The most current versions of the documents need to be readily accessible by those that are expected to follow them. Many organizations have placed these documents electronically on their intranets or shared file folders to facilitate communication of the most current documents. Placement of these documents plus checklists, forms, and sample documents can save time for the individual and be an added value provided by the security department.

Policies

Policies define *what* at a high level the organization needs to accomplish and serves as management's intentions to control the operation of the organization to meet business objectives. The *why* should be stated in the form of a policy summary statement or purpose. If end users understand the why, they are more apt to follow the policy. As children, we were told what to do by our parents and we just did it. As we grew older, we challenged those beliefs (as 4- and 5-year-olds and again as teenagers) and needed to understand the reasoning. The rules had to make sense to us. Today's organizations are no different; people need to understand the why before they can really commit.

Security Policy Best Practices

Someone once said, "Writing security policies is like making sausage. You don't know want to know what goes into it, but what comes out is pretty good!" Writing policies does not have to be a mystery, and there are several guidelines for creating good security policies practiced in the industry.

- *Clearly define policy creation practice*—A clearly defined process for initiating, creating, reviewing, recommending, approving, and distributing the policies communicates the responsibilities of all parties necessary and the time expectations of their participation. This can be accomplished by process flows, swim lanes, flowcharts, or written documentation.
- *Write policies to survive 2 to 3 years*—Policies are high-level statements of the objectives of the organization. The underlying methods and technologies to implement the controls to support the policies may change. By including these in the

other related documents (procedures, standards, guidelines, and baselines), the policy statements will need less frequent change. This avoids frequent updates and subsequent distribution to the organization.

- *Use directive wording*—Policies represent expectations to be complied with. As such, statements such as must, will, and shall communicate this requirement versus using weaker directives such as should, may, or can. This latter type of language is better reserved for guidelines or areas where there are options.
- *Avoid technical implementation details*—Policies should be written to be technology independent, as the implemented technology may change over time.
- *Keep length to a minimum*—Policies published online should be limited in length to two to three pages maximum per policy. The intent for the policies is for the end user to understand and not to create long documents for the sake of documentation.
- *Provide navigation from the policy to the supporting documents*—If the implementation of the policy is placed online, then hyperlinking the procedures, standards, guidelines, and baselines can be an effective method to ensure that the appropriate procedures are being followed. Some of the internal security procedures would not be appropriate for general knowledge, such as the procedure for monitoring intrusions or reviewing log files, and these need to be accessible by the security department and properly secured from general distribution.
- *Thoroughly review before publishing*—Proofreading policies by multiple individuals can catch errors that may not be readily seen by the author.
- *Conduct management review and sign off*—Senior management must endorse the policies if they are to be effectively accepted by all management levels and subsequently the end users of the organization.
- *Avoid techno speak*—Policies are oriented to communicate to nontechnical users. Technical jargon is acceptable in technical documentation but not in high-level security policies.
- *Review incidents and adjust policies*—Review of the security incidents that have occurred may indicate the need for a new

policy, a revision to an existing policy, or the need to redistribute the current policy to reinforce compliance.

- *Periodically review policies*—A formalized review process provides a mechanism to ensure that the security policies are still in alignment with the business objectives.
- *Develop sanctions for noncompliance*—Effective policies have consistent sanction policies to enable action when the policies are not followed. These sanctions may include "disciplinary action up to and including termination." Stronger language can also be added for prosecution for serious offenses.

Policies provide the foundation for a comprehensive and effective security program. The company is protected from surprises and gives the necessary authority to the security activities of the organization. By communicating the company policies as directives, accountability and personal responsibility for adhering to the security practices is established. The policies are utilized in determining or interpreting any conflicts that may arise. The policies also define the elements, scope, and functions of the security management.

Types of Security Policies

Security policies may consist of different types, depending upon the specific need for the policy (NIST, 2003). The different security policies work together to meet the objectives of the comprehensive security program. Different policy types include:

- *Organizational or program policy*—This policy is issued by a senior management individual who creates the authority and scope for the security program. The purpose of the program is described and the assigned responsibility is defined for carrying out the information security mission. The goals of confidentiality, integrity, and availability would be addressed in the policy. Specific areas of security focus may be stressed, such as the protection of confidential information for a credit card company or heath insurance company, or the availability focus for a company maintaining mission-critical, high-availability systems. The policy should be clear as to the facilities, hardware, software, information, and personnel that are in scope for the security program. In most cases, the scope will be the entire organization, however, in larger organizations the security program may be limited in scope to a division or geographic location. The organization policy sets out the high-level authority to define the appropriate sanctions for failure to comply with the policy.

- *Functional, issue-specific policies*—Although the organizational security policies are broad in scope, the functional or issue-specific policies address areas of particular security concern requiring clarification. The issue-specific policies may be focused on the different domains of security and address areas such as access control, contingency planning, segregation of duties principles, and so forth. They may also address specific technical areas of existing and emerging technologies, such as use of the Internet, e-mail and corporate communication systems, wireless access, or remote system access. For example, an acceptable use policy may define the responsibilities of the end user for using the corporate computer systems for business purposes only, or may allow the person some incidental personal use provided the restrictions of ensuring usage is free from viruses, spyware, downloading inappropriate pictures or software, or sending chain letters through e-mail. These policies will depend upon the business needs and the tolerance for risk. The policies contain the statement of the issue, the statement of the organization's position on the issue, the applicability of the issue, compliance requirements, and sanctions for not following the policy.
- *System specific policies*—Areas where it is desired to have clearer direction or greater control for a specific technical or operational area may have more detailed policies. These policies may be targeted for a specific application or platform. For example, a system-specific policy may address which departments are permitted to input or modify information in the check writing application for the disbursement of accounts payable payments.

The more detailed and issue specific the policy, the higher likelihood that the policy will require more frequent changes. Typically, high-level organizational security policies will survive for several years, whereas those focused on the use of technology will change much more frequently as technology matures and new technology is added to the environment. Even if an organization is not currently utilizing a technology, policies can explicitly strengthen the message that the technology is not to be used and is prohibited. For example, a policy regarding removable media such as USB drives, or one regarding the use of wireless devices or camera phones in the workplace, would reinforce the management intentions around the acceptance or nonacceptance of these devices.

Standards

Whereas policies define what an organization needs, the standards take this a step further and define the how. Standards provide the agreements that provide interoperability within the organization through the use of common protocols.

Standards are the hardware and software security mechanisms selected as the organization's method of controlling security risks. Standards are prevalent in many facets of our daily lives, such as the size of the tires on automobiles; specifications of the height, color, and format of the stop sign; and the wiring details of the RJ11 plug on the end of the phone jack cable. Standards provide consistency in the implementation as well as permit interoperability with reduced confusion. There are many security standards that could be chosen to implement a particular solution. For example, when selecting a control for remote access identification and authentication, an organization could decide to utilize login IDs and passwords, strong authentication through a security token over dialup, or a virtual private network (VPN) solution over the Internet.

Standards simplify the operation of the security controls within the company and increase the efficiency. It is more costly to support multiple software packages, which do essentially the same activity. Imagine if each user was told to go to the local computer store and purchase the antivirus product that they liked the best. Some users would ask the sales person's opinion, some would buy the least expensive to meet their budget needs, and others might get the most expensive assuming this would provide the greatest protection. Without a consistent product standard for antivirus products, the organization would be unsure as to the level of protection provided. Additionally, each of these different products would have different installation, update, and licensing considerations contributing to complex management. It makes much sense to have consistent products chosen for the organization versus leaving the product choice to every individual.

Determination of which standards meet the organization's needs must be driven by the security policies agreed by management. The standards provide the specification of the technology to effectively enable the organization to become successful in meeting the requirements of the policy. If in the example of the remote access the organization was restricting information over the Internet or had many users in rural areas with limited Internet access, then the VPN standard over the Internet may not be a plausible solution. Conversely, for end users transmitting large amounts of information, the dial-up solution may be impractical. The policy defines the boundaries within which the standards must be supportive.

Standards may also refer to those guidelines established by a standards organization and accepted by management. Standards creators include organizations such as the National Institute of Standards and Technology (NIST), International Organization for Standardization (ISO), Institute of Electrical and Electronics Engineers (IEEE), American National Standards Institute (ANSI), and National Security Agency (NSA).

Procedures

Procedures are step-by-step instructions in support of the policies, standards, guidelines, and baselines. The procedure indicates how the policy will be implemented and who does what to accomplish the tasks. The procedure provides clarity and a common understanding to the operation required to effectively support the policy on a consistent basis. Procedures are best developed when the input of each of the interfacing areas are included in the development of the procedure. This reduces the risk that important steps, communication, or required deliverables are left out of the procedure.

Companies must be able to provide assurance that they have exercised due diligence in the support and enforcement of company policies. This means that the company has made an effort to be in compliance with the policies and has communicated the expectations to the workforce. Having documented procedures communicated to the users, business partners, and anyone utilizing the systems as appropriate, minimizes the legal liability of the corporation.

Creating documented procedures is more than a documentation exercise for the sake of documentation. The process itself creates a common understanding between the developers of the procedure of the methods used to accomplish the task. Individuals from different organizational units may be very familiar with their work area but not as familiar with the impact of a procedure on a department. This is the "beach ball effect," where organizations sometimes appear as a large beach ball, and the individuals working in different departments can only see their side of the beach ball and may not understand the other parts of the organization. The exercise of writing down a single, consistent procedure has the added effect of establishing agreement between the parties. Many times at the beginning of the process, individuals will think they all understand the process, only to come to understand that people were really executing different, individual processes to accomplish the task.

Consistent documentation of the procedures permits the ability to improve the procedures. Once everyone understands the initial procedure, enhancements can be applied and communicated to everyone. This provides a method to incorporate the best thinking on the single procedure versus having multiple procedures for the same operation with a mixture of good and bad practices.

Baselines

Baselines provide descriptions of how to implement security packages to ensure that implementations are consistent throughout the organization. Different software packages, hardware platforms and networks have different methods of ensuring security. There are many different options and settings which must be determined to provide the desired protection. An analysis of the available configuration settings and subsequent settings desired form the basis for future, consistent implementation of the standard. For example, turning off the telnet service may be specified in the hardening baseline document for the network servers. A procedure for exceptions to the baseline would need to be followed in the event that the baseline could not be followed for a particular device, along with the business justification. The baselines are the specific rules necessary to implement the security controls in support of the policy and standards, which have been developed.

Testing of the implemented security controls on a periodic basis assures that the baselines are implemented according to the documented baselines. The baselines themselves should be reviewed periodically to ensure that they are sufficient to address emerging threats and vulnerabilities. In large environments with multiple individuals performing systems administration and responding to urgent requests, there is an increased risk that one of the baseline configurations may not be implemented properly. Internal testing identifies these vulnerabilities and provides a mechanism to review why the control was or was not properly implemented. Failures in training, adherence to baselines and associated procedures, change control, documentation, or skills of the individual performing the changes may be identified through the testing.

Guidelines

Guidelines are discretionary or optional controls used to enable individuals to make judgments with respect to security actions. A good exercise is to replace the word *guideline* with the word *optional*. If by doing so, the statements contained in the "optional" category are what is desired to happen at the user's discretion, then it is an appropriate guideline. If on the other hand, the statements are considered as required to adequately protect the security of the organization, then this should be defined as part of a policy, standard, or baseline.

Guidelines are also those recommendations, best practices, and templates provided by other organizations such as the Control Objectives for Information and Related Technology (COBIT), the Capability Maturity Model (CMM), ISO 17799, British Standard 7799, security configuration recommendations such as those from the NIST or NSA, organizational guidelines, or other governmental guidelines.

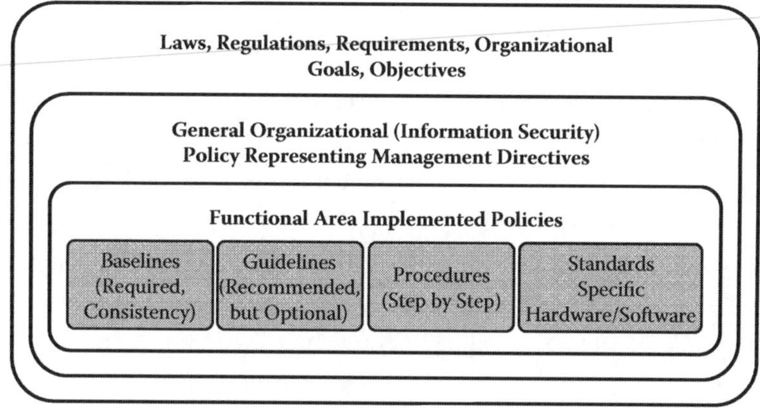

Figure 6.1 Relationships between policies, standards, procedures, baselines, and guidelines.

Combination of Policies, Standards, Baselines, Procedures, and Guidelines

Policies, standards, baselines, procedures, and guidelines are closely related to each other and may be developed as the result of new regulations, external industry standards, new threats and vulnerabilities, emerging technologies, upgraded hardware and software platforms, or risk assessment changes. Sometimes these different areas are combined into single documents for ease of management of all the documents. Keeping policies separate from the implementation components (standards, baselines, and procedures) increases the flexibility and reduces the cost of maintenance as the policies typically change less frequently than the supporting processes to achieve compliance with the policy. The relationships between the policies, standards, baselines, procedures, and guidelines and the laws and regulations providing the requirement to implement these governing activities is shown in Figure 6.1.

Policy Analogy A useful analogy to remember the differences between policies, standards, guidelines, and procedures is to think of a company that builds cabinets, which has a hammer policy. The different components may be as follows:

- *Policy*—"All boards must be nailed together using company-issued hammers to ensure end product consistency and worker safety." Notice the flexibility provided to permit the company to define the hammer type with changes in technology or safety issues. The purpose is also communicated to the employees.

- *Standard*— "Eleven-inch fiberglass hammers will be used; only hardened-steel nails will be used with the hammers; automatic hammers are to be used for repetitive jobs >1 hour." Technical specifics are provided to clarify the expectations that make sense for the current environment and represent management's decision.
- *Guideline*—"To avoid splitting the wood, a pilot hole should be drilled first." The guideline is a suggestion and may not apply in all cases or all types of wood. This does not represent a requirement, but rather a suggested practice.
- *Procedure*—"(1) Position nail in upright position on board. (2) Strike nail with full swing of hammer. (3) Repeat until nail is flush with board. (4) If thumb is caught between nail and board, see Nail First-Aid Procedure." The procedure indicates the process of using the hammer and the nail to clarify what is expected to be successful. Following this procedure, with the appropriate standard hammers, and practicing guidelines where appropriate, will fulfill the policy.

Analogies such as this can be effective when leading the team to develop security policies to ensure that they are on the same wavelength and not mixing policies, procedures, standards, and guidelines. These can also be useful in security awareness training to indicate when a particular user should refer to a policy, standard, procedure, or guideline.

An Approach for Developing Information Security Policies

Let us assume for a moment that the guidance in the preceding sections were followed, and the organization now has a set of information security policies that are easy to read, kept current, and generally available in a nice format on the Web. However, if no one seems to be reading them or following them, what could be the problem? Many times the root cause is a lack of management support. How could this be? After all, if the information security officer has been designated with the role of developing and distributing information security policies, why would there be a low acceptance rate?

The answer usually lies in the fact that while the information security officer may have done an excellent job researching and developing security policies, the same diligence was not applied in ensuring that the rest of management was on board with the policies prior to rollout. The security officer may decide to push out the policies once his department has developed them. As such, the policies become those "owned" by the security officer and not the rest of the management. These are then treated as departmental policies that have no greater enforcement requirements than the policies and procedures that are created by their organizational area. Then, when there is a conflict between the departmental desires and the security policy, the departmental desires win. For example, if an organization has to get information quickly to a customer, it can fax or e-mail the information as part of its normal procedure. However, the information security policy may require that all transmissions over an open network, as in the case of e-mail, or that only the transmission of all confidential information be encrypted with the most stringent government standard encryption, such as Federal Information Processing Standard (FIPS) 140-2 encryption requirements. The department sending the information may have a disagreement with the security department on the information classification of "confidential" in the information security policy, or may feel that the requirement is a bit over the top and does not agree with the policy at all, as it would hamper the speed of doing business and cause inferior relationships with customers. Who is right? In this case, neither; the security officer failed to obtain agreement with the policy before the procedures were executed and the executive from the other department is incorrect in not adhering to the policy. Unfortunately, this situation is all too common. The good news is that this can be avoided by following a different approach to developing and distributing the security policies.

Utilizing the Security Council for Policies

Management support is essential in the development of information security policies. So, how is that attained? One method that is very effective is to form a security committee, also known as an information security council as introduced in Chapter 4. The security council can review the policies proposed by the information security department.

The benefits of this approach are (1) consensus of the policies are first built at the front-line supervisor/middle management/technical staff level, (2) senior management has greater comfort that the policies will be accepted by the organization as the management team has reviewed them before approval, and (3) it builds grassroots ownership of the information security policies. Although the information security council can also serve as oversight for other security initiatives, serve as a sounding board, and prioritize information security efforts, it can be especially effective in vetting and discussing the information policies that are needed by the organization.

The Policy Review Process

Now that the organization has identified an individual responsible for the development and implementation of security policies the security council has been created, and an understanding of what makes a good policy has been communicated, there needs to be a process for reviewing the policies. This process may be developed during the creation of the security council. What is important is that the policy development process is thought out ahead of time to determine who will (1) create, (2) review and recommend, (3) approve the final version, (4) publish, and (5) read and accept the policies. The time spent in this process, *up front,* will provide many dividends down the road. Many organizations jump right in and someone in the security department or information technology department to draft then email the policy without taking these steps. Proceeding along that path ends up with a policy that is not accepted by the organization's management and thus will not be accepted by the organization's end users. Why? Because the necessary discussion, debate, and acceptance of the policies by the leaders of the organization never took place. In the end, the question of management commitment again surfaces, when there was never a process in place to obtain the commitment.

The process could be depicted in a swim-lane-type chart showing the parties responsible, activities, records created through each activity, and decision boxes; or a flowchart format. Senior management will want this presented at a high level, typically no more than one to two pages of a process diagram. The process will vary by organizational

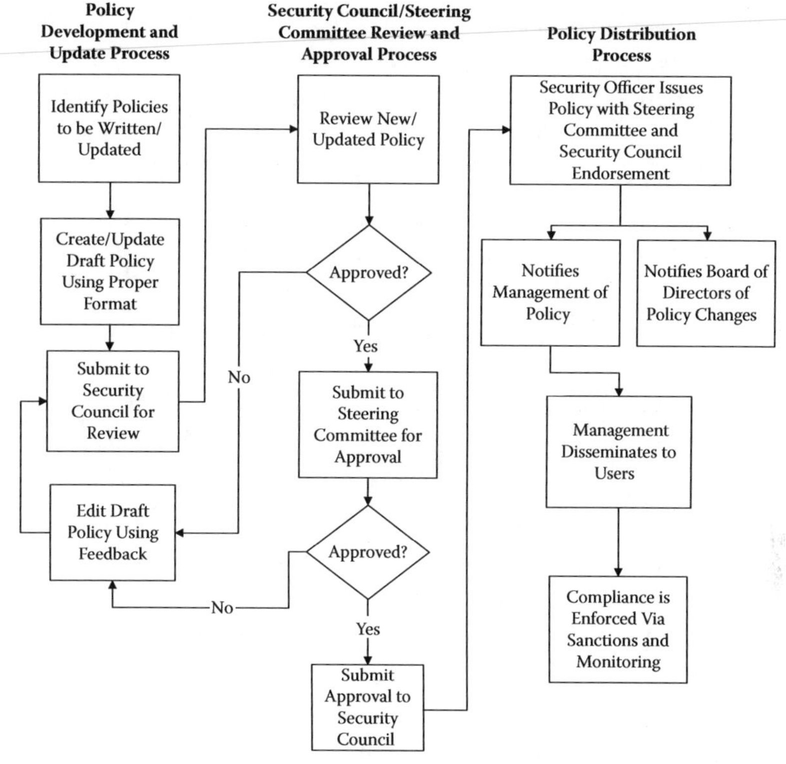

Figure 6.2 Security council policy development, approval, and distribution process.

structure, geographic location, size, and culture of decision making. However, a successful process for review should contain the following steps, as depicted in Figure 6.2.

1. *Policy needs to be determined*—Anyone can request the need for a policy to the information security department. Business units may have new situations that are not covered by an existing security policy. If no security policies exist in the organization, the information security department needs to take the lead and establish a prioritization of policies that are necessary.
2. *Create, modify existing policy*—The information security department creates an initial draft for a new policy that can be reacted to. Caution must be taken not to copy and distribute these policies taken from books or Internet sources as is as they may not be completely appropriate, enforceable, or supported by procedures within the organization.

3. *Internal review by security department*—People within the security department will have varying levels of technical expertise, business acumen, and understanding of the organizational culture. By reviewing within the team first, many obvious errors or misunderstandings of the policy can be avoided before engaging management's limited review time. This also increases the credibility of the information systems security department by bringing a quality product for review. It also saves time on minor grammatical reviews and focuses the management review on substantive policy issues.
4. *Security council reviews and recommends policy*—This is arguably the most critical step in the process. This is where the policy begins the *acceptance step* within the organization. The policies are read, line by line, during these meetings and discussed to ensure that everyone understands the intent and rationale for the policy. Management's commitment begins here. Why? Because the management feels like part of the process and have a chance to provide input, as well as thinking about how the policy would impact their individual departments. Contrast this method with just sending out the policy and saying "this is it" and the difference becomes readily apparent. These are the same management people that are being counted on to continue to support the policy once it is distributed to the rest of the workforce. Failing in this step will guarantee failure in having a real policy.

If we buy into the notion that a security council is a good practice, logical, practical, and appears to get the job done, what is the downside? Some may argue that it is a slow process, especially when senior management may be pushing to "get something out there to address security" to reduce the risks. It is a slow process while the policies are being debated. However, the benefits of (1) having a real policy that the organization can support, (2) buy-in from the management on a continuing basis, (3) reduced need to rework the policies later, and (4) increased understanding by management of the policies' meanings and why they are important outweigh the benefits of blasting out an e-mail containing policies that were copied from another source, the name of the company changed, and distributed without prior collaboration. Policies created in the later context rarely become "real" and followed within the organization, as they were not developed with thorough analysis of how they would be supported by the business in their creation.

5. *Information technology steering committee approves policy*—A committee made up of the senior leadership of the organization is typically formed to oversee the strategic investments in information technology. Many times these committees struggle with balancing decisions on tactical firefighting on short term issues versus dealing with strategic issues, and this perspective needs to be understood when addressing this type of committee. The important element in the membership of this committee is that it involves the decision leaders of the organization. These are the individuals that the employees will be watching to see if they support the policies that were initially generated from the security department. Their review and endorsement of the policies is critical to obtain support in implementing the policies. Also, they may be aware of strategic plans or further operational issues not identified by middle management (through the security council) that may make a policy untenable.

   Since time availability of the senior leadership is typically limited, these committees meet at most on a monthly basis, but more typically on a quarterly basis. Therefore, sufficient time for planning policy approval is necessary. This may seem to run counter to the speed at which electronic policies are distributed. However, as in the case with the security council review, the time delay is essential in obtaining long-term commitment.

6. *Publish policy*—Organizations that go directly from step 2 to this step end up with shelfware, or if e-mailed, "electronic dust." By the time the policy gets to this step, the security department should feel very confident that the policy will be understood by the users and supported by management. Users may agree or disagree with the policy, but will understand the need to follow it because it will be clear how the policy was created and reviewed. Care must be taken when publishing

policies electronically, as it is not desirable to publish the same policy over and over with minor changes to grammar and terminology. Quality reviews need to be performed early in the development process so that the security council and information technology steering committee can devote their time to substantive issues of the policy versus pointing out the typos and correcting spelling. End users should be given the same respect and should expect to be reviewing a document free from error. The medium may be electronic but that does not change the way people want to manage their work lives. With the amount of e-mail already in our lives, we should try to limit the amount of "extra work" that is placed upon the readers of the policies.

The Web-based policy management tools provide the facilities to publish the policies very quickly. Since tracking of reading the policies is a key feature of these products, once the policy is published, they typically cannot be changed unless a new policy is created! This has major implications for the distribution of the policy. This means that *any change made* will require the republishing of the policy. Imagine thousands of users in the organization that now have to reread the policy due to a minor change. This situation should be avoided with the review process in place in the preceding steps. The electronic compliance tracking software is usually built this way (and rightly so), so that it is clear which policy version the user actually signed off on.

It should be clear by now that even though some of the policy development tools support a workflow process within the tool to facilitate approvals of the policies through the various stages (such as draft, interim reviews, and final publishing), there is no substitute for the oral collaboration on the policies. Electronic communications are very flat and do not provide expression of the meaning behind the words. Through the discussions within the various committees, the documented text becomes clearer beyond just those with technical skills. The purpose is more apt to be appropriately represented in the final policies through the collaborative process.

Information Security Policy Process

Security policy development is a repetitive process, where existing policies are updated and new ones are created as needed. The majority of the work is in creating the initial security policies, and hopefully, if these policies were written to the appropriate level, modification of the policies should be minimal. The majority of the work in policy development is evaluating the policies against the introduction of new technologies, law and regulation changes, and changes to the business. Most often, the existing polices will suffice and not require major change. This rate of small change can cause organizations to not pay the appropriate attention to the policy review and update.

As a final note, it should be clear through the activities presented in this chapter that the information security officer is the facilitator of the information security policy development, but should not own them. The security policies should be owned by the organization, which in most cases, is represented by the CEO and the executive management. There will be much less challenging of the security policy if it is owned and issued at this level, than if it is owned by the security officer, who may reside at a lower level within the organization (except for large organizations where the CISO may be part of the executive team).

All other security procedures, standards, guidelines, and implementations are dependent upon the construction of a consistent, easy-to-understand, coherent, and comprehensive information security policy. The time investment in this step is very valuable and the impact to the organization should not be underestimated. Following the steps in this chapter will lead to more efficient and effective information security policy development and subsequent acceptance.

Suggested Reading

1. Peltier, T. R. 2007. *Information security policies and procedures: A practitioner's reference*, 2nd ed. Boca Raton, FL: Auerbach.
2. Wood, C. C. 2009. *Information security policies made easy*, version 11. Houston, TX: Information Shield.
3. Fitzgerald, T. 2004. Ten steps to effective Web-based security policy development and distribution. *EDPACS* 31(9): 1–22.

4. Fitzgerald, T., Goins, B., and Herold, R. 2007. Information security and risk management. In *Official ISC²® Guide to the CISSP CBK*, H. A. Tipton and K. Henry, eds., 9–17. Boca Raton, FL: Auerbach.
5. National Institute of Standards and Technology (NIST). March 2009. Special Publication 800-16 Rev1 (draft): Information security training requirements: A role- and performance-based model (draft). http://csrc.nist.gov/publications/drafts/800-16-rev1/Draft-SP800-16-Rev1.pdf
6. National Institute of Standards and Technology (NIST). October 2003. Special Publication 800-50: Building an information technology security awareness and training program. http://csrc.nist.gov/publications/nistpubs/800-50/NIST-SP800-50.pdf
7. Gupta, U. 2010. Blog: Lessons learned from BP oil spill. Healthcare Info Security (June 21). http://blogs.healthcareinfosecurity.com/posts.php?postID=592

7

Security Compliance Using Control Frameworks

The cautious seldom err.

Confucius, 551–479 BC

Security Control Frameworks Defined

Control frameworks and security standards are often interchangeable terms depending upon the creator. Just to confuse things further, ISO 27001, from the International Organization for Standardization, posits an information security management "system" (ISMS) and the controls are contained within the ISO 27002 Code of Practice (ISO, 2005). The National Institute of Standards and Technology (NIST) Special Publication 800-53 (NIST, 2009), titled Recommended Security Control for Federal Information Systems, breaks the controls into 18 control families and 3 classes (managerial, operational, and technical) of controls. COBIT, Control Objectives for Information and related Technology framework, defines a control framework as a tool for business process owners that facilitates the discharge of their responsibilities through the provision of a supporting control model. Alternatively, COBIT defines a standard as a business practice or technology product that is an accepted practice endorsed by the enterprise or information technology (IT) management team.

COBIT adapted the control from the Committee of Sponsoring Organizations of the Treadway Commission (COSO) report "Internal Control–Integrated Framework" (COSO, 1992) to mean "the policies, procedures, practices, and organizational structures designed to provide assurance that business objectives will be achieved and that undesired events will be prevented or detected and corrected."

For the purposes of this discussion, control frameworks, controls, and standards are interchangeable, as the intent of each of them is to provide some definition to a practice or set of practices that if performed will protect the organization's information assets. These consist of documented, executed, tested, implemented, and monitored controls that reduce the risk of threats succeeding against company vulnerabilities.

Security Control Frameworks and Standards Examples

The following are some examples of the control frameworks and standards that address information security requirements.

Heath Insurance Portability and Accountability Act (HIPAA)

The Heath Insurance Portability and Accountability Act (HIPAA) final rule for adopting security standards was published February 20, 2003, which required a series of administrative, technical, and physical security procedures for entities to use to assure the confidentiality of protected health information (PHI). The standard was intentionally nontechnology specific and intended to provide scalability to small providers and large providers alike.

Federal Information Security Management Act of 2002 (FISMA)

Primary purpose of the Federal Information Security Management Act (FISMA) is to provide a comprehensive framework for ensuring the effectiveness of security controls over information resources that support federal operations and assets. The law also provided funding for NIST to develop the minimum necessary controls required to provide adequate security. The government publishes an annual report card based upon its assessment of compliance with the framework.

National Institute of Standards and Technology (NIST) Recommended Security Controls for Federal Information Systems (800-53)

The NIST Special Publication 800-53 standards and guidelines reference the minimum set of controls that must be implemented to protect the federal system based upon the risk level determined.

Implementation of the 18 families of security controls establishes a level of "security due diligence" for federal agencies and the contractors that perform work for the government. These standards are very comprehensive, freely available, and an excellent resource to supplement other control frameworks.

Federal Information System Controls Audit Manual (FISCAM)

Issued by the U.S. Government Accountability Office (formerly known as the U.S. General Accounting Office), the Federal Information System Controls Audit Manual (FISCAM) provides guidance for information systems auditors to evaluate the IT controls used in support of financial statement audits (GAO, 1999). This is not an audit standard, but is included here because auditors are typically testing the control environment in government audits using this standard. There has been increased emphasis on the use of NIST 800-53 controls and the NIST 800-53A assessments. However, FISCAM is still utilized by government auditors, and, therefore, it is worthwhile to understand the contents.

ISO/IEC 27001:2005 Information Security Management Systems—Requirements

ISO/IEC 27001:2005 provides a model for establishing, implementing, operating, monitoring, reviewing, maintaining, and improving an information security management system (ISMS). This was an evolution from British Standard (BS) 7799-2 and ISO 17799.

The UK Department of Trade and Industry Code of Practice (CoP) for information security, which was developed from support of industry in 1993, became BS 7799 in 1995. The BS 7799 standard was subsequently revised in 1999 to add certification and accreditation components, which became part 2 of the BS 7799 standard. Part 1 of the BS 7799 standard became ISO 17799 and was published as ISO 17799:2000 as the first international information security management standard by the ISO and International Electrotechnical Commission (IEC). ISO 17799 standard was modified in June 2005 as ISO/IEC 17799:2005 containing 134 detailed information security controls based upon the following 11 areas:

- Information security policy
- Organizing information security
- Asset management
- Human resources security
- Physical and environmental security
- Communications and operations management
- Access control
- Information systems acquisition, development, and maintenance
- Information security incident management
- Business continuity management
- Compliance

ISO standards are grouped together by topic areas and the ISO/IEC 27000 series has been designated as the information security management series. For example, ISO 27002:2005 Information Technology—Security Techniques—Code of Practice for Information Security Management replaced the ISO/IEC 17799:2005 Information Technology—Security Techniques—Code of Practice for Information Security Management document. This is consistent with how ISO has named other topic areas, such as the ISO 9000 series for quality management. ISO/IEC 27001:2005 was released in October 2005 and specifies the requirements for establishing, implementing, operating, monitoring, reviewing, maintaining, and improving a documented information security management system taking into consideration the company's business risks. This management standard was based on the BS 7799 part 2 standard and provides information on building information security management systems and guidelines for auditing the system.

ISO/IEC 27002:2005 Information Technology—Security Techniques—Code of Practice for Information Security Management

ISO/IEC 27002:2005 provides 11 security control clauses, as noted earlier. The code of practice specifies the controls necessary and the implementation guidance by specifying the controls with may be chosen to build the ISMS specified through application of ISO/IEC 27001:2005.

Control Objectives for Information and Related Technology (COBIT)

COBIT is a framework and supporting toolset that allow managers to bridge the gap with respect to control requirements, technical issues, and business risks, and then communicate that level of control to stockholders. COBIT can be used to integrate other standards as an umbrella framework.

COBIT is published by the IT Governance Institute and contains a set of 34 high-level control objectives, one for each of the IT processes, such as define a strategic IT plan, define the information architecture, manage the configuration, manage facilities, and ensure systems security. Ensure systems security has been broken down further into control objectives such as manage security measures, identification, authentication and access, user account management, data classification, and firewall architectures.

The COBIT framework examines the effectiveness, efficiency, confidentiality, integrity, availability, compliance, and reliability aspects of the high-level control objectives. The model defines four domains for governance, namely, planning and organization, acquisition and implementation, delivery and support, and monitoring. Processes and IT activities and tasks are then defined within these domains. The framework provides an overall structure for IT control and includes control objectives, which can be utilized to determine effective security control objectives that are driven from the business needs.

COBIT gained increasing popularity through implementation to demonstrate compliance with Sarbanes–Oxley regulations, which were enacted in 2002 to require management and the external auditor to report on internal controls over financial reporting.

Payment Card Industry Data Security Standard (PCI DSS)

The Payment Card Industry Data Security Standard (PCI DSS) is a set of comprehensive requirements for enhancing payment account security, formed by several major credit card issuers, to facilitate the broad adoption of a comprehensive security standard designed to protect cardholder data. The standard applies to all parties that are involved in credit card processing, such as merchants, processors, acquirers, issuers, and service providers as well as other entities that store, process, or transmit cardholder data. The standard contains requirements to address each of the following areas:

- Build and maintain a secure network (proper network device configuration)
- Protect cardholder data (storage and encrypted transmission across open networks)
- Maintain a vulnerability management program (e.g., secure systems, antivirus software)
- Implement strong access control measures (logical and physical access, need to know)
- Regularly monitor and test networks (regularly test, track, and monitor access)
- Maintain an information security policy (maintain a policy that addresses information security for all personnel)

The reviews are to be performed annually to ensure that cardholder data is protected. Depending upon the size of the entity participating in the program, the review may need to be conducted by an external assessor.

Information Technology Infrastructure Library (ITIL)

The Information Technology Infrastructure Library (ITIL) is a set of books published by the British government's Stationary Office between 1989 and 1992 to improve IT service management. The framework contains a set of best practices for IT core operational processes such as change, release, and configuration management; incident and problem management; capacity and availability management; and IT financial management. ITIL's primary contribution is showing how the controls can be implemented for the service management IT processes.

Security Technical Implementation Guides (STIGs) and National Security Agency (NSA) Guides

Security Technical Implementation Guides (STIGs) and National Security Agency (NSA) Guides are configuration standards for the

Department of Defense Information Assurance. They are freely available and used as the basis for technical standards for many private organizations. These standards, if implemented, support many of the high-level requirements specified within requirements such as FISMA, HIPAA, PCI, NIST, COBIT, ISO 27001, and GLBA (Gramm–Leach–Bliley Act).

Federal Financial Institutions Examination Council (FFIEC) IT Examination Handbook

The Federal Financial Institutions Examination Council (FFIEC) is empowered to provide uniform principles, standards, and reporting forms for the examination of financial institutions by the Board of Governors of the Federal Reserve System (FRB), the Federal Deposit Insurance Corporation (FDIC), the National Credit Union Administration (NCUA), the Office of the Comptroller of the Currency (OCC), and the Office of Thrift Supervision (OTS). Several booklets have been issued by the council, including Audit, Business Continuity Planning, Development and Acquisition, Electronic Banking, Management, Operations, Outsourcing Technology Services, Retail Payment Systems, Supervision of Technology Service Providers, Wholesale Payment Systems. Information Security was also added as a booklet in July 2006, which includes guidance for the security process, risk assessment, security strategy, security controls implementation, and security monitoring as well as the examination procedures and related laws. The handbook issued by the FFIEC serves as a supplement to the member agencies expectations for meeting the GLBA 501(b) requirements. These documents provide the detail necessary to evaluate an information security program.

The World Operates on Standards

The fact about standards is that they are useful and the world is made up of many of them, from the minimum weight in the passenger seat that must be met before the airbag protection will become active, to the specification of the size of a #8 screw, to the standard formats for electronic data interchange of electronic transactions between healthcare providers, payers. and clearinghouses. Standards ensure that products are built to specifications and allow us to simplify the complexity of the world by creating a common deliverable and common language. Imagine if every time a manufacturer wanted a product built they had to design a screw that could be potentially different from any other screw a manufacturer created. Not only would this process be very expensive, it would also be very time consuming for the customer and the supplier, and would be very error-prone. Nonstandardized processes also slow the delivery of the product or service. Henry Ford recognized many years ago that there were efficiencies and increases in quality by creating vehicles that looked the same and were painted the same color (black). Although the cars were available in other colors, the primary color produced was black for efficiency. Imagine if stoplights were each made with different colors to represent stop, slow down, and go. Imagine roadways that used different types of striping to indicate passing versus nonpassing lanes based upon the state in which you live. The world would be very chaotic with each individual interpreting the colors and passing lanes as they drove, many times potentially making the wrong decision.

Sometimes we like the standards, sometimes we do not. Sometimes they just do not make intuitive sense to us nor do they seem effective. For example, the Transportation Security Administration (TSA) originally did not allow nail clippers on the airplane and reversed the decision in 2005 after negative public opinion (however, there are varying accounts as to whether it was the TSA that banned nail clippers or if thee ban was pre-TSA). Lighters were also subsequently allowed in July 2007 by the Federal Aviation Administration. Laws, regulations, and the standards that support them are sometimes developed without the extensive analysis of their necessity, or in reaction to a major event and the need to do something, only to be rescinded later for their lack of effectiveness. This is understandable, as government and private industry must react to new situations, making decisions on the data available at the time. In defense of the TSA, decisions to limit what was brought on an airplane had to be made quickly on the heels of September 11, 2001, and its focus was on objects that had the potential to harm. Thus, the standard of no nail clippers was enacted. As time went on, this standard was modified to reflect a reevaluated risk. Liquid restrictions such as being able to carry only a 1 quart bag of 3.4 oz bottles of shampoo and other liquids on board were placed on travelers due to an incident with liquid explosives (TSA, 2009).

Standards Are Dynamic

Over time, the standards evolve, and they change to meet the societal and technological needs. Although the intent of many security standards appears to stay the same over time, the underlying technologies that must be supported are constantly changing. Just as in the "no liquids" ban on airplanes was first introduced, and then evolved into "as long as the liquids are 3 oz or less and fit in a 1 qt plastic bag," and then may morph into "no requirements at all" due to investments in more advanced scanning technology, information security standards also need to change. Alternatively, increased protections may be added, such as the x-ray body scanners and pat downs, which were added at most airports in late 2010.

Most control frameworks are written at a higher, broader level, which provides flexibility to implement controls to satisfy the specific technological request. For example, the ISO 27002:2005 Information Technology—Security Techniques (Code of Practice) control 10.5.1d indicates that "the back-ups should be stored in a remote location, at a sufficient distance to escape any damage from a disaster at the main site." This leaves much interpretation up to the implementer of the standard. How far away is far enough? Before Hurricane Katrina inflicted extensive damage on New Orleans, Louisiana, and other surrounding areas in 2005, many individuals felt that storage a few miles away was sufficient. Today, when companies are assessing their business continuity plans, they typically point to Katrina and quickly decide that 50 to 100-plus miles away would greatly reduce the risk. Others have invested in new replication technologies and the availability of inexpensive storage to ensure availability of the information.

Changing environments necessitate the ability to change the implementation strategies to meet the lower cost of technology, increased effectiveness of controls, and conformance to emerging regulations.

The How Is Typically Left Up to Us

As the aforementioned example illustrates, the good news is that the standards may be written to be flexible over time. The bad news is that they are written to be flexible over time. In other words, standards often lack the specificity of the 'how' that would be useful to implementing the standard. Obviously, this is by design. However, it leaves the implementer of the standard to figure out, based upon the available alternatives, what the best method of implementation should be for their particular environment and cost constraints.

The *best practices* terminology has received criticism over the past several years, as the beauty is in the eye of the beholder. A practice that works for one organization may not fit for another. One organization may implement a policy banning USB drives due to their small size, whereas another may allow them as long as the contents are automatically encrypted with the company-approved software. Still another may prohibit their use by policy to most users, but allow adoption by those who establish a business need (as specified in ISO 27002:2005 10.7.1f), as well as taking the additional step of controlling access through active directory authorization and a vendor product. Which is the best practice? It depends on the organizational culture, appetite for risk, cost constraints, and so forth. It may also be the case that the individuals within the organization do not have access to sensitive information, thus limiting the exposure.

Therefore, the best practice for an organization must take in many factors not defined within the individual standard. Typically, an organization would be prudent to follow the trends within their particular vertical industry, and pay attention to what the "herd" is doing. If 70% of the sheep are heading for the hills, it may be worth heading in that direction. It is also important to understand why another 10% is going in another direction (assuming 20% are standing still) and may be headed to a better best practice. In the tape backup example, maybe the 10% that are utilizing online, high-speed compressed disk-to-disk backup strategies are the best practice that is right for the organization.

Whatever these practices are named for our individual organizations, each must recognize that the practices must satisfy the standard and where they do not, sufficient business justification and risk acceptance must be documented. In this manner, the standards become the reference point for making informed business decisions.

Key Question: Why Does the Standard Exist?

Before deciding how to implement the standard, it is a useful exercise to examine the selected control within the standard and analyze why the control exists in the first place. What threat is it addressing? What would the risk be to my organization if I decided to ignore addressing the control? In other words, how is implementing the control increasing the security, protection, or information assurance of the information assets within the organization? Understanding the "what if I don't" can quickly lead to a deeper understanding of the intent of the control versus trying to ensure compliance with every detail of the control.

For example, if there is a control within the standard that says that logs of activity to the system must be retained for 1 year and access must be restricted to only those with a need to know, understanding why this standard exists will contribute to how it should be implemented. If the intent of the control is to be able to go back and analyze incidents, then the individuals who need read access are the systems security operations team or those responding to the incidents. The files may also need to be online if there is a frequent occurrence of investigation. Alternatively, the logs may not be able to be reviewed due to resource (human) constraints and may necessitate the investment in a Security Information and Event Management (SIEM) tool that aggregates and correlates the information.

Understanding the intent of the control also assists in interpreting the terminology used within the control. Many different organizations, committees, and geographic representations promulgate the standards. The NIST uses terminology in the 800-53 standard (Recommended Security Controls for Federal Information Systems) with roots in the government sector that would be familiar to many accustomed to working for or contracting with government agencies. Contrast that with the IT Governance Institute's COBIT framework (ITGI, n.d.), which is reviewed by an internationally represented committee.

Compliance Is Not Security, But It Is a Good Start

Checking off each of the controls specified within a standard is analogous to completing the weekend honey-do list at home—it may be done at the end of the weekend, but wait for the household auditor to see if it was done well. When HIPAA, GLBA, FISMA, PCI DSS, and other regulations arrived on the scene, some organizations reviewed the "compliancy with the standard" as the primary goal and subsequently created a checklist approach to satisfying the controls with the minimum that would be needed for compliancy, without the benefit of a real risk assessment. The danger in this is that the security controls implemented may prove to be ineffective to addressing the vulnerabilities of the organization and the threats that they face.

However, even though compliance with standards may not be sufficient to mitigate the risk level to an acceptable level for the organization, the fact that the organization is adopting a control framework provides the opportunity to create a baseline and enhance the security level over time. Without such a framework in place, there is less chance that the environment will be secure, as items can be missed too easily.

Integration of Standards and Control Frameworks

Each of the standards and control frameworks contributes in their own way and the astute security professional will become familiar with each of them. COBIT provides an excellent overall governance framework that ties together business goals, governance drivers, business outcomes, and IT resources, processes, and goals. ISO 27001 provides a nice control framework for establishing an ISMS, ensuring that risks are assessed, controls are implemented, management is actively involved, and the documentation is up to date. NIST 800-53 provides the detailed controls with tailored enhancements with the specifications for assessing the controls (800-53A document). The HIPAA Final Federal Security Rule provides the framework for implementing protection for the healthcare vertical industry. FISMA relies on the controls specified by NIST to comply with the regulation instead of creating a new set of controls. The ITIL provides the control areas for providing effective and efficient service delivery, and overlaps the security areas specified in the other control areas.

Several organizations, such as NIST and the IT Governance Institute, have recognized the commonality of these standards as evidenced by their work in mapping controls between HIPAA, NIST 800-53, COBIT, FISMA, ITIL, and others. Although the wording, level of the control, and measures for assessment may have different criteria, there is much commonality amongst the controls. For example, controls regarding configuration management and the need to develop baselines may not be specifically called out in HIPAA and FISMA as they are in ISO27001 and NIST, however, the need for securing the computing devices are represented within the controls for technical controls and the implementation of systems security plans.

Auditing Compliance

Once a control framework or set of standards has been chosen and implemented, it is imperative that the framework be internally and externally audited on a regular basis. Gaps in process are typically uncovered during these audits, and if these gaps are mitigated quickly, the security program becomes more complete over time. Care must be taken to address reasonable risk, as it is rare that an organization will execute every control every time. What is important is that there are mitigating or compensating controls that catch the anomalies before they become major issues, and prompt follow-up and correction actions are taken. Audit testing of the control frameworks will take many forms including interviewing, determining and testing samples, performing vulnerability assessments, review of policies and procedures, and conducting external penetration tests. Each audit should be viewed as an opportunity to determine the effectiveness of the control framework and potentially modify the existing controls. Preparing for the auditing of the controls is covered in more depth in Chapter 11.

Adoption Rate of Various Standards

Whatever the industry, it seems that there are always many standards from which to choose. Each standard has occurred due to a lack of security in a certain area, and laws or rules were put in place. HIPAA emerged due to a concern about creating electronic medical records/claims information and the privacy concerns that would result over aggregating the data. PCI emerged as cardholder information was being stored and not properly protected. FISMA was enacted to provide a common evaluation of the security across government agencies and their contractors.

ISO 27001/2 Certification

The aforementioned laws needed standards containing a listing of controls that could be implemented, such as ISO 27001/2, NIST-800-53 Controls, COBIT, PCI, ITIL, and HITRUST (Health Information Trust Alliance), to protect the information assets that were being targeted (government, financial, healthcare, or all industries). However, the adoption rates of the different standards have varied from organization to organization. For example, some organizations are basing their security program on ISO27001/2, whereas others use COBIT as a framework, and others still are using NIST 800-53 controls. Others, such as those in healthcare, might be using the NIST 800-53 controls mapped to HIPAA (as available from the NIST website in document 800-66) to satisfy the requirements of HIPAA. Others yet are using the HITRUST model to determine compliance. So, this begs the question, why isn't everyone using NIST 800-53? Or ISO 27001/2?

To answer this question, it is useful to look at the number of companies that are currently ISO 27001 certified, which varies greatly by country. For example, Japan has the most number of certifications (3720), followed by India (509), China (494), United Kingdom (455), Taiwan (401), and then the list drops off with Germany at 145 and so forth. The United States has approximately 100 companies that are certified in its information security management system. With the number of years that the ISO security standard has been around (approximately 20 years), one would think the adoption rate would be much higher. The reality is that many companies are utilizing the standard to frame their security programs; however, they have not taken the step to obtain certification. The rationale, anecdotally expressed at numerous security conferences, is (1) it can be a timely, rigorous process involving extra (unnecessary) expense; (2) the benefit of certification is not easily determined, as the auditors will still pull samples and audit according to their audit program; and (3) there is currently no law or mandate requiring that ISO 27001/2 be utilized and certified as the control standard. Without a law requiring its use, organizations have chosen the ISO 27001/2 standard to demonstrate compliance with areas such as HIPAA, Sarbanes–Oxley Act of 2002 (Section 404), GLBA, SAS070 requirements, but have stopped short of pursuing certification. Audits are expensive in terms of audit time, business interruption time, and cost, and an ISO audit represents an extra expense over and above the other required audits.

NIST Certification

U.S. government agencies are all too familiar with NIST 800-53 controls, as they are required by FISMA to be implemented by all federal agencies and their contractors. There is no requirement that the federal agencies implement the set of ISO 27001/2 controls; however, they are mapped to the NIST 800-53 controls as a reference. There is much overlap in these controls. However, the NIST controls are at a more detailed level than the ISO controls. In fact, the NIST controls are an excellent supplement to the ISO controls if this is the framework that is selected. There does not exist, at this time, a NIST security "certification" per say of the 800-53 controls; however, there is a process by which the government certifies the systems security plan and risk assessment, which embody the 800-53 controls and how they are implemented within the general support system defined by the systems security plan.

NIST 800-53 controls and guidance offer an excellent integration opportunity to supplement the ISO and COBIT controls in building the information security program. Although the controls are required for use in federal agencies, they are also very applicable to the private sector and best of all they are freely available for download from the NIST site on the Internet.

Control Framework Convergence

Why can't we have just one standard? On the surface, this appears to be a simple, logical question. As Eckhart Tolle (2005) promotes in his book *A New Earth* that individuals create stress in their lives by not accepting "what is." The reality is that laws and regulations will continue to emerge from different organizations, and as security professionals, adapting to the emerging laws and regulations and applying the appropriate standards and control frameworks will be key. This is not to say that efficiencies cannot be gained, as controls can be implemented that would support multiple control frameworks. Sometimes, a control only needs to be tweaked to satisfy multiple controls and standards.

Over time, the practices that are common do emerge and become generally accepted. Even as recent as a few years ago, laptops were not universally encrypted by companies, with IT departments citing the expense, complexity, lack of necessity, files stored on the network by company policy, and so on. So what was the tipping point that changed the practice to companies encrypting the laptops? It was when the Veterans Administration lost a laptop containing information on 26.5 million veterans in 2006 causing a public outrage. Today, few companies would want to admit that they are not encrypting their laptops due to the shift in the herd mentality to encryption. The sheep have headed for the hills, and the slow sheep are vulnerable to being left behind. Upon reviewing the standards and control frameworks, it is clear that the requirements for protecting mobile devices and media were specified prior to 2006. It could be argued that proactive attention to these frameworks would save much in the long run. The Veterans Administration suffered in terms of public reputation and financially ($20 million lawsuit to settle claims), all which could have been avoided. What happened to this government agency could happen to any of our organizations if the controls are not in place. Adherence to the control frameworks and standards increases the likelihood that breaches will not have a devastating effect on the confidentiality, integrity, or availability of the information assets.

The 11-Factor Compliance Assurance Manifesto

The regulations, control frameworks, standards, technical implementation guides, and penalties for noncompliance provide insight into what needs to be achieved to provide the organizational compliance assurance to the various security-related regulations. Now this begs the next question: What actions need to be taken to achieve and maintain compliance with the regulations?

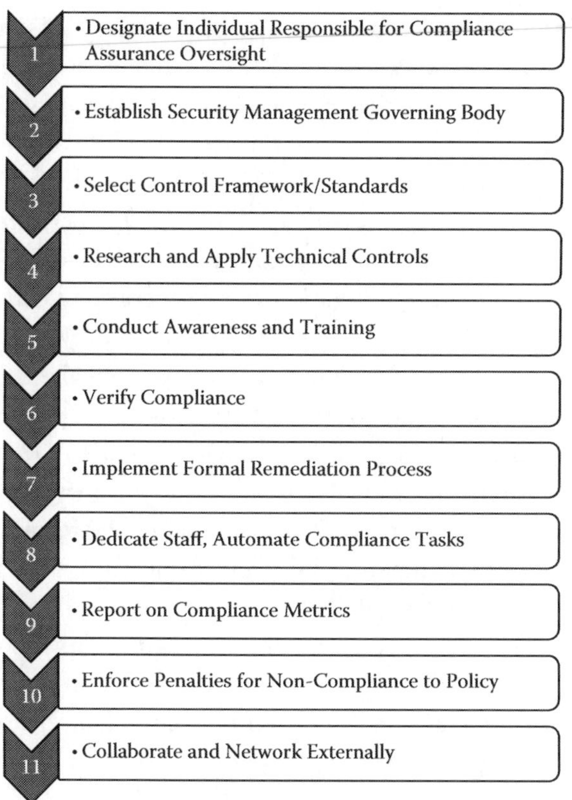

Figure 7.1 11-Factor Security Compliance Assurance Manifesto.

To answer that question, the 11-Factor Security Compliance Assurance Manifesto (Fitzgerald, 2008), as shown in Figure 7.1, sets out the principles by which compliance assurance may be achieved.

1. *Designate the individual responsible for compliance assurance oversight*—Whereas many of the policy-type regulations may not appear to change on a frequent basis, the supporting documents, technical specifications, and current areas of concern do change over time. New laws are also created, such as the new incident breach reporting laws implemented as part of the HITECH Act (Chapter 13), where state-by-state adoption of some form of the law is enacted. Similarly, when the HIPAA privacy rule was being made effective, each state had groups that were focused on creating a preemption analysis. Staying on top of these changes and ensuring that someone

is directing the security compliance efforts is essential. In medium-sized organizations, this is likely to be the manager or director of security, whereas in larger organizations the chief information security officer, chief security officer, or security officer is likely be responsible for ensuring that the security compliance assurance activities are performed. The chief information officer's organization and the other business units carry out the mitigation work as appropriate.

2. *Establish a security management governing body*—To achieve support for the implementation of security policies throughout the organization and to ensure that the security policies do not disrupt the business, it is advisable to establish an information security council. Councils made up of representatives from IT, business units, human resources, legal departments, physical security, internal audit, ethics and compliance, and information security can be effective in achieving compliance with the regulations. Their oversight and interaction provide feedback as to whether the security activities planned are feasible and whether there is a high probability of compliance success.
3. *Select control framework and standards*—The frameworks mentioned, such as COSO, ITIL, ISO 17799, COBIT, NIST, and FISCAM, offer an excellent place to map the security controls that are in place to the framework, uncover the gaps in compliance, and create action plans to increase the security assurance with these objectives. Multiple control frameworks can be selected for different levels of detail. For example, COBIT may be selected to provide a governing framework, whereas ISO 17799 controls may be mapped to the framework (already available from the IT governance institute) and then linked to the NIST control objective families and supported by the Defense Information Systems Agency (DISA) STIGs. The mapping provides a mechanism to review how a set of technical controls supports the higher-level statements in the other frameworks. The same controls serve multiple purposes. Comprehensive frameworks are created through this process, enabling the other compliance assurance activities.
4. *Research and apply technical controls*—There are many approaches at the technical level for being compliant with the control

objectives. Analysis must be performed to determine the best control based upon the risk profile of the organization. For example, achieving compliance with a requirement to provide adequate off-site backups of information in the event of a disaster could be achieved in a small regional office by placing a daily tape in a fireproof safe and rotating the weekly tape off site. Alternatively, a small office may decide to store the backup tapes remotely with a tape storage facility, transmit the backup information securely over the Internet for backups, or assign an individual to take home the backup tape nightly. Each of the scenarios has its own costs and risks inherent in the control selection.

5. *Conduct awareness and training*—The documented security policies and procedures are necessary; however, if individuals do not truly understand their responsibilities to comply with the security controls, the likelihood that the appropriate processes will be followed is greatly diminished.
6. *Verify compliance*—Vulnerability assessments, penetration testing, and internal audit reviews of the security controls ensure that the policies and procedures that were created are being followed. Implemented security on the computing platform can be tested and compared with the documented baselines, configurations, and change control records to provide assurance that the security controls are being maintained per the requirements implemented through the control frameworks.
7. *Implement a formal remediation process*—When weaknesses in the security controls are discovered through internal audits, external audits, vulnerability assessments, risk assessments, or other internal reviews, the issue must be logged and tracked to completion. Accountability should be placed at a middle management or senior management level to ensure the appropriate attention and priority are placed on remedying the issue. Completion dates must be assigned (preferably no later than 90 days after creation of the action plan). Documentation of the remediation (evidence) must be provided when the issue has been resolved. The existence of formal tracking of the security issues provides the assurance that security is an ongoing, management-supported process.

8. *Dedicate staff, automate compliance tasks*—Compliance initiatives are very time consuming and drain the organization of resources to collect evidence, provide explanations, participate in interviews, and locate the policies and procedures that support the regulations. Without an organized automated process, this activity becomes even more challenging and time is wasted on inefficiencies. The same information may be requested multiple times to answer similar questions, where one report may have provided a reasonable answer. Initially, more staff should be allocated to the compliance efforts to provide a focus to the activity. When the compliance tasks are added to the regular jobs of predominantly IT staff, they may be given lower priority and resources. As automation increases, the staff required to support the compliance efforts should either remain constant or decrease. A constant staff may be needed to ensure that the new regulations and changes are adequately addressed.
9. *Report on compliance metrics*—Dashboards of red, yellow, and green, or heat maps are useful tools to demonstrate where security is weak within the organization and where more focus should be placed. These metrics should be reported in a manner that is meaningful to the business, such as unavailability issues, which could impact major, mission critical applications, or confidentiality concerns that may affect the consumer trust in the brand.
10. *Enforce penalties for noncompliance to policy*—Does one grin and bear it when the security control objectives are not followed or grit one's teeth? This is one area that needs teeth! There must be sanctions in place for those that do not follow the security policies. Associates must also be trained that compliance with the security controls is part of their job responsibilities. The individual responsible for compliance assurance must ensure that the guidelines are established for sanctions and that the appropriate parties follow through with the sanction (which may be the manager, and legal and human resources representatives).
11. *Collaborate and network externally*—Many organizations must comply with the same regulations. Why not leverage that experience? Working with peers within the industry vertical for dealing with industry-specific regulations and across

industries for understanding various methods to implement the control frameworks, standards, and technical controls can be invaluable. For example, nonprofit organizations, such as the HIPAA Collaborative of Wisconsin, were formed to bring together healthcare providers, payers, and clearinghouses to discuss approaches to implementing HIPAA. The presentations, network contacts, and information sharing that happen are phenomenal. Attending conferences and industry associations such as the Information Systems Security Association (ISSA), Information Systems Audit and Control Association (ISACA), Computer Security Institute (CSI), Management Information System Training Institute (MISTI), SANS (SysAdmin, Audit, Network, Security) Institute, and others helps to gain a common understanding of the regulation and implementation approaches. This also provides input as to what the herd is doing to be compliant with the regulation.

The Standards/Framework Value Proposition

Control frameworks and standards provide the roadmap to build a successful information security program. Once in place, continuous review of the policies, standard operating procedures, and implementation of the controls will enhance the effectiveness of the program. Monitoring through audits accompanied by corrective actions and tracking enables refinement of the control framework and standards to reduce the risk of a security event impacting the business in a significant way. Think of the various security control frameworks as each contributing in some way to the infrastructure of a super six-lane freeway. Rather than manage our security programs by ourselves, on an old gravel road at 20 miles per hour, it is time to get on the superhighway supported by the strong plethora of control frameworks and standards and enjoy the ride!

Suggested Reading

1. Federal Information Security Management Act of 2002 (FISMA). November 27, 2002. http://csrc.nist.gov/groups/SMA/fisma/index.html
2. National Institute of Standards and Technology (NIST), Special Publications, http://csrc.nist.gov/publications/PubsSPs.html

3. National Institute of Standards and Technology (NIST). August 2009. Recommended security controls for federal information systems, Special publication 800-53. http://csrc.nist.gov/publications/PubsSPs.html
4. National Institute of Standards and Technology (NIST). July 2008. Guide for assessing controls in federal information systems. http://csrc.nist.gov/publications/nistpubs/800-53A/SP800-53A-final-sz.pdf
5. Defense Information Systems Agency (DISA), Security technical implementation guides (STIGs), http://iase.disa.mil/stigs/stig
6. National Security Agency, Security configuration guides, http://www.nsa.gov/snac
7. International Organization for Standardization (ISO). ISO/IEC 27001:2005 Information security management systems—Requirements. http://www.iso.org/iso/iso_catalogue/catalogue_tc/catalogue_detail.htm?csnumber=42103
8. International Organization for Standardization (ISO). ISO/IEC 27002:2005 Information technology security techniques—Code of practice for information security management. http://www.iso.org/iso/iso_catalogue/catalogue_tc/catalogue_detail.htm?csnumber=50297
9. U.S. General Accounting Office. January 1999. Federal Information System Controls Audit Manual (FISCAM), GAO/AIMD-12.19.6. http://www.gao.gov/special.pubs/12_19_6.pdf
10. U.S. Government Accountability Office. February 2009. Federal Information System Controls Audit Manual (FISCAM), GAO-09-232G. http://www.gao.gov/new.items/d09232g.pdf
11. Information Technology Infrastructure Library, http://www.itil-officialsite.com/home/home.asp
12. Tolle, E. 2005. *A new earth: Awakening to your life's purpose.* New York: Penguin.
13. PCI Data Security Standards Council, https://www.pcisecuritystandards.org/security_standards/documents.php
14. International Register of ISMS Certificates, http://iso27001certificates.com
15. Fitzgerald, T. 2008. Compliance assurance: Taming the beast. In *Information security handbook*, H. Tipton and M. Krause, eds., chap. 28. Boca Raton, FL: Auerbach.
16. IT Governance Institute. 2000. COBIT® framework: Governance, control and audit for information and related technology.
17. TSA urban legends (nail clippers, knitting needles and corkscrews). 2009. TSA Blog (May 9). http://blog.tsa.gov/2009/05/tsa-urban-legends-nail-clippers.html
18. Lighters, nail clippers and lithium batteries. 2008. The TSA Blog (January 31). http://blog.tsa.gov/2008/01/lighters-nail-clippers-and-lithium.html
19. IT Governance Institute. COBIT® 4.1, http://www.itgi.org
20. Committee of Sponsoring Organizations of the Treadway Commission (COSO). 1992. Internal control—Integrated framework.

8
Managerial Controls
Practical Security Considerations

> It is tempting, if the only tool you have is a hammer, to treat everything as if it were a nail.
>
> **Abraham Harold Maslow, 1908–1970**

The previous chapter provided an overview of the security standards and framework landscape, and illustrated the importance of adhering to a set of security controls to enhance security and demonstrating compliance to the organization and to the auditors. Each of the different standards has controls at different levels of detail. The standards chosen by an organization may be aligned to a particular vertical industry or generally applicable across industries as shown in Table 8.1.

Security Control Convergence

The next three chapters cover the minimum controls that should be considered for a functioning information security program. These chapters cover the detailed controls for the managerial, operational, and technical classes of controls across 18 families of controls. The basis of the controls is from the National Institute of Standards and Technology (NIST) 800-53 Recommended Controls for Federal Information Systems and Organizations. Although these controls were developed with the U.S. government in mind, this control set forms one of the most comprehensive, detailed control specifications that currently exist. An organization may decide that this level of control is not necessary for its organization. However, it is very useful to start with these controls and by performing a risk assessment of the control, determine whether the control is necessary. If the controls are approached in this manner, which could also be referred to as a bottom-up approach, it is unlikely that key controls will be missed.

As noted in the previous chapter on controls, a preferred approach would be to use the NIST 800-53 security controls in conjunction with ISO/IEC 27001 controls (from Annex A; published by the International Organization for Standardization and the International Electrotechnical Commission), the COBIT controls, and the security requirements that are specified for the specific industry. If the controls are used in this manner, the best of all worlds can be achieved. COBIT (Control Objectives for Information and related Technology) can be used to supply the overall information technology (IT) framework and provide the accepted structure for future auditing of the framework to establish compliance (i.e., Sarbanes–Oxley). ISO 27001 can provide the notion of a formalized information security management system (ISMS) and a description of the processes that could be chosen to make up the ISMS. The NIST 800-53 controls can take the controls to a lower, more granular level to support the security processes as well as provide some criteria for assessing the lower level controls via the 800-53A special publication providing auditors guidance on assessing the controls. Finally, the vertical industry set of controls, such as the Health Insurance Portability and Accountability Act (HIPAA) Final Security Rule can provide the higher-level requirements necessary to be in compliance with the promulgated regulation. Each of these standards, control frameworks, or regulations are not in conflict with one another but can be very complimentary. Granted they exist at different levels of detail, come from a different focus, and may have more or less stringent requirements from one another, by implementing the sum of these requirements, the security program can be made very effective and reduce the risk of loss. An illustration of an example relationship between NIST 800-53, COBIT, ISO 27001, and HIPAA are shown in Figure 8.1.

Controls may be tailored to fit the needs of the organization and controls may or may not be applicable. For example, an organization that outsources the data center processing to another organization may not have to set up contracts and testing of disaster recovery with another off-site data center. However the organization would need to

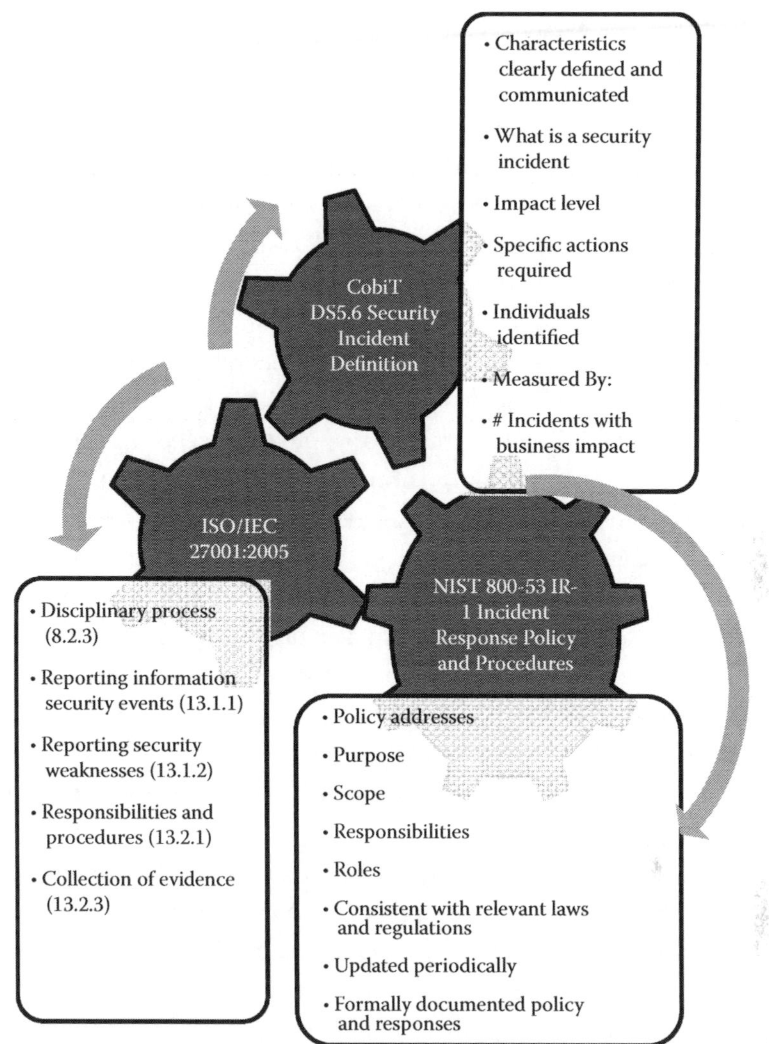
• Characteristics clearly defined and communicated
• What is a security incident
• Impact level
• Specific actions required
• Individuals identified
• Measured By:
• # Incidents with business impact
CobiT DS5.6 Security Incident Definition
ISO/IEC 27001:2005
NIST 800-53 IR-1 Incident Response Policy and Procedures
• Disciplinary process (8.2.3)
• Reporting information security events (13.1.1)
• Reporting security weaknesses (13.1.2)
• Responsibilities and procedures (13.2.1)
• Collection of evidence (13.2.3)
• Policy addresses
• Purpose
• Scope
• Responsibilities
• Roles
• Consistent with relevant laws and regulations
• Updated periodically
• Formally documented policy and responses

Figure 8.1 NIST 800-53, COBIT, and ISO 27001 relationship example.

ensure that the function is being provided by the data center that they are contracting their workload to. The organization should be asking how often the data is being backed up, how often is it restored, and how often disaster recovery tests are performed. It may be asked to participate in the tests for the contracted data center. In other words, it is important to review the intent of the control, and then determine who, what, where, why, and when the control is being performed.

Security Control Methodology

The controls in the next three chapters are presented by (1) a discussion of the control family area (e.g., access control) and the practical security considerations for addressing this family are;, (2) a table showing the mapping between the NIST 800-53 control and ISO/IEC 27001, COBIT 4.1, and HIPAA as an example of a vertical industry mapping. In some cases, there was no related ISO/IEC 27001 mapping, and this is noted in the table. When there was a COBIT mapping, this is noted. Likewise, when there was no specific HIPAA reference, one was not noted.

The practical security considerations provide a discussion for each of the 18 control families as a guide for approaching the creation of controls within each area. The 18 control families are shown in Table 8.2. The size and resources of the organization will dictate how much can be invested within each control. Larger companies are expected to devote more resources to the security controls and implement more automated solutions to address the issues. Smaller organizations need to decide what is feasible to adequately protect the resources and may need to engage external resources to provide the adequate protection. For example, a small community bank may not be able to afford an in-house staff to perform vulnerability assessment testing on the infrastructure, but may be able to secure the Internet entry point into the organization and ensure that the 15 employees receive adequate information security awareness training. This approach would not be sufficient for an organization of 40,000 employees spread across 100 locations. The risk assessment for these two organizations would lead to different conclusions. Clearly the security officer would like to spend as much money on the security controls as possible, however, the reality of balancing the other company demands with overspending on information security will limit the investment. Therefore, the practical security discussion provides an interpretation of what the NIST 800-53 controls, COBIT controls, ISO 27001 controls, and in this case the HIPAA controls are really trying to achieve and some considerations for implementation.

Security Assessment and Authorization Controls

The security assessment and authorization control family (CA) controls shown in Table 8.3 ensures that the policies and procedures are developed and followed, security controls are reviewed by the organization on a periodic basis, and that a person in position of high enough authority has approved the security controls for operation of the system. In effect this approval is contingent upon the acceptance of the risk assessment and the security control environment being adequate to present a reasonable level of risk to the approver. Government entities will have a formalized assessment and authorization process (formerly known as security certification and accreditation). However, each organization should develop a process whereby the security controls and the residual risk are approved and accepted by senior management. This creates awareness of the controls and the risk that the organization is accepting.

The security assessments may be done internally or externally, depending upon the expertise available to perform the assessments. In either case, the individuals performing the assessment should be independent so that bias does not impact the assessment. When gaps are found with the security controls, these need to be documented formally through a document such as a plan of action and milestones (POA&M). By reviewing the plans on a monthly basis, the organization can direct the appropriate attention to the controls. A process should be developed for closing the plans upon receipt of the documentation demonstrating that the issue was fixed, along with a reporting mechanism to management for items on the monthly POA&M, especially those items showing delayed status or ones that have missed the estimated implementation date.

The intent of these controls is to ensure that there is some oversight on the assessment process and that the items that are determined to be gaps are promptly closed. A goal of this process should be to close items within 90 days from issue identification. Although not all issues will be able to be mitigated within that timeframe, this can be set as a standard to address most security issues that an organization will face. For those items that could take longer, the process could be built to require business justification and subsequent executive management approval (i.e., from the chief technology officer, chief information officer, or chief executive officer) for any initiatives that will take longer than 90 days to implement.

Planning Controls

The old adage "If you don't know where you are going, all roads will lead you there" certainly applies to the security planning control family (PL) shown in Table 8.4. Security can happen by chaos, but as indicated by the Capability Maturity Model Integration (CMMI), an organization can become more effective by adopting a more proactive, planned approach.

The key document in this section is the systems security plan (SSP) containing descriptions of the business, computing infrastructure, major applications, and key controls that support the documentation of the environment. The document needs to be updated annually or whenever there are significant changes in the environment. These may be caused by changes in applications, outsourcing of information technology, mergers and acquisitions, adding a managed security service provider (MSSP), and so forth. The plan should not be viewed as merely a documentation exercise that is performed by one individual in the security department, but rather as an opportunity to engage individuals from different business and IT departments to construct the plan. It is not uncommon for different people to have different understandings of what systems are in place, technology infrastructure, and security controls to support the business application or support system defined in the plan. In other words, the process of constructing the plan can be an eye-opening experience.

The security team should also have a weekly meeting to discuss the current initiatives and their status, including a review of the dates and deliverables. For security to be viewed as an ongoing program versus a point-in-time initiative to resolve the issues created by a recent incident, then the security program should be expected to be managed as a business. This can be as simple as creating a red–green–yellow colored spreadsheet (for behind, completed, and in process) and shared at a weekly meeting or as elaborate as using project management software for each project and having a biweekly comprehensive review. What is important is that there is a constant focus on what the activities are that are in process as well as what activities need to be added within the next 0–6, 6–12, and 12–18 month time frames to keep them on the radar.

Risk Assessment Controls

Risk assessments are the topic of much discussion these days and rightfully so. The risk assessment should represent a documented meeting of the minds between information security and senior management. This is the process that, in very simple terms, documents the risks to the organization, documents the mitigating controls, identifies the residual risk, and provides an understanding of what needs to be done to bring the security profile of the organization in line with its risk appetite. The risk management process was discussed extensively in Chapter 5 and the risk assessment control family controls are depicted in Table 8.5.

Vulnerability scanning is performed as part of the risk assessment to provide the status of the technical controls and where improvements need to be made. The risk assessment may be performed on an annual basis; however, the vulnerability scanning should be done more frequently due to the vulnerabilities introduced daily that could impact the computing environment. A minimum quarterly scanning frequency with a subsequent 90 fix-cycle to address the vulnerabilities found during the scan would be preferred. If the organization is able to perform the scanning on a weekly or daily basis through the use of automated tools, this would be a good goal to strive toward. Once the process is in place and the initial list of vulnerabilities is mitigated, the amount of time required to remove the subsequent vulnerabilities should decrease and become more manageable. An organization may choose to use multiple tools to provide increased security, whereby one tool might not pick up the same vulnerability as another.

As with the systems security plans, the risk assessment constitutes a key security document and should be approved by senior management including the CEO, CIO, and business owner of the system. The systems security department should view itself as the facilitator of the risk assessment, but the final acceptance of risk is whoever is designated within senior management to assume that role. Senior management has a fiduciary responsibility to protect the organization's resources from loss, and the Risk Assessment document is a key document in its ability to consciously understand and accept the appropriate level of risk.

System and Services Acquisition Controls

The system and services acquisition control family (SA) controls shown in Table 8.6 ensure that the computer code supporting the

Table 8.1 Vertical Industry Control Standard Alignment

STANDARD/CONTROL FRAMEWORK/REGULATION	VERTICAL INDUSTRY
Health Insurance Portability and Accountability Act (HIPAA) addressable and required standards	Health insurance
Payment Card Industry Data Security Standards	Financial
National Institute of Standards and Technology (NIST) Recommended Security Controls for Federal Information Systems (800-53)	Government, federal contractors (detailed controls may be applied to all industries) to support Federal Information Security Management Act (FISMA)
ISO/IEC 27001:2005 information security management systems—Requirements and ISO 27002:2005 Information technology—Security techniques—Code of practice for information security management	International standard may be applied to all industries
Control Objective for Information and related Technology (COBIT)	International standard may be applied to all industries; used heavily to evaluate and demonstrate compliance with internal controls for Sarbanes–Oxley regulation
Information Technology Infrastructure Library (ITIL)	Adopted largely by IT operational areas to improve service, applicable across industries
Federal Financial Institutions Examination Council (FFIEC) IT Examination Handbook (supports Gramm–Leach–Bliley Act)	Financial
North American Electric Reliability Corporation (NERC) Critical Infrastructure Program (CIP)	U.S. bulk power systems

business environment, whether running internally or externally, has been created by following a system development life cycle whereby the appropriate security controls are analyzed, designed, implemented, and tested according to a defined process.

Software usage and licensing is also addressed to make sure that only the authorized software in the appropriate quantities is running within the environment. This can be controlled by tracking spreadsheets, discovery tools, and removing administrative access from most users machines and creating policies of the approved software that may be requested from the desktop support team, help desk, or the group managing the software licenses. Allowing end users to install software, even versions of approved software, on their own might introduce vulnerabilities as they may be installing a version with vulnerabilities not internally reviewed or an older version. Software installs should be centrally controlled for vulnerability management and license tracking. Having too many unused licenses installed costs

Table 8.2 NIST 800-53 18 Control Families

IDENTIFIER	FAMILY	CLASS
AC	Access control	Technical
AT	Awareness and training	Operational
AU	Audit and accountability	Technical
CA	Security assessment and authorization	Management
CM	Configuration management	Operational
CP	Contingency planning	Operational
IA	Identification and authorization	Technical
IR	Incident response	Operational
MA	Maintenance	Operational
MP	Media protection	Operational
PE	Physical and environmental protection	Operational
PL	Planning	Management
PS	Personnel security	Operational
RA	Risk assessment	Management
SA	System and services acquisition	Management
SC	System and communications protection	Technical
SI	System and information integrity	Operational
PM	Program management	Management

Source: NIST Special Publication 800-53 Revision 3, Table 1-1. August 2009. Includes May, 1, 2010, updates.

the company money as well as the potential for fines by the software vendors for not having enough licenses.

Program Management Controls

The program management (PM) control family was added in NIST 800-53 Rev3 to provide the controls in support of managing an information security program (see Table 8.7). The other controls could be viewed as tactical implementation of security controls, whereby this control ensures that there is someone designated with the role of information security and carries out the mission of managing the information security program. The ISMS within ISO 27000 has long had the requirements for the establishment of an information security program. Chapter 2 of this book discussed creating the information security strategy, and Chapters 3 and 4 addressed the management roles and responsibilities to achieve the appropriate structure and relationships to carry out the program.

Table 8.3 Security Assessment and Authorization Controls

CONTROL FAMILY	COMPLIANT (YES/NO)	CONTROL	MAPPINGS
Security assessment and authorization		CA-1 Security Assessment and Authorization Policies and Procedures The organization develops, disseminates, and reviews/updates [Assignment: organization defined frequency]: a. Formal, documented security assessment and authorization policies that address purpose, scope, roles, responsibilities, management commitment, coordination among organizational entities, and compliance; and b. Formal, documented procedures to facilitate the implementation of the security assessment and authorization policies and associated security assessment and authorization controls. Practical security considerations:	ISO/IEC 27001 A.5.1.1, A.5.1.2, A.6.1.1, A.6.1.3 A.6.1.4, A.8.1.1, A.10.1.1, A.15.1.1, A.15.2.1 COBIT P010.12 HIPAA 1 64.308(a)(8)
Security assessment and authorization		CA-2 Security Assessments The organization: a. Develops a security assessment plan that describes the scope of the assessment including: • Security controls and control enhancements under assessment • Assessment procedures to be used to determine security control effectiveness • Assessment environment, assessment team, and assessment roles and responsibilities b. Assesses the security controls in the information system [Assignment: organization-defined frequency] to determine the extent to which the controls are implemented correctly, operating as intended, and producing the desired outcome with respect to meeting the security requirements for the system;	ISO/IEC 27001 A.6.1.8, A.10.3.2, A.15.2.1, A.15.2.2 COBIT DS5.5 HIPAA 164.308(a)(8)

Table 8.3 (continued) Security Assessment and Authorization Controls

CONTROL FAMILY	COMPLIANT (YES/NO)	CONTROL	MAPPINGS
		c. Produces a security assessment report that documents the results of the assessment; and d. Provides the results of the security control assessment, in writing, to the authorizing official or authorizing official designated representative. Practical security considerations:	
Security assessment and authorization		CA-3 Information System Connections The organization: a. Authorizes connections from the information system to other information systems outside of the authorization boundary through the use of interconnection security agreements; b. Documents, for each connection, the interface characteristics, security requirements, and the nature of the information communicated; and c.Monitors the information system connections on an ongoing basis verifying enforcement of security requirements. Practical security considerations:	ISO/IEC 27001 A.6.2.1, A.6.2.3, A.10.6.1, A.10.8.1, A.10.8.2, A.10.8.5, A.11.4.2 HIPAA 164.308(b)(1), 164.308(b)(4), 164.314(a)(2)(ii)
Security assessment and authorization		CA-5 Plan of Action and Milestones The organization: a. Develops a plan of action and milestones for the information system to document the organization's planned remedial actions to correct weaknesses or deficiencies noted during the assessment of the security controls and to reduce or eliminate known vulnerabilities in the system; and b. Updates existing plan of action and milestones [Assignment: organization-defined frequency] based on the findings from security controls assessments, security impact analyses, and continuous monitoring activities. Practical security considerations:	ISO/IEC 27001 (None) COBIT ME2.7

Continued

Table 8.3 (continued) Security Assessment and Authorization Controls

CONTROL FAMILY	COMPLIANT (YES/NO)	CONTROL	MAPPINGS
Security assessment and authorization		CA-6 Security Authorization The organization: a. Assigns a senior-level executive or manager to the role of authorizing official for the information system; b. Ensures that the authorizing official authorizes the information system for processing before commencing operations; and c. Updates the security authorization [Assignment: organization-defined frequency]. Practical Security Considerations:	ISO/IEC 27001 A.6.1.4, A.10.3.2 COBIT AI7.7, DS5.5 HIPAA 164.308(a)(8), 164.308(a)(2)
Security assessment and authorization		CA-7 Continuous Monitoring The organization establishes a continuous monitoring strategy and implements a continuous monitoring program that includes: a. A configuration management process for the information system and its constituent components; b. A determination of the security impact of changes to the information system and environment of operation; c. Ongoing security control assessments in accordance with the organizational continuous monitoring strategy; and d. Reporting the security state of the information system to appropriate organizational officials [Assignment: organization-defined frequency]. Practical Security Considerations:	ISO/IEC 27001 A.6.1.8, A.15.2.1, A.15.2.2 COBIT PO1.3, DS5.5 HIPAA 164.308(a)(8), 164.308(a)(1)(ii)(D)

Table 8.4 Planning Controls

CONTROL FAMILY	COMPLIANT (YES/NO)	CONTROL	MAPPINGS
Planning		PL-1 Security Planning Policy and Procedures The organization develops, disseminates, and reviews/updates [Assignment: organization-defined frequency]: a. A formal, documented security planning policy that addresses purpose, scope, roles, responsibilities, management commitment, coordination among organizational entities, and compliance; and b. Formal, documented procedures to facilitate the implementation of the security planning policy and associated security planning controls.	ISO/IEC 27001 A.5.1.1, A.5.1.2, A.6.1.1, A.6.1.2, A.6.1.3, A.8.1.1, A.10.1.1, A.15.1.1, A.15.2.1 COBIT DS5.2, PC5 HIPAA 164.316(a)
Planning		PL-2 System Security Plan The organization: a. Develops a security plan for the information system that • Is consistent with the organization's enterprise architecture; • Explicitly defines the authorization boundary for the system; • Describes the operational context of the information system in terms of missions and business processes; • Provides the security categorization of the information system including supporting rationale; • Describes the operational environment for the information system; • Describes relationships with or connections to other information systems;	

Continued

Table 8.4 (continued) Planning Controls

CONTROL FAMILY	COMPLIANT (YES/NO)	CONTROL	MAPPINGS
		• Provides an overview of the security requirements for the system; • Describes the security controls in place or planned for meeting those requirements including a rationale for the tailoring and supplementation decisions; • Is reviewed and approved by the authorizing official or designated representative prior to plan implementation; b. Reviews the security plan for the information system [Assignment: organization-defined frequency]; and c. Updates the plan to address changes to the information system/environment of operation or problems identified during plan implementation or security control assessments.	ISO/IEC 27001 (None) COBIT PO1.4, DS5.2 HIPAA 164.310(a)(2), 164.316(a)(ii)
Planning		PL-4 Rules of Behavior The organization: a. Establishes and makes readily available to all information system users, the rules that describe their responsibilities and expected behavior with regard to information and information system usage; and b. Receives signed acknowledgment from users indicating that they have read, understand, and agree to abide by the rules of behavior, before authorizing access to information and the information system.	ISO/IEC 27001 A.6.1.5, A.6.2.2, A.7.1.3. A.8.1.1, A.8.1.3, A.8.2.1, A.9.1.5, A.10.8.1, A.11.7.1, A.11.7.2, A.12.4.1, A.13.1.2, A.15.1.5 COBIT PO6.5, DS5.2, PC4 HIPAA 164.306(a)(4)
Planning		PL-5 Privacy Impact Assessment The organization conducts a privacy impact assessment on the information system in accordance with OMB policy.	ISO/IEC 27001 A.15.1.4

Table 8.4 (continued) Planning Controls

CONTROL FAMILY	COMPLIANT (YES/NO)	CONTROL	MAPPINGS
Planning		PL-6 Security-Related Activity Planning The organization plans and coordinates security-related activities affecting the information system before conducting such activities in order to reduce the impact on organizational operations (i.e., mission, functions, image, and reputation), organizational assets, and individuals.	ISO/IEC 27001 A.6.1.2, A.15.3.1 HIPAA 164.308(a)(1)(ii)(B), 164.310(a)(2)(ii)

Table 8.5 Risk Assessment Controls

CONTROL FAMILY	COMPLIANT (YES/NO)	CONTROL	MAPPINGS
Risk assessment		RA-1 Risk Assessment Policy and Procedures The organization develops, disseminates, and reviews/updates [Assignment: organization-defined frequency]: a. A formal, documented risk assessment policy that addresses purpose, scope, roles, responsibilities, management commitment, coordination among organizational entities, and compliance; and b. Formal, documented procedures to facilitate the implementation of the risk assessment policy and associated risk assessment controls.	ISO/IEC 27001 A.5.1.1, A.5.1.2, A.6.1.1, A.6.1.3, A.8.1.1, A.10.1.1, A.14.1.2, A.15.1.1, A.15.2.1 COBIT PC5, P09.1 HIPAA 164.316(a), 164.308(a)(1)(i)
Risk assessment		RA-2 Security Categorization The organization: a. Categorizes information and the information system in accordance with applicable federal laws, executive orders, directives, policies, regulations, standards, and guidance; b. Documents the security categorization results (including supporting rationale) in the security plan for the information system; and c. Ensures the security categorization decision is reviewed and approved by the authorizing Official or authorizing official designated representative.	ISO/IEC 27001 A.7.2.1, A.14.1.2 COBIT P09.2 HIPAA 164.308(a)(1)(ii)(A), 164.308(a)(7)(ii)(E)

Table 8.5 (continued) Risk Assessment Controls

CONTROL FAMILY	COMPLIANT (YES/NO)	CONTROL	MAPPINGS
Risk assessment		RA-3 Risk Assessment The organization: a. Conducts an assessment of risk, including the likelihood and magnitude of harm, from the unauthorized access, use, disclosure, disruption, modification, or destruction of the information system and the information it processes, stores, or transmits; b. Documents risk assessment results in [Selection: security plan; risk assessment report; Assignment: organization-defined document]; c. Reviews risk assessment results [Assignment: organization-defined frequency]; and d. Updates the risk assessment [Assignment: organization-defined frequency] or whenever there are significant changes to the information system or environment of operation (including the identification of new threats and vulnerabilities), or other conditions that may impact the security state of the system.	ISO/IEC 27001 A.6.2.1, A.10.2.3, A.12.6.1, A.14.1.2 COBIT P09.3, P09.4, AI1.1 HIPAA 164.316(a), 164.308(a)(1)(ii)(A)
Risk assessment		RA-5 Vulnerability Scanning The organization: a. Scans for vulnerabilities in the information system and hosted applications [Assignment: organization-defined frequency and/or randomly in accordance with organization-defined process] and when new vulnerabilities potentially affecting the system/applications are identified and reported;	

Continued

Table 8.5 (continued) Risk Assessment Controls

CONTROL FAMILY	COMPLIANT (YES/NO)	CONTROL	MAPPINGS
		b. Employs vulnerability scanning tools and techniques that promote interoperability among tools and automate parts of the vulnerability management process by using standards for: • Enumerating platforms, software flaws, and improper configurations; • Formatting and making transparent, checklists and test procedures; and • Measuring vulnerability impact c. Analyzes vulnerability scan reports and results from security control assessments; d. Remediates legitimate vulnerabilities [Assignment: organization-defined response times] in accordance with an organizational assessment of risk; and e. Shares information obtained from the vulnerability scanning process and security control assessments with designated personnel throughout the organization to help eliminate similar vulnerabilities in other information systems (i.e., systemic weaknesses or deficiencies).	ISO/IEC 27001 A.12.6.1, A.15.2.2 COBIT P09.3, DS5.5

Table 8.6 System and Services Acquisition Controls

CONTROL FAMILY	COMPLIANT (YES/NO)	CONTROL	MAPPINGS
System and services acquisition		SA-1 System and Services Acquisition Policy and Procedures The organization develops, disseminates, and reviews/updates [Assignment: organization defined frequency]: a. A formal, documented system and services acquisition policy that includes information security considerations and that addresses purpose, scope, roles, responsibilities, management commitment, coordination among organizational entities, and compliance; and b. Formal, documented procedures to facilitate the implementation of the system and services acquisition policy and associated system and services acquisition controls.	ISO/IEC 27001 A.5.1.1, A.5.1.2, A.6.1.1, A.6.1.3, A.6.2.1, A.8.1.1, A.10.1.1, A.12.1.1, A.12.5.5, A.15.1.1, A.15.2.1 COBIT AI2.5, AI5.1, PC5
System and services acquisition		SA-2 Allocation of Resources The organization: a. Includes a determination of information security requirements for the information system in mission/business process planning; b. Determines, documents, and allocates the resources required to protect the information system as part of its capital planning and investment control process; and c. Establishes a discrete line item for information security in organizational programming and budgeting documentation.	ISO/IEC 27001 A.6.1.2, A.10.3.1 COBIT PO1.1, PO5.2
System and services acquisition		SA-3 Life Cycle Support The organization: a. Manages the information system using a system development life cycle methodology that includes information security considerations;	

Continued

Table 8.6 (continued) System and Services Acquisition Controls

CONTROL FAMILY	COMPLIANT (YES/NO)	CONTROL	MAPPINGS
		b. Defines and documents information system security roles and responsibilities throughout the system development life cycle; and c. Identifies individuals having information system security roles and responsibilities.	ISO/IEC 27001 A.12.1.1 COBIT PO8.3, AI2.7
System and services acquisition		SA-4 Acquisitions The organization includes the following requirements and/or specifications, explicitly or by reference, in information system acquisition contracts based on an assessment of risk and in accordance with applicable federal laws, executive orders, directives, policies, regulations, and standards: a. Security functional requirements/ specifications; b. Security-related documentation requirements; and c. Developmental and evaluation-related assurance requirements.	ISO/IEC 27001 A.12.1.1, A.12.5.5 COBIT AI2.4, AI5.4 HIPAA 164.314(a)(2)(i)
System and services acquisition		SA-5 Information System Documentation The organization: a. Obtains, protects as required, and makes available to authorized personnel, administrator documentation for the information system that describes: • Secure configuration, installation, and operation of the information system; • Effective use and maintenance of security features/functions; and • Known vulnerabilities regarding configuration and use of administrative (i.e., privileged) functions; and	

Table 8.6 (continued) System and Services Acquisition Controls

CONTROL FAMILY	COMPLIANT (YES/NO)	CONTROL	MAPPINGS
		b. Obtains, protects as required, and makes available to authorized personnel, user documentation for the information system that describes: • User-accessible security features/functions and how to effectively use those security features/functions; • Methods for user interaction with the information system, which enables individuals to use the system in a more secure manner; and • User responsibilities in maintaining the security of the information and information system; and c. Documents attempts to obtain information system documentation when such documentation is either unavailable or nonexistent.	ISO/IEC 27001 A.10.7.4, A.15.1.3 COBIT DS5.7
System and services acquisition		SA-6 Software Usage Restrictions The organization: a. Uses software and associated documentation in accordance with contract agreements and copyright laws; b. Employs tracking systems for software and associated documentation protected by quantity licenses to control copying and distribution; and c. Controls and documents the use of peer-to-peer file sharing technology to ensure that this capability is not used for the unauthorized distribution, display, performance, or reproduction of copyrighted work.	ISO/IEC 27001 A.12.4.1, A.12.5.5, A.15.1.2 COBIT DS9.3
System and services acquisition		SA-7 User-Installed Software The organization enforces explicit rules governing the installation of software by users.	ISO/IEC 27001 A.12.4.1, A.12.5.5, A.15.1.5 COBIT DS9.3

Continued

Table 8.6 (continued) System and Services Acquisition Controls

CONTROL FAMILY	COMPLIANT (YES/NO)	CONTROL	MAPPINGS
System and services acquisition		SA-8 Security Engineering Principles The organization applies information system security engineering principles in the specification, design, development, implementation, and modification of the information system.	ISO/IEC 27001 A.10.4.1, A.10.4.2, A.11.4.5, A.12.5.5 COBIT AI2.4
System and services acquisition		SA-9 External Information System Services The organization: a. Requires that providers of external information system services comply with organizational information security requirements and employ appropriate security controls in accordance with applicable federal laws, executive orders, directives, policies, regulations, standards, and guidance; b. Defines and documents government oversight and user roles and responsibilities with regard to external information system services; and c. Monitors security control compliance by external service providers.	ISO/IEC 27001 A.6.1.5, A.6.2.1, A.6.2.3, A.8.1.1, A.8.2.1, A.10.2.1, A.10.2.2, A.10.2.3, A.10.6.2, A.10.8.2, A.12.5.5 COBIT DS1.6, DS2.3, ME3.1, ME3.3 HIPAA 164.308(b)(4), 164.314(a)(1), 164.314(a)(2)(i), 164.314(a)(2)(ii)
System and services acquisition		SA-10 Developer Configuration Management The organization requires that information system developers/integrators: a. Perform configuration management during information system design, development, implementation, and operation; b. Manage and control changes to the information system; c. Implement only organization-approved changes; d. Document approved changes to the information system; and e. Track security flaws and flaw resolution.	ISO/IEC 27001 A.12.4.3, A.12.5.1, A.12.5.5

Table 8.6 (continued) System and Services Acquisition Controls

CONTROL FAMILY	COMPLIANT (YES/NO)	CONTROL	MAPPINGS
System and services acquisition		SA-11 Developer Security Testing The organization requires that information system developers/ integrators, in consultation with associated security personnel (including security engineers): a. Create and implement a security test and evaluation plan; b. Implement a verifiable flaw remediation process to correct weaknesses and deficiencies identified during the security testing and evaluation process; and c. Document the results of the security testing/evaluation and flaw remediation processes.	ISO/IEC 27001 A.10.3.2, A.12.5.5 COBIT AI2.8
System and services acquisition		SA-12 Supply Chain Protection The organization protects against supply chain threats by employing [Assignment: organization-defined list of measures to protect against supply chain threats] as part of a comprehensive, defense-in-breadth information security strategy.	ISO/IEC 27001 A.12.5.5
System and services acquisition		SA-13 Trustworthiness The organization requires that the information system meets [Assignment: organization-defined level of trustworthiness].	ISO/IEC 27001 A.12.5.5
System and services acquisition		SA-14 Critical Information System Components The organization: a. Determines [Assignment: organization-defined list of critical information system components that require re-implementation]; and b. Re-implements or custom develops such information system components.	ISO/IEC 27001 (None)

Table 8.7 Program Management Controls

CONTROL FAMILY	COMPLIANT (YES/NO)	CONTROL	MAPPINGS
Program management		PM-1 Information Security Program Plan The organization: a. Develops and disseminates an organization-wide information security program plan that: • Provides an overview of the requirements for the security program and a description of the security program management controls and common controls in place or planned for meeting those requirements; • Provides sufficient information about the program management controls and common controls (including specification of parameters for any assignment and selection operations either explicitly or by reference) to enable an implementation that is unambiguously compliant with the intent of the plan and a determination of the risk to be incurred if the plan is implemented as intended; • Includes roles, responsibilities, management commitment, coordination among organizational entities, and compliance; • Is approved by a senior official with responsibility and accountability for the risk being incurred to organizational operations (including mission, functions, image, and reputation), organizational assets, individuals, other organizations, and the nation; b. Reviews the organization-wide information security program plan [Assignment: organization-defined frequency]; and	ISO/IEC 27001 A.5.1.1, A.5.1.2, A.6.1.1, A.6.1.3 A.8.1.1, A.15.1.1, A.15.2.1

Table 8.7 (continued) Program Management Controls

CONTROL FAMILY	COMPLIANT (YES/NO)	CONTROL	MAPPINGS
		c. Revises the plan to address organizational changes and problems identified during plan implementation or security control assessments.	
Program management		PM-2 Senior Information Security Officer The organization appoints a senior information security officer with the mission and resources to coordinate, develop, implement, and maintain an organization-wide information security program.	ISO/IEC 27001 A.6.1.1, A.6.1.2, A.6.1.3
Program management		PM-3 Information Security Resources The organization: a. Ensures that all capital planning and investment requests include the resources needed to implement the information security program and documents all exceptions to this requirement; b. Employs a business case/Exhibit 300/Exhibit 53 to record the resources required; and c. Ensures that information security resources are available for expenditure as planned.	ISO/IEC 27001 (None)
Program management		PM-4 Plan of Action and Milestones Process The organization implements a process for ensuring that plans of action and milestones for the security program and the associated organizational information systems are maintained and document the remedial information security actions to mitigate risk to organizational operations and assets, individuals, other organizations, and the nation.	ISO/IEC 27001 (None)
Program management		PM-5 Information System Inventory The organization develops and maintains an inventory of its information systems.	ISO/IEC 27001 A.7.1.1, A.7.1.2

Continued

Table 8.7 (continued) Program Management Controls

CONTROL FAMILY	COMPLIANT (YES/NO)	CONTROL	MAPPINGS
Program management		PM-6 Information Security Measures of Performance The organization develops, monitors, and reports on the results of information security measures of performance.	ISO/IEC 27001 (None)
Program management		PM-7 Enterprise Architecture The organization develops an enterprise architecture with consideration for information security and the resulting risk to organizational operations, organizational assets, individuals, other organizations, and the nation.	ISO/IEC 27001 (None)
Program management		PM-8 Critical Infrastructure Plan The organization addresses information security issues in the development, documentation, and updating of a critical infrastructure and key resources protection plan.	ISO/IEC 27001 (None)
Program management		PM-9 Risk Management Strategy The organization: a. Develops a comprehensive strategy to manage risk to organizational operations and assets, individuals, other organizations, and the nation associated with the operation and use of information systems; and b. Implements that strategy consistently across the organization.	ISO/IEC 27001 A.6.2.1, A.14.1.2
Program management		PM-10 Security Authorization Process The organization: a. Manages (i.e., documents, tracks, and reports) the security state of organizational information systems through security authorization processes; b. Designates individuals to fulfill specific roles and responsibilities within the organizational risk management process; and c. Fully integrates the security authorization processes into an organization-wide risk management program.	ISO/IEC 27001 A.6.1.4

Table 8.7 (continued) Program Management Controls

CONTROL FAMILY	COMPLIANT (YES/NO)	CONTROL	MAPPINGS
Program management		PM-11 Mission/Business Process Definition The organization: a. Defines mission/business processes with consideration for information security and the resulting risk to organizational operations, organizational assets, individuals, other organizations, and the nation; and b. Determines information protection needs arising from the defined mission/business processes and revises the processes as necessary, until an achievable set of protection needs is obtained.	ISO/IEC 27001 (None)

Suggested Reading

1. National Institute of Standards and Technology (NIST). August 2009. Special Publication 800-53 Rev3: Recommended security controls for federal information systems and organizations. http://csrc.nist.gov/publications/nistpubs/800-53-Rev3/sp800-53-rev3-final_updated-errata_05-01-2010.pdf
2. IT Governance Institute. 2007. Mapping of NIST SP 800-53Rev 1 with COBIT® 4.1. http://www.itgi.org
3. National Institute of Standards and Technology (NIST). October 2008. An introductory resource guide for implementing the Health Insurance Portability and Accountability Act (HIPAA) Security Rule. http://csrc.nist.gov/publications/nistpubs/800-66-Rev1/SP-800-66-Revision1.pdf
4. International Organization for Standardization (ISO). ISO/IEC 27001:2005 Information security management systems—Requirements. http://www.iso.org/iso/iso_catalogue/catalogue_tc/catalogue_detail.htm?csnumber=42103
5. International Organization for Standardization (ISO). ISO/IEC 27002:2005 Information technology—Security techniques—Code of practice for information security management. http://www.iso.org/iso/iso_catalogue/catalogue_tc/catalogue_detail.htm?csnumber=50297
6. Department of Health and Human Services, Office of the Secretary. February 20, 2003. 45 CFR Parts 160, 162, and 164 Health insurance reform: Security standards; Final rule. *Federal Register* 68(24). http://www.hhs.gov/ocr/privacy/hipaa/administrative/securityrule/securityrulepdf.pdf
7. Capability Maturity Model Integration (CMMI), http://www.sei.cmu.edu/cmmi/

9

Technical Controls

Practical Security Considerations

For a successful technology, reality must take precedence over public relations, for nature cannot be fooled.

Richard Phillips Feynman, Report on space shuttle *Challenger* disaster (1986)

The controls specified in this chapter are the technical controls, or those controls that govern the ongoing technical mechanisms impacting security. This chapter, along with the preceding Chapter 8 on managerial controls and the subsequent Chapter 10 on operational controls, completes the controls necessary for building the foundation for an information security program. Each listing of the operational control family is preceded with some practical security considerations for reviewing the family of controls. These controls are also mapped to COBIT 4.1, ISO 27001, and Health Insurance Portability and Accountability Act (HIPAA) where a relationship between them exists.

Access Control Controls

The access control (AC) family could be in some ways viewed as the primary focus of information security for the first several decades. This is the most tested area of information security and uncovers how well the security policies have been implemented. The AC control family requires that accounts are set up according to preestablished business reasons and that they are set up for individuals who have a need to know the information they are requesting. Identity management systems of recent years have been implemented to ensure that access was properly controlled and that terminated and transferred users no longer had access after their company or department tenure. Role-based systems provide the ability to model user access based upon a consistent profile. The profile can be as simple as creating a small number of roles, defining the access required by those roles, and then running a macro to create the access for the account requiring the access.

The AC family also promotes technical controls in place such that accounts are locked in the event that someone is attempting to access the account and repeatedly failing. The system notification messages should be made available when the user logs into the system as well as for other entry points, such as a logging onto a server (via the use of banner pages). The wireless, mobile device and remote device controls are in place to ensure that each entry point into the computing environment has been addressed by policy and procedures for gaining access. These procedures ensure that there is a consistent path for requesting and approving the access. The controls for the AC family are shown in Table 9.1.

Audit and Accountability Controls

The audit and accountability controls family (AU), as shown in Table 9.2, specifies controls to ensure that the events are being monitored and failures are being followed up. Due to the volume of audit records that may be generated, choices need to be made as to what items are most important to be audited. Logon failures, for example, may be monitored, but a threshold of 25 in a week may be used for the level requiring investigation. Alternatively a trending report may be developed and whereas the daily occurrence may be low, say 2, just under the threshold of 3 invalid login attempts before a lockout, resulting in over 60 during a month's time. This could be the work of someone internally attempting to guess someone's password and having over 750 tries in a year.

Reviewing audit records can be a very time-consuming task and automation of some sort, whether it be through a Security Information and Event Management (SIEM) product or an off-the-shelf reporting tool used to reduce the input records to focus solely on the exceptions over the thresholds, the activity must be performed beyond merely logging of the records. Logging the records for forensic review in the event that other sources point to an incident may cause the organization to miss valuable information such as that previously described that the audit records could be pointing to.

Audit record storage and retention periods need to be defined. These may follow a multilevel strategy, whereby the online audit records are held for 90 days, followed by 1-year retention on a storage area network (SAN) device, and then rolled off to tape for longer term archival in the event of an incident. By the time 1 year has passed, it is a small likelihood that these records would be needed, unless requested through litigation to support e-discovery efforts. The record retention policies of the legal department need to be known before devising a strategy.

Identification and Authentication

The identification and authentication control family (IA) is shown in Table 9.3. These controls provide assurance that the individuals are each uniquely identified and are authenticated in a manner such that it is likely that the person accessing the computer system is who they say they are. This works with the access control family of controls to provide the appropriate access.

The strength of the authenticator may vary and may include media access control (MAC) addressing, public key infrastructure (PKI) methods, or may be using multifactor authentication through the use of a software or hardware token. The transmission of information would also need encryption controls to ensure that the authenticator is not being intercepted and used for playback.

System and Communications Protections

The systems and communications protections control family (SC) contains the controls shown in Table 9.4. These controls ensure that the endpoints of the communication systems are secured as well as sufficient management of the applications internally (e.g., application portioning). The content needs to be secured in transit and at rest (for data classified at a higher risk level) using encryption.

The security architecture needs to be reviewed to determine the appropriate access between servers, applications, placement of devices, and network zones. Local, host-based firewalls are typically placed on mobile devices in addition to the network firewall protections. These protections need to be depicted in the systems security plan to demonstrate how the boundaries are being protected as well as the transmission of data.

Table 9.1 Access Control Controls

CONTROL FAMILY	COMPLIANT (YES/NO)	CONTROL	MAPPINGS
Access control		AC-1 Access Control Policy and Procedures The organization develops, disseminates, and reviews/updates [Assignment: organization defined frequency]: a. A formal, documented access control policy that addresses purpose, scope, roles, responsibilities, management commitment, coordination among organizational entities, and compliance; and b. Formal, documented procedures to facilitate the implementation of the access control policy and associated access controls.	ISO/IEC 27001 A5.1.1, A5.1.2, A.6.1.1, A.6.1.3, A.8.1.1, A10.1.1, A.10.8.1, A.11.1.1, A.11.2.1, A11.2.2, A11.4.1, A.11.7.1, A.11.7.2, A.15.1.1, A.15.2.1 COBIT PC5, DS11.6 HIPAA 164.308(a)(4)(ii)(B), 164.308(a)(4)(ii)(C), 164.312(a)(1), 164.308(a)(3)(i), 164.308(a)(3)(ii)(A), 164.308(a)(4)(i)
Access control		AC-2 Account Management The organization manages information system accounts, including: a. Identifying account types (i.e., individual, group, system, application, guest/anonymous, and temporary); b. Establishing conditions for group membership; c. Identifying authorized users of the information system and specifying access privileges; d. Requiring appropriate approvals for requests to establish accounts; e. Establishing, activating, modifying, disabling, and removing accounts; f. Specifically authorizing and monitoring the use of guest/anonymous and temporary accounts;	ISO/IEC 27001 A.8.3.3, A.11.2.1, A.11.2.2, A.11.2.4, A15.2.1 COBIT DS5.4 HIPAA 164.308(a)(4)(ii)(B), 164.308(a)(4)(ii)(C), 164.308(a)(5)(ii)(C), 164.312(a)(2)(i), 164.312(a)(2)(ii), 164.308(a)(3)(ii)(B), 164.308(a)(4)(i)

Table 9.1 (continued) Access Control Controls

CONTROL FAMILY	COMPLIANT (YES/NO)	CONTROL	MAPPINGS
		g. Notifying account managers when temporary accounts are no longer required and when information system users are terminated, transferred, or information system usage or need-to-know/need-to-share changes; h. Deactivating: (i) temporary accounts that are no longer required; and (ii) accounts of terminated or transferred users; i. Granting access to the system based on: (i) a valid access authorization; (ii) intended system usage; and (iii) other attributes as required by the organization or associated missions/business functions; and j. Reviewing accounts [Assignment: organization-defined frequency].	
Access control		AC-3 Access Enforcement The information system enforces approved authorizations for logical access to the system in accordance with applicable policy.	ISO/IEC 27001 A.10.8.1 A.11.4.4, A.11.4.6, A.11.5.4, A.11.6.1, A.12.4.2 COBIT PO2.3, AI2.4, DS11.6 HIPAA 164.308(a)(4)(ii)(B), 164.308(a)(4)(ii)(C), 164.310(a)(2)(iii), 164.310(b), 164.312(a)(1), 164.312(a)(2)(i), 164.312(a)(2)(ii), 164.312(a)(2)(iv), 164.308(a)(3)(ii)(A)

Continued

Table 9.1 (continued) Access Control Controls

CONTROL FAMILY	COMPLIANT (YES/NO)	CONTROL	MAPPINGS
Access control		AC-4 Information Flow Enforcement The information system enforces approved authorizations for controlling the flow of information within the system and between interconnected systems in accordance with applicable policy.	ISO/IEC 27001 A.10.6.1, A.10.8.1, A.11.4.5, A.11.4.7, A.11.7.2, A.12.4.2, A.12.5.4 COBIT DS5.10 HIPAA 164.308(a)(4)(ii)(B), 164.310(b), 164.308(a)(3)(ii)(A)
Access control		AC-5 Separation of Duties The organization: a. Separates duties of individuals as necessary, to prevent malevolent activity without collusion; b. Documents separation of duties; and c. Implements separation of duties through assigned information system access authorizations.	ISO/IEC 27001 A.6.1.3, A.8.1.1, A.10.1.3, A.11.1.1, A.11.4.1 COBIT P04.11 HIPAA 164.308(a)(4)(ii)(A), 164.312(a)(1), 164.308(a)(3)(i), 164.308(a)(4)(i)
Access control		AC-6 Least Privilege The organization employs the concept of least privilege, allowing only authorized accesses for users (and processes acting on behalf of users) who are necessary to accomplish assigned tasks in accordance with organizational missions and business functions.	ISO/IEC 27001 A.6.1.3, A.8.1.1, A.11.1.1, A.11.2.2, A.11.4.1, A.11.4.4, A.11.4.6, A.11.5.4, A.11.6.1, A.12.4.3 COBIT P04.11 HIPAA 164.308(a)(4)(ii)(A), 164.312(a)(1), 164.308(a)(3)(i), 164.308(a)(4)(i)

Table 9.1 (continued) Access Control Controls

CONTROL FAMILY	COMPLIANT (YES/NO)	CONTROL	MAPPINGS
Access control		AC-7 Unsuccessful Login Attempts The information system: a. Enforces a limit of [Assignment: organization-defined number] consecutive invalid login attempts by a user during a [Assignment: organization-defined time period]; and b. Automatically [Selection: locks the account/node] for an [Assignment: organization-defined time period]; locks the account/node until released by an administrator; delays next login prompt according to [Assignment: organization-defined delay algorithm] when the maximum number of unsuccessful attempts is exceeded. The control applies regardless of whether the login occurs via a local or network connection.	ISO/IEC 27001 A.11.5.1
Access control		AC-8 System Use Notification The information system: a. Displays an approved system use notification message or banner before granting access to the system that provides privacy and security notices consistent with applicable federal laws, executive orders, directives, policies, regulations, standards, and guidance and states that: (i) users are accessing a U.S. government information system; (ii) system usage may be monitored, recorded, and subject to audit; (iii) unauthorized use of the system is prohibited and subject to criminal and civil penalties; and (iv) use of the system indicates consent to monitoring and recording;	ISO/IEC 27001 A.6.2.2, A.8.1.1, A.11.5.1, A.15.1.5

Continued

Table 9.1 (continued) Access Control Controls

CONTROL FAMILY	COMPLIANT (YES/NO)	CONTROL	MAPPINGS
		b. Retains the notification message or banner on the screen until users take explicit actions to log on to or further access the information system; and c. For publicly accessible systems: (i) displays the system use information when appropriate, before granting further access; (ii) displays references, if any, to monitoring, recording, or auditing that are consistent with privacy accommodations for such systems that generally prohibit those activities; and (iii) includes in the notice given to public users of the information system, a description of the authorized uses of the system.	
Access control		AC-9 Previous Logon (Access) Notification The information system notifies the user, upon successful logon (access), of the date and time of the last logon (access).	ISO/IEC 27001 A.11.5.1
Access control		AC-10 Concurrent Session Control The information system limits the number of concurrent sessions for each system account to [Assignment: organization-defined number].	ISO/IEC 27001 A.11.5.1
Access control		AC-11 Session Lock The information system: a. Prevents further access to the system by initiating a session lock after [Assignment: organization-defined time period] of inactivity or upon receiving a request from a user; and b. Retains the session lock until the user reestablishes access using established identification and authentication procedures.	ISO/IEC 27001 A.11.3.2, A.11.3.3, A.11.5.5 HIPAA 164.310(b), 164.312(a)(2)(iii)

Table 9.1 (continued) Access Control Controls

CONTROL FAMILY	COMPLIANT (YES/NO)	CONTROL	MAPPINGS
Access control		AC-14 Permitted Actions without Identification or Authentication The organization: a. Identifies specific user actions that can be performed on the information system without identification or authentication; and b. Documents and provides supporting rationale in the security plan for the information system, user actions not requiring identification and authentication.	ISO/IEC 27001 A.11.6.1
Access control		AC-16 Security Attributes The information system supports and maintains the binding of [Assignment: organization-defined security attributes] to information in storage, in process, and in transmission.	ISO/IEC 27001 A.7.2.2 COBIT PO2.3, DS11.6 HIPAA 164.310(b)
Access control		AC-17 Remote Access The organization: a. Documents allowed methods of remote access to the information system; b. Establishes usage restrictions and implementation guidance for each allowed remote access method; c. Monitors for unauthorized remote access to the information system; d. Authorizes remote access to the information system prior to connection; and e. Enforces requirements for remote connections to the information system.	ISO/IEC 27001 A.10.6.1, A.10.8.1, A.11.1.1, A.11.4.1, A.11.4.2, A.11.4.4, A.11.4.6, A.11.4.7, A.11.7.1, A.11.7.2 HIPAA 164.310(b)

Continued

Table 9.1 (continued) Access Control Controls

CONTROL FAMILY	COMPLIANT (YES/NO)	CONTROL	MAPPINGS
Access control		AC-18 Wireless Access The organization: a. Establishes usage restrictions and implementation guidance for wireless access; b. Monitors for unauthorized wireless access to the information system; c. Authorizes wireless access to the information system prior to connection; and d. Enforces requirements for wireless connections to the information system.	ISO/IEC 27001 A.10.6.1, A.10.8.1, A.11.1.1, A.11.4.1, A.11.4.2, A.11.4.4, A.11.4.6, A.11.4.7, A.11.7.1, A.11.7.2
Access control		AC-19 Access Control for Mobile Devices The organization: a. Establishes usage restrictions and implementation guidance for organization-controlled mobile devices; b. Authorizes connection of mobile devices meeting organizational usage restrictions and implementation guidance to organizational information systems; c. Monitors for unauthorized connections of mobile devices to organizational information systems; d. Enforces requirements for the connection of mobile devices to organizational information systems; e. Disables information system functionality that provides the capability for automatic execution of code on mobile devices without user direction; f. Issues specially configured mobile devices to individuals traveling to locations that the organization deems to be of significant risk in accordance with organizational policies and procedures; and	ISO/IEC 27001 A.10.4.1, A.11.1.1, A.11.4.3, A.11.7.1 HIPAA 164.310(b)

Table 9.1 (continued) Access Control Controls

CONTROL FAMILY	COMPLIANT (YES/NO)	CONTROL	MAPPINGS
		g. Applies [Assignment: organization-defined inspection and preventative measures] to mobile devices returning from locations that the organization deems to be of significant risk in accordance with organizational policies and procedures.	
Access control		AC-20 Use of External Information Systems The organization establishes terms and conditions, consistent with any trust relationships established with other organizations owning, operating, and/or maintaining external information systems, allowing authorized individuals to: a. Access the information system from the external information systems; and b. Process, store, and/or transmit organization-controlled information using the external information systems.	ISO/IEC 27001 A.7.1.3, A.8.1.1, A.8.1.3, A.10.6.1, A.10.8.1, A.11.4.1, A.11.4.2
Access control		AC-21 User-Based Collaboration and Information Sharing The organization: a. Facilitates information sharing by enabling authorized users to determine whether access authorizations assigned to the sharing partner match the access restrictions on the information for [Assignment: organization-defined information sharing circumstances where user discretion is required]; and b. Employs [Assignment: list of organization-defined information sharing circumstances and automated mechanisms or manual processes required] to assist users in making information sharing/collaboration decisions.	ISO/IEC 27001 A.11.2.1, A.11.2.2

Continued

Table 9.1 (continued) Access Control Controls

CONTROL FAMILY	COMPLIANT (YES/NO)	CONTROL	MAPPINGS
Access control		AC-22 Publicly Accessible Content The organization: a. Designates individuals authorized to post information onto an organizational information system that is publicly accessible; b. Trains authorized individuals to ensure that publicly accessible information does not contain nonpublic information; c. Reviews the proposed content of publicly accessible information for nonpublic information prior to posting onto the organizational information system; d. Reviews the content on the publicly accessible organizational information system for nonpublic information [Assignment: organization-defined frequency]; and e. Removes nonpublic information from the publicly accessible organizational information system, if discovered.	ISO/IEC 27001

Table 9.2 Audit and Accountability Controls

CONTROL FAMILY	COMPLIANT (YES/NO)	CONTROL	MAPPINGS
Audit and accountability		AU-1 Audit and Accountability Policy and Procedures The organization develops, disseminates, and reviews/updates [Assignment: organization defined frequency]: a. A formal, documented audit and accountability policy that addresses purpose, scope, roles, responsibilities, management commitment, coordination among organizational entities, and compliance; and b. Formal, documented procedures to facilitate the implementation of the audit and accountability policy and associated audit and accountability controls.	ISO/IEC 27001 A.5.1.1, A.5.1.2, A.6.1.1, A.6.1.3, A.8.1.1, A.10.1.1, A.10.10.2, A.15.1.1, A.15.2.1, A.15.3.1 COBIT PC2, PC5 HIPAA 164.312(b)
Audit and accountability		AU-2 Auditable Events The organization: a. Determines, based on a risk assessment and mission/business needs, that the information system must be capable of auditing the following events: [Assignment: organization-defined list of auditable events]; b. Coordinates the security audit function with other organizational entities requiring audit-related information to enhance mutual support and to help guide the selection of auditable events; c. Provides a rationale for why the list of auditable events is deemed to be adequate to support after-the-fact investigations of security incidents; and	ISO/IEC 27001 A.10.10.1, A.10.10.4, A.10.10.5, A.15.3.1 COBIT AI2.3 HIPAA 164.312(b), 164.308(a)(5)(ii)(C)

Continued

Table 9.2 (continued) Audit and Accountability Controls

CONTROL FAMILY	COMPLIANT (YES/NO)	CONTROL	MAPPINGS
		d. Determines, based on current threat information and ongoing assessment of risk, that the following events are to be audited within the information system: [Assignment: organization defined subset of the auditable events defined in AU-2(a) to be audited along with the frequency of (or situation requiring) auditing for each identified event].	
Audit and accountability		AU-3 Content of Audit Records The information system produces audit records that contain sufficient information to, at a minimum, establish what type of event occurred, when (date and time) the event occurred, where the event occurred, the source of the event, the outcome (success or failure) of the event, and the identity of any user/subject associated with the event.	ISO/IEC 27001 A.10.10.4, A.10.10.5, A.15.3.1 A.10.10.1 HIPAA 164.312(b)
Audit and accountability		AU-4 Audit Storage Capacity The organization allocates audit record storage capacity and configures auditing to reduce the likelihood of such capacity being exceeded.	ISO/IEC 27001 A.10.10.1, A.10.3.1 HIPAA 164.312(b)
Audit and accountability		AU-5 Response to Audit Processing Failures The information system: a. Alerts designated organizational officials in the event of an audit processing failure; and b. Takes the following additional actions: [Assignment: organization-defined actions to be taken (e.g., shut down information system, overwrite oldest audit records, stop generating audit records)].	ISO/IEC 27001 A.10.3.1, A.10.10.1

Table 9.2 (continued) Audit and Accountability Controls

CONTROL FAMILY	COMPLIANT (YES/NO)	CONTROL	MAPPINGS
Audit and accountability		AU-6 Audit Review, Analysis, and Reporting The organization: a. Reviews and analyzes information system audit records [Assignment: organization-defined frequency] for indications of inappropriate or unusual activity, and reports findings to designated organizational officials; and b. Adjusts the level of audit review, analysis, and reporting within the information system when there is a change in risk to organizational operations, organizational assets, individuals, other organizations, or the nation based on law enforcement information, intelligence information, or other credible sources of information.	ISO/IEC 27001 A.10.10.2, A.10.10.5, A.13.1.1, A.15.1.5 COBIT DS5.5 HIPAA 164.308(a)(5)(ii)(C), 164.312(b), 164.308(a)(1)(ii)(D)
Audit and accountability		AU-7 Audit Reduction and Report Generation The information system provides an audit reduction and report generation capability.	ISO/IEC 27001 A.10.10.2 HIPAA 164.312(b), 164.308(a)(1)(ii)(D)
Audit and accountability		AU-8 Time Stamps The information system uses internal system clocks to generate time stamps for audit records.	ISO/IEC 27001 A.10.10.1, A.10.10.6
Audit and accountability		AU-9 Protection of Audit Information The information system protects audit information and audit tools from unauthorized access, modification, and deletion.	ISO/IEC 27001 A.10.10.3, A.13.2.3, A.15.1.3, A.15.3.2
Audit and accountability		AU-10 Non-Repudiation The information system protects against an individual falsely denying having performed a particular action.	ISO/IEC 27001 A.10.9.1, A.12.2.3 COBIT DS5.11, AC6

Continued

Table 9.2 (continued) Audit and Accountability Controls

CONTROL FAMILY	COMPLIANT (YES/NO)	CONTROL	MAPPINGS
Audit and accountability		AU-11 Audit Record Retention The organization retains audit records for [Assignment: organization-defined time period consistent with records retention policy] to provide support for after-the-fact investigations of security incidents and to meet regulatory and organizational information retention requirements.	ISO/IEC 27001 A.10.10.1, A.10.10.2, A.15.1.3
Audit and accountability		AU-12 Audit Generation The information system: a. Provides audit record generation capability for the list of auditable events defined in AU-2 at [Assignment: organization-defined information system components]; b. Allows designated organizational personnel to select which auditable events are to be audited by specific components of the system; and c. Generates audit records for the list of audited events defined in AU-2 with the content as defined in AU-3.	ISO/IEC 27001 A.10.10.1, A.10.10.4, A.10.10.5
Audit and accountability		AU-13 Monitoring for Information Disclosure The organization monitors open source information for evidence of unauthorized exfiltration or disclosure of organizational information [Assignment: organization-defined frequency].	ISO/IEC 27001 (None)
Audit and accountability		AU-14 Session Audit The information system provides the capability to: a. Capture/record and log all content related to a user session; and b. Remotely view/hear all content related to an established user session in real time.	ISO/IEC 27001 (None)

Table 9.3 Identification and Authentication Controls

CONTROL FAMILY	COMPLIANT (YES/NO)	CONTROL	MAPPINGS
Identification and authentication		IA-1 Identification and Authentication Policy and Procedures The organization develops, disseminates, and reviews/updates [Assignment: organization defined frequency]: a. A formal, documented identification and authentication policy that addresses purpose, scope, roles, responsibilities, management commitment, coordination among organizational entities, and compliance; and b. Formal, documented procedures to facilitate the implementation of the identification and authentication policy and associated identification and authentication controls.	ISO/IEC 27001 A.5.1.1, A.5.1.2, A.6.1.1, A.6.1.3, A.8.1.1, A.10.1.1, A.11.2.1, A.15.1.1, A.15.2.1 COBIT DS5.3, PC5
Identification and authentication		IA-2 Identification and Authentication (Organizational Users) The information system uniquely identifies and authenticates organizational users (or processes acting on behalf of organizational users).	ISO/IEC 27001 A.11.3.2, A.11.5.1, A.11.5.2, A.11.5.3 COBIT AI2.4, DS5.3 HIPAA 164.308(a)(5)(ii)(D), 164.312(a)(2)(i), 164.312(d)
Identification and authentication		IA-3 Device Identification and Authentication The information system uniquely identifies and authenticates [Assignment: organization defined list of specific and/or types of devices] before establishing a connection.	ISO/IEC 27001 A.11.4.3 HIPAA 164.312(a)(2)(i), 164.312(d)
Identification and authentication		IA-4 Identifier Management The organization manages information system identifiers for users and devices by: a. Receiving authorization from a designated organizational official to assign a user or device identifier;	ISO/IEC 27001 A.11.5.2 COBIT DS5.3, DS5.4 HIPAA 164.308(a)(5)(ii)(D), 164.312(a)(2)(i), 164.312(d)

Continued

Table 9.3 (continued) Identification and Authentication Controls

CONTROL FAMILY	COMPLIANT (YES/NO)	CONTROL	MAPPINGS
		b. Selecting an identifier that uniquely identifies an individual or device; c. Assigning the user identifier to the intended party or the device identifier to the intended device; d. Preventing reuse of user or device identifiers for [Assignment: organization-defined time period]; and e. Disabling the user identifier after [Assignment: organization-defined time period of inactivity].	
Identification and authentication		IA-5 Authenticator Management The organization manages information system authenticators for users and devices by: a. Verifying, as part of the initial authenticator distribution, the identity of the individual and/or device receiving the authenticator; b. Establishing initial authenticator content for authenticators defined by the organization; c. Ensuring that authenticators have sufficient strength of mechanism for their intended use; d. Establishing and implementing administrative procedures for initial authenticator distribution, for lost/compromised or damaged authenticators, and for revoking authenticators; e. Changing default content of authenticators upon information system installation; f. Establishing minimum and maximum lifetime restrictions and reuse conditions for authenticators (if appropriate); g. Changing/refreshing authenticators [Assignment: organization-defined time period by authenticator type];	

Table 9.3 (continued) Identification and Authentication Controls

CONTROL FAMILY	COMPLIANT (YES/NO)	CONTROL	MAPPINGS
		h. Protecting authenticator content from unauthorized disclosure and modification; and i. Requiring users to take, and having devices implement, specific measures to safeguard authenticators.	ISO/IEC 27001 A.11.2.1, A.11.2.3, A.11.3.1, A.11.5.2, A.11.5.3 HIPAA 164.308(a)(5)(ii)(D)
Identification and authentication		IA-6 Authenticator Feedback The information system obscures feedback of authentication information during the authentication process to protect the information from possible exploitation/use by unauthorized individuals.	ISO/IEC 27001 A.11.5.1 HIPAA 164.308(a)(5)(ii)(D)
Identification and authentication		IA-7 Cryptographic Module Authentication The information system uses mechanisms for authentication to a cryptographic module that meet the requirements of applicable federal laws, executive orders, directives, policies, regulations, standards, and guidance for such authentication.	ISO/IEC 27001 A.12.3.1, A.15.1.1, A.15.1.6, A.15.2.1 HIPAA 164.308(a)(5)(ii)(D)
Identification and authentication		IA-8 Identification and Authentication (Non-Organizational Users) The information system uniquely identifies and authenticates non-organizational users (or processes acting on behalf of non-organizational users).	ISO/IEC 27001 A.10.9.1, A.11.4.2, A.11.5.1, A.11.5.2

Table 9.4 System and Communications Protection Controls

CONTROL FAMILY	COMPLIANT (YES/NO)	CONTROL	MAPPINGS
System and communications protection		SC-1 System and Communications Protection Policy and Procedures The organization develops, disseminates, and reviews/updates [Assignment: organization defined frequency]: a. A formal, documented system and communications protection policy that addresses purpose, scope, roles, responsibilities, management commitment, coordination among organizational entities, and compliance; and b. Formal, documented procedures to facilitate the implementation of the system and communications protection policy and associated system and communications protection controls.	ISO/IEC 27001 A.5.1.1, A.5.1.2, A.6.1.1, A.6.1.3, A.8.1.1, A.10.1.1, A.15.1.1, A.15.2.1 COBIT DS5.2, PC5
System and communications protection		SC-2 Application Partitioning The information system separates user functionality (including user interface services) from information system management functionality.	ISO/IEC 27001 A.10.4.1, A.10.4.2 COBIT AI2.4
System and communications protection		SC-3 Security Function Isolation The information system isolates security functions from nonsecurity functions.	ISO/IEC 27001 A.10.4.1, A.10.4.2, A.10.9.1, A.10.9.2 COBIT DS5.7
System and communications protection		SC-4 Information in Shared Resources The information system prevents unauthorized and unintended information transfer via shared system resources.	ISO/IEC 27001 (None)
System and communications protection		SC-5 Denial of Service Protection The information system protects against or limits the effects of the following types of denial of service attacks: [Assignment: organization-defined list of types of denial of service attacks or reference to source for current list].	ISO/IEC 27001 A.10.3.1
System and communications protection		SC-6 Resource Priority The information system limits the use of resources by priority.	ISO/IEC 27001 (None)

Table 9.4 (continued) System and Communications Protection Controls

CONTROL FAMILY	COMPLIANT (YES/NO)	CONTROL	MAPPINGS
System and communications protection		SC-7 Boundary Protection The information system: a. Monitors and controls communications at the external boundary of the system and at key internal boundaries within the system; and b. Connects to external networks or information systems only through managed interfaces consisting of boundary protection devices arranged in accordance with an organizational security architecture.	ISO/IEC 27001 A.6.2.1, A.10.4.1, A.10.4.2, A.10.6.1, A.10.8.1, A.10.9.1, A.10.9.2, A.10.10.2, A.11.4.5, A.11.4.6 COBIT DS5.10
System and communications protection		SC-8 Transmission Integrity The information system protects the integrity of transmitted information.	ISO/IEC 27001 A.10.4.2, A.10.6.1, A.10.6.2, A.10.9.1, A.10.9.2, A.12.2.3, A.12.3.1 COBIT AC6 HIPAA 164.312(c)(1), 164.312(c)(2), 164.312(e)(2)(i)
System and communications protection		SC-9 Transmission Confidentiality The information system protects the confidentiality of transmitted information.	ISO/IEC 27001 A.10.6.1, A.10.6.2, A.10.9.1, A.10.9.2, A.12.3.1 COBIT DS5.11, AC6 HIPAA 164.312(e)(1), 164.312(e)(2)(ii)
System and communications protection		SC-10 Network Disconnect The information system terminates the network connection associated with a communications session at the end of the session or after [Assignment: organization-defined time period] of inactivity.	ISO/IEC 27001 A.10.6.1, A.11.3.2, A.11.5.1, A.11.5.5

Continued

Table 9.4 (continued) System and Communications Protection Controls

CONTROL FAMILY	COMPLIANT (YES/NO)	CONTROL	MAPPINGS
System and communications protection		SC-11 Trusted Path The information system establishes a trusted communications path between the user and the following security functions of the system: [Assignment: organization-defined security functions to include at a minimum information system authentication and reauthentication].	ISO/IEC 27001 (None) COBIT AC6, DS5.11
System and communications protection		SC-12 Cryptographic Key Establishment and Management The organization establishes and manages cryptographic keys for required cryptography employed within the information system.	ISO/IEC 27001 A.12.3.2 COBIT DS5.8 HIPAA 164.312(e)(2)(ii)
System and communications protection		SC-13 Use of Cryptography The information system implements required cryptographic protections using cryptographic modules that comply with applicable federal laws, executive orders, directives, policies, regulations, standards, and guidance.	ISO/IEC 27001 A.12.3.1, A.15.1.6 COBIT DS5.8 HIPAA 164.312(a)(2)(iv), 164.312(e)(2)(ii)
System and communications protection		SC-14 Public Access Protections The information system protects the integrity and availability of publicly available information and applications.	ISO/IEC 27001 A.10.4.1, A.10.4.2, A.10.9.1, A.10.9.2, A.10.9.3
System and communications protection		SC-15 Collaborative Computing Devices The information system: a. Prohibits remote activation of collaborative computing devices with the following exceptions: [Assignment: organization-defined exceptions where remote activation is to be allowed]; and b. Provides an explicit indication of use to users physically present at the devices.	ISO/IEC 27001 (None)
System and communications protection		SC-16 Transmission of Security Attributes The information system associates security attributes with information exchanged between information systems.	ISO/IEC 27001 A.7.2.2, A.10.8.1 COBIT DS5.11

Table 9.4 (continued) System and Communications Protection Controls

CONTROL FAMILY	COMPLIANT (YES/NO)	CONTROL	MAPPINGS
System and communications protection		SC-17 Public Key Infrastructure Certificates The organization issues public key certificates under an [Assignment: organization-defined certificate policy] or obtains public key certificates under an appropriate certificate policy from an approved service provider.	ISO/IEC 27001 A.12.3.2
System and communications protection		SC-18 Mobile Code The organization: a. Defines acceptable and unacceptable mobile code and mobile code technologies; b. Establishes usage restrictions and implementation guidance for acceptable mobile code and mobile code technologies; and c. Authorizes, monitors, and controls the use of mobile code within the information system.	ISO/IEC 27001 A.10.4.2 COBIT DS5.9
System and communications protection		SC-19 Voice Over Internet Protocol The organization: a. Establishes usage restrictions and implementation guidance for Voice over Internet Protocol (VoIP) technologies based on the potential to cause damage to the information system if used maliciously; and b. Authorizes, monitors, and controls the use of VoIP within the information system.	ISO/IEC 27001 A.10.6.1
System and communications protection		SC-20 Secure Name/Address Resolution Service (Authoritative Source) The information system provides additional data origin and integrity artifacts along with the authoritative data the system returns in response to name/address resolution queries.	ISO/IEC 27001 A.10.6.1

Continued

Table 9.4 (continued) System and Communications Protection Controls

CONTROL FAMILY	COMPLIANT (YES/NO)	CONTROL	MAPPINGS
System and communications protection		SC-21 Secure Name/Address Resolution Service (Recursive or Caching Resolver) The information system performs data origin authentication and data integrity verification on the name/address resolution responses the system receives from authoritative sources when requested by client systems.	ISO/IEC 27001 A.10.6.1
System and communications protection		SC-22 Architecture and Provisioning for Name/Address Resolution Service The information systems that collectively provide name/address resolution service for an organization are fault-tolerant and implement internal/external role separation.	ISO/IEC 27001 A.10.6.1
System and communications protection		SC-23 Session Authenticity The information system provides mechanisms to protect the authenticity of communications sessions.	ISO/IEC 27001 A.10.6.1 COBIT AC6
System and communications protection		SC-24 Fail in Known State The information system fails to a [Assignment: organization-defined known state] for [Assignment: organization-defined types of failures] preserving [Assignment: organization-defined system state information] in failure.	ISO/IEC 27001 (None)
System and communications protection		SC-25 Thin Nodes The information system employs processing components that have minimal functionality and information storage.	ISO/IEC 27001 (None)
System and communications protection		SC-26 Honeypots The information system includes components specifically designed to be the target of malicious attacks for the purpose of detecting, deflecting, and analyzing such attacks.	ISO/IEC 27001 (None)

Table 9.4 (continued) System and Communications Protection Controls

CONTROL FAMILY	COMPLIANT (YES/NO)	CONTROL	MAPPINGS
System and communications protection		SC-27 Operating System-Independent Applications The information system includes: [Assignment: organization-defined operating system independent applications].	ISO/IEC 27001 (None)
System and communications protection		SC-28 Protection of Information at Rest The information system protects the confidentiality and integrity of information at rest.	ISO/IEC 27001 (None)
System and communications protection		SC-29 Heterogeneity The organization employs diverse information technologies in the implementation of the information system.	ISO/IEC 27001 (None)
System and communications protection		SC-30 Virtualization Techniques The organization employs virtualization techniques to present information system components as other types of components, or components with differing configurations.	ISO/IEC 27001 (None)
System and communications protection		SC-31 Covert Channel Analysis The organization requires that information system developers/integrators perform a covert channel analysis to identify those aspects of system communication that are potential avenues for covert storage and timing channels.	ISO/IEC 27001 (None)
System and communications protection		SC-32 Information System Partitioning The organization partitions the information system into components residing in separate physical domains (or environments) as deemed necessary.	ISO/IEC 27001 (None)
System and communications protection		SC-33 Transmission Preparation Integrity The information system protects the integrity of information during the processes of data aggregation, packaging, and transformation in preparation for transmission.	ISO/IEC 27001 (None)

Continued

Table 9.4 (continued) System and Communications Protection Controls

CONTROL FAMILY	COMPLIANT (YES/NO)	CONTROL	MAPPINGS
System and communications protection		SC-34 Non-Modifiable Executable Programs The information system at [Assignment: organization-defined information system components]: a. Loads and executes the operating environment from hardware-enforced, read-only media; and b. Loads and executes [Assignment: organization-defined applications] from hardware-enforced, read-only media.	ISO/IEC 27001 (None)

Suggested Reading

1. National Institute of Standards and Technology (NIST). August 2009. Special Publication 800-53 Rev3: Recommended security controls for federal information systems and organizations. http://csrc.nist.gov/publications/nistpubs/800-53-Rev3/sp800-53-rev3-final_updated-errata_05-01-2010.pdf
2. IT Governance Institute. 2007. Mapping of NIST SP 800-53Rev 1 with COBIT 4.1, http://www.itgi.org
3. National Institute of Standards and Technology (NIST). October 2008. An introductory resource guide for implementing the Health Insurance Portability and Accountability Act (HIPAA) security rule. http://csrc.nist.gov/publications/nistpubs/800-66-Rev1/SP-800-66-Revision1.pdf
4. International Organization for Standardization (ISO). ISO/IEC 27001:2005 Information security management systems—Requirements. http://www.iso.org/iso/iso_catalogue/catalogue_tc/catalogue_detail.htm?csnumber=42103
5. International Organization for Standardization (ISO). ISO/IEC 27002:2005 Information technology security techniques—Code of practice for information security management. http://www.iso.org/iso/iso_catalogue/catalogue_tc/catalogue_detail.htm?csnumber=50297
6. Department of Health and Human Services, Office of the Secretary. February 20, 2003. 45 CFR Parts 160, 162, and 164 Health insurance reform: Security standards; Final rule. *Federal Register* 68(24). http://www.hhs.gov/ocr/privacy/hipaa/administrative/securityrule/securityrulepdf.pdf

10

Operational Controls

Practical Security Considerations

There is no such thing as a free lunch.

Attributed to Milton Friedman, 1912–2006

The controls specified in this chapter are the operational controls or those controls that govern the ongoing operational processes impacting security spanning multiple departments. This chapter, along with the preceding security control chapters (Chapter 8 on managerial controls and Chapter 9 on technical controls) complete the controls necessary for building the foundation for an information security program. Each listing of the operational control family is preceded with some practical security considerations for reviewing the family of controls. These controls are also mapped to COBIT 4.1, ISO 27001:2005, and Health Insurance Portability and Accountability Act (HIPAA) where a relationship between them exists.

Awareness and Training Controls

The awareness and training control family (AT) shown in Table 10.1 serves to ensure that individuals within the organization have the appropriate level of training. All users of the organization need some level of training, and this includes all management levels and all end users. Records need to be maintained demonstrating that everyone has taken the training. End users need awareness training primarily so that they know what is expected of them, when a security breach has occurred, and how to report the breach. Executive management will also need the same training, potentially supplemented with training around risk management as it relates to security. Role-based training can provide technical staff with security-specific education, such as the network administrator on securing a firewall, or the security analyst with Security Information and Event Management (SIEM) training, or the server engineer on securing Windows/Unix servers. Additionally, management may need training for a new identity management system or handling terminations. The entire organization may need additional refresher training on a monthly basis.

End user awareness training should be provided prior to accessing the computer system and on an annual basis at a minimum. In Chapter 12 more ideas for security training are provided.

Configuration Management Controls

The configuration management control family controls (CM), as shown in Table 10.2, provide control of the configuration setting baselines and their ongoing integrity. Once the baseline is decided upon, there should be a periodic review to ensure that the baselines are being kept up with the latest changes by the issuing agency (e.g., Defense Information Systems Agency). The appropriate team members for the particular baseline (server, desktop, firewall, database, mainframe, etc.) should meet and determine the changes required to the baseline. The new baseline can then be constructed and applied according to the baseline procedures to all the devices of that type. Exceptions to the baseline standard need to be documented. The deviations from the baseline can be captured with automated tools, provided the upfront work has been done to populate the tool with the existing baseline.

Change control is a difficult area to ensure that changes are properly authorized for change and subsequently approved for production implementation prior to implementation. Programmers and those responsible for the infrastructure components may be pressed for time to implement a change and not receive proper approval beforehand. A change control board (CCB) can be very beneficial in this case, with individuals tracking the production implementations and following up on individuals that have not received the appropriate approvals. Managing the change control process provides the traceability of subsequent changes to the system.

Contingency Planning Controls

The contingency planning control family (CP) ensures that the systems can be brought up in a reasonable amount of time in the event of a disaster. These controls, shown in Table 10.3, typically require that some form of testing be done to ensure that the system can be brought up in a reasonable time. The testing identifies gaps in the documentation and highlights information that may have been left out, such as a file or the knowledge of an administrator password that halted the testing. If an outsourced data center company handles these functions, testing should still be performed to determine whether the network at the site will be available in the event of a disaster.

Business continuity plans should be written for each department to ensure they are ready in the event of a disaster, not only in terms of the computing platform, but where will they work and how the equipment will be configured or delivered to a remote location, or for a work-at-home scenario.

Incident Response Controls

The incident response control family (IR), as shown in Table 10.4, ensures that the organization has a predefined mechanism in place to respond to an incident. Security incidents can range from not sending sensitive information encrypted through e-mail to having the infrastructure penetrated through the use of structured query language (SQL) injection on the public facing website, for example. Not all incidents will be of the magnitude to invoke the formation of a computer security incident response team (CSIRT), however, the CSIRT procedure created by the organization should spell out the conditions by which the CSIRT team will be invoked. A senior management crisis management team for significant events, such as threats of violence, bomb threats, and emergency weather conditions, should be established. These teams need to be in place prior to the incidents occurring.

Incidents should be simulated by creating a scenario and walking though what would be done in the event of a crisis or a technical outage caused by an event, such as malware, antivirus, or an advanced persistent threat (APT) targeted toward the organization.

Maintenance Controls

The maintenance control family (MA) shown in Table 10.5 ensures that the equipment is properly maintained by having contracts in place, service level agreements, spare parts available, and routine maintenance performed. Exposing the device to the employees of an external vendor carries the risk that the software, firmware, or data may be modified to create a subsequent entry point into the system, or information could be disclosed. The device also needs to be properly maintained and serviced on a regular basis to ensure appropriate availability. Contracts should be in place for spare parts availability, with 4 hours not being an unreasonable time frame in most cases. In the case of workstations or desktops, for most organizations, having alternate equipment on-site can alleviate the need for immediate spare parts from a vendor. In this case, there should be agreements with hardware manufacturers to replace the items under warranty and documented procedures for handling the return of equipment.

There should be contracts in place for each computing platform in the environment. Mainframe contracts typically come in the form of a master services agreement with an annual renewal signoff. Procedures should also be in place for when vendors are required to service the equipment on-site to ensure they are escorted, as well as procedures for vendor remote access. Vendors that require infrequent connections to the equipment could be granted one-time ID/passwords along with secure tokens to access the equipment. The access should be also be logged, specifying the individual using the ID and the business reason for the access.

Media Protection Controls

The media protection control family (MP) controls shown in Table 10.6 address information wherever it may be stored. As the perimeter of the organization is disappearing with information moving closer to the end user (i.e., the information resides on laptops, USB drives, compact disks, DVDs, smartphones, and other types of flash memory chips), care must be taken to ensure that only those authorized individuals have the ability to copy information to these external sources. Due to the massive amount of information that can be stored on a portable drive (multiterabytes), or a USB stick (upward of 64 GB), these devices must be carefully managed.

Workstations can be locked down with technology to permit only certain users to write to an external device or CD/DVD writer. Due to the mobile nature and size of these devices, an encryption method should be chosen by the organization to encrypt either the media using the software that comes with the USB drive or the files themselves prior to placing on the media. At least 128-bit encryption, and AES-256 encryption is desirable. Some encryption products are FIPS 140-2 certified, which provides the highest level of encryption and suitable for most organizations.

Policies regarding media disposal need to ensure that appropriate tracking and sanitization of the devices is performed prior to disposal, along with retention of the disposal records. The organization should be able to know where the devices are located from birth to death of the device. This is no easy task in larger organizations where devices are reimaged frequently and redeployed to other users.

Media protection also extends to paper forms of information and policies and procedures to support clean desk policies (i.e., no visible confidential information during the day, locked up during business off-hours), shredding of documents, and which items are approved for dumpster disposal. On-site shredding of paper, tapes, and CDs avoids the tracking of information sent off-site and the risks of information being intercepted or not being properly shredded.

Physical and Environmental Protection Controls

The physical and environmental protection control family (PE) controls listed in Table 10.7 address the need for physical controls around the facility for employees, contractors, and visitors, as well as the environmental controls for the computing equipment in the local area networks (LAN) rooms and data centers. Just as the logical access controls need to be addressed with authorizations for access, periodic recertifications, terminating access, and restricting access to sensitive areas, the physical access controls need these same controls. An organization may employ multiple methods of achieving the physical controls, from security guards, proximity readers, piggybacking policies, visitor sign-in, temporary badge issuance, guard stations, and so forth. One of the more difficult areas of managing the physical security for an organization is the lack of integration between the physical security systems capturing the ingress/egress to the buildings and the identity management systems authorizing the approval. Manual reconciliation between the systems is necessary to demonstrate that the access was removed from the physical system. As companies merge, investments are required to merge the security systems of multiple offices. Small offices may also not have the same capabilities as systems purchased for the larger offices and may need to be managed separately.

The fire suppression, temperature, and water controls generally are focusing upon the data center and LAN room needs. Organizations need to decide on how power outages will be addressed (uninterruptable power supply [UPS]), and diesel generators, equipment that must also have contracts and periodic servicing and testing. LAN closets need to be secured to only staff requiring access to perform their jobs along with unused ports disabled.

Personnel Security Controls

The personnel security control family (PS) controls listed in Table 10.8 seek to place human resource policies and procedures around the employees to ensure that the individuals have backgrounds without damaging criminal histories, that their access is appropriately removed when they are no longer working for the company or have transferred to a different division, and finally to ensure that they understand their responsibilities with respect to the security controls while they are working for the company and after they have left the company.

Background checks must be completed before the employee is permitted to work for the company. To ensure that this happens, the information security department could withhold the login ID and password until the human resources department has provided evidence that the background check has been completed. This would serve as a secondary control to ensure the action took place. Individuals also need to be rescreened on a periodic basis. The simplest way to achieve this is to perform rescreens on those determined to be in sensitive positions (e.g., the information technology [IT] department, finance department, administrators) at the same time. Otherwise, the overhead of tracking individuals based upon anniversary dates, without an automated system to administer this process, could be manually intensive. For any contractors that are performing work on behalf of the company, the company may either request a background check, or require that the contracting firm provide evidence that a background check has been completed and is satisfactory.

Sanction policies must be in place to provide enforcement of the controls. The information security department should view itself as the provider of the supporting evidence for the infraction; however, the incident is best handled between human resources or ethics/compliance with the individual and his or her manager. The security department can provide support for the events that occurred.

Due to the strong linkage between the employees on-boarding, compliance with security controls while an associate, and the termination procedures and the access provisioning of the information security department, an equally strong relationship between human resources and information security should be maintained. Documenting the information flows between the human resource information systems (HRIS) and the identity management system can identify gaps in the processes.

System and Information Integrity Controls

System and information integrity controls (SI) listed in Table 10.9 focus on providing controls to protect the systems environment and handling such issues as malicious code; spam; systems monitoring; flaw remediation; and ensuring that applications are coded correctly with appropriate input validation, error handling, and consistent failure prevention. Antivirus, malware, and spyware products should be installed at the entry points, such as servers, desktops, and firewalls, to restrict the entry of malicious traffic, in addition to the security awareness programs on these topics. Processes need to be built to manage the exceptions (e.g., when the antivirus is not applied to the desktops within a specified frequency, such as 1 to 3 days after distribution to the servers) to ensure that all desktops are appropriately being addressed within the system. There may be issues with the software pushing the updates or the asset inventory that needs to be rectified. End users should be made aware of the effects of malicious code as well as having the technical infrastructure to support them in the event a wrong decision is made.

Application code must be written such that information that would be useful to an intruder is not displayed. Input data needs to be validated to avoid buffer overruns and other programming errors, which could provide elevated command line access. This all works in concert with the systems development life cycle process, whereby secure coding guidelines would be established and certified to, either by attestation or the completion of a checklist indicating which guidelines were incorporated into the development.

Table 10.1 Awareness and Training Controls

CONTROL FAMILY	COMPLIANT (YES/NO)	CONTROL	MAPPINGS
Awareness and training		AT-1 Security Awareness and Training Policy and Procedures The organization develops, disseminates, and reviews/updates [Assignment: organization defined frequency]: a. A formal, documented security awareness and training policy that addresses purpose, scope, roles, responsibilities, management commitment, coordination among organizational entities, and compliance; and b. Formal, documented procedures to facilitate the implementation of the security awareness and training policy, and associated security awareness and training controls.	ISO/IEC 27001 A.5.1.1, A.5.1.2, A.6.1.1, A.6.1.3, A.8.1.1, A.10.1.1, A.15.1.1, A.15.2.1 COBIT DS7.1, PC5 HIPAA 164.308(a)(5)(i)
Awareness and training		AT-2 Security Awareness The organization provides basic security awareness training to all information system users (including managers, senior executives, and contractors) as part of initial training for new users, when required by system changes, and [Assignment: organization-defined frequency] thereafter.	ISO/IEC 27001 A.6.2.2, A.8.1.1, A.8.2.2, A.9.1.5, A.10.4.1 COBIT P07.4 HIPAA 164.308(a)(5)(i), 164.308(a)(5)(ii)(B)
Awareness and training		AT-3 Security Training The organization provides role-based security-related training: (i) before authorizing access to the system or performing assigned duties; (ii) when required by system changes; and (iii) [Assignment: organization-defined frequency] thereafter.	ISO/IEC 27001 A.8.1.1, A.8.2.2, A.9.1.5 COBIT P07.4, DS7.2 HIPAA 164.308(a)(5)(i)
Awareness and training		AT-4 Security Training Records The organization: a. Documents and monitors individual information system security training activities including basic security awareness training and specific information system security training; and b. Retains individual training records for [Assignment: organization-defined time period].	ISO/IEC 27001 (None) COBIT DS7.2 HIPAA 164.308(a)(5)(i)

Table 10.1 (continued) Awareness and Training Controls

CONTROL FAMILY	COMPLIANT (YES/NO)	CONTROL	MAPPINGS
Awareness and training		AT-5 Contacts with Security Groups and Associations The organization establishes and institutionalizes contact with selected groups and associations within the security community: • To facilitate ongoing security education and training for organizational personnel; • To stay up to date with the latest recommended security practices, techniques, and technologies; and • To share current security-related information including threats, vulnerabilities, and incidents.	ISO/IEC 27001 A.6.1.7 HIPAA 164.308(a)(5)(i)

Table 10.2 Configuration Management Controls

CONTROL FAMILY	COMPLIANT (YES/NO)	CONTROL	MAPPINGS
Configuration management		CM-1 Configuration Management Policy and Procedures The organization develops, disseminates, and reviews/updates [Assignment: organization defined frequency]: a. A formal, documented configuration management policy that addresses purpose, scope, roles, responsibilities, management commitment, coordination among organizational entities, and compliance; and b. Formal, documented procedures to facilitate the implementation of the configuration management policy and associated configuration management controls.	ISO/IEC 27001 A.5.1.1, A.5.1.2, A.6.1.1, A.6.1.3, A.8.1.1, A.10.1.1, A.10.1.2, A.12.4.1, A.12.5.1, A.15.1.1, A.15.2.1 COBIT® DS9.1, PC5,PO2.1, AI6.1
Configuration management		CM-2 Baseline Configuration The organization develops, documents, and maintains under configuration control, a current baseline configuration of the information system.	ISO/IEC 27001 COBIT DS9.1, PO1.6, PO2.1
Configuration management		CM-3 Configuration Change Control The organization: a. Determines the types of changes to the information system that are configuration controlled; b. Approves configuration-controlled changes to the system with explicit consideration for security impact analyses; c. Documents approved configuration-controlled changes to the system; d. Retains and reviews records of configuration-controlled changes to the system; e. Audits activities associated with configuration-controlled changes to the system; and	ISO/IEC 27001 A.10.1.1, A.10.1.2, A.10.3.2, A.12.4.1, A.12.5.1, A.12.5.2, A.12.5.3 COBIT DS9.2, AI6.1, AI6.3

Table 10.2 (continued) Configuration Management Controls

CONTROL FAMILY	COMPLIANT (YES/NO)	CONTROL	MAPPINGS
		f. Coordinates and provides oversight for configuration change control activities through [Assignment: organization-defined configuration change control element (e.g., committee, board] that convenes [Selection (one or more): [Assignment: organization-defined frequency]; [Assignment: organization-defined configuration change conditions]].	
Configuration management		CM-4 Security Impact Analysis The organization analyzes changes to the information system to determine potential security impacts prior to change implementation.	ISO/IEC 27001 A.10.1.2, A.10.3.2, A.12.4.1, A.12.5.2, A.12.5.3 COBIT DS5.5, DS9.3
Configuration management		CM-5 Access Restrictions for Change The organization defines, documents, approves, and enforces physical and logical access restrictions associated with changes to the information system.	ISO/IEC 27001 A.10.1.2, A.11.1.1, A.11.6.1, A.12.4.1, A.12.4.3, A.12.5.3
Configuration management		CM-6 Configuration Settings The organization: a. Establishes and documents mandatory configuration settings for information technology products employed within the information system using [Assignment: organization-defined security configuration checklists] that reflect the most restrictive mode consistent with operational requirements; b. Implements the configuration settings; c. Identifies, documents, and approves exceptions from the mandatory configuration settings for individual components within the information system based on explicit operational requirements; and	

Continued

Table 10.2 (continued) Configuration Management Controls

CONTROL FAMILY	COMPLIANT (YES/NO)	CONTROL	MAPPINGS
		d. Monitors and controls changes to the configuration settings in accordance with organizational policies and procedures.	ISO/IEC 27001 (None)
Configuration management		CM-7 Least Functionality The organization configures the information system to provide only essential capabilities and specifically prohibits or restricts the use of the following functions, ports, protocols, and/or services: [Assignment: organization-defined list of prohibited or restricted functions, ports, protocols, and/or services].	ISO/IEC 27001 (None)
Configuration management		CM-8 Information System Component Inventory The organization develops, documents, and maintains an inventory of information system components that: a. Accurately reflects the current information system; b. Is consistent with the authorization boundary of the information system; c. Is at the level of granularity deemed necessary for tracking and reporting; d. Includes [Assignment: organization-defined information deemed necessary to achieve effective property accountability]; and e. Is available for review and audit by designated organizational officials.	ISO/IEC 27001 A.7.1.1, A.7.1.2
Configuration management		CM-9 Configuration Management Plan The organization develops, documents, and implements a configuration management plan for the information system that: a. Addresses roles, responsibilities, and configuration management processes and procedures;	ISO/IEC 27001 A.6.1.3. A.7.1.1, A.7.1.2, A.8.1.1, A.10.1.1, A.10.1.2, A.10.3.2, A.12.4.1, A.12.4.3, A.12.5.1, A.12.5.2, A.12.5.3

Table 10.2 (continued) Configuration Management Controls

CONTROL FAMILY	COMPLIANT (YES/NO)	CONTROL	MAPPINGS
		b. Defines the configuration items for the information system and when in the system development life cycle the configuration items are placed under configuration management; and c. Establishes the means for identifying configuration items throughout the system development life cycle and a process for managing the configuration of the configuration items.	

Table 10.3 Contingency Planning Controls

CONTROL FAMILY	COMPLIANT (YES/NO)	CONTROL	MAPPINGS
Contingency planning		CP-1 Contingency Planning Policy And Procedures The organization develops, disseminates, and reviews/updates [Assignment: organization defined frequency]: a A formal, documented contingency planning policy that addresses purpose, scope, roles, responsibilities, management commitment, coordination among organizational entities, and compliance; and b. Formal, documented procedures to facilitate the implementation of the contingency planning policy and associated contingency planning controls.	ISO/IEC 27001 A.5.1.1, A.5.1.2, A.6.1.1, A.6.1.3, A.8.1.1, A.9.1.4, A.10.1.1, A.10.1.2, A.14.1.1, A.14.1.3, A.15.1.1, A.15.2.1 COBIT® PC5,DS4.1 HIPAA 164.308(a)(7)(i)
Contingency planning		CP-2 Contingency Plan The organization: a. Develops a contingency plan for the information system that: • Identifies essential missions and business functions and associated contingency requirements; • Provides recovery objectives, restoration priorities, and metrics; • Addresses contingency roles, responsibilities, assigned individuals with contact information; • Addresses maintaining essential missions and business functions despite an information system disruption, compromise, or failure; • Addresses eventual, full information system restoration without deterioration of the security measures originally planned and implemented; and • Is reviewed and approved by designated officials within the organization;	ISO/IEC 27001 A.6.1.2, A.9.1.4, A.10.3.1, A.14.1.1, A.14.1.2, A.14.1.3, A.14.1.4, A.14.1.5 COBIT DS4.2 HIPAA 164.308(a)(7)(ii)(B), 164.308(a)(7)(ii)(C), 164.308(a)(7)(ii)(E), 164.310(a)(2)(i), 164.312(a)(2)(ii)

Table 10.3 (continued) Contingency Planning Controls

CONTROL FAMILY	COMPLIANT (YES/NO)	CONTROL	MAPPINGS
		b. Distributes copies of the contingency plan to [Assignment: organization-defined list of key contingency personnel (identified by name and/or by role) and organizational elements]; c. Coordinates contingency planning activities with incident handling activities; d. Reviews the contingency plan for the information system [Assignment: organization-defined frequency]; e. Revises the contingency plan to address changes to the organization, information system, or environment of operation and problems encountered during contingency plan implementation, execution, or testing; and f. Communicates contingency plan changes to [Assignment: organization-defined list of key contingency personnel (identified by name and/or by role) and organizational elements].	
Contingency planning		CP-3 Contingency Training The organization trains personnel in their contingency roles and responsibilities with respect to the information system and provides refresher training [Assignment: organization defined frequency].	ISO/IEC 27001 A.8.2.2, A.9.1.4, A.14.1.3 COBIT DS4.6 HIPAA 164.308(a)(7)(ii)(D)
Contingency planning		CP-4 Contingency Plan Testing and Exercises The organization: a. Tests and/or exercises the contingency plan for the information system [Assignment: organization-defined frequency] using [Assignment: organization-defined tests and/or exercises] to determine the plan's effectiveness and the organization's readiness to execute the plan; and	ISO/IEC 27001 A.6.1.2, A.9.1.4, A.14.1.1, A.14.1.3, A.14.1.4, A.14.1.5 COBIT DS4.2, DS4.5 HIPAA 164.308(a)(7)(ii)(D)

Continued

Table 10.3 (continued) Contingency Planning Controls

CONTROL FAMILY	COMPLIANT (YES/NO)	CONTROL	MAPPINGS
		b. Reviews the contingency plan test/exercise results and initiates corrective actions.	
Contingency planning		CP-6 Alternate Storage Site The organization establishes an alternate storage site including necessary agreements to permit the storage and recovery of information system backup information.	ISO/IEC 27001 A.9.1.4, A.14.1.3 COBIT DS4.1, DS4.9 HIPAA 164.308(a)(7)(ii)(B), 164.310(a)(2)(i)
Contingency planning		CP-7 Alternate Processing Site The organization: a. Establishes an alternate processing site including necessary agreements to permit the resumption of information system operations for essential missions and business functions within [Assignment: organization-defined time period consistent with recovery time objectives] when the primary processing capabilities are unavailable; and b. Ensures that equipment and supplies required to resume operations are available at the alternate site or contracts are in place to support delivery to the site in time to support the organization-defined time period for resumption.	ISO/IEC 27001 A.9.1.4, A.14.1.3 COBIT DS4.1, DS4.8 HIPAA 164.308(a)(7)(ii)(B), 164.310(a)(2)(i)
Contingency planning		CP-8 Telecommunications Services The organization establishes alternate telecommunications services including necessary agreements to permit the resumption of information system operations for essential missions and business functions within [Assignment: organization-defined time period] when the primary telecommunications capabilities are unavailable.	ISO/IEC 27001 A.9.1.4, A.10.6.1, A.14.1.3 COBIT DS4.1, HIPAA 164.308(a)(7)(ii)(B)

Table 10.3 (continued) Contingency Planning Controls

CONTROL FAMILY	COMPLIANT (YES/NO)	CONTROL	MAPPINGS
Contingency planning		CP-9 Information System Backup The organization: a. Conducts backups of user-level information contained in the information system [Assignment: organization-defined frequency consistent with recovery time and recovery point objectives]; b. Conducts backups of system-level information contained in the information system [Assignment: organization-defined frequency consistent with recovery time and recovery point objectives]; c. Conducts backups of information system documentation including security-related documentation [Assignment: organization-defined frequency consistent with recovery time and recovery point objectives]; and d. Protects the confidentiality and integrity of backup information at the storage location.	ISO/IEC 27001 A.9.1.4, A.10.5.1, A.14.1.3, A.15.1.3 COBIT DS4.2, DS11.5 HIPAA 164.308(a)(7)(ii)(A), 164.310(d)(2)(iv), 164.312(c)(1)
Contingency planning		CP-10 Information System Recovery and Reconstitution The organization provides for the recovery and reconstitution of the information system to a known state after a disruption, compromise, or failure.	ISO/IEC 27001 A.9.1.4, A.14.1.3 COBIT DS4.8, DS11.5 HIPAA 164.308(a)(7)(ii)(B), 164.308(a)(7)(ii)(C)

Table 10.4 Incident Response Controls

CONTROL FAMILY	COMPLIANT (YES/NO)	CONTROL	MAPPINGS
Incident response		IR-1 Incident Response Policy And Procedures The organization develops, disseminates, and reviews/updates [Assignment: organization defined frequency]: a. A formal, documented incident response policy that addresses purpose, scope, roles, responsibilities, management commitment, coordination among organizational entities, and compliance; and b. Formal, documented procedures to facilitate the implementation of the incident response policy and associated incident response controls.	ISO/IEC 27001 A.5.1.1, A.5.1.2, A.6.1.1, A.6.1.3, A.8.1.1, A.10.1.1, A.13.1.1, A.13.2.1, A.15.1.1, A.15.2.1 COBIT® PO9.5, PO9.6, DS5.6, DS8.2, PC5 HIPAA 164.308(a)(6)(i)
Incident response		IR-2 Incident Response Training The organization: a. Trains personnel in their incident response roles and responsibilities with respect to the information system; and b. Provides refresher training [Assignment: organization-defined frequency].	ISO/IEC 27001 A.8.2.2 HIPAA 164.308(a)(6)(i)
Incident response		IR-3 Incident Response Testing and Exercises The organization tests and/or exercises the incident response capability for the information system [Assignment: organization-defined frequency] using [Assignment: organization-defined *tests* and/or exercises] to determine the incident response effectiveness and documents the results.	ISO/IEC 27001 (None) HIPAA 164.308(a)(6)(i)
Incident response		IR-4 Incident Handling The organization: a. Implements an incident handling capability for security incidents that includes preparation, detection and analysis, containment, eradication, and recovery;	ISO/IEC 27001 A.6.1.2, A.13.2.2, A.13.2.3 COBIT PO9.5, PO9.6, DS8.2 HIPAA 164.308(a)(6)(ii)

Table 10.4 (continued) Incident Response Controls

CONTROL FAMILY	COMPLIANT (YES/NO)	CONTROL	MAPPINGS
		b. Coordinates incident handling activities with contingency planning activities; and c. Incorporates lessons learned from ongoing incident handling activities into incident response procedures, training, and testing/exercises, and implements the resulting changes accordingly.	
Incident response		IR-5 Incident Monitoring The organization tracks and documents information system security incidents.	ISO/IEC 27001 (None) COBIT DS8.2, DS8.4 HIPAA 164.308(a)(6)(ii), 164.308(a)(1)(ii)(D)
Incident response		IR-6 Incident Reporting The organization: a. Requires personnel to report suspected security incidents to the organizational incident response capability within [Assignment: organization-defined time-period]; and b. Reports security incident information to designated authorities.	ISO/IEC 27001 A.6.1.6, A.13.1.1 COBIT DS5.6 HIPAA 164.308(a)(1)(ii)(D), 164.308(a)(6)(ii), 164.314(a)(2)(i)
Incident response		IR-7 Incident Response Assistance The organization provides an incident response support resource integral to the organizational incident response capability that offers advice and assistance to users of the information system for the handling and reporting of security incidents.	ISO/IEC 27001 (None) COBIT DS8.1 HIPAA 164.308(a)(6)(ii)
Incident response		IR-8 Incident Response Plan The organization: a. Develops an incident response plan that: • Provides the organization with a roadmap for implementing its incident response capability; • Describes the structure and organization of the incident response capability.	ISO/IEC 27001 (None)

Table 10.5 Maintenance Controls

CONTROL FAMILY	COMPLIANT (YES/NO)	CONTROL	MAPPINGS
Maintenance		MA-1 System Maintenance Policy And Procedures The organization develops, disseminates, and reviews/updates [Assignment: organization defined frequency]: a. A formal, documented information system maintenance policy that addresses purpose, scope, roles, responsibilities, management commitment, coordination among organizational entities, and compliance; and b. Formal, documented procedures to facilitate the implementation of the information system maintenance policy and associated system maintenance controls.	ISO/IEC 27001 A.5.1.1, A.5.1.2, A.6.1.1, A.6.1.3, A.8.1.1, A.9.2.4, A.10.1.1, A.15.1.1, A.15.2.1 COBIT® PC5 HIPAA 164.310(a)(2)(iv)
Maintenance		MA-2 Controlled Maintenance The organization: a. Schedules, performs, documents, and reviews records of maintenance and repairs on information system components in accordance with manufacturer or vendor specifications and/or organizational requirements; b. Controls all maintenance activities, whether performed on site or remotely and whether the equipment is serviced on site or removed to another location; c. Requires that a designated official explicitly approves the removal of the information system or system components from organizational facilities for off-site maintenance or repairs; d. Sanitizes equipment to remove all information from associated media prior to removal from organizational facilities for off-site maintenance or repairs; and	ISO/IEC 27001 A.9.2.4 COBIT AI2.10 HIPAA 164.310(a)(2)(iv)

Table 10.5 (continued) Maintenance Controls

CONTROL FAMILY	COMPLIANT (YES/NO)	CONTROL	MAPPINGS
		e. Checks all potentially impacted security controls to verify that the controls are still functioning properly following maintenance or repair actions.	
Maintenance		MA-3 Maintenance Tools The organization approves, controls, monitors the use of, and maintains on an ongoing basis, information system maintenance tools. Supplemental guidance: The intent of this control is to address the security-related issues arising from the hardware and software brought into the information system specifically for diagnostic and repair actions (e.g., a hardware or software packet sniffer that is introduced for the purpose of a particular maintenance activity). Hardware and/or software components that may support information system maintenance, yet are a part of the system (e.g., the software implementing "ping," "ls," "ipconfig," or the hardware and software implementing the monitoring port of an Ethernet switch) are not covered by this control. Related to MP-6.	ISO/IEC 27001 A.9.2.4, A.11.4.4
Maintenance		MA-4 Non-Local Maintenance The organization: a. Authorizes, monitors, and controls non-local maintenance and diagnostic activities; b. Allows the use of non-local maintenance and diagnostic tools only as consistent with organizational policy and documented in the security plan for the information system; c. Employs strong identification and authentication techniques in the establishment of non-local maintenance and diagnostic sessions;	ISO/IEC 27001 A.9.2.4, A.11.4.4

Continued

Table 10.5 (continued) Maintenance Controls

CONTROL FAMILY	COMPLIANT (YES/NO)	CONTROL	MAPPINGS
		d. Maintains records for non-local maintenance and diagnostic activities; and e. Terminates all sessions and network connections when non-local maintenance is completed.	
Maintenance		MA-5 Maintenance Personnel The organization: a. Establishes a process for maintenance personnel authorization and maintains a current list of authorized maintenance organizations or personnel; and b. Ensures that personnel performing maintenance on the information system have required access authorizations or designates organizational personnel with required access authorizations and technical competence deemed necessary to supervise information system maintenance when maintenance personnel do not possess the required access authorizations.	ISO/IEC 27001 A.9.2.4, A.12.4.3 HIPAA 164.308(a)(3)(ii)(A)
Maintenance		MA-6 Timely Maintenance The organization obtains maintenance support and/or spare parts for [Assignment: organization-defined list of security-critical information system components and/or key information technology components] within [Assignment: organization-defined time period] of failure.	ISO/IEC 27001 A.9.2.4 HIPAA 164.310(a)(2)(iv)

Table 10.6 Media Protection Controls

CONTROL FAMILY	COMPLIANT (YES/NO)	CONTROL	MAPPINGS
Media protection		MP-1 Media Protection Policy And Procedures The organization develops, disseminates, and reviews/updates [Assignment: organization defined frequency]: a. A formal, documented media protection policy that addresses purpose, scope, roles, responsibilities, management commitment, coordination among organizational entities, and compliance; and b. Formal, documented procedures to facilitate the implementation of the media protection policy and associated media protection controls.	ISO/IEC 27001 A.5.1.1, A.5.1.2, A.6.1.1, A.6.1.3, A.8.1.1, A.10.1.1, A.10.7.1, A.10.7.2, A.10.7.3, A.11.1.1, A.15.1.1, A.15.1.3, A.15.2.1 COBIT® DS11.1, DS11.6, PC5 HIPAA 164.310(d)(1)
Media protection		MP-2 Media Access The organization restricts access to [Assignment: organization-defined types of digital and non-digital media] to [Assignment: organization-defined list of authorized individuals] using [Assignment: organization-defined security measures].	ISO/IEC 27001 A.7.2.2, A.10.7.1, A.10.7.3 COBIT DS11.6 HIPAA 164.308(a)(3)(ii)(A)
Media protection		MP-3 Media Marking The organization: a. Marks, in accordance with organizational policies and procedures, removable information system media and information system output indicating the distribution limitations, handling caveats, and applicable security markings (if any) of the information; and b. Exempts [Assignment: organization-defined list of removable media types] from marking as long as the exempted items remain within [Assignment: organization-defined controlled areas].	ISO/IEC 27001 A.7.2.2, A.10.7.1, A.10.7.3 COBIT DS11.6 HIPAA 164.310(c), 164.310(d)(1)

Continued

Table 10.6 (continued) Media Protection Controls

CONTROL FAMILY	COMPLIANT (YES/NO)	CONTROL	MAPPINGS
Media protection		MP-4 Media Storage The organization: a. Physically controls and securely stores [Assignment: organization-defined types of digital and non-digital media] within [Assignment: organization-defined controlled areas] using [Assignment: organization-defined security measures]; b. Protects information system media until the media are destroyed or sanitized using approved equipment, techniques, and procedures.	ISO/IEC 27001 A.10.7.1, A.10.7.3, A.10.7.4, A.15.1.3 COBIT DS11.2, DS11.6 HIPAA 164.310(c), 164.310(d)(1), 164.310(d)(2)(iv)
Media protection		MP-5 Media Transport The organization: a. Protects and controls [Assignment: organization-defined types of digital and non-digital media] during transport outside of controlled areas using [Assignment: organization-defined security measures]; b. Maintains accountability for information system media during transport outside of controlled areas; and c. Restricts the activities associated with transport of such media to authorized personnel.	ISO/IEC 27001 A.9.2.5, A.9.2.7, A.10.7.1, A.10.7.3, A.10.8.3 COBIT DS11.4, DS11.6 HIPAA 164.310(d)(1), 164.310(d)(2)(iii), 164.312(c)(1)
Media protection		MP-6 Media Sanitization The organization: a. Sanitizes information system media, both digital and nondigital, prior to disposal, release out of organizational control, or release for reuse; and b. Employs sanitization mechanisms with strength and integrity commensurate with the classification or sensitivity of the information.	ISO/IEC 27001 A.9.2.6, A.10.7.1, A.10.7.2, A.10.7.3 COBIT DS11.4, DS11.6, HIPAA 164.310(d)(1), 164.310(d)(2)(i)

Table 10.7 Physical and Environment Protection Controls

CONTROL FAMILY	COMPLIANT (YES/NO)	CONTROL	MAPPINGS
Physical and environmental protection		PE-1 Physical And Environmental Protection Policy And Procedures The organization develops, disseminates, and reviews/updates [Assignment: organization defined frequency]: a. A formal, documented physical and environmental protection policy that addresses purpose, scope, roles, responsibilities, management commitment, coordination among organizational entities, and compliance; and b. Formal, documented procedures to facilitate the implementation of the physical and environmental protection policy and associated physical and environmental protection controls.	ISO/IEC 27001 A.5.1.1, A.5.1.2, A.6.1.1, A.6.1.3, A.8.1.1, A.9.1.4, A.9.2.1, A.9.2.2, A.10.1.1, A.11.1.1, A.11.2.1, A.11.2.2, A.15.1.1, A.15.2.1 COBIT® DS12.1, DS12.5, PC5 HIPAA 164.310(a)(1) 164.310(a)(2)(ii) 164.310(a)(2)(iii)
Physical and environmental protection		PE-2 Physical Access Authorizations The organization: a. Develops and keeps current a list of personnel with authorized access to the facility where the information system resides (except for those areas within the facility officially designated as publicly accessible); b. Issues authorization credentials; c. Reviews and approves the access list and authorization credentials [*Assignment: organization defined frequency*], removing from the access list personnel no longer requiring access.	ISO/IEC 27001 A.9.1.5, A.11.2.1, A.11.2.2, A.11.2.4 COBIT DS12.3 HIPAA 164.310(a)(1), 164.310(a)(2)(iii)
Physical and environmental protection		PE-3 Physical Access Control The organization: a. Enforces physical access authorizations for all physical access points (including designated entry/exit points) to the facility where the information system resides (excluding those areas within the facility officially designated as publicly accessible);	ISO/IEC 27001 A.9.1.1, A.9.1.2, A.9.1.3, A.9.1.5, A.9.1.6, A.11.3.2, A.11.4.4 COBIT DS12.2 HIPAA 164.310(a)(1), 164.310(a)(2)(iii), 164.310(b), 164.310(c)

Continued

Table 10.7 (continued) Physical and Environment Protection Controls

CONTROL FAMILY	COMPLIANT (YES/NO)	CONTROL	MAPPINGS
		b. Verifies individual access authorizations before granting access to the facility; c. Controls entry to the facility containing the information system using physical access devices and/or guards; d. Controls access to areas officially designated as publicly accessible in accordance with the organization's assessment of risk; e. Secures keys, combinations, and other physical access devices; f. Inventories physical access devices [Assignment: organization-defined frequency]; and g. Changes combinations and keys [Assignment: organization-defined frequency] and when keys are lost, combinations are compromised, or individuals are transferred or terminated.	
Physical and environmental protection		PE-4 Access Control for Transmission Medium The organization controls physical access to information system distribution and transmission lines within organizational facilities.	ISO/IEC 27001 A.9.1.3, A.9.1.5, A.9.2.3 COBIT DS5.7, DS12.2 HIPAA 164.310(a)(1), 164.310(c)
Physical and environmental protection		PE-5 Access Control for Output Devices The organization controls physical access to information system output devices to prevent unauthorized individuals from obtaining the output.	ISO/IEC 27001 A.9.1.2, A.9.1.3, A.10.6.1, A.11.3.2 COBIT DS12.2 HIPAA 164.310(b), 164.310(c), 164.310(a)(1)
Physical and environmental protection		PE-6 Monitoring Physical Access The organization: a. Monitors physical access to the information system to detect and respond to physical security incidents; b. Reviews physical access logs [Assignment: organization-defined frequency]; and	ISO/IEC 27001 A.9.1.2, A.9.1.5, A.10.10.2 COBIT DS12.3 HIPAA 164.310(a)(2)(iii)

Table 10.7 (continued) Physical and Environment Protection Controls

CONTROL FAMILY	COMPLIANT (YES/NO)	CONTROL	MAPPINGS
		c. Coordinates results of reviews and investigations with the organization's incident response capability.	
Physical and environmental protection		PE-7 Visitor Control The organization controls physical access to the information system by authenticating visitors before authorizing access to the facility where the information system resides other than areas designated as publicly accessible.	ISO/IEC 27001 A.9.1.2, A.9.1.5, A.9.1.6 COBIT DS12.3 HIPAA 164.310(a)(2)(iii)
Physical and environmental protection		PE-8 Access Records The organization: a. Maintains visitor access records to the facility where the information system resides (except for those areas within the facility officially designated as publicly accessible); and b. Reviews visitor access records [Assignment: organization-defined frequency].	ISO/IEC 27001 A.9.1.5, A.10.10.2, A.15.2.1 COBIT DS12.3 HIPAA 164.310(a)(2)(iii)
Physical and environmental protection		PE-9 Power Equipment and Power Cabling The organization protects power equipment and power cabling for the information system from damage and destruction.	ISO/IEC 27001 A.9.1.4, A.9.2.2, A.9.2.3 COBIT DS12.4
Physical and environmental protection		PE-10 Emergency Shutoff The organization: a. Provides the capability of shutting off power to the information system or individual system components in emergency situations; b. Places emergency shutoff switches or devices in [Assignment: organization-defined location by information system or system component] to facilitate safe and easy access for personnel; and c. Protects emergency power shutoff capability from unauthorized activation.	ISO/IEC 27001 A.9.1.4 COBIT DS12.4

Continued

Table 10.7 (continued) Physical and Environment Protection Controls

CONTROL FAMILY	COMPLIANT (YES/NO)	CONTROL	MAPPINGS
Physical and environmental protection		PE-11 Emergency Power The organization provides a short-term uninterruptible power supply to facilitate an orderly shutdown of the information system in the event of a primary power source loss. Supplemental guidance: This control, to include any enhancements specified, may be satisfied by similar requirements fulfilled by another organizational entity other than the information security program. Organizations avoid duplicating actions already covered.	ISO/IEC 27001 A.9.1.4, A.9.2.2 COBIT DS12.4
Physical and environmental protection		PE-12 Emergency Lighting The organization employs and maintains automatic emergency lighting for the information system that activates in the event of a power outage or disruption, and that covers emergency exits and evacuation routes within the facility.	ISO/IEC 27001 A.9.2.2 COBIT DS12.4
Physical and environmental protection		PE-13 Fire Protection The organization employs and maintains fire suppression and detection devices/systems for the information system that are supported by an independent energy source.	ISO/IEC 27001 A.9.1.4 COBIT DS12.4
Physical and environmental protection		PE-14 Temperature and Humidity Controls The organization: a. Maintains temperature and humidity levels within the facility where the information system resides at [Assignment: organization-defined acceptable levels]; and b. Monitors temperature and humidity levels [Assignment: organization-defined frequency].	ISO/IEC 27001 A.9.2.2 COBIT DS12.4

Table 10.7 (continued) Physical and Environment Protection Controls

CONTROL FAMILY	COMPLIANT (YES/NO)	CONTROL	MAPPINGS
Physical and environmental protection		PE-15 Water Damage Protection The organization protects the information system from damage resulting from water leakage by providing master shutoff valves that are accessible, working properly, and known to key personnel.	ISO/IEC 27001 A.9.1.4 COBIT DS12.4
Physical and environmental protection		PE-16 Delivery and Removal The organization authorizes, monitors, and controls [Assignment: organization-defined types of information system components] entering and exiting the facility, and maintains records of those items.	ISO/IEC 27001 A.9.1.6, A.9.2.7, A.10.7.1 COBIT DS12.2
Physical and environmental protection		PE-17 Alternate Work Site The organization: a. Employs [Assignment: organization-defined management, operational, and technical information system security controls] at alternate work sites; b. Assesses as feasible, the effectiveness of security controls at alternate work sites; and c. Provides a means for employees to communicate with information security personnel in case of security incidents or problems.	ISO/IEC 27001 A.9.2.5, A.11.7.2 HIPAA 164.310(a)(2)(i)
Physical and environmental protection		PE-18 Location of Information System Components The organization positions information system components within the facility to minimize potential damage from physical and environmental hazards and to minimize the opportunity for unauthorized access.	ISO/IEC 27001 A.9.2.1, A.11.3.2 COBIT DS12.1 HIPAA 164.310(c)
Physical and environmental protection		PE-19 Information Leakage The organization protects the information system from information leakage due to electromagnetic signals emanations.	ISO/IEC 27001 A.12.5.4 COBIT DS12.2

Table 10.8 Personnel Security Controls

CONTROL FAMILY	COMPLIANT (YES/NO)	CONTROL	MAPPINGS
Personnel security		PS-1 Personnel Security Policy and Procedures The organization develops, disseminates, and reviews/updates [Assignment: organization defined frequency]: a. A formal, documented personnel security policy that addresses purpose, scope, roles, responsibilities, management commitment, coordination among organizational entities, and compliance; and b. Formal, documented procedures to facilitate the implementation of the personnel security policy and associated personnel security controls.	ISO/IEC 27001 A.5.1.1, A.5.1.2, A.6.1.1, A.6.1.3, A.8.1.1, A.10.1.1, A.15.1.1, A.15.2.1 COBIT® PC5, P04.6, P07.3 HIPAA 164.308(a)(3)(ii)(A) 164.308(a)(3)(ii)(B) 164.308(a)(3)(ii)(C)
Personnel security		PS-2 Position Categorization The organization: a. Assigns a risk designation to all positions; b. Establishes screening criteria for individuals filling those positions; and c. Reviews and revises position risk designations [Assignment: organization-defined frequency].	ISO/IEC 27001 A.8.1.1 COBIT P04.13, P07.3 HIPAA 164.308(a)(3)(ii)(B)
Personnel security		PS-3 Personnel Screening The organization: a. Screens individuals prior to authorizing access to the information system; and b. Rescreens individuals according to [Assignment: organization-defined list of conditions requiring rescreening and, where rescreening is so indicated, the frequency of such rescreening].	ISO/IEC 27001 A.8.1.2 COBIT P07.6 HIPAA 164.308(a)(3)(ii)(B)

Table 10.8 (continued) Personnel Security Controls

CONTROL FAMILY	COMPLIANT (YES/NO)	CONTROL	MAPPINGS
Personnel security		PS-4 Personnel Termination The organization, upon termination of individual employment: a. Terminates information system access; b. Conducts exit interviews; c. Retrieves all security-related organizational information system-related property; and d. Retains access to organizational information and information systems formerly controlled by terminated individual.	ISO/IEC 27001 A.8.3.1, A.8.3.2, A.8.3.3 COBIT P07.8 HIPAA 164.308(a)(3)(ii)(C)
Personnel security		PS-5 Personnel Transfer The organization reviews logical and physical access authorizations to information systems/facilities when personnel are reassigned or transferred to other positions within the organization and initiates [Assignment: organization-defined transfer or reassignment actions] within [Assignment: organization-defined time period following the formal transfer action].	ISO/IEC 27001 A.8.3.1, A.8.3.2, A.8.3.3 COBIT P07.8 HIPAA 164.308(a)(3)(ii)(C)
Personnel security		PS-6 Access Agreements The organization: a. Ensures that individuals requiring access to organizational information and information systems sign appropriate access agreements prior to being granted access; and b. Reviews/updates the access agreements [Assignment: organization-defined frequency].	ISO/IEC 27001 A.6.1.5, A.8.1.1, A.8.1.3, A.8.2.1, A.9.1.5, A.10.8.1, A.11.7.1, A.11.7.2, A.15.1.5 COBIT DS5.4 HIPAA 164.308(a)(3)(ii)(A), 164.308(a)(3)(ii)(B), 164.308(a)(4)(ii)(B), 164.310(b), 164.310(d)(2)(iii), 164.314(a)(1), 164.314(a)(2)(i), 164.314(a)(2)(ii)

Continued

Table 10.8 (continued) Personnel Security Controls

CONTROL FAMILY	COMPLIANT (YES/NO)	CONTROL	MAPPINGS
Personnel security		PS-7 Third-Party Personnel Security The organization: a. Establishes personnel security requirements including security roles and responsibilities for third-party providers; b. Documents personnel security requirements; and c. Monitors provider compliance.	ISO/IEC 27001 A.6.2.3, A.8.1.1, A.8.2.1, A.8.1.3 COBIT PO4.14, DS2.2 HIPAA 164.308(a)(3)(ii)(A), 164.308(a)(4)(ii)(B), 164.308(b)(1), 164.314(a)(1), 164.314(a)(2)(i), 164.314(a)(2)(ii)
Personnel security		PS-8 Personnel Sanctions The organization employs a formal sanctions process for personnel failing to comply with established information security policies and procedures.	ISO/IEC 27001 A.8.2.3, A.15.1.5 HIPAA 164.308(a)(1)(ii)(C)

Table 10.9 System and Information Integrity Controls

CONTROL FAMILY	COMPLIANT (YES/NO)	CONTROL	MAPPINGS
System and information integrity		SI-1 System And Information Integrity Policy And Procedures The organization develops, disseminates, and reviews/updates [Assignment: organization defined frequency]: a. A formal, documented system and information integrity policy that addresses purpose, scope, roles, responsibilities, management commitment, coordination among organizational entities, and compliance; and b. Formal, documented procedures to facilitate the implementation of the system and information integrity policy and associated system and information integrity controls.	ISO/IEC 27001 A.5.1.1, A.5.1.2, A.6.1.1, A.6.1.3, A.8.1.1, A.10.1.1, A.15.1.1, A.15.2.1 COBIT® P02.4, PC5 HIPAA 164.312(c)(1)
System and information integrity		SI-2 Flaw Remediation The organization: a. Identifies, reports, and corrects information system flaws; b. Tests software updates related to flaw remediation for effectiveness and potential side effects on organizational information systems before installation; and c. Incorporates flaw remediation into the organizational configuration management process.	ISO/IEC 27001 A.10.10.5, A.12.5.2, A.12.6.1, A.13.1.2
System and information integrity		SI-3 Malicious Code Protection The organization: a. Employs malicious code protection mechanisms at information system entry and exit points and at workstations, servers, or mobile computing devices on the network to detect and eradicate malicious code: • Transported by electronic mail, electronic mail attachments, Web accesses, removable media, or other common means; or	ISO/IEC 27001 A.10.4.1 COBIT DS5.9 HIPAA 164.308(a)(5)(ii)(B)

Continued

Table 10.9 (continued) System and Information Integrity Controls

CONTROL FAMILY	COMPLIANT (YES/NO)	CONTROL	MAPPINGS
		• Inserted through the exploitation of information system vulnerabilities; b. Updates malicious code protection mechanisms (including signature definitions) whenever new releases are available in accordance with organizational configuration management policy and procedures; c. Configures malicious code protection mechanisms to: • Perform periodic scans of the information system [Assignment: organization-defined frequency] and real-time scans of files from external sources as the files are downloaded, opened, or executed in accordance with organizational security policy; and • [Selection (one or more): block malicious code; quarantine malicious code; send alert to administrator; [Assignment: organization-defined action]] in response to malicious code detection; and d. Addresses the receipt of false positives during malicious code detection and eradication and the resulting potential impact on the availability of the information system.	
System and information integrity		SI-4 Information System Monitoring The organization: a. Monitors events on the information system in accordance with [Assignment: organization defined monitoring objectives] and detects information system attacks; b. Identifies unauthorized use of the information system;	ISO/IEC 27001 A.10.10.2, A.13.1.1, A.13.1.2 COBIT P02.4, DS5.5, DS5.10 HIPAA 164.308(a)(5)(ii)(B), 164.308(a)(1)(ii)(D)

Table 10.9 (continued) System and Information Integrity Controls

CONTROL FAMILY	COMPLIANT (YES/NO)	CONTROL	MAPPINGS
		c. Deploys monitoring devices: (i) strategically within the information system to collect organization-determined essential information; and (ii) at ad hoc locations within the system to track specific types of transactions of interest to the organization; d. Heightens the level of information system monitoring activity whenever there is an indication of increased risk to organizational operations and assets, individuals, other organizations, or the nation based on law enforcement information, intelligence information, or other credible sources of information; and e. Obtains legal opinion with regard to information system monitoring activities in accordance with applicable federal laws, executive orders, directives, policies, or regulations.	
System and information integrity		SI-5 Security Alerts, Advisories, and Directives The organization: a. Receives information system security alerts, advisories, and directives from designated external organizations on an ongoing basis; b. Generates internal security alerts, advisories, and directives as deemed necessary; c. Disseminates security alerts, advisories, and directives to [Assignment: organization-defined list of personnel (identified by name and/or by role)]; and d. Implements security directives in accordance with established time frames, or notifies the issuing organization of the degree of noncompliance.	ISO/IEC 27001 A.6.1.6, A.12.6.1, A.13.1.1, A.13.1.2 HIPAA 164.308(a)(5)(ii)(A)

Continued

Table 10.9 (continued) System and Information Integrity Controls

CONTROL FAMILY	COMPLIANT (YES/NO)	CONTROL	MAPPINGS
System and information integrity		SI-6 Security Functionality Verification The information system verifies the correct operation of security functions [Selection (one or more): [Assignment: organization-defined system transitional states]; upon command by user with appropriate privilege; periodically every [Assignment: organization-defined time-period]] and [Selection (one or more): notifies system administrator; shuts the system down; restarts the system; [Assignment: organization-defined alternative action(s)]] when anomalies are discovered.	ISO/IEC 27001 (None)
System and information integrity		SI-7 Software and Information Integrity The information system detects unauthorized changes to software and information.	ISO/IEC 27001 A.10.4.1, A.12.2.2, A.12.2.3 COBIT P02.4 AI2.4, DS5.9 HIPAA 164.312(c)(1), 164.312(c)(2), 164.312(e)(2)(i)
System and information integrity		SI-8 Spam Protection The organization: a. Employs spam protection mechanisms at information system entry and exit points and at workstations, servers, or mobile computing devices on the network to detect and take action on unsolicited messages transported by electronic mail, electronic mail attachments, web accesses, or other common means; and b. Updates spam protection mechanisms (including signature definitions) when new releases are available in accordance with organizational configuration management policy and procedures.	ISO/IEC 27001 (None) COBIT DS5.9 HIPAA 164.308(a)(5)(ii)(B)

Table 10.9 (continued) System and Information Integrity Controls

CONTROL FAMILY	COMPLIANT (YES/NO)	CONTROL	MAPPINGS
System and information integrity		SI-9 Information Input Restrictions The organization restricts the capability to input information to the information system to authorized personnel.	ISO/IEC 27001 A.10.8.1, A.11.1.1, A.11.2.2, A.12.2.2 COBIT AC1, AC2
System and information integrity		SI-10 Information Input Validation The information system checks the validity of information inputs.	ISO/IEC 27001 A.12.2.1, A.12.2.2 COBIT AC3, AC4, AC6
System and information integrity		SI-11 Error Handling The information system: a. Identifies potentially security-relevant error conditions; b. Generates error messages that provide information necessary for corrective actions without revealing [Assignment: organization-defined sensitive or potentially harmful information] in error logs and administrative messages that could be exploited by adversaries; and c. Reveals error messages only to authorized personnel.	ISO/IEC 27001 (None) COBIT AC5
System and information integrity		SI-12 Information Output Handling and Retention The organization handles and retains both information within and output from the information system in accordance with applicable federal laws, executive orders, directives, policies, regulations, standards, and operational requirements.	ISO/IEC 27001 A.10.7.3, A.15.1.3, A.15.1.4, A.15.2.1 COBIT AC5, DS11.1, DS11.6
System and information integrity		SI-13 Predictable Failure Prevention The organization: a. Protects the information system from harm by considering mean time to failure for [Assignment: organization-defined list of information system components] in specific environments of operation; and b. Provides substitute information system components, when needed, and a mechanism to exchange active and standby roles of the components.	ISO/IEC 27001 (None)

Suggested Reading

1. National Institute of Standards and Technology (NIST). August 2009. Special Publication 800-53 Rev 3: Recommended security controls for federal information systems and organizations. http://csrc.nist.gov/publications/nistpubs/800-53-Rev3/sp800-53-rev3-final_updated-errata_05-01-2010.pdf
2. IT Governance Institute. 2007. Mapping of NIST SP 800-53 Rev 1 with COBIT 4.1. http://www.itgi.org
3. National Institute of Standards and Technology (NIST). October 2008. An introductory resource guide for implementing the Health Insurance Portability and Accountability Act (HIPAA) security rule. http://csrc.nist.gov/publications/nistpubs/800-66-Rev1/SP-800-66-Revision1.pdf
4. International Organization for Standardization (ISO). ISO/IEC 27001:2005 Information Security Management Systems—Requirements, http://www.iso.org/iso/iso_catalogue/catalogue_tc/catalogue_detail.htm?csnumber=42103
5. International Organization for Standardization (ISO). ISO/IEC 27002:2005 Information technology—Security techniques—Code of practice for information security management, http://www.iso.org/iso/iso_catalogue/catalogue_tc/catalogue_detail.htm?csnumber=50297
6. Department of Health and Human Services, Office of the Secretary. February 20, 2003. 45 CFR Parts 160, 162, and 164 Health insurance reform: Security standards; Final rule. *Federal Register* 68(24). http://www.hhs.gov/ocr/privacy/hipaa/administrative/securityrule/securityrulepdf.pdf

11
The Auditors Have Arrived, Now What?

Truth exists, only falsehood has to be invented.

Georges Braque, 1882–1963

Auditors perform an essential role in protecting the information assets of the organization, which should be embraced versus feared. Many times when an audit is scheduled, whether internally or externally initiated, the response is one of fear of what the auditors will find as gaps in the information security program. Analogous to how many people feel when they are scheduled for their annual performance review, anxiety is almost certain to be a normal response. Why is it that way? The answer is simple: No one likes to criticized for what they have put their best efforts into, and just like the potentially stressful performance reviews, audits have the potential to be taken very personally and viewed as a negative experience. A recent comment by an information security colleague summed this up very well, in reference to the auditors judging his work by saying, "Whose baby are you calling ugly?"

The truth is that audits typically do cause anxiety and cause people's stress levels and outward emotions to reflect the pressure of being "judged." The truth is also that these can be extremely valuable learning experiences by which those leading information security programs can learn greatly from the auditors. Auditors are typically very detail oriented and as a result may see items that may be overlooked by big-picture people. Auditors also typically follow a methodical, systematic approach to analyzing what that organization asserts are the controls that are in place. The systematic approach allows them to uncover what may be assumed is actually occurring by the company. For example, a manager may assume a policy in place that requires that all access be terminated for an exiting employee within 72 hours is being followed. When the auditor reviews the policy, he or she may find that there was no documented standard operating procedure, thus raising doubts that a consistent procedure was actually being followed. The auditor may also find that while logical access was promptly removed, there was no equivalent procedure within physical security, creating a gap. Many times the auditor will request a full population of employees and request a random sample based upon the frequency of the process, say 25 or 45 for a daily process, and test to determine if the requirement was consistently met.

How often do the operational departments within an organization perform an independent test of the product or service they are creating? Companies are doing their utmost best to just get the product of service out the door. This creates a situation where compliance with the company policies, procedures, standards, and guidelines is assumed and not regularly tested. In this respect, we should be welcoming the auditors with open arms.

A byproduct of performing audits on a regular basis is that managers are more apt to pay attention to ensure that the standard operating procedures are actually accurate and reviewed on a periodic basis (minimally on an annual basis). Knowing that they will be judged on the basis of what process is written versus the current process, if different, even if the current process is better, will encourage managers to take the documentation more seriously. Documentation should be regarded as management directives to ensure that the appropriate activities are being performed at the right time.

Through experience gained through dozens of audits involving the Big Four accounting firms, audit firms occupying the middle-market tier, and boutique technical auditing firms, it is safe to say that no two audits are conducted the same or necessarily have the same goals in mind. However, there are some basic commonalities as to the flow of an audit and how the information security department should interact with the auditors. The next few sections walk through the anatomy of an IT audit and how the security professional should best prepare for the audit.

Anatomy of an Audit

From a security officer's point of view, the audit can be separated into five phases: (1) audit planning, (2) on-site arrival, (3) audit execution,

(4) entrance/status/exit conferences, and (5) report issuance and finding remediation. It is useful to look at the audit as a project, with a discrete set of steps, a beginning, and an end. Viewing the audit as an activity in this manner permits the prioritizing, scheduling, and resourcing of the audit similar to other projects within the company. The success of an audit depends upon having knowledgeable individuals available to answer the questions for which they are most qualified at the appropriate time.

External audits involve an up-front period of negotiations for the scope and pricing of the audit. This process is normally administered through the company's internal audit department in response to a contractual requirement for awarded business (e.g., government contract with Federal Information Security Management Act [FISMA] provisions or Health Insurance Portability and Accountability Act [HIPAA] compliance requirements). Since the internal audit department may have many internal and external audits scheduled during a given year, the audit may not occur at the best time for the information technology (IT) department to have the resources available. Partnership with internal audit, information security, information technology, and compliance areas can help mitigate the scheduling disruptions that can occur. Once the external audit dates are set, there is typically limited flexibility to move the schedule, as the external audit firms also must balance their resources with the needs of other clients. Teams are typically only put together a few weeks in advance at the most for the audit firm, but once they are, they tend to be locked in.

The phases shown in Figure 11.1 assume that the contract and schedule are now in place, and information security and the other departments need to prepare for the audit.

Audit Planning Phase

The audit planning phase ensures that the auditors have most, if not all, of the requested information delivered to them when they arrive for the audit. With sufficient resources dedicated to the up-front planning phase, the audit runs more smoothly as more time can be dedicated toward accurately answering the auditor's questions and responding to follow-up requests versus scrambling for documentation or having less-than-optimal facilities for the auditors to conduct the audit.

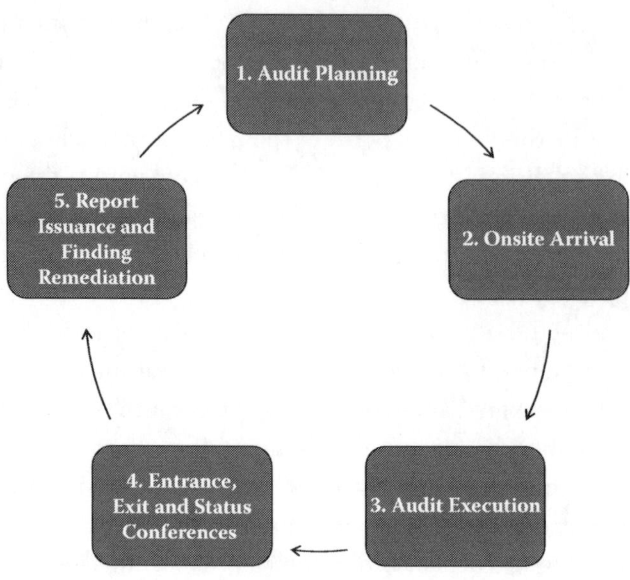

Figure 11.1 Security audit phases and activities.

Preparation of Document Request List

The first step is to establish an audit coordinator for the information security/IT portion of the audit. This individual is usually someone within the IT organization that understands the interoperability of the technical infrastructure, operations, and management of IT. Internal audit departments traditionally have focused upon the financial and operational audit areas and may or may not have the IT auditing skills. Even if they do have individuals with these skills, their role is to audit the organization. The role of the audit coordinator is to respond to the requests of the auditors, which may be internal or external. To mitigate any conflict of interest questions (auditors preparing responses to their own managed audits), an audit coordinator position is established. The function of this individual is to coordinate all audit requests, ensure timely receipt and delivery of the artifacts, schedule meetings, communicate issues, and generally ensure that a smooth process is followed.

Anywhere from 3 to 5 weeks ahead of the audit, the auditors will prepare and deliver a request for documentation. The request goes by such names as prepared by client (PBC) listing, client assistance list (CAL), and agreed upon procedures (AUP). Regardless of the name, the intent of the request is the same: a document typically in the form of a Word document or spreadsheet that contains the auditors' request for documentation that they would like to have available when they start the audit. It is in everyone's best interest to comply with the request and have 100% of the items requested available when the auditors start the audit. This permits the auditors to start right away reviewing and understanding the materials provided. By supplying all of the information at the beginning, it can also reduce the stress level by avoiding hurry-up requests that must be immediately supplied to the auditors. There will also be additional requests by the auditors that will consume valuable time during the audit, so it makes sense to solicit the materials in advance and give the departments as much of the 3 to 5 weeks time as necessary to collect the artifacts. Failure to adequately allow ample preparation time causes the organization to respond on the fly and not necessarily provide the best responses due to the short time frame allowed during the audit to provide the responses.

If any of the audit requests are not clear, the audit coordinator may need to schedule a meeting to discuss the deliverables requested. The scope may not be clearly understood by the auditors or the client. As new auditors are brought into an engagement, they must quickly come up to speed with the organization, processes, and the business operations. Since the request list is typically based upon a generic template, assumptions may be made about the processing that is performed by the company being audited. For example, it may be assumed that the company is following a system development life cycle (SDLC) process to develop software, when in fact the organization may have outsourced the development and maintenance activities to a system integrator and is running these processes at the data center. If the audit of the data center is also in scope, the SDLC processes can be obtained through a separate audit of the data center.

The requests are usually organized into sections deemed as important by the auditor and may or may not be numbered. The number of items requested varies, but typically 50 to 200 requests for different security elements are normal. There is little consistency between audit firms as to what is requested, as each audit firm has constructed its audit program based upon what it considers to be important, modified by the focus desired by the organization or branch of government requesting the audit. The number of auditors and scope may dictate how much testing is performed within the audit. An audit that has 2 to 3 auditors on site for 1 to 3 weeks will involve substantially less testing than a 4-week audit with 10 auditors on site.

An example of an audit request for documentation can be seen in Figure 11.2. A description of the contents of the request, an associated control ID, dates requested and dates received, and a field for comments are typical. One item that is not stated is how this document will be used within the audit! The auditors do not necessarily tie the request to the control item being tested, nor do they necessarily want to make this clear. After all, this is an audit to test the operations, and if they are testing to determine if the controls are adequate to protect the information assets, then it should be irrelevant if the company knows what control is being tested when the documentation request is made—the organization should have the document in question. On the other hand, it helps to know the context of the request in order to supply the correct documentation.

Once the request list is received, the items should be assigned an internal control number for tracking. This helps tremendously during the audit to track and determine what has and what has not been provided. The next step is to determine which (1) director, (2) manager, and (3) subject matter expert, or primary point of contact is in the best position, knowledge-wise, to respond to the request. The documentation request list can be modified to place these accountable and responsible positions in columns for each request so that it is clear who will own this deliverable. Although it may seem obvious, it is vitally important to establish who the correct owners are up front or time ends up being wasted when a manager indicates the day before the deliverable is due that they are not the correct owner. This action is unfair to the manager who now needs to scramble to complete the request and does not promote the generation of a quality product.

The updated spreadsheet with the internal tracking numbers, accountable management, and subject matter experts is then distributed to the organization by the audit coordinator, typically within 1 week after receiving the initial request list. Managers should be given a couple of days to receive the listing and confirm that the items are theirs, and if not, recommend who should own the requested item. At this point they are not fulfilling the request but rather merely indicating whether it is theirs to supply. It is best to place the responsibility

REQ NO	DESCRIPTION	PROCESS	CONTROL	DATE REQUESTED	DATE RECEIVED	DIRECTOR/ MANAGER	POC	DOCUMENT NAMES	DOCS COMPLETE?
1	Risk assessment	RA	RA-3	3/01/12	3/02/12	Johnson/ Costigan	Miller	2011RA_Final.doc	Yes
2	Patch management procedures (Unix, Windows, SQL, Sybase, DB2, Oracle, Mainframe)	CM, SI	CM-1, SI-1	3/01/12	3/04/12	Harrison/ LePerla	Beske	PM_Unix145.doc, PM_ Unix145.xls,MFV7_RACF.doc	Under review
3	Record of personnel termination actions (use TERM.XLS Sample)	PS	PS-4	3/01/12	03/02/12	Murray/ Potter	Williams	Terms100112_To_Present. xls;AuthTickets_030112.pdf	No, documentation not complete
4	Incident response records and documents	IR	IR-5	3/01/12	03/01/12	Westphal/ Jovi	Diller	IRlog0212.xls; POL_IR034_V5.doc	Under review
5	Listing of desktops/ laptops and antivirus information	SI	SI-3	3/01/12	03/04/12	Harrison/ LePerla	Beske	SysAntiVirus_daily_ report_022812. xls;AssetListing_ Desktop_020112.pdf	Under review
6	Business continuity plan, disaster recovery plan, and mock tests	CP	CP-1, CP-2	3/01/12		Symmonds/ Rozek	Sims		Not received

Figure 11.2 Document request list example.

with the assigned manager to reach agreement with the department manager that should own the request and inform the audit coordinator. This avoids multiple conversations between the audit coordinator and each party that can potentially increase the time to gain agreement due to unavailability of all parties to the conversation.

Now that the documentation requests each have an owner associated with them, each owner can now begin the process of collecting the artifacts for submission. The audit coordinator should create an audit artifact repository of some sort to capture and organize the artifacts. This may be a simple directory structure, containing one folder for each item on the request list (the folder will most likely contain multiple documents to satisfy the request) or may be a more elaborate homegrown database or vendor-created database. Either of these methods are preferred to subject matter experts sending the requests via e-mail, as the file sizes can typically exceed internal 5 to 10 megabyte limitations of the e-mail service or the storage of the audit participants. Additionally, when others need to look up the audit artifacts that have been supplied, without a central network storage area, they may have been the recipient of the initial e-mail and will have to request the information be forwarded again. This in turn, increases the company's storage requirements and is very inefficient.

Gather Audit Artifacts

Once each manager has accumulated all of the artifacts assigned to him or her for the audit, the manager needs to confirm with the audit coordinator that the collection is complete. At this point, the audit coordinator can review the contents and determine whether all of the information has been provided. This quality assurance process increases the likelihood that the information will not have to be re-requested. The auditor coordinator looks for such discrepancies as:

- Accuracy spot check—Check to determine if information supplied matches the information requested.
- Empty folders—Contents may have been placed in a different audit directory, accidently deleted, moved to another folder, or misplaced. It all happens.

- An insufficient artifact—The audit coordinator has typically seen a similar request across audits over time and is usually in the best position to determine whether this artifact is complete.
- Time period not valid—If the audit is from October 1, 2012, to March 31, 2013, and a standard operating procedure updated April 8, 2013, is supplied, the new procedure would not have been effective during the period.
- Sizes too large—If the file sizes are too large, say >10 MB, then it may be difficult if the files need to be subsequently e-mailed to the auditor. It is best to break these directories into subdirectories prior to the audit.
- Outdated policies/procedures—A quick review of the last update date would indicate whether this might be an old artifact.

Whereas the management and subject matter experts are responsible to ensure that the audit artifacts are accurate and comply with the information request, the spot checking by the audit coordinator is a value-added step that can find problems with the information prior to presentation to the auditors. Figure 11.3 shows a data model representation of the audit artifacts.

Provide Information to Auditors

Once all of the information has been collected by the audit coordinator for all of the items requested on the document request list, the audit coordinator can burn an initial CD, DVD, or USB drive containing all of the information. Since much of the information will be highly confidential (network diagrams, access control lists, employee listings, background checks, logs, etc.), the information must be encrypted. Encryption programs have substantially fallen in price in the past few years, so there is little justifiable reason to not protect this information. Programs such as WinZip, SecureZip, PKZip, or programs based upon the zip format are used by most audit firms and can be opened by their auditors. This should be verified with the auditors prior to starting the engagement, as not all encryption programs are compatible. For example, Winzip or SecureZip cannot open a file encrypted using Pointsec software because it used as a proprietary

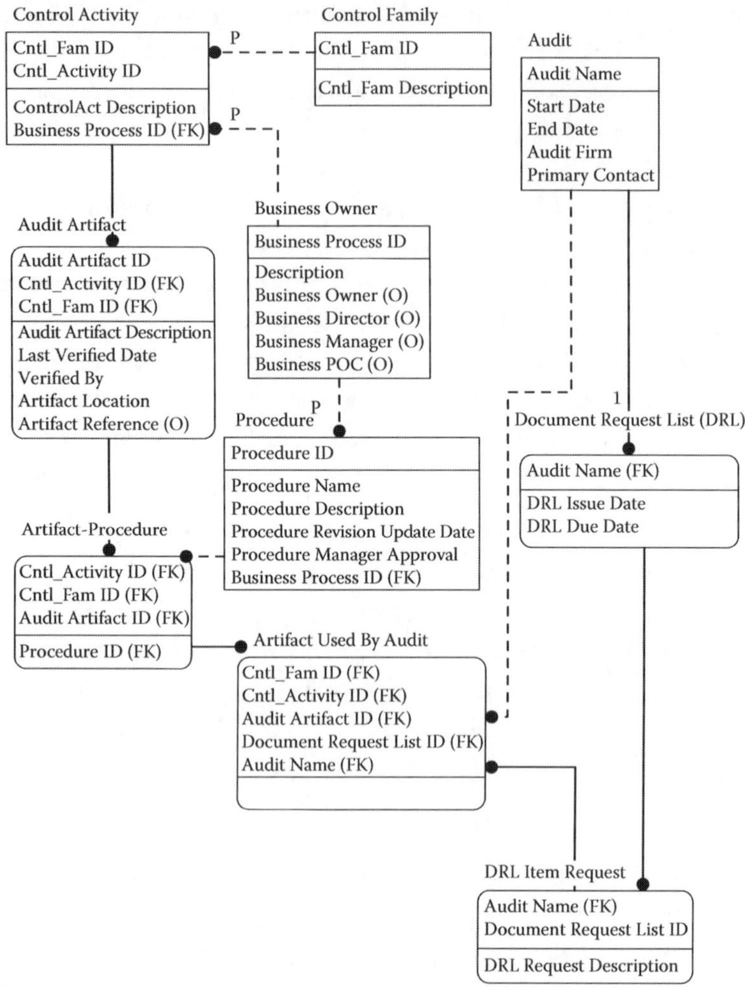

Figure 11.3 Audit artifact data model.

nonzip internal format. However, a file encrypted by Winzip (version 9.0 or greater) or SecureZip can be opened by either program since the internal format used in both products is based on the zip format. Providing multiple copies to the auditors is typically appreciated to enable them to ramp up quickly while on site without having to spend time copying sizable files across a network or wait for others to complete copying the files to their disks. Although most auditors in the profession utilize encrypted hard disks on their PCs to store the client files, it is advisable to confirm this with the auditors before providing them with the information.

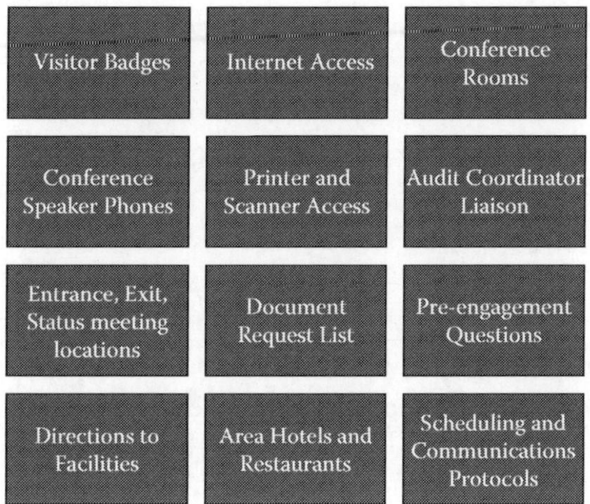

Figure 11.4 Preaudit visit logistical items.

On-Site Arrival Phase

Auditors may schedule a pre-on-site meeting ahead of the audit to ensure that the appropriate logistics have been taken care of. A listing of the items typically requested by the auditors in advance is shown in Figure 11.4. The next sections discuss considerations for some of the key items requested by the auditors that are needed during the on-site arrival. In reality, these items are planned for in the audit planning phase, and utilized within the on-site arrival phase.

Internet Access

Even though the auditors are engaged at the client site, they still have responsibilities to the home office and need to communicate with other senior-level auditors and partners. They may need to share files, access e-mail, conduct conference calls, access home office software, and so forth. One method of providing this access is to provide internal network access and subsequent access to the Internet. This involves setting up the auditors similar to how contractors may be connected to the system—with a user account on the network and access to the Internet. The problem with this configuration is that the auditors are now resident on the network and may have access to more network files than desired. Auditors should be treated with the same security need-to-know and least-privilege principles that are applied to other users of the organization's information assets.

An alternative solution that serves to provide the access the auditors need while simultaneously limiting the exposure of internal information outside the scope of the audit is to provide network access via a wireless broadband router. This relatively inexpensive solution provides the auditors with the access required and keeps the auditors from having to be set up on the organization's computer network. Not only does this save time in set up, but it provides a fast solution to deploy to the auditors. In other words, the day they arrive on site, the wireless broadband router can be plugged in and they are ready to begin work. The router also permits sharing of the broadband connection between the auditors. It is advisable to have one broadband router per every four auditors to ensure adequate bandwidth when downloading and uploading large files.

Once the availability of this device is known within the company, it is not unusual for the IT department to have more requests than there are routers. Given the inexpensive nature of an inexpensive piece of hardware (under $200 as of this writing) and the aircard monthly fees (generally $60/month or less depending upon pricing discounts and usage), it makes sense to ensure that there are extra routers that can be shipped to alternate audit locations to support the audit. The hidden costs of requesting accounts, setting up audit access, terminating accounts, requesting auditor names, and so forth are greater than the one time cost of the routers and monthly charges.

Reserve Conference Rooms

Depending upon the size and duration of the audit, a small or large conference room may be needed. Failure to provide a room with enough space for both the auditors and the auditees can create an environment that increases the stress levels of both parties. The proper size conference room for the interviews may not be known until the interview schedule has been created. Most organizations do not have extra conference rooms so these should be scheduled at the start of the audit.

The auditors may request that a room also be reserved for their private conversations that are separate from the room reserved for the interviews and the other auditors. This permits sidebar discussions without disturbing the rest of the team. However, it is not unusual to see auditors with headphones on in large conference rooms to block out the distractions of the other auditors.

If possible, locate a conference room that is away from the individuals performing a bulk of the work that is being audited. This avoids embarrassing situations where someone may make a comment related to an aspect that is currently being audited and being overheard by the auditor. Although the comment may be accurate, it may be taken out of context by the auditor or substantiate an issue that the auditor was investigating. Staff should also be courteous to the auditors and respect the noise levels and conversations outside the conference room.

Temperature control is always a consideration. Although it may be tempting to smoke out or freeze up the auditors, this strategy is ill advised. While this may be obvious, keep in mind that there will be more individuals in the room at one time with the auditors and auditees and body heat will tend to raise the temperature.

Physical Access

The degree of physical access needs to be defined in advance: What building? What times? Must the access be escorted? How long can they keep their badges? Some auditors will be using their own experiences with the badging process to evaluate the physical visitor, consultant, employee and contractor security controls. If the visitor log policy indicates that an individual is supposed to obtain a badge and sign out at the end of each day and this function is not required of the auditors, then this may result in an audit finding based upon the lack of control enforcement. Or, if the policy is that the auditor must be escorted and the auditor finds that during the course of the audit he was free to roam the building, this could also result in a finding.

Special auditor badges with predefined access and required to conform to a separate auditor visitor policy is recommended. Auditors generally work until the early evening hours or start early, so a 7 a.m. to 7 p.m. access policy would satisfy most auditor needs. As far as escorting, auditors are being entrusted with vast amounts of confidential information to perform an audit, so the risk of damage by allowing the auditors in the building without an escort is low. Auditors could be granted access badges that permit entry the week during their audit and be required to return the badges at the end of the fieldwork. Agreements with the auditors should be made that they will confine their activities to the conference rooms, restrooms, and break rooms without needing an escort, but if they need to visit other operational areas that they must have an escort. The escort would preferably be the audit coordinator or his or her designate.

Conference Phones

Ever been on a phone conference and someone is shuffling papers, having a conversation on a cell phone, or hear dogs barking in the background? We all have, and it does not help the subject matter being discussed. A good quality conference phone, such as a Polycom, should be placed in each conference room where interviews will be held. Since interviews generally involve geographically dispersed individuals or will involve someone calling in while traveling, there will need to be a phone for the conference. The speakerphones on office phones are not designed to handle a room of people between 4 and 8 feet away from the phone. A better setup is to have a conference phone with two microphones attached by 3- to 4-foot cords. The acoustics of the room should also be tested to ensure that outside, heating or air conditioning, or fan noise is not interfering with the sound quality level.

Schedule Entrance, Exit, Status Meetings

Entrance, exit, and status meetings should be scheduled at least a week in advance of the start of the audit, preferably 2 weeks or more, so that the appropriate management and technical staff can make themselves available to attend. Consideration should be given to those individuals who reside in different time zones, with the avoidance of a pre-8 a.m. meeting in any time zone if possible. Individuals should be at their best for the audit calls and for most staff this would be during their normal workday hours.

Set Up Interviews

As with the entrance, exit, and status meetings, as many interviews as possible should be scheduled prior to the start of the audit. The document request list provides the procedures, reports, samples, and other evidence, but does not have the element of human interaction and explanation of what is written in the documents. The interview provides the auditor with the opportunity to ask clarifying questions of the information provided. This also represents an opportunity to provide an overall big picture description of a control or management area. For example, the information security manager could provide an overview of access management or security administration and how user IDs and logins are obtained; the business continuity/disaster recovery manager could explain all of the activities involved in ensuring continuity of operations; or the human resources manager could explain how a new hire is on boarded into the organization with reference checks, background checks, confidentiality statements, and PeopleSoft human resource/payroll transactions. Potential overview areas to be scheduled are listed in Figure 11.5.

Interviews should be scheduled for 1 to 1.5 hours each with at least 30 minutes in between each interview to permit the auditors a chance to digest what they have heard and subsequently review their notes. They will also need time to prepare for the next interview. Generally,

MANAGERIAL	TECHNICAL	OPERATIONAL
• Overview of security function and IT organization (initial meeting) • Risk assessment • Systems security plans • Audit monitoring and issue tracking • Annual assessments • Security planning and program management	• Logical access • SDLC and change management • Network monitoring • Intrusion detection and incident response • Walkthroughs of logging, Security Information and Event Management (SIEM), and vulnerability management tools • Access recertification	• Human resources procedures • Physical access • Disaster recovery/business continuity planning • Business process walkthroughs • Data center walkthrough • Security awareness • Baseline configuration reviews • Asset management (software and hardware)

Figure 11.5 Potential security audit interview areas.

the interviews should be scheduled during the first week of a multi-week audit so that the appropriate understanding of the environment controls and processes are understood by the audit early on in the process. This can avoid sample pulls of the wrong information or invalid assumptions when evaluating the documents provided, leading to rework for both parties. Given these constraints, it is generally advisable to spread the interviews out during the first week, with no more than two scheduled for a morning or an afternoon. Afternoon or morning status meetings will also be scheduled during these days as well. Given that the first day is a travel day, many auditors will request that no more than one interview be scheduled the afternoon of the first day in addition to the entrance meeting. The status meeting is typically not scheduled on the first day, as there is nothing to report. The auditors also prefer this time to begin reviewing the document request list items.

Finally, it is also useful to create a spreadsheet to map the individuals to the date and time of the interview to ensure that there are no availability issues. It should also be noted whether that person is required to be physically present for the interview. There is usually more interaction with a face-to-face interview and more rapport is established with the auditor. At a minimum the primary point of contact should be present in the interview, with the secondary individuals available by phone. The audit coordinator should also be present in the interviews to monitor how the audit is performing as well as to initiate the conference calls, record the attendees, and continuously look for ways to improve the audit process.

Audit Execution Phase

The audit execution phase begins after the on-site arrival phase and continues until the end of the audit. Although the on-site arrival phase may last 1 to 4 weeks, the audit execution phase may extend several weeks or months past the on-site portion depending upon the scope of the audit. The extended time is necessary for off-site quality reviews by the audit firm. Even if the testing is completed during the on-site period, it may be several months before the draft, final draft, or final report is issued.

Additional Audit Meetings

With appropriate planning in scheduling the meetings, the meetings should flow from the entrance to the exit conference according to the schedule. Additional meetings will have to be scheduled as the auditor reviews the documents requested and performs tests of the audit plan. The security manager is best served by letting the auditor request these additional meetings, as they are only necessary if the auditor is having difficulty interpreting the information provided. In other words, volunteering to set up meetings to walk through every document requested when the auditor has not specifically requested the meeting only takes away from valuable audit time the auditor has to complete the audit. The auditor may have reviewed the information provided and decided that the evidence was sufficient and therefore needed no further explanation.

Establish Auditor Communication Protocol

Messages on the Internet get from person A to person B through a standard communications protocol. Teenage text messages are sent by understanding an agreed upon set of communications, some that make us LOL. To be really effective in working with the auditors to ensure that they have the right information, at the right place, at the right time, we need to establish an effective way of communicating. Failure to do so ends up with the auditor saying things like "I requested that information 5 days ago and haven't seen it," possibly evoking the response, "But we sent it to your team three times already." Who is right? At this point, it does not really matter, what matters is that the process of communication failed. At the end of the day, if the auditor does not receive the information requested during the audit time period, he cannot validate that the documented control is in place and working.

To increase the likelihood that the aforementioned scenario does not occur, the following activities should be agreed upon with the auditor no later than the first day of the audit. A good time to discuss this protocol is after the entrance meeting, between the audit coordinator and the lead auditor and the audit team.

- Track every information request from the auditor during the audit in a spreadsheet separate from the auditor document request list.
- Assign a unique number to each information request to enable tracking.
- Ensure during the audit that it is clear which information request referred to is being analyzed by referring to the tracking number.
- Implement a scheme (e.g., a, b, c, 01, 02, 03) to track follow-up requests for information already provided. This helps to keep the information organized together.
- Require the auditors to put all requests in writing and assign a number to ensure that it is clear what the auditor is requesting.
- Determine the number of times a day the auditor would like to receive outstanding requests. Limiting to once or twice a day unless there are many requests increases both auditor and auditee efficiency.
- Require that all incoming and outgoing requests go through the audit coordinator so that they can be tracked.

The net effect of these items is that all information is tracked and the status is immediately known. When the status meetings are held and the auditor and the audit coordinator have tracked the requests, they can be compared to see where the gaps are and reconciled. Accurate tracking by a central person avoids the he-said-she-said discussion, as well as creating the impression that the company is working diligently to ensure that the auditor has the information on a timely basis. From an economic perspective, it is just better business to have to request and furnish the information one time.

Establish Internal Company Protocol

Just as it is important to have a protocol established with the auditors, it is equally important that the following protocol is followed internally:

- All audit requests for additional information are sent only from the audit coordinator.
- All responses to requests for additional information are sent to the auditor from the audit coordinator.

- E-mail subject lines contain the year, audit name, tracking number, brief description of item to permit searching for requests.
- Information is placed in a directory related to the tracking number and a reply to the request from the audit coordinator from the person providing the information indicates that the information is complete and ready to be provided to the auditor.
- A protocol is established for moving the request from "completed status" to "sent to the auditor" by the audit coordinator.
- Audit requests are expected to be fulfilled within 24 hours (exceptions may be acceptable for items that must be retrieved from off site or other contractors/outsourced operations).

Figure 11.6 shows the flow of information from the initial request through fulfillment. By tracking each request in a spreadsheet and subsequently maintaining a tracking number throughout the process,

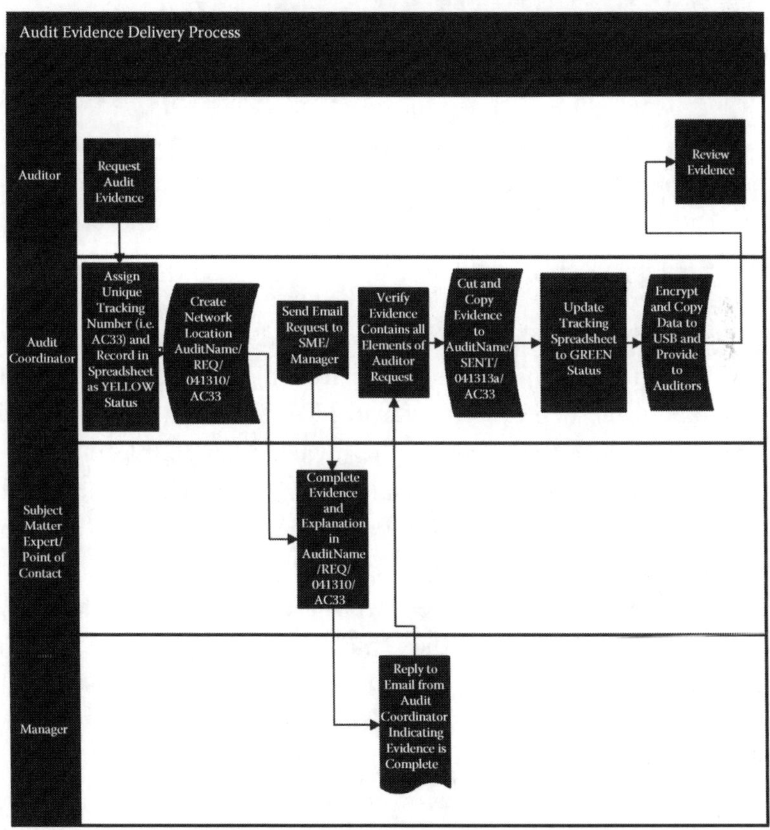

Figure 11.6 Information request flow.

information is less likely to be lost. As shown in the diagram, when the audit coordinator assigns the request, it is logged in a spreadsheet with a tracking number. The same number, in this case AC33, is used as the folder name under the directory REQ\041313 where 041313 is date the item was requested (April 13, 2013). Once the audit coordinator receives the e-mail response from the point of contact assigned to fulfill the request in the folder that the information is complete, he proceeds to move the folder to the SENT\[today's date] folder. He then provides this information to the auditor along with other items that are complete.

Using this method of SENT and REQ folders (1) provides a mechanism (a place) for the point of contact to place the items requested, and (2) provides knowledge that the information was subsequently provided to the auditor. The folder structure also serves as an additional validation of the tracking spreadsheet (e.g., no contents in the REQ folder indicate the request was completed).

Media Handling

The documents provided for the auditors' review during the course of an audit contain confidential information that could cause harm if disclosed outside the organization or beyond the audit firm. For this reason, all information provided to the auditors should be encrypted, preferably with a product that is FIPS 140-2 compliant. This greatly reduces the risk that this information will be disclosed during the useful life. Documents such as security plans, baseline configurations, script output, and firewall rules contain highly confidential information.

Media may be passed to the auditors on site by burning the information onto a CD or USB drive. In either case, it is not necessary to encrypt each file individually, but rather each submission to the auditor could be encrypted by encrypting the high level folder and all subdirectories. For example, the contents were copied to the \Security Audits\2013\SENT\041910a folder, where a equals the first submission of the day to the auditors, then this folder could be encrypted and the contents copied to a CD or USB drive.

Establishing a common password for the entire project makes the encryption process much easier and also increases the probability that after the audit files will be readable because one-time passwords may not be well documented. The password should be communicated to the team in a separate e-mail. The password should also be constructed as a strong password due to the nature of the audit artifacts that are being collected. A password comprised of at least eight characters (preferably ten), at least one uppercase, one lowercase, one numeric, and one special character should be sufficient. A password constructed in this way also tends to void the use of pet names, dictionary names, birthdays, and so forth.

It is not advisable to send the audit artifacts by e-mail, as the average user has a plethora of e-mails on a daily basis and tracking who sent what when and to whom becomes a challenge. As previously mentioned, the better approach is to use the e-mail system for the audit coordinator to distribute the requests to the points of contact, requesting that the audit artifacts be placed in the appropriate REQ\Date\ItemTrackingNo on the server for subsequent handling. These can be placed on the server in an unencrypted format, as the audit coordinator will encrypt the entire contents of the SENT\Date+suffix folder when the items are sent. It is also not uncommon for the size of many of these files or file collections to exceed the 10 MB range, which is typically a constraint imposed on the e-mails today.

It is to the company's advantage to provide as much information to the auditors while on site due to these files easily fitting on 16, 32, or 64 GB USB drives. Once the auditor has left the site, the files may have to be broken into 10 MB file sizes or less, the files encrypted, and multiple e-mails sent to the off-site auditors. This situation can be avoided by adequate preparation and confirmation that the auditors have received all of the required documents during the status meetings and the site exit meeting. The file size may be so large (>100 MB) that it only makes sense to burn this information to a CD or copy to a USB and send it via overnight mail. This is not desirable, as there are still delays for the auditor in receiving the information, plus this adds unnecessary expense in having to provide rework. Some audit firms have secure FTP servers, and to avoid the necessity of validating the security of that environment, the audit coordinator could view the FTP transmission as that of being over an open network (even if it is encrypted), and subsequently still encrypt the file folder containing the audit evidence before FTPing the file. In this manner, the information is sure to meet the security requirements of the audited organization.

Audit Coordinator Quality Review

The point of contacts or subject matter experts that are supplying the information are in the best position to ascertain whether they are meeting the audit request, as they are the ones that are closest to the business process. The audit coordinator still needs to briefly review the information provided to the auditors as a second look to catch errors such as those similar to those previously noted in reviewing the initial document request list. Given that it may take an overnight process to extract requested information, and the auditors may not review the information provided immediately, it behooves the organization to provide the information requested correctly the first time. The QA process works to ensure completeness of the response.

The Interview Itself

Auditees are expected to answer questions truthfully and failure to do so may constitute obstruction of a federal audit with U.S.-government-initiated audits, or constitute a company or industry ethics violation. Audits are intended to improve the organization's control environment, and lying or misrepresenting the facts would serve little purpose and not lead to making needed improvements in processes that would be identified by the audits.

With truthfulness as the foundation for the audit, the auditee respondent should only answer the questions that are asked. Providing details outside of the request not only wastes the auditors time with fluff that may be irrelevant to the testing the auditor is performing, but it may also expose other areas of vulnerability that are beyond the scope of the audit. Some auditors are known for going on fishing expeditions, whereby they may ask, "I have just one more question," a line made famous by the TV show *Columbo*, which originally aired in the 1970s. This line of questioning is primarily intended to reveal a flaw within the system by poking around. So why would we not want to know all the areas where we have issues? The answer is not so much that we do not want to know, but rather we want to be on a fair playing field with our competitors. Say, for example, that our firm is being audited for Payment Card Industry Data Security Standard (PCIDSS) compliance by a qualified auditor or our contractual requirements mandates that a Statement on Auditing Standards, No. 70 (SAS 70, PCAOB, n.d.) be performed to get the business, we would want to be evaluated based upon an audit program that our competitors are being evaluated against. Therefore, it is important that individuals that are selected for interview are able to answer the questions posed by the auditors, but not so verbose that they start talking about unrelated items or bring up other vulnerabilities outside of the scope of the audit. Most people are proud of their work and want to talk about it with whoever will listen. An audit interview, outside of the interview sections where overviews of the processes are provided, is not the time to explain all the details of a process unless requested by the auditor.

Mock interview sessions are advantageous for those individuals that have not been involved in an audit before, as well as a refresher for those who engaged in them infrequently. In a mock interview, an individual can portray the auditor, asking a series of questions requesting evidence that a control activity was performed. This can help put the interviewee more at ease during the audit. The mock interview may also trigger additional information request ideas that were previously missed to support the organization's control position.

Entrance, Exit, and Status Conferences

The entrance, exit, and status conferences are scheduled throughout the audit and provide the essential information to the various stakeholders to keep the audit on track. The worst-case scenario is to get to the end of an audit and have a list of findings that were not previously discussed. At this point the opportunity is lost to provide more information that may have cleared the issue, leading the more expensive process to tracking the issue, reporting evidence demonstrating that the proper controls were in place, and subsequently obtaining agreement on closure of the issue.

Entrance Meeting

The audit entrance meeting provides the opportunity to ensure that the organization knows the audit scope, expectations, and key dates. The entrance meeting is often scheduled late Monday morning to early afternoon to allow for traveling. Auditors generally travel Sunday night to Thursday evening or Monday morning to Friday evening to provide for some balance since on-site auditors for Big Four accounting firms are traveling 80% to 100% of the time depending upon the contracts. Hopefully the audit coordinator has communicated as much as possible to the organization prior to the arrival of the entrance meeting, because the preparation activities as previously mentioned needed to ensure that the documentation would be available for the entrance meeting. Some auditors will request that the documentation request list be provided as soon as possible, sometimes ahead of the entrance meeting, however, as is more often the case, the auditors tend to start looking at the materials after the entrance meeting has begun. Why? Because their time is usually fully committed to a prior client the weeks preceding this engagement. As a result, there is limited time to look at the files that are provided to them, and most auditors will agree that receiving the files the day they are on site will give them plenty to keep busy. In addition, this also provides more time to ensure that the document request list has been adequately prepared, reviewed, and QAed prior to providing to the auditors. The exception to this may be when scripts are requested to be run against infrastructure devices, such as Unix/Windows servers, firewalls, routers, and the output is needed for them to begin their analysis.

Senior management should be invited to the entrance meeting so that they are aware of the scope and timeline of the audit. All managers who have a role in providing information, attending interviews, or providing staff should also be included. Depending upon the organization, it generally does not hurt to encourage everyone that has a key role in providing information to the auditors to attend as well. The entrance call is scheduled for 30 minutes to 1 hour, however, in practice the call is normally 10 to 15 minutes as there is not much to discuss at this point. The scope has been agreed to per prior audit engagement contracts or conversations and should not be a surprise at this juncture. The meeting is more of a formality to kickoff the audit project and answer any questions that need to be clarified.

From an organization's point of view, the audit entrance meeting should not be considered complete if there are still lingering questions regarding (1) audit scope, (2) timing of fieldwork, (3) delivery dates of the draft and final reports (may be approximate), (4) documentation requested, (5) samples that will be requested, and (6) departments that must be involved. Failure to have an understanding of any of these items by this point can lead to unnecessary confusion.

Exit Meeting

An audit may have multiple exit meetings depending upon the duration of the audit. If the audit involves on-site fieldwork of several weeks, but the audit itself takes several months to complete, the auditors may hold a site exit meeting to reaffirm the results of their fieldwork, while scheduling a formal exit conference at the end of their analysis and prior to issuance of the audit report. The purpose of the exit meeting is to signal either the end of the audit activities and ensure that both the auditor and auditee come away with the same understanding. These are usually scheduled in late morning or midday on the final day of the audit, again permitting auditor cleanup and travel time in the afternoon.

Status Meetings

Status meetings provide a more frequent opportunity for the auditor and the auditee to ensure that there are no surprises or misunderstandings at the exit conference. Knowing what issues the auditors are facing early in the process provides an opportunity to provide other documentation that may better answer the auditors' request or permit further dialogue to clarify the control in question. It also provides the opportunity for the audit coordinator to validate that the auditor has received the information requested and the information provided was satisfactory.

Some organizations prefer a daily status meeting; however, in practice, if the audit coordinator is communicating on a frequent basis with the auditor, a formal meeting every other day should be sufficient. These are scheduled near the end of the normal workday (4 p.m. or 4:30 p.m.) for 30 minutes so that other management staff can call in. This is true even if the auditors may be working until 6 or 7 p.m. to ensure the most attendance possible. The meetings should be focused on what observations, gaps, or findings have been noted or what documentation has been requested and is still outstanding. An agenda and updated document request list should be provided by the auditor in advance of each status update meeting to ensure that the conversation is focused on the important issues.

Report Issuance and Finding Remediation Phase

All control deficiencies should be known and communicated by the exit conference. If for some reason testing could not be completed, there could be additional deficiencies noted after the auditors have left the site. If this is the case, for reasons mentioned in the media handling section, this complicates the audit and should be avoided. Proactive inquiry of the auditors to ensure they have all the necessary information, especially by the start of the last week of the audit, should be done. The auditors should be focused on completing their work papers the last week of the audit versus performing additional testing. This usually occurs because of disagreement in earlier testing or the selection of a new sample that was deemed insufficient (e.g., population was assumed to be employees and contractors, but only employees were provided).

At the exit conference, the auditor should provide a listing of control deficiencies (also referred to as gaps, observations, exceptions, or findings, depending upon the nomenclature used by the auditor). These might end up as findings on the final report. Auditors might have to evaluate the findings with other organizations that have been included in the scope of the audit. For example, for a chief financial officer's audit contracted by the federal government, the audit firm may wait until it has been to all the sites to ensure that it has been consistent in its approach and fair to each contractor. Another reason for not receiving the findings at the exit conference is that further peer reviews may need to be performed, or the senior partners may need to review the work papers containing the audit testing and evidence collected.

A draft report is subsequently issued with the findings. There should be no surprises if the audit team and the organization have worked together. Usually when surprises end up on the report, it is the result of (1) lack of clear communicating in the beginning as to what conditions would create a finding, (2) a prior issue was surfaced but not communicated that it was a finding, (3) documentation requested were not provided, (4) misunderstanding that an earlier agreement was or was not reached when discussing a gap, or (5) the auditor held the issue to the end to avoid confrontation. In my experience through many audits, number 5 does occur, but usually one of the other items is the primary reason for surprises. Surprises should be left for birthdays and holidays and not audit findings.

Once the draft report is received by the organization from the auditor, the auditee has 5 to 10 business days to provide a response. The response provides the auditee an opportunity to agree or disagree to the audit finding and explain why. These comments are included in the reissued draft report, which should be issued 5 to 10 days after receipt of the auditee's comments. If the organization agrees with the finding, it is best to also note a corrective action plan (CAP) at this time. The corrective action plan explains at a high level what will be done to mitigate the deficiency and when this will be completed. The CAP will need to be submitted within 30 days after the final report is reissued with the auditee comments, so if there is agreement, this may as well be included in the draft report. This provides the reader who is not so familiar with the audit an early understanding as to what steps will be taken.

The final report issuance varies by audit firm and the contractual requirements. Internal review of the draft report and work papers adds off-site time after the fieldwork to ensure the audit report is accurate. Sometimes this process can take months between the issuance of the draft and the final report. Firms that are security conscious will not wait for the final report to begin action on the issues. CAPs are typically due within 30 days after final report issuance, and it is preferable to mitigate the vulnerability within 90 days from the cap due date. Obviously, long security implementations will be the exception but should not be the rule. Ninety days should be sufficient for mitigating most vulnerabilities given the appropriate priority. Each of the CAPs should be tracked to ensure that the person responsible is completing the milestones and the target date is still on track. As the CAPS are completed, the audit artifacts including changed processes, reports, project plans, and evidence of implementation should be retained to provide to the auditor for next year's review. The auditor will then take these items and use them as partial evidence to close the finding.

Suggested Reading

1. U.S. Government Accountability Office. February 2009. GAO Federal Information Systems Controls Audit Manual (FISCAM). http://www.gao.gov/special.pubs/fiscam.html
2. Public Company Accounting Oversight Board. Auditing standards, http://pcaobus.org/Standards/Auditing/Pages/default.aspx

12
EFFECTIVE SECURITY COMMUNICATIONS

> The meeting of two personalities is like the contact of two chemical substances: if there is any reaction, both are transformed.
>
> **Carl Gustav Jung, 1875–1961**

Why a Chapter Dedicated to Security Communications?

If the phrase *security communications* conjures thoughts of the network, protocols, blocking, terminating communications, ensuring messages get from point A to point B intact, and must be available 24/7, you are correct. However, the topic is not about computer communications but rather human communications. Information security governance depends upon humans to deliver the right message to the right individuals at the right time in the right manner for the messages to be heard and acted upon.

Imagine for a moment that the information security department creates a plethora of security policies representing the equivalent of creating the Mona Lisa to an artist or creating a team of athletes that wins the Super Bowl. Imagine then that what would have happened if no one had ever seen the Mona Lisa that was stored in an attic or the team that was capable of winning the Super Bowl never showed up for its games? A similar fate can fall upon the information security program if information security policies, ideas, and initiatives are not properly communicated. True information security governance may look good on paper, with policies drafted and technical solutions appearing to be in place, but if these are not communicated properly, security governance is really not occurring.

Security communication takes on many forms such as the publishing of information security policies, selling the next information investment to management, explaining the current status of security audit issues to the board of directors, crafting security e-mail messages of the latest security concerns, or simply having a conversation about a security issue with a security colleague or business unit manager. It should be clear that every communication by every individual associated with the information security team has the potential to either (a) provide increased credibility and support to the information security program or (b) cause the information security area to be viewed as a roadblock or lessen trust that the security group has the organization's best interests front and center.

Communication skills are constantly evaluated as we are growing up—from formal penmanship, written communication skills, listening skills, plays well with others, and speaks up when called upon as a child to the formal performance reviews where written and oral communication skill competencies are evaluated on an annual basis. The continuous evaluation of these skills indicates the importance of them. After all, how effective can we be in the workplace if we cannot effectively communicate with others? Hence, due to this importance, this chapter is dedicated toward how security professionals can improve their communication skills to convey the appropriate security messages throughout the organization. Different aspects of communication are explored and by understanding the different communication styles that are occurring within the company, the security executive and professional can be more effective in constructing and delivering the appropriate message.

End User Security Awareness Training

One of the debates over the past decade has been whether information security awareness training has been effective. Much of this concern is generally started from an analysis of the number of security incidents in a given year and then concluding whether the end users were receiving the message and acting in a secure manner in their day-to-day jobs. The conclusion then usually suggests that technical controls need to be implemented to take out the risk of "human error." Unfortunately, these conclusions are made without the benefit of a scientifically controlled experiment, whereby the "test group" of users of the same organization received no security awareness training were evaluated against a "control group" in order to determine whether there would have been more or fewer incidents experienced by the control group. Obviously, technical controls are very important to the information security program, and are necessary to address the aspects such as antivirus, encryption, firewalls, security mechanisms, physical security, authentication, and monitoring, but given that technical controls cannot fully address the end-user behaviors, security awareness training must be in place to reduce the risk. Information also comes in nontechnical forms (oral and paper documents) that cannot be secured by technical means or without the diligence and assistance of the end user. For example, a policy may state that all documents transported between the office and home need to be transported in a locked container. If the end user is not aware of the policy or does not understand the rationale for the policy, she might decide it is not necessary and not place the documents in a locked box. Alternatively, an individual may load boxes of documents in his car in the wintertime, leaving the engine running to keep it warm while hr runs back into the house to retrieve more boxes for loading. Meanwhile, the end user may be taking an increased risk that the car will be stolen and the confidential documents exposed. Since there are no technical controls to prevent this (other than the end user locking the door in between trips), security needs to be continuously reinforced with the end user to reduce the risk of this type of error.

Awareness Definition

Security awareness training is different from security training. The National Institute of Standards and Technology Special Publication 800-50: Building an Information Security Technology Security Awareness and Training Program (NIST, 2003) provides the following definition:

> Awareness is not training. The purpose of awareness presentations is simply to focus attention on security. Awareness presentations are intended to allow individuals to recognize IT security concerns and respond accordingly. In awareness activities, the learner is the recipient of information, whereas the learner in a training environment has a more active role. Awareness relies on reaching broad audiences with attractive packaging techniques. Training is more formal, having a goal of building knowledge and skills to facilitate job performance.

In short, the basic objective of security awareness training is to (1) provide enough information to the end users as to what they and others should and should not do and recognize what would constitute a security incident, and (2) know what they should do if they recognize or suspect that a security incident has occurred. If these two objectives have been met, then the information security awareness program has been successful.

Delivering the Message

Information security programs fall short of the message when the security message is not crafted in a manner that grabs the end users' attention or fails to provide them with the necessary information. Let's face it, many security people progressed to higher levels within the organization due to their technical abilities, not based upon their communication or marketing skills. Providing information security awareness is essentially marketing—inducing the recipient of the message to buy something (in this case buy into) what they ordinarily may not have thought to buy on their own. Savvy marketers craft the message not in pages of boring technical, jargon-filled presentations, but rather in short, high-impact, sound-bite type messages that grab our attention and are retained. Security professionals must do the same. The following seven steps, adapted from NIST security awareness guidance, provide a process for delivering an effective information security program.

Step 1: Security Awareness Needs Assessment

Assessing security awareness is often an overlooked step when first implementing a security awareness program. Without knowing where the highest risk areas or areas that have been causing the most incidents are, valuable time with the end users could be wasted. The needs can be determined from multiple sources, as described next.

New or Changed Policies If the organization is rolling out a new identity management system or a new incident reporting process, this may be a good time to explain how this will work. Or a new law or regulation could mandate new reporting requirements that would need to be communicated.

Past Security Incidents Past breaches can provide a wealth of information from which to construct the security awareness program. These are also very useful in obtaining the end users' attention, as it demonstrates that security issues are occurring within their organization versus a theoretical concept that "this could happen." It also reduces the likelihood that the end user will think that the security department is sensationalizing the news. Care should be taken when presenting actual incidents within the company that it is not possible for the end users to deduce the person or in which department that the individual was working. This could cause some ethical and legal issues in disclosing personal human resource issues. The objective is to explain the incident so that the same type of incident does not reoccur through someone else's behavior. Incidents of the same type that have a high number of occurrences would be excellent candidates for targeted security awareness training.

Systems Security Plans Systems security plans (SSPs) document the current state of an information security system and can take the form of a major application (MA) or general support system (GSS). Since these plans define the overall business objective of the system, the infrastructure, and the managerial, technical, and operational controls required to support the system, these documents can provide excellent sources of the types of information that needs to be shared with the end users. For example, if there are many business partners that are part of the infrastructure, the end users may need to be made aware of which email communications are secure or what is permissible to discuss with the business partner due to intellectual property rights that are defined in the systems security plan.

Audit Findings and Recommendations If there are recurring audit issues that have not been mitigated, these should be included in the security awareness training. Since auditors cannot audit 100% of everything, samples are taken that represent a statistical significance if an issue is found. The issues found may or may not have occurred across every department; however, that does not mean that the issue is not broader than the audit issue found. For example, the auditors may pull a sample of policies and procedures and determine that they have not been updated on an annual basis for a couple of departments.

Odds are, just as when a pest exterminator sees one mouse, there are likely to be many more, so is it likely that other areas have not been following the process of annual updates. Typically these are issues of security governance across the organization; the tone at the top has not made this a priority or there have not been the processes in place to monitor and ensure this is completed on an annual basis. Repeat audit issues should always be addressed either to a targeted group or broadly across the organization, depending upon the issue.

Event Analysis Similar to security incidents, event analysis of the monitoring logs can highlight areas of concern. These are likely to evolve into targeted training more than security awareness training. For example, logs indicating that firewall vulnerability is repeatedly being exploited by external hackers may indicate the need to train the network group on device configurations.

Industry Trends Introduction of new technology into the marketplace can provide a rich source for discussion. Discussing the use of social media in the workplace, such as Facebook, LinkedIn, or Myspace will provide relevant discussion of issues that most end users can relate to. Alternatively a discussion of the use (or nonuse) of personal e-mail and the acceptable use policy to govern appropriate Internet behavior will be of interest to the end users. The security officer has to keep abreast of the current industry trends to ensure that the risks are mitigated, as new technologies are often released first and then security controls are added second. The reality of this situation is that products are usually in a race to become the first to capture market share and may not have implemented the necessary security controls. As an example, consider the evolution of the Windows operating system and how it took almost nine releases over a period of more than two decades to build-in many of the security concepts that are expected today.

Management Concerns Managers should be polled to determine what issues they are aware of that need more focus. They may be concerned with documents not being properly disposed or laptops not being put away at the end of the day or securely transported.

Organizational Changes After reorganizations, employees are oftentimes reporting to a new manager that may operate differently. This is a good time to reinforce the security concepts. Locations may have closed during the reorganizations or whole departments eliminated, thus creating potential changes in the security procedures.

Step 2: Program Design

Communications can either happen through the best intentions or be designed. By approaching the security awareness program as something that must be designed, the chances of leaving out critical components are lessened. A car would not be produced without a design; a TV show would not be delivered without a script to guide the flow of the contents.

Target Audience A cliché in providing presentations is to know your audience. The security awareness presentation delivered to a group of airline mechanics may be different than to a group of customer service representatives. The analogies or stories used in the presentation to connect with the audience may be different. For example, relating the information security concepts of physical protection to ensure that no unauthorized people are in the hangar that could cause loss of life by tampering with the airplane engine parts may be effective with the airline mechanics. The customer service representatives may relate to the importance of verifying the caller with identifying information so as to not release confidential information to the wrong person. Alternatively, talking about sending faxes to the wrong healthcare provider would have little relevance to the airline mechanics.

Frequency of Sessions Security awareness training should be performed minimally once a year and preferably during a time in the business cycle that will not cause an increased burden in meeting the company objectives. For example, having a training session for a group of accountants at fiscal yearend or right before tax season would not be welcomed. If face-to-face sessions are used, scheduling of the sessions needs to be planned so that there is ample time for individuals to plan the training into their schedules.

Number of Users Face-to-face sessions work best when the number is kept to 30 or less. A group of this size allows for interaction and more exchange of information between the participants. Schedules should be drawn up 6 to 8 weeks in advance of the training to ensure the greatest attendance and to obtain the appropriate facilities.

Method of Delivery Face-to-face sessions work best, however, these are also time consuming, as multiple sessions are needed to cover the workforce in groups of 25 to 30 people. The security officer and his staff have to dedicate significant resources to this task, especially if the associates are spread out across multiple locations. As a result of cost reductions, some security departments have gravitated to online learning management systems to deliver PowerPoint-type contact to the end user. The difficulty with this approach is that users may simply click through the material without providing their full attention, which is much harder to do in an interactive security awareness session. Even though quizzes can be incorporated into the material to determine whether the end user was paying attention, it is difficult to ascertain if the end user was truly engaged. The more engaged the participants in the learning process, the greater the likelihood that the material will be retained.

Resources Required The labor, materials, locations, and budget required for the program need to be reviewed. At this stage the full costs may not be known, however, the budget parameters should be determined. It would not be unreasonable to spend 1% to 2% of the information security budget on security awareness training and a greater percentage on a small budget.

Step 3: Develop Scope

The security awareness program must be scoped or there is a risk that the message will be lost in delivering the training. Scoping utilizes the needs assessment captured in step 1 and determines what topics are provided.

Determine Participants Needing Training Once the scope of the training has been initially defined, the population that is required to attend or participate in the training needs to be defined. Depending upon the company desire or the law or regulation, all employees, including contractors requiring systems access may be subject to the training. If a subcontractor relationship exists with another firm that is performing work on the organization's behalf, then it should be determined whether the subcontractor should provide its own security awareness training (as the subcontractors are employees or contracted to that firm) or should the company that hired the subcontractor require the security awareness training provided to its own employees.

New hires present a special situation that must be addressed. The organization may require annual refresher training for the existing employees and contractors, but the new hires also need the security awareness training from day one. New hires should not be allowed access to the system until they have had some form of security awareness training. One technique that is very effective is to have the hiring manager provide security awareness training to the employee (e.g., in the form of a PowerPoint presentation); have the employee sign an attestation that they have read the security requirements, understand them, and will abide by them; and have the manager fax or e-mail the signed copy to the security administration or access management department or whichever department is responsible for account establishment. Once the fax or e-mail is received, then the department can release the login ID and password to the manager to provide to the employee. The employee would then log on and change the one-time password. In this manner, the new hire has the appropriate onboarding security awareness training that may not line up with the scheduled annual awareness training, which they would take during the next cycle with everyone else.

Business Units Security awareness training is generally developed for the current cycle (i.e., annual training) and provided to everyone in the organization. However, there may be special situations where the training is customized to a particular department because of different concerns.

Select Theme One of the most important aspects in designing a security awareness program is to select a theme for the training. A list of themes is shown in Table 12.1. This helps to focus the training around a subject and keeps the scope from drifting. Selecting a theme does not limit the creativeness of the training, but rather permits

Table 12.1 Security Awareness Themes

Appropriate Internet usage	Viruses, worms, Trojans, malicious code	Spyware	Phishing attacks
E-mail security	Identity Theft	Confidentiality, information sensitivity	Spam
Social engineering	Incidents and incident response	Shoulder surfing	Government regulations
Wireless security	Tablet computing	Smartphones	Laptop security
Copyright protections and licensing	Need-to-know access	Individual security responsibility	Password management
E-mail etiquette	Clean desk policy	Home network usage	Protecting yourself and your company in a disaster
Handling of protected health information or credit card data	Latest information security events in the news	What is risk?	Obtaining access to information

the designer to build the program around a common concept while introducing other security-related items into the program. For example, while constructing a security awareness training program using the theme "Internet and E-mail Security," the concepts of antivirus, confidentiality, non-sharing of passwords, encryption, phishing, and website malware can be introduced into the training.

The common mistake is that the fire hose method of security awareness education is used, and all possible aspects of security are communicated during a 1 to 2 hour presentation or during a webinar. The end users eyes glaze over and little is retained other than "be sure to not let someone piggyback behind you when walking in the building" or "hit CTL–ALT–DELETE and Lock when stepping away from the computer." The themed approach avoids this scenario.

Step 4: Content Development

Once the theme is chosen for the security awareness training, the content should be developed to be as impactful as possible to achieve the highest retention rate after training. Face-to-face training affords the ability to combine video, music, props, and attendee interaction to create an unforgettable learning environment (versus the two-dimensional Internet training delivery mechanisms). Game shows, use of online videos, and interactive skits to grab the participants' attention work very well. Once the security awareness training grabs attendees' attention, it is not uncommon to see that people enjoy coming to the sessions and are the first ones to sign up in subsequent years.

Security awareness should be fun! One of the first places to start to build the security training session is to go to the toy store and the party store to buy some toys. As silly as this may sound, when people walk into the room feeling like they are about to play a game, their mood changes from "Is this going to be another boring security PowerPoint presentation?" to one of "Hey, this looks like fun!" Their curiosity takes over and as a result, they are more likely to pay attention.

Security is a serious subject, but that does not mean that it has to be presented that way to be impactful. If the security professional is uncomfortable with giving presentations that appear silly or humorous, then another possibility is to enlist someone from corporate communications or marketing for support. Imagine being in the place of the end user that is required to attend mandatory awareness training. Programs should be constructed in such a manner that the end-user wants to attend the security awareness training.

Step 5: Communication and Logistics Plan

A one-page slide announcing the theme of the program should be developed as well as posters indicating the dates of the program. If multiple locations are part of the program, the poster could look something analogous to rock concert tour dates to generate interest.

E-mails to the end users at least 1 month prior to the awareness session should be mailed, along with follow-up reminders at 2- and 1-week intervals. People are often very busy and may appreciate the e-mail reminders to sign up for the awareness session. Provisions for make-up signups should also be planned by scheduling one or two make-up sessions after the regular sessions have concluded. The e-mail reminders should stress promptness in attending the sessions.

Each location should have signup sheets for the session to ensure that sessions are appropriately filled and do not exceed the size of the room. A good rule of thumb is to only have enough signups for five less than the capacity of the session. For example, if the room will comfortably seat 30 people in the session, then permit 25 to sign up. Why? Because there will always be some individuals that will add their names below the line exceeding the capacity. This can cause problems if tables and exercises were set up for a group size of 25, but 30 show up. By planning for a maximum of 30 people, and allowing 25 to sign up with a 5-person contingency, there would be no problem if 30 people showed up.

Travel arrangements to the various sites are also determined in this step, making reservations at least 30 to 60 days in advance to reduce the costs of the program.

Step 6: Awareness Delivery

Details at this stage are very critical, as the security awareness session should be managed as a production with contingencies for items that may go wrong. The trainer should arrive at the room location at least 1 hour before the start of the session so that the room can be set up in advance of people arriving for the first session. Items such as visual props, table arrangements, candy or food, evaluation sheets, and presentation copies need to be arranged around the room. The LCD projector and computer need to be tested to ensure the video, audio, and presentation operation are working correctly.

Sessions should be no more than 1 hour, as the attention span starts to fade after 45 to 60 minutes. Sessions should also be scheduled 30 minutes apart to allow for (a) those individuals that arrive early to "get a good seat," (b) those individuals that stay after the last session to ask one-on-one questions, and (c) set up for the next session. The trainer should be available at the start of each session to greet each person as they enter the room, and if the trainer is still running around setting up tables, projectors, and props, he or she will not be available. Greeting each person helps to make the program personable and starts the connection process, which increases the likelihood the individual will pay more attention.

The delivery should be scripted, but be spontaneous at the same time. Each subsequent delivery can incorporate what worked and remove what did not work in the prior sessions.

Sessions should start 5 minutes after the posted start time of the session and end 5 minutes prior to the end. Starting 5 minutes into the session accounts for the latecomers that would miss the start of the session. In high school, students have 5 minutes to get to their next class, but once people get into the work world, they are faced with back-to-back meetings with no built-in travel time. Ending 5 minutes early provides time for them to fill out the evaluations.

Step 7: Evaluation/Feedback Loops

Evaluations provide insight into what is and is not working with the security awareness program. The quality adage "If you can't measure it, you can't improve it" applies to information security as well. Did the end users enjoy the training? Did they learn what was expected? Was there anything that could have been improved (content, logistics, delivery, understanding, etc.)?

One method that is highly successful is to provide a trade of sorts, or an exchange, at the door as the attendees are leaving, exchanging a security trinket for an evaluation. They may place the evaluation facedown in the chair, but they do not receive the trinket unless they provide an evaluation. A small percentage will be blank; however this technique usually results in 95% to 100% return of the evaluations.

The evaluations can then be tracked in a database by location, and assessments of the training can be performed. Numerical scores are tabulated (e.g., 4 out of 5 on a 5-point scale) and open-ended question responses are recorded. Quizzes several months after the training can be issued to determine whether the preceding training was effective.

Security Awareness Training Does Not Have to Be Boring

By injecting some creativity into the security awareness program, the training can be fun for the participants and fun for the creators. As a side benefit, engaging security professionals where this is not their daily role can broaden their own interpersonal and communication skills. The approach demonstrated in the aforementioned seven steps aides in the understanding and retention of the security message, which is the primary goal of creating a fun security awareness program.

Targeted Security Training

Security awareness training provides the broad security training that is sufficient for most of the organization. However, to ensure that the proper skills are retained by the organization to carry out the implementation of the security policies, targeted training needs to be developed for certain groups, primarily those individuals managing others and those who are directly involved in an information security function.

Security administrators need targeted training in areas such as Microsoft Active Directory, Resource Access Control Facility (RACF), Access Control Facility (AC2), and UNIX administration to be able to set up and administer accounts correctly. Depending upon the level of the staff and the expectations, the depth of the training may vary. For example, the security administrator that is setting up accounts may need training on how to use the identity management system but not necessarily the technical details of Active Directory. On the other hand, the security analyst who is responsible for building automated queries and processes may need a seminar in Active Directory. Information security governance cannot occur if individuals are not competent within their assigned jobs. This does not mean that everyone needs the 5-day class, where a PowerPoint or 2-hour hands-on training session may suffice.

Managers of employees and contractors typically require additional training, usually an hour or less PowerPoint or learning management system–type course to address issues such as access authorization using the identity management system and the handling on on-boarding and terminations. During the on-boarding process, security awareness training, ensuring that background checks are completed, and providing the new hires initial access are subjects that may be covered. When the employee or contractor is terminated, the manager usually has some responsibility to enter information into the system and collect physical property such as badges, credit cards, laptops, and tokens. Communicating these requirements through training can reduce the risk that these activities are not occurring and increasing the exposure to the systems after the employee leaves the company.

There are also specialized types of training depending upon the department that may need to occur, such as training of the handling of a customer care application, data center operations, and emergency response training. Not everyone in the organization would need to do what is required in the event of an emergency in the data center, such as a fire, however, the computer operators would need to know what to do to protect the data center and minimize the loss as well as how to safely evacuate.

Continuous Security Reminders

A daily e-mail from the help desk explaining the latest security incident would cause most users to set up an e-mail filter to move this type of e-mail to the delete bucket. A balance of the security message must be achieved whereby when the users see an information security message, they are likely to read it and act upon it accordingly.

E-mails of the latest incidents as applied to the organization can be very beneficial, especially if employees can relate to the issues in their own home environment. The breach involving Epsilon in 2011 where there was an exposure to the e-mail accounts of millions of customers to firms such as Chase, Citigroup, and Verizon, caused e-mail messages to be spammed and appeared to be coming from these organizations. This represented a great opportunity for organizations to communicate what was occurring and educate the end users about protecting their accounts. Since this occurred to many users as part of their personal computer involvement outside of work, this also has a side benefit of demonstrating the organization's caring for the associate. These opportunities should be leveraged, which increase the likelihood of compliance to the security policies.

Utilize Multiple Security Awareness Vehicles

The potential avenues for security communication can fill a book by themselves. Some of the avenues for communication include

- Company newsletters
- Posters
- Learning management system online presentations
- Brown bag lunches
- Links on corporate intranet sites
- Weekly e-mails
- Logon page or scrolling marquee messages
- Hosting a "security day"
- Monthly, short three- to five-page presentations
- Online quizzes
- Online "scavenger hunts"
- Security contests

Each of these methods should be considered as supplemental to the classroom-type training that is delivered face-to-face in person annually. Posters should also be used sparingly and typically in support of a specific security awareness campaign. Posters that utilize slogans tend to have limited lasting power beyond the campaign period. Posters can serve as a great advertisement for ongoing online training or classroom training, but by themselves have limited value. If posters are used, care should be taken to track where the posters have been displayed so that they can be removed in a timely manner. The messages should be impactful and address different security concerns beyond the "don't share your password" type of message. Relating the security message back to how implementing security controls serves to protect the information for the customers that entrust their information to us can be very impactful.

Security Officer Communication Skills

As discussed in Chapter 3 on Defining the Security Management Organization and also in Chapter 4 on Interacting with the C-Suite, the security officer must be able to interact with multiple levels of management. Oftentimes when employees respond to the first survey that an organization issues on employee satisfaction, a frequent issue that surfaces is lack of communication. What does this really mean? That the associate did not feel listened to? That their ideas were not acted upon? That there was not an avenue to provide input? That the manager or supervisor was not sharing relevant news in a timely manner? It could be any one or more of those items or something else.

The security officer must be able to communicate with individuals in different levels of the organizational hierarchy, from the board of directors to the end users and everywhere in between. There are different personalities that must be communicated with, different styles of working and different ways that people deliver, receive, and process information. The subsequent techniques can improve the ability of the security officer or any security professional to communicate with others.

Talking versus Listening

Many people appear to believe that they are best communicating when they are talking, however, when we are listening and the other person feels that he or she has been heard, our ability to communicate is much greater. Unfortunately, we block ourselves from effective listening by not paying full attention to the person speaking. Those who are good listeners tend to draw other people to them; people confide in them and they become a trusted member of the team. By not listening, it sends the message that what they have to say is not very important. Critical information is then missed and opportunities to demonstrate that the person is cared about is also missed. True listening involves providing our full attention.

Roadblocks to Effective Listening

There are 12 roadblocks that get in our way of effective listening, that make it hard for us to truly listen to what the other person is saying (McKay, 1995). Because listening is so crucial in communications, we should continuously be aware of our behavior when another person is speaking.

1. *Comparing*—While the other person is talking, you are trying to determine if you have had that situation before, and was it worse or not. They may be talking about an issue that you have had before, and the thought is running though your mind, "Hey, it isn't that tough to complete that, why are they having a problem." By comparing, it is difficult to listen to what their problem is, as the mind is busy analyzing our own past experiences.
2. *Mind reading*—Instead of focusing on what the person is saying, the listener is focused on trying to understand the meaning behind what they are saying and interpret what different situation is driving the comments. For example, they may be saying "I have worked long hours to review these security violation reports, and I am tired of reworking them," while the listener is thinking, "Oh, they just had a long day because they are going to school in the evenings and are probably just tired." This may not be the case at all, and in fact the real issue is that the rework is preventing other work from being performed.
3. *Rehearsing*—The mind is too busy thinking of what the listener will say next, that they are not focusing on the message

that is being delivered. In this case, the listener "appears" to be interested in what is being said.

4. *Filtering*—The listener listens just long enough to hear whether the person is angry, unhappy, or in danger. Once the emotion is determined, then the listening stops and focuses on other activities or plans that the person is thinking about. The listener only hears half of what is being said.
5. *Judging*—Judging occurs when someone is prejudged before they even start talking. A negative label is placed on the person who devalues what they may have to say. If the person is seen as unqualified, incompetent, or lacking necessary skills by the listener, they may discount what they have to say. This causes insights to be missed that could provide valuable insight to the solution.
6. *Dreaming*—When the talker mentions a thought that causes you to think of something in your own life that is unrelated to what they are saying, this is dreaming. They may be talking about what happens if the contract that the company is bidding on is not won, what will happen to the security staffing levels, but before they get to ask the questions, your mind has drifted off to the last company that you worked for that lost a huge contract and how you hated going through the reduction in force motions with your staff.
7. *Identifying*—Similar to dreaming, in this case every thing the person is telling gets related back by the listener to an experience in their own life. This is commonly shown when people are talking about a situation and then a similar situation is parroted back from the listener's life.
8. *Advising*—In this scenario, the listener is too busy thinking of the solution to the problem from the first few sound bites that they miss important information or fail to pickup on how the listener is feeling.
9. *Sparring*—Quickly disagreeing by the listener causes the listener to search for items to disagree with. This can take the form of a put-down where the talker does not feel listened to and possibly humiliated.
10. *Being right*—This person will go to great lengths to demonstrate that they are right, including standing by their

convictions, not listening to criticism, making excuses, shouting, and twisting the facts.

11. *Derailing*—The conversation is ended by changing the subject and avoiding the conflict. This is sometimes done by joking to avoid the discomfort of having to discuss the subject.
12. *Placating*—The listener is very agreeable, as you want people to like you, see you as nice, pleasant, and supportive. Listening may be at the level just enough to get the idea of what is being said, however, you are not fully engaged.

By being conscious of these blocks, they can be avoided to become a better listener. There are also four steps to becoming a better listener, as discussed in the next few sections.

Generating a Clear Message

Effective oral communication depends upon generating a series of clear, straightforward messages that expresses the thoughts, feelings, and observations that need to be conveyed. Since over 90% of what we "hear" is not from the words, but from the volume, pitch, and rhythm of the message and the body movements, including facial expression, it is important that our messages are congruent. We cannot be verbalizing the need for a new, exciting security initiative with our posture slouched in the chair and expect the recipient of the message to be as excited as we are (or potentially not). Double messages should be avoided without hidden agendas. Over the long-term, hidden agendas serve to undermine the security department's credibility.

Influencing and Negotiating Skills

Not everyone is going to automatically sign up for the information security initiatives, especially if this means spending money that could be allocated to other programs, involves an increase in the number of rules or adds perceived overhead to their business operations. To successfully negotiate when discussing a position, the security officer must be able to separate the problem from the individual. Direct attacks based upon prior experience with a particular department will not help gain its support. The key is to look at the security initiative that is being proposed from the perspective of the person that you are trying to influence. It is also dangerous to try to read the other person's mind as noted in the previous section and come to prejudged conclusions of their support or nonsupport of the project. It is OK to postulate in advance what the stakeholders may think about the situation to assist with the preparations; however, it is not prudent to come to foregone conclusions about their reaction.

Consider various options to implementing a strategy that may be pliable to the stakeholder. There is always more than one way to perform something. A request by a business manager may be met with resistance by the security officer. However, by brainstorming various options, one of these solutions may be palatable, with some investigation, for both the business manager and the security officer. Once options are determined, these can be generated into requirements that are not demands but rather where the solution is mutually agreeable.

Written Communication Skills

Written communication takes on several forms in today's word from e-mail, texting, twittering, social media (Facebook, Myspace, LinkedIn) posting, report writing, policy/procedure writing, and memo writing. E-mail is the predominant written form of communication and is much different than writing a memo or a policy and procedure. Care must be taken to know the audience and the purpose of the written communication. Although e-mail is a very quick method to communicate across the organization, it is amazing how many e-mails people send that have incorrect grammar, misspelled words, or use negative language. Since there is no tone button on the e-mail that is sent, words must be chosen carefully so as to not alienate the recipient. A simple request may turn into hurt feelings if not written in a clear, nonconfrontational manner. E-mails are also received almost as quickly as the send button is pressed, so extra care needs to be made taken constructing the message. Although it may be easy to become emotional over an issue, these are best handled by picking up the phone if they cannot be addressed using a fact-based, diplomatic written approach.

Presentation Skills

Presentations come with the territory and security officers will find themselves in the position of having to deliver a presentation to senior management. Since management has limited time, presentations need to be focused with, "What do I hope to obtain or convey with this presentation?" Sometimes presentations will be an impromptu-type, such as the 30-second elevator speech, or it may be at the other extreme in the form of a memorized speech. Most presentations are combination of the two, whereby the presentation slides serve to guide the presentation, with much of the material being an impromptu delivery (albeit prepared) by the presenter. Presentation dos and don'ts are shown in Table 12.2.

Table 12.2 Presentation Dos and Don'ts

DO THIS	DON'T DO THIS
Know the audience: General end users? Technically oriented users? Management?	Assume that the audience has the same level of understanding.
Engage the audience by asking questions.	Speak nonstop for 45 minutes or more (beyond the normal attention span).
Use a mixture of audio, video, and visual artifacts to make a point.	Exclusively using PowerPoint.
Translate the technical issues by using analogies, stories, and relating to common everyday language.	Use technical security jargon when unnecessary.
Make eye contact and use a friendly demeanor.	Read the presentation slide by slide or from note cards.
Answer their questions using the no-dumb-question rule.	Act superior to the questioner by failing to recognize their comments as valid, albeit they may be coming from a different perspective or disagree.
Ask questions early to get the audience engaged.	Completely, but briefly, answer their questions.
If unsure of an answer, open the question up to the group.	Lose credibility by talking about subjects that you have little experience with.
Leave time for questions and end the presentation 5 minutes early to permit time for attendees to make their next meeting.	Speak right up until the end of the hour and not get the conclusion or discussion of options completed.
Focus on a few main objectives for the presentation.	Provide histories (organization, computing) that are not related to the current discussion.
Keep the type text at least 24 font point.	Use graphics that are hard to see or are distracting (e.g., excessive use of animation).
Speak with a microphone in larger rooms so the audience in the back of the room can hear.	Assume that your voice is loud enough; some individuals may not be able to pick up the modulation properly.

Applying Personality Type to Security Communications

Ideas emanating from the early work of Carl Jung, a Swiss psychologist, were extended through the development of an instrument to indicate personality type differences by Isabel Myers and her mother Katharine Cook Briggs in 1943 (Myers, 1995). This later became known as the Myers–Briggs Type Indicator, or MBTI, which has been taken by millions of people. The MBTI is a very powerful tool, which at its simplest form breaks down all of the personalities into 16 types. Understanding each of these 16 types can help the security organization communicate more effectively with different individuals based upon their type. In other words, it helps to know how they may be wired to understand how they take in information, make decisions, where they get their energy from, and how they organize their lives.

The Four Myers–Briggs Type Indicator (MBTI) Preference Scales

The complete psychology explanation of the 16 types is well beyond the scope of this book, but there are many useful books written on the MBTI type noted at the end of this chapter. However it is useful to provide a brief primer on the 16 types and, more important, what the implications are for the information security department. There are four scales, with each person having a natural preference for one of the two opposites on each scale. While we all use each of the opposites at different times, one scale feels more natural to us most of the time. This natural tendency becomes our preference or the place where we are the most comfortable. The combination of the four scales, with two opposite values, yields 16 combinations of letters. Each set of letters yields a describable personality, not in a stereotypical manner, but rather a mechanism to explain the personality and what may be expected behavior, career interests, reactions to certain events, and so forth from that personality type. It is important to note that no "preference" is better than another, it is just different. Each of us uses all of the dimensions of preference at some point, and we flex our behaviors depending upon the situation. For example, an introverted parent may flex their extraversion when providing discipline to a child.

Table 12.3 Where Do I Prefer to Focus My Energy (Inner or Outer World)?

EXTRAVERSION (E)—TUNED INTO OUTER WORLD OF PEOPLE AND EVENTS	INTROVERSION (I)—DRAWN TO INNER WORLD OF IDEAS AND EXPERIENCES
Seek interaction	Like to be alone
Enjoy groups	Enjoy one-on-one conversation
Act or speak first, then think	Think first, then speak or act
Sociable and expressive	Think to themselves
Expend energy	Conserve energy
Focus outwardly	Focus inwardly
Take initiative in work and relationships	Quiet, reserved
Like variety and action	Like to focus on one thing at a time
Outgoing	Enjoy reflecting
Breath of information	Depth of information

Extraversion versus Introversion Scale The first preference is about where you prefer to get your energy: the external world (extraversion, E) or from the inside world (introversion, I). Extraverts tend to get energy from the people, interactions, and events, whereas introverts tend to derive their energy from their internal thought, feelings, and reflections. It is sometimes said that extraverts are processing information as they are talking, while introverts tend to crystallize the idea internally first before speaking. Introverts draw their energy from being alone, while the extravert may feel drained by spending long periods without interaction. Table 12.3 shows some of the characteristics of extraverts and introverts (Kroger and Thuesen, 1992).

Sensing versus Intuition Scale This preference indicates how information is gathered. Sensing (S) individuals prefer to take in information through their senses, such as seeing, hearing, smelling, and so forth, to see what is actually happening. They are observant of what is going on around them and very good at determining the practicality of the situation. Information presented is preferred to be delivered in a very specific manner. Sensors tend to prefer to be presented with the facts and details of what they are reviewing. About 70% of the world prefers to gather information this way.

Individuals that prefer to see the big picture to take in information most likely prefer intuition (N) to gather information. They focus on

Table 12.4 What Kind of Information Do I Normally Pay Attention To?

SENSING (S)—FOCUS ON CONCRETE, REAL, ACTUAL	INTUITION (N)—FOCUS ON ABSTRACT, RELATIONSHIPS, PATTERNS
Prefer facts, concrete data	Prefer insights
Value practical applications	Value imaginative insight
Present oriented	Future oriented
Focus on reality, details, specifics	Focus on the big picture, possibilities
Like step-by-step instructions	Like to jump around, move in anywhere
Pragmatic	Speculative
Value common sense	Value innovation

the relationship between various facts, facts that may not appear to have any relationship to the sensor. They are good at seeing new possibilities and new ways of doing things. Table 12.4 shows some of the characteristics of sensing and intuition preferences.

Thinking versus Feeling Scale How decisions are made is attributed to the decision-making preference, which has two ends of the scale, thinking (T) and feeling (F). Thinkers tend to look at the logical ramifications of a course of action. The goal of the thinker is to make a decision from an objective viewpoint and tend not to get personally involved in the decision. They are often called firm minded and seek clarity in the decision. They are good at figuring out what is wrong with something so that problem-solving abilities can then be applied.

The feelers tend to approach decision making based upon what is important to them and to the other people. While the decision making of the thinker may gravitate toward what is right, lawful, or concludes with justice, the feeler may base the decision on person-centered values to achieve harmony and recognition of other individuals through understanding, appreciating, and supporting others. In short, feelers tend to prefer empathy over intellect. Table 12.5 shows some of the characteristics of thinkers and feelers.

Judging versus Perceiving Scale The last preference indicates the preference as to how you orient your world. Judgers (J) want to regulate and control life by living in a scheduled, organized, and structured way. They do not like things unsettled and want order in their lives. They enjoy their ability to stick to a schedule and get things done. For the judgers there is usually a right way and a wrong way to do things.

Table 12.5 How Do I Make Decisions?

THINKING (T)—ANALYTICAL, LOGICAL CONSEQUENCES, PRINCIPLED	FEELING (F)—CONSIDER IMPORTANCE TO THEM, OTHER PEOPLE AND VALUES
Firm minded	Gentle hearted
Objective, convinced by logic	Subjective, convinced by values
Laws, justice, policy	Humane, social values
Reasonable	Compassionate
Logical problem solvers	Assess impact on people
Don't take things personally	Likely to take things personally
Good at critiquing	Good at appreciating

Table 12.6 How Do I Organize My World?

JUDGING (J)—PLANNED, ORDERLY, CONTROLLED LIFE	PERCEIVING (P)—FLEXIBLE, SPONTANEOUS, EXPERIENCE LIFE
Seek closure, things settled	Seek openness
Value structure, goals	Like flexibility, tentative
Scheduled, methodical	Spontaneous, flexible
Systematic	Casual
Like closure and have things decided	Like to have their options open, able to change
Avoid last-minute stresses	Energized by last-minute pressures
Enjoy completing projects	Enjoy starting projects

Perceivers (P) prefer to be flexible and adaptable in different situations. They want to be able to be spontaneous and flexible to rise to the opportunity as it presents itself. They are called perceivers due to their ability to keep collecting new information, rather than draw premature conclusions on a subject. In other words, they prefer the open-endedness and ability to change their decision based upon new information. Table 12.6 shows some of the characteristics of judgers and perceivers.

Determining Individual MBTI Personality

Using the aforementioned descriptions and characteristics, by now it should be possible to determine your approximate MBTI or set of four letters describing your personality. This can be used as a guide for the next section in determining the individual temperament. The actual determination of the letters is more accurately determined by taking an assessment of the MBTI® by Consulting Psychologists Press, containing more than 200 preference questions and determining the letters with more accuracy (CPP, 1993). In real life, we have to learn to approximate the Myers–Briggs of our peers, unless we ask them if they know what theirs are, as they are not going to take a 200-plus question assessment for us! Over time, speed reading the types for individuals become easier and a very valuable tool for interacting with others.

The Four Temperaments In an effort to distill the 16 types into commonalities for ease of discussion, David Keirsey portioned the 16 types into four temperaments by grouping the Sensing-Perceiving (SPs), Sensing-Judging (SJs), Intuition-Thinking (NTs), and Intuition-Feeling (NFs) (Keirsey, 1998). Although there are individual differences due to the other two letters that make up each set of 4 letters (for an individual's personality), there was a strong commonality within these groups, which simplifies the discussion of their temperament.

Following is a brief description of some of the characteristics of personality types that fall into each of the four temperaments, along with the implications as to how security should be communicated with each temperament. For example, the SJ temperament consists of those individuals who have the ESTJ, ISTJ, ESFJ, or ISFJ personality preferences. For example, the ESTJ natural preferences are to obtain their energy from extraversion, gather information through sensing (concrete, detail-oriented), make decisions based upon thinking (logical, analytical values), and orient their world through Judging (schedule oriented, organized). The ESTJs share some common characteristics with the other SJs (ISTJ, ESFJ, ISFJ), even though they may vary on one of the other dimensions.

SJ "Guardian" Temperament Those personality preferences sharing the SJ temperament (ESTJ, Supervisor; ISTJ, Inspector; ESFJ, Provider; ISFJ, Protector) share characteristics of being reliable, organized, task focused, and hard working at their best. At their worst, they may be perceived as being judgmental, controlling, inflexible, or close minded. They typically respect the laws and traditions of society, like to be in charge, have a standard way of doing things, expect others to be realistic, strive to belong and to contribute, have high expectations of themselves and others, are critical of mistakes and may fail to reward expected duties, have difficulty refusing to take on other assignments, and do not like surprises. They are also good at anticipating problems.

While people of any temperament can be successful at any job, there are some careers that attract this temperament more than others. The SJ temperament may choose careers as a project manager, regulatory compliance officer, budget analyst, chief information officer, bank manager/loan officer, government employee, administrative assistant, nurse, auditor, pharmacist, engineer, or an accountant. These are jobs typically involving adhering to a set of rules and standards without a large amount of ambiguity, which is attractive to the SJ temperament. SJs are also attracted toward positions that can create financial security.

When communicating information security issues with the SJ temperament, it is important that if something was done wrong, that regret is expressed and a simple I'm sorry is used. This can set things straight and allow the SJ to move forward. SJs should be appreciated for their responsibility and willingness to handle the details of the situation in the form of compliments. For example, individuals in the security group managing the very detailed logging and monitoring may be of the SJ temperament as evidenced by their willingness to handle and organize the vast amount of detail.

Commitments must be kept with SJs to win their trust. If the CEO is an SJ and there were promises made to implement a security initiative by the end of March so that a new product could be launched in May, the CEO who shares this personality type preference will most likely be less forgiving than the SP type, for example, when the deadline is not met.

Communications with SJs should be specific and practical, as *Dragnet*'s Joe Friday would iterate, "Just the facts ma'am. Just the facts." SJs are also resistant to change and need to be brought into change more slowly with logical reasons for the change. However, once the change has been embraced, they can be one of the strongest supporters of the change.

SP "Artisan" Temperament The SP temperament (ESTP, Promoter; ISTP, Crafter; ESFP, Performer; ISFP, Composer) personality types may be viewed as the action seekers. They may be viewed as optimistic, generous, fun loving, adventurous, realistic, and adaptable at their best, or hyperactive, impatient, impulsive, and scattered at their worst. They enjoy life in the here and now, highly value freedom and action, like risk and challenge, are spontaneous, may be perceived as indecisive, are observant, ask the right questions to get what they need, respond well to crisis, like short-term projects, and dislike laws and standard ways of doing things. This is sharp contrast to the SJ temperament previously discussed, which thrives on standards and ensuring that the rules are being followed.

For career selections, the SPs tend to gravitate toward careers that permit them to experience life versus a means toward an end. Potential career choices for the SJ may include emergency room nurse, medical assistant, photographer, police officer, public relations specialist, fire/insurance fraud investigator, news anchor, airline mechanic, marine biologist, or paramedic/firefighter. In the security field, individuals wanting the excitement of responding to a disaster recovery situation or an intrusion may gravitate toward this area.

When communicating with the SP temperament, appreciation should be shown for their enthusiasm, common sense, and ability to deal with crisis. Joining in some of their activities may be appropriate, such as an invitation to meet them and a group of security vendors after work. Business executives of this type may be part of the golf club or bowling league, and this would be a good opportunity to network with these individuals and build rapport to create a nonadversarial environment. Given choices and alternatives, those sharing the SP temperament will want to do things their own way in their own timeframe. Issues should be pinpointed and overwhelming them with information avoided. They also do not like being told how to change or what to do.

NF "Idealist" Temperament Those sharing the NF temperament (ENFJ, Teacher; INFJ, Counselor; ENFP, Champion; INFP, Healer), known as the ideal seekers, share the characteristics of being compassionate, loyal helpful, genuine, warmhearted, and nurturing at their best, or may be perceived as moody, depressed, or oversensitive at their worst. They are stimulated by new ideas, take an antiauthoritarian attitude, often side with the underdog, see possibilities in institutions and people, search for meaning and authenticity, self-actualize, maintain close contact with others, give freely and need positive appreciation, and are good listeners.

NF temperaments may gravitate toward jobs such as psychologist, sociologist, facilitator, career counselor, travel agent, human resources recruiter, teacher (health, art, drama, foreign language), social worker, or hotel and restaurant manager.

When communicating with the NF temperament, cards, gifts, compliments and adoration go a long way. They are sensitive to criticism, so extra tact is necessary. Patience is needed to understanding of their need to express their feelings. Their support can be gained by appealing to their creativity and vision of their ideals.

NT "Rational" Temperament Individuals sharing the NT temperament group (ENTJ, Field Marshal; INTJ, Mastermind; ENTP, Inventor; INTP, Architect), known as the knowledge seekers, have strengths of being innovative, inquisitive, analytical, bright, independent, witty and competent at their best, or they may be perceived as arrogant, cynical, critical, distant, or self-righteous at their worst. They work well with ideas and concepts, value knowledge and competency, understand and synthesize complex information, anticipate future trends, focus on long-term goals, like to start projects (although not as good on follow-through), not always aware of other's feelings, aim for mastery, and deal with the day-to-day details but have little interest in them.

Knowledge seekers may be found as an executive, senior manager, personnel manager, sales/marketing manager, technical trainer, network integration specialist, technical writer, investment banker, attorney, psychiatrist, database administrator, credit analyst, technical project manager, architect, or Web developer/computer programmer.

When communicating a security concern or initiative with the NT temperament, the security professional should attempt to appreciate their objectivity, quick minds, and knowledge. Since they value mastery in what they do, conversations that are intellectually stimulating should be pursued, feelings should be avoided in conversation, and debate with them, letting them know frequently you value their insights. Many of the technical staff involved in connecting patterns together, such as the network engineers or database administrators, can become supportive of the security program by simply asking them for their input and genuinely incorporating their insights into the security strategy and subsequent implementations.

Summing Up the MBTI for Security

Communication is so important and goes well beyond providing a written report or an oral presentation; it is how we interact with others on a daily basis. As the security program must remain credible to be effective, we must ensure that we are communicating the security messages clearly, and in a manner in which they will be heard. We tend to communicate by default by the manner that we are comfortable receiving. Unfortunately, and fortunately, we are not all the same, and we take in and process information differently. To be successful within the organization, the security officer and his or her team need to be able to communicate at an appropriate level with others within the organization. Understanding the differences in personalities will increase the effectiveness of the security message that needs to be delivered.

Suggested Reading

1. McKay, M., Davis, M., and Fanning, P. 1995. *How to communicate: The ultimate guide to improving your personal and professional relationships.* New York: MJF Books.
2. National Institute of Standards and Technology (NIST). October 2003. Special Publication 800-50: Building an information security technology security awareness and training program. http://csrc.nist.gov/publications/nistpubs/800-50/NIST-SP800-50.pdf
3. National Institute of Standards and Technology (NIST). October 1995. Special Publication 800-12: An introduction to computer security: The NIST handbook. http://csrc.nist.gov/publications/nistpubs/800-12/handbook.pdf
4. Herold, R. 2005. *Managing an information security and privacy awareness and training program.* Boca Raton, FL: Auerbach.
5. Tieger, P. D., and Barron-Tieger, B. 1998. *The art of speedreading people: Harness the power of personality type and create what you want in business and in life.* Boston: Little, Brown and Company.
6. Tieger, P. D., and Barron-Tieger, B.1998. *Do what you are: Discover the perfect career for you through the secrets of personality type.* Boston: Little, Brown and Company.

7. Myers, I. B., and Myers, P. 1995. *Gifts differing: Understanding personality type*, 2nd ed. Palo-Alto, CA: Davies-Black.
8. Kroeger, O., and Thuesen, J. M. 1992. *Type talk at work*. New York: Tilden Press.
9. Bolton, R., and Bolton, D. G. 1996. *People styles at work: Making bad relationships good and good relationships better*. New York: Ridge Associates.
10. Keirsey, D. 1998. *Please understand me II: Temperament, character, intelligence*. Del Mar, CA: Pometheus Nemesis.
11. Myers, I. B.1993. *Introduction to type,* 5th ed. Palo Alto, CA: Consulting Psychologists Press, Inc.

13

The Law and Information Security

If you give to a thief he cannot steal from you, and he is then no longer a thief.

William Saroyan, 1908–1981

Over the past several decades, and particularly in the last decade, there has been an increased focus on information security in concert with the fear that individual privacy could be compromised. As information has become more electronic and networks such as the Internet provide access points to personal computers and company computer networks, the attention of lawmakers has been raised. The fear is that this massive aggregation and interconnection of information will lead to exposures of sensitive information.

Numerous laws have been put in place. In some cases, these laws overlap, adding to the complexity for the security officer attempting to build a one-size-fits-all information security program. The governance strategy must ensure the compliance with existing laws, as well as remain abreast of the emerging laws and regulations that are on the horizon. When the regulations are published, they come with a mandated compliance date and depending upon the size of the organization and the scope of the mandate, can be very time consuming to complete between the period of final law issuance and the required implementation. Therefore, it is in the best interest of the security officer to review draft regulations and proactively anticipate what types of requirements have a good chance of remaining in the final version of the law to provide more time to implement the new requirements. An added benefit of this approach is that by being well versed in the upcoming provisions, the security officer has the opportunity to provide input by way of comments to the proposal, usually within a 60-day period for federal regulations, to help shape the legislation.

For example, thousands of comments were received shortly after the Health Insurance Portability and Accountability Act (HIPAA) Security Rule was published in 2003, which changed the format and contents of the Final Security Rule. This also provides the opportunity for the security officer to assist his or her business partners to comply with the regulation, having gained experience with the details of the regulation.

Some regulations that must be complied with are not laws per se, but are regulations formulated by an industry body. The Payment Card Industry Data Security Standard (PCI DSS) is good example of this, whereby the standard was formed by the major credit card issuers to ensure security between the merchants and card processors. Even though the standard is not a law, it is a requirement established by the issuers that must be complied with to participate within the industry.

The subsequent sections present a brief synopsis of some of the key laws that have driven information security in recent years, as well as some of the high-level controls that are required. These sections should be regarded as an executive guide to the information security laws impacting information security decisions. Many times individuals are working within their own vertical industry and are unaware of the laws, regulations, control frameworks, and standards that are being discussed in other industries. Each of the laws has a specific purpose, genealogy, and differences with the other standards, but after working with these different laws, it is also clear that by following a consistent framework, whether it be COBIT (ITGI, n.d.), NIST 800-53 (NIST, 2009), ISO 27000/27001 (ISO, 2005), PCI, Information Security Forum (ISF) Good Security Practice (ISF, 2007), or some other framework, there are requirements in these frameworks that if followed, would more than likely to satisfy the law or regulation in most cases. This is due to the fact that many of these laws and regulations are grounded in security principles to begin with and it should be no surprise that these requirements are presented within the regulation. The difference will typically be that the control framework will be more prescriptive and granular than the higher-level law. This is necessary, otherwise technology advances and innovation would be impeded by having the law state requirements in terms of today's technology. The law or regulation would also not be very flexible. These are the strengths of keeping the laws written at a more generic level, however, this is also criticized as a weakness since the law does not describe specifically what to do.

The security officer and the security department are often in a position where they are interpreting the law's requirements for senior management. The legal staff will know the ins and outs of the legal system, which can be very helpful, particularly with their understanding of contract laws. Customers entrust their data to a business with the expectation that the information is adequately protected and used for business purposes. This expectation does not change even if the business decides to subcontract and share the information with another entity. From the perspective of the consumer, they still have that expectation and do not care who is at fault if there is an incident. The legal staff must be involved in contracts of services or products of other organizations to ensure that the appropriate information security language is included. The language includes clauses that require the subcontractor to protect the confidentiality, integrity and availability of the information, ensure there is the right to audit the controls of the subentity, and establish communication protocols and expectations between the subcontractor and the contracting business in the event there is a breach. The security department can provide the technical expertise to the legal department or the assurance as to how the laws or regulations are being met.

Since it is difficult to have real privacy of information without security, the security officer needs to keep abreast of the privacy laws as well. HIPAA is a prime example whereby the security regulations followed the privacy regulations, as it was viewed as important to protect the security of the information to achieve privacy. The fear by Congress was that the aggregation and moving the transactions to an electronic format would create privacy concerns if the security was not addressed.

Civil Law versus Criminal Law

Criminal laws exist for the purpose of punishing the perpetrator of the crime, hoping to also serve as a deterrent to others considering committing the same crime. Since computer crime prosecution is not very prevalent and very few criminals go to jail, some of the criminal penalties associated with the various laws do not seem to serve as a large deterrent. As more criminals are prosecuted and sent to jail, maybe the criminal penalties will provide the deterrent that the law prescribes. It seems that the conduct would need to be egregious and willful to move to a standard of criminal prosecution. In large cases, such as the Heartland Payment Systems fraud where Albert Gonzalez received 20 years, it is obvious that an example was made of the fraud to deter others from engaging in similar activity (Mosaritolo, 2010).

Another reason for the lack of criminal prosecution may be that for criminal law the plaintiff must demonstrate beyond a reasonable doubt to a jury of their peers that an offense occurred, which given the complexities of hacking, this may be difficult to explain in understandable terms to the jury. Prosecutors have to weigh the odds of a successful outcome before investing valuable time and resources into the case.

The more likely scenario is the leveling of civil monetary damages in the form of statutory damages that may be assessed as a matter of law. If the law has been violated, then there is entitlement to the award. This may also present itself by way of fines, such as the Federal Trade Commission's assessment of $15 million in fines for Eli Lilly's accidental e-mail/website disclosure of customers who were using an antidepressant drug (FTC, 2002).

Civil cases are must more likely to be pursued to make the victim whole, as the standard of proof is much different. Whereas criminal cases must determine beyond a reasonable doubt, civil cases only require that a preponderance of the evidence is sufficient to find the person guilty of the infraction.

Electronic Communications Privacy Act of 1986 (ECPA)

The Electronic Communications Privacy Act of 1986 (ECPA; Public Law 99-508), also known as the Wiretap Act, was passed by Congress to extend the protections of the wiretap law to electronic communication forms, such as e-mail, text, video, audio, and data. Under the law, messages may not be intercepted in transmission or in stored form while in transit. Law enforcement would need to obtain a court order to obtain information such as account activity logs showing the IP addresses that were visited by a subscriber of Internet services or the e-mail addresses from who the subscriber exchanged emails. Law enforcement can also obtain a court order to compel cellular phone companies to provide records showing the cell phone location information for calls made from a person's cell phone. In an effort to increase the foreign intelligence gathering activities after the events of 9/11, the U.S. Patriot Act was made law by President George W. Bush on October 26, 2001. The U.S. Patriot Act weakened the restrictions and increased law enforcement's ability to obtain telephone, e-mail communications, and records such as medical and financial. For example, a search warrant could be issued for voicemail communications, bypassing the more stringent Wiretap Act.

The Computer Security Act of 1987

Congress enacted a law that reaffirmed the National Institute for Standards and Technology (NIST) as being responsible for the protection of unclassified, nonmilitary government systems and information. The National Security Agency (NSA), which provided for the protection of classified information for the military, provided technical assistance to the nonmilitary parts of government, as Congress decided that is it was more appropriate to have a nonmilitary agency responsible for the creation of guidance for protecting civilian information. The Computer Security Act of 1987 became Public Law 100-235 (NIST, 1987). The key implications of the act was that it required that minimum acceptable security practices would be established for federal computer systems, systems security plans would be constructed for the these systems defining the security controls in use, and that appropriate training would be provided. Computer systems were defined to include the computers, ancillary equipment, software, firmware, services, and included the computer systems operated by any federal agency or a contractor of a federal agency that processes information on behalf of the federal government.

Several attempts have been made to amend the Computer Security Act (1997, 1999, and 2001) to address technical changes that had occurred since 1987 and to designate a single agency to lead the computer security activities. These measures passed the House of Representatives and made their way through the Senate subcommittees, but were not presented to the Senate for a vote. No attempts have been made to change the law since 2001. This may be due in part to having more focus on the Federal Information Security Management Act of 2002.

The Privacy Act of 1974

The Privacy Act of 1974 provides restrictions on the federal government in the collection, maintenance, and use of the information collected on individuals (FTC, 1974). The act provides protection from disclosure of information that is defined within a "record set." Information cannot be released unless it was specifically requested by a court and with an individual's express consent. Whereas the Health Insurance Portability and Accountability Act of 1996 (HIPAA) provided protections for the release of health care information, the release of information contained within government systems such as Medicare and Medicaid was already protected by the Privacy Act of 1974. The attempts to provide a balance between the federal government's need to collect information but at the same time not collect too much information or release information that constitutes an invasion of privacy. From a historical perspective, the act was born during the aftermath of Watergate, where information was collected on individuals related to the Watergate scandal. Also, with the interconnectivity between systems and networks in the 1970s and the subsequent introduction of the PC that followed the act in the early '80s, there was concern over the potential aggregation of information by the use of a single identifier, such as the social security number. The act established fair information practices by placing some structure on how agencies managed their records, provided individuals with increased access to the records held by federal agencies; provided the means to amend records that were not accurate, relevant, timely, or complete; and restricted their disclosure to appropriate individuals.

Sarbanes–Oxley Act of 2002 (SOX)

Public law 107-204 was enacted on July 30, 2002, and is referred to as the Public Company Accounting Reform and Investor Protection Act by the Senate, and the Corporate Auditing Accountability and Responsibility Act in the House of Representatives, but is most widely known as the Sarbanes–Oxley Act (SOX), (SEC, 2002). The bill came about as there were a number of accounting scandals that cost investors and employees of companies such as Enron, Tyco International, and WorldCom dearly. Arthur Andersen, a well known and respected audit firm and auditor for Enron, ceased doing business after the Enron scandal. SOX established the Public Company Accounting Oversight Board (PCAOB) to provide independent oversight of public accounting firms providing auditing services. The act also established standards to ensure auditor independence and avoid conflicts of interest, with a key provision restricting companies that provide consulting from providing audit services. Executives were also required to take individual responsibility for the accuracy and completeness of the financial reports, which was represented by their signing off and attesting to the documents. Within organizations, this resulted in a series of management signoffs to ensure that appropriate governance was achieved. For the chief financial officer and chief executive officer to sign-off on the documents, it was not unusual for them to also require attestations of the management staff as well.

The most significant section of the law is section 404, which requires an assessment of the internal controls. This part of the law has received criticism in recent years for the costs associated with compliance. Initially, many auditing firms took a very conservative view of what was required to be in compliance, resulting in some cases extensive auditing, documentation, and testing of the automated controls. However, the increased attention to the internal controls has had a positive effect on the controls that in the past were overridden by management. The laws did represent more risk to the audit firms, as more work needed to be done to ensure that there was no undetected fraud being committed.

The PCAOB approved auditing standard No. 5 on July 25, 2007, replacing the guidance provided in standard No. 2 issued in 2004. The guidance refers to the report of the Committee of Sponsoring Organizations of the Treadway Commission (also known as the COSO report) as a framework for demonstrating the internal controls.

The European Union has passed a law named Directive 84/253/EEC, also called the 8th Company Law Directive. This is sometimes referred to as EuroSOX, however, this name is somewhat of a misnomer when compared to the United States version of SOX.

The difference is that the legislative process takes time and must be addressed by each country. Whereas the U.S. version was a single law that was mandated at once, the European directive is met by various laws within each country. The adoption of the directive has been varied and not had the same focus or effect as SOX in the United States. The international standards such as ISO 27001/27002, COBIT, and COSO appear to be the predominant standards used to demonstrate adequate internal controls.

Gramm–Leach–Bliley Act (GLBA)

The Gramm–Leach–Bliley Act (GLBA; Public Law 106-1020), also known as the Financial Services Act, was enacted on November 12, 1999, which repealed part of the Glass–Steagall Act of 1933, which provided the ability for banks to function as an investment bank, commercial bank, and insurance company. The act also provided the Financial Privacy Rule, which permitted individuals to opt out of having their information shared with unaffiliated parties. Individuals need to be notified each time the privacy policy is changed and must be given the opportunity to opt out. As such, the Financial Privacy Rule established a privacy policy between the individual and the company. Section 501(b) of the GLBA required the Federal Deposit Insurance Corporation (FDIC), Board of Governors of the Federal Reserve System (FRB), Office of the Comptroller of the Currency (OCC), and Office of Thrift Supervision (OTS) to develop standards for the examination to ensure that adequate safeguards are being implemented. The examination procedures were developed to determine the involvement of the board of directors, evaluate the risk management process, evaluate the adequacy of the program to manage and control risk, assess measures taken to oversee service providers, and determine where an effective process exists to adjust the program.

The Safeguards Rule of the GLBA requires the development of a written information security plan and must protect the current and past client's financial information. Title 15, chapter 94, subchapter I, section 6801(b) requires that the financial institution "establish appropriate standards for the financial institutions subject to their jurisdiction relating to administrative, technical and physical safeguards (1) to insure the security and confidentiality of customer records and information; (2) to protect against any anticipated threats or hazards to the security or integrity of such records; and (3) to protect against unauthorized access to or use of such records or information which could result in substantial harm or inconvenience to any customer." The Federal Financial Institutions Examination Council (FFIEC) IT Examination Handbook discussed in Chapter 7 can be used as a basis to meet the GLBA requirements.

Health Insurance Portability and Accountability Act of 1996

The Health Insurance Portability and Accountability Act of 1996 (HIPAA) was enacted by Congress (Public Law 104-191) with two purposes in mind: (1) to reform health insurance to protect insurance coverage for workers and families when they change or lose their jobs, and (2) to simplify the administrative processes by adopting standards to improve the efficiency and effectiveness of the nation's health care system. Title I of HIPAA contains provisions to address health insurance reform, whereas Title II addresses national standards for electronic transactions, unique health identifiers, privacy, and security. Title II is known as Administrative Simplification and is intended to reduce the costs of health care through the widespread use of electronic data interchange. Administrative simplification was added to the Title XI of the Social Security Act through Subtitle F of Title II of the enacted HIPAA law.

Although the initial intent of the Administrative Simplification was to reduce the administrative costs associated with processing health care transactions, Congress recognized that standardizing and electronically aggregating health care information would increase the risk of disclosure of confidential information, and the patient's privacy rights needed to be protected. Security provisions were needed not only to protect the confidentiality of information but also to ensure that information retained the appropriate integrity. Consider the situation where the diagnosis or vital sign information is changed on a medical record, and subsequent treatment decisions are based upon this information. The impact of not being able to rely on the information stored within the health care environment could have life-threatening consequences. Thus, privacy issues are primarily centered on the confidentiality of information to ensure that only the appropriate individuals have access to the information, whereas the security standards take on a larger scope to also address issues of integrity and availability of information.

The proposed security and electronic signature standards were originally published in the *Federal Register* on August 12, 1998. The security rule was delayed on several occasions, as resources were committed to and focused on the proposed transaction and code set and privacy rules, both of which generated a large number of public comments. These public comments must be reviewed, and the numbers can be large. Several thousand comments were received on the privacy rule and on the proposed security rule. The security rule was initiated during the Clinton administration and was carried over into the Bush administration, which created political challenges for expedient passage of the rule. As a result, the language was rewritten during 2002 to coincide with the privacy rule (issued on December 28, 2000, and was subsequently modified on August 14, 2002, with a compliance date for most covered entities of April 14, 2003), which needed to go through the Health ad Human Services clearance process prior to final rule publication. The Final Security Rule was submitted by the Centers for Medicare and Medicaid Services to the Office of Management and Budget (OMB) in early 2003 and was published in the *Federal Register* as 45 CFR Parts 160, 162, and 164 on February 20, 2003. The regulations became effective on April 21, 2003, and covered entities were required to comply with the requirements by April 21, 2005, and small health plans had until April 21, 2006.

The Administrative Simplification (Part C of Title XI of the Social Security Act) provisions state that covered entities that maintain or transmit health information are required to "maintain reasonable and appropriate administrative, physical and technical safeguards to ensure the integrity and confidentiality of the information and to protect against any reasonable anticipated threats or hazards to the security or integrity of the information and unauthorized use or disclosure of the information." The administrative, technical, and physical safeguards were divided into addressable and required implementation specifications. The addressable standards were more flexible; however, the required safeguards had to be implemented according to the rule. The contractors supporting Medicare claims processing (fiscal intermediaries and carriers now known as Medicare administrative contractors) were given the directive that all of the required and addressable security controls were to be regarded as required, setting a higher, and more stringent standard for the protection of Medicare information maintained by the contractors.

Since the Final Security Rule was written to be consistent with the Privacy Rule, the focus of security standards applied to health information in support of the Administrative Simplification requirements were shifted to protected health information (PHI) and specifically to electronic PHI. The applicability statement of the Final Security Rule states: "A covered entity must comply with the applicable standards, implementation specifications, and requirements of this subpart with respect to electronic protected health information." Covered entities are defined as (1) a health plan, (2) a health care clearinghouse, and (3) a health care provider who transmits any health information in electronic form in connection with a transaction covered by part 162 of title 45 of the Code of Federal Regulations (CFR).

The security rule was meant to be scalable such that small providers would not be burdened with excessive costs of implementation, and the large providers, health plans, and clearinghouses could take steps appropriate to their business environments. For example, a small office may be able to control access and enforce segregation of duties between the staff with a manually documented process with supervisory review, whereas a larger organization would most likely need automated support through an identity management system, management approval processes, and automated reporting tools to achieve the same level of assurance. Decisions have to be made to reasonably protect the information and document how the decisions were determined. Although it was earlier recognized that security is always a risk-based decision, it is sometimes difficult to determine what will be "reasonable" under the circumstances.

One of the criticisms of the HIPAA Final Security Rule since its mandated implementation has been the lack of enforcement. When the HIPAA law was first issued, many organizations were very focused on achieving HIPAA compliance and formed steering committees, hired consultants and tracked compliance. Investigations were handled on a complaint-basis only, which resulted in a small number of complaints given the number of health care providers. In February 2006, HHS issued the Final Rule for HIPAA enforcement, setting the civil monetary penalties and procedures for investigations. Since the Office of Civil Rights (OCR), which is in charge of the enforcement, has tried to work out arrangements between the offender and the victim versus pursue prosecution, there have been few prosecutions under the law. In 2007, Piedmont Hospital in Atlanta was the first to undergo a HIPAA-type audit, which caused concern across health care as to whether the government would be actively auditing health care organizations. To date, this fear has not materialized.

Health Information Technology for Economic and Clinical Health (HITECH) Act

As part of the American Recovery and Reinvestment Act of 2009, Subtitle D of the Health Information Technology for Economic and Clinical Health (HITECH) Act extended the HIPAA security and privacy rules to the business associates of the covered entities. Breach notification requirements were also added to the HITECH Act, requiring the Federal Trade Commission and HHS to issue guidance on the breach notification requirements. Additionally, the organization must account for disclosures when using an electronic health record (EHR). The HITECH Act strengthened the civil monetary penalties by raising the maximum fine from $25,000 under HIPAA to $1.5 million under HITECH. The first civil monetary penalty (CMP) of this magnitude was issued by the HHS Office for Civil Rights to Cignet Health (Cignet) for violating the HIPAA privacy rule in the amount of $4.3 million. OCR issued a notice of proposed determination on October 20, 2010, finding that Cignet violated 41 patients' rights by denying them access to their medical records that were requested between September 2008 and October 2009. These violations resulted in $1.3 million in fines, and Cignet's failure to fully cooperate in the investigation netted it an additional $3 million in fines (Vijayan, 2011).

Federal Information Security Management Act of 2002 (FISMA)

The primary purpose of the Federal Information Security Management Act of 2002 (FISMA), enacted as Title III of the E-Government Act of 2002, is to provide a comprehensive framework for ensuring the effectiveness of security controls over information resources that support federal operations and assets (NIST, 2002). The law also provided funding for NIST to develop the minimum necessary controls required to provide adequate security. The government publishes an annual report card based upon its assessment of compliance with the framework. Multiple bills have been introduced into Congress in recent years to change FISMA from what is perceived to be largely a paper-based compliance reporting mechanism to one that is more reflective of the risks and incorporates the concept of continuous monitoring and standardized methods to measure the security of the systems. FISMA applies not only to the federal government but also to those contracted to perform actions on behalf of the government. The key requirements are shown in Figure 13.1.

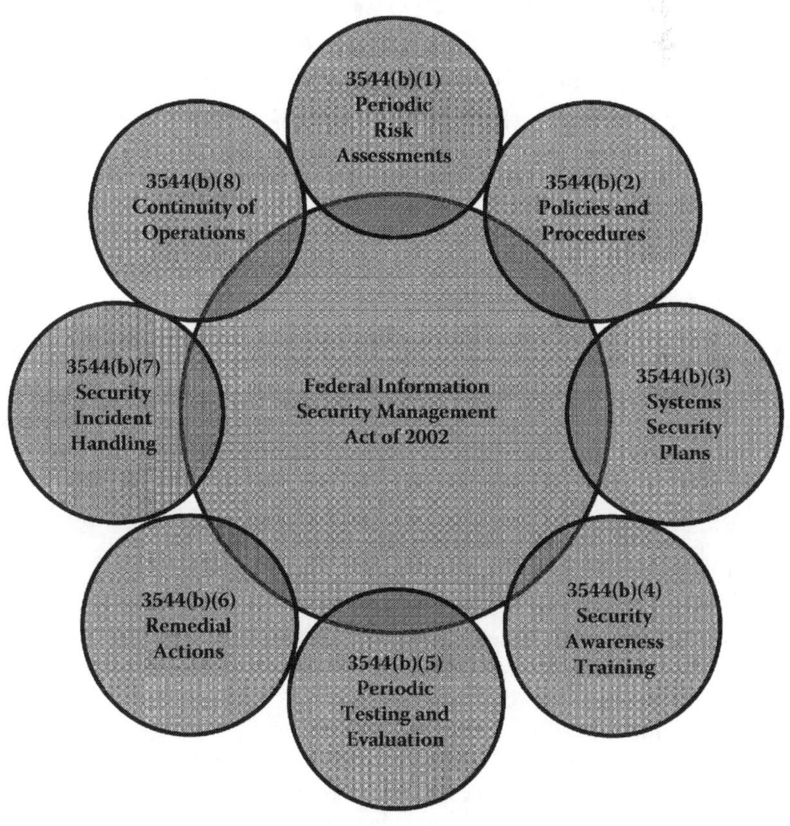

Figure 13.1 Federal Information Security Management System (FISMA) control areas.

Summary

Although the preceding discussion of some of the information security laws is not a comprehensive list, the laws represented provide the majority of the driving legislation in force today, and should give the perception that information security is being addressed by laws and regulations in multiple industries and governments. Different laws permit different causes of action for enforcement of the security rules. For example, until recently with the introduction of the HITECH Act, a HIPAA violation could not be used to sue for a private cause of action. Now state attorney generals have the authority to sue using the HIPAA law as the basis. In January 2010, the Connecticut Attorney General Richard Blumenthal sued Health Net of Connecticut alleging it failed to secure patient information when it lost a hard drive containing personal information on 1.5 million patients and waited 6 months to inform the consumers of the breach.

The laws have come about in large part because information security is not something that businesses will normally invest in just because 'it is the right thing to do.' Without this legislation, it is likely that the security posture of the impacted industries would not be where they are today, albeit there is much work that needs to be done. Smaller organizations often find it difficult to obtain the appropriate resources to comply with the regulations, and larger organizations may become complacent after the initial implementation following a new law's introduction if the appropriate security oversight and governance mechanisms noted in the other chapters are not put in place.

Suggested Reading

1. National Institute of Standards and Technology (NIST). August 2009. Special Publication 800-53 Rev 3: Recommended security controls for federal information systems and organizations. http://csrc.nist.gov/publications/nistpubs/800-53-Rev3/sp800-53-rev3-final_updated-errata_05-01-2010.pdf
2. Moscaritolo, A. 2010. Hacker Albert Gonzalez receives 20 years in prison. *SC Magazine* (March 25). http://www.scmagazineus.com/hacker-albert-gonzalez-receives-20-years-in-prison/article/166571/
3. Federal Information Security Management Act of 2002 (FISMA). November 27, 2002. http://csrc.nist.gov/groups/SMA/fisma/index.html

4. International Organization for Standardization (ISO). ISO/IEC 27001:2005 Information Security Management Systems Requirements. http://www.iso.org/iso/iso_catalogue/catalogue_tc/catalogue_detail.htm?csnumber=42103
5. PCI Data Security Standards Council, https://www.pcisecuritystandards.org/security_standards/documents.php
6. COBIT 4.1, IT Governance Institute, http://www.itgi.org
7. Federal Trade Commission. 1974. The Privacy Act of 1974, as amended. http://www.ftc.gov/foia/privacy_act.shtm, http://www.justice.gov/opcl/privstat.htm
8. Federal Trade Commission. 2002. Eli Lilly settles FTC charges concerning security breach. http://www.ftc.gov/opa/2002/01/elililly.shtm
9. National Institute of Standards and Technology (NIST). June 11, 1987. Computer Security Act of 1987. http://csrc.nist.gov/groups/SMA/ispab/documents/csa_87.txt
10. Securities Exchange Commission. 2002. Public Law 107-204—July 30, 2002 (Sarbanes–Oxley Act). http://www.sec.gov/about/laws/soa2002.pdf
11. HITRUST Central, http://hitrustalliance.net/
12. Vijayan, J. 2011. HIPAA privacy actions seen as warning: HHS hit Cignet with $4.3M penalty; Mass. General settles for $1M. *Computerworld* (February 25). http://www.computerworld.com/s/article/9211359/HIPAA_privacy_actions_seen_as_warning
13. Information Security Forum. Standard of Good Practice. https://www.isfsecuritystandard.com/SOGP07/index.htm
14. National Institute of Standards and Technology (NIST). 2002. H.R.2458-48. Federal Information Security Management Act of 2002. http://csrc.nist.gov/drivers/documents/FISMA-final.pdf

14

Learning from Information Security Incidents

The public seldom forgive twice.

Johann Kaspar Lavater, 1741–1801

The common method of building an information security program is to (1) review the laws and regulations that apply to the particular organization and determine which ones are pertinent, (2) develop a gap analysis or assessment to determine which controls are missing, (3) create an information security policy representing the required laws and regulations, and (4) developing and implementing controls to satisfy the policy that has been developed.

This process may appear somewhat simplified and make it sound as if it is a simple, quick exercise, when in fact this process can occur iteratively over several years to move an organization to a place where it feels comfortable with the security controls. And just as the organization is beginning to feel comfortable, new technologies are introduced, mergers and acquisitions take place, and new breaches are reported in the news.

This chapter focuses on security incidents that have occurred over the past several years. Why are these important? After all, these are other companies' incidents occurring on different infrastructures with different applications and "our security is so much tighter ... especially than our competition's!" Reality is, we can learn so much from what other people have experienced without having to experience it for ourselves. We do not have to drink alcohol to excess, smoke, or use illegal drugs to know that these can be harmful to us. We do not have to run a red light to know that it could be fatal. As children, we are taught not to "jump in a river because someone else told us to." We are human beings with the ability to assimilate information and learn from the mistakes of others. The daily newspaper provides an excellent vehicle to learn from others' mistakes.

While it is useful to read as many technical magazines and books on information security as possible, one does not need to go further than reading *USA Today* to get a very good idea of the security issues that are occurring. There is rarely a single day that goes by that there is not a *USA Today* article that is highlighting an information security concern. Organizations obviously do not want to be the ones that are associated with the security issues; however, organizations should view these newspapers and magazines as opportunities to learn what issues are of interest to the general public to avoid them ever occurring in the first place. Daily scanning of the newspaper for incidents provides a very proactive way to develop the appropriate controls to minimize the occurrence of the events within the organization and keep out of the newspapers.

Verizon also provides an annual report on data breaches that is very interesting and provides much intelligence as to where the breaches appear to be coming from and the types of exploits that are occurring. Since it started in 2004, Verizon has analyzed over 1700 breaches and over 900 million compromised records. According to its latest report, 92% of the breaches were external, 50% utilized some form of hacking, 49% used malware, and 83% of the victims were targets of opportunity (Verizon Business, 2011). It is fascinating to note that 92% of the attacks were not highly difficult, 86% were not even discovered by the organizations themselves but rather by third parties, and 96% of the breaches were avoidable by simple or intermediate controls. This data suggests that organizations that can understand what incidents are occurring and have the appropriate information security governance structures in place to implement and monitor the appropriate controls have the ability to significantly reduce the likelihood these incidents will occur. Implementation of security controls does not necessarily involve large expenditures for technical solutions, but rather the understanding of the controls necessary and ensuring their consistent application. Examining the incidents of other companies can provide insight as to where the people, process, or technology breakdowns may be occurring within the organization. Just because an incident is not yet known does not mean that it has not yet occurred, citing that in 86% of the cases they were discovered by third parties. For the small organization that does not have the scale of business connections a large organization may have, it may have data being stolen without its knowledge and without knowledge that it was the target until someone else in a business relationship reports an issue.

Information security governance depends upon effectively communicating the policies, procedures, and controls throughout the company and ensuring that they are being followed. One method of gaining the attention of others needed to support the policies is to provide them with an understanding that the threats are not theoretical, but rather are real and occur more than they may be aware. Security governance failures at other organizations, as represented by their security incidents, and especially those that share the same vertical industry, size, revenue, and geographic characteristics can provide the incentive necessary to examine how the organization is ensuring that that same situation will not occur there.

Recent Security Incidents

The security incidents that follow can be used as examples within the organization to explain the need for different security controls. These incidents are only a handful of the incidents that are reported each year, each chosen due either by their widespread coverage of the issue or to provide a good cross-section of security issues as a reference.

Texas State Comptroller

Issue: Texas State Comptroller's Office exposes 3.5 million personal records
Company: State of Texas
Date: January 2010; discovered March 31, 2011
Impact: $1.8 million
Lessons learned: The comptroller's office left information including Social Security numbers, driver's license numbers, birth dates, and mailing addresses on their servers unprotected for over a year before it was noticed. Information that was transferred from three other state agencies was stored on the computers unencrypted, which was in violation of the procedures. The comptroller's office subsequently hired consulting firms ($290,000), established a call center for inquiries ($393,000), and spent $1.2 million to notify those whose information

had been exposed (Rashid, 2011). As expected, the security officer and security staff were terminated following the incident.

This was clearly a case where the organization knew the proper actions, however, due to a lack of following the prescribed procedures, the organization was placed at risk. Based upon the fact that the exposure was not discovered until a year later also suggests that there was a lack of ongoing internal review of the security procedures and subsequent security testing that the procedures were being followed. Several years earlier, a Texas attorney general sent a memo to ensure that sensitive databases were protected in reaction to other breaches that were occurring. This illustrates that the reaction to a security incident by issuing a memo may provide the appearance that action is being taken and may satisfy management that they are performing due diligence in being aware of potential threats, but without adequate implementation of information security governance in the form of policies, procedures, and internal review processes, the issuance of a memo by itself is not very effective. The support is admirable and may even be politically motivated versus amounting to increased protection of the organization's resources.

Sony PlayStation Network

Issue: Sony PlayStation Network and Qriocity servers breached
Company: Sony
Date: April 17–19, 2011
Impact: E-mail addresses, birth dates, login, and password details revealed
Lessons learned: Hackers were able to gain access to a Sony server exposing the names, email addresses, birth dates, login/password information, and credit card information for Sony's online gamers. Since information was retrieved about the gamers and their purchasing histories, this opened the possibility of targeted phishing attacks based upon their prior purchasing histories and tastes in music and online video games. Subsequent spear phishing attacks could cause some gamers to give up bank account and Social Security information in the future. Many websites use the e-mail address as the identifier to log into their websites, and end users may use the same password to authenticate for simplicity across these sites, exposure of the e-mail

address information and login information can provide the hackers with the means to access other accounts for fraudulent purposes.

Sony has had to provide several public apologies since taking the site offline. The real damage to the company is the failure of trust in the network as well as the time it takes to investigate the breach while the network is offline. Even though the credit card information may be encrypted as Sony indicated, the cost of lawsuits and public relations most certainly will have long-term effects. One question that should be answered is why did Sony store the credit card information, even encrypted, in the first place. Since other processing companies typically handled processing, there really was no need to store this information. Also, was this the result of a targeted phishing attack against someone with administrative access to the information? If so, what extra controls were in place, in terms of policies, training, separation of IDs, frequency of administrative password changes, logging and monitoring detection, and so forth to mitigate the risk of a targeted attack?

Although the long-term financial impact of the breach is unclear, what is not unclear is that in the minds of 77 million members of the Sony PlayStation Network, Sony failed to protect their information. As Sony offered free credit protection as well as reimbursement of up to $1 million per person for identity restoration costs, legal fees, and lost wages within 12 months of the incident, the final costs of the breach could be substantial (Kitten, 2011).

One could make the assumption that Sony was lax in its application of appropriate security controls. However, it would be difficult to assume that an organization the size of Sony did not allocate extensive resources toward protecting the network. The incident should demonstrate how fragile our networks are. The security staff may close the doors 99.9% of the time, but the one time that someone lets down their guard, that door becomes opened and a public relations nightmare ensues. This incident also suggests that multiple doors need to be in place, whereby there is a system of checks and balances, and roadblocks that make it difficult to penetrate the system undetected. Sony attempted to bring up the system initially in early May 2011, however it was unable to because the hackers had penetrated the systems deeper than Sony originally thought. Clearly, 100% of the end users will not perform what is asked for in the policies 100% of the time, so there must be other controls within the environment such as antivirus filtering, spyware detection, vulnerability scanning, logging and monitoring, baseline configurations, administrative access controls, data classification, restricted file access, help desk procedures, and so forth to mitigate the risk of an elevation of privileges when they are targeted and give up their keys. For example, the end user's car keys may open the car door, but the steering wheel manual locking device prevents the car from going further. The cliché "defense in depth" is very real and security departments need to review multiple strategies to answer, "What if they were able to get through this door, then what?"

Student Loan Social Security Numbers Stolen

Issue: 3.3 million Social Security numbers stolen from student loan program
Company: Education Credit Management
Date: March 2010
Impact: Social Security numbers revealed
Lessons learned: The information was not stolen from external Internet access but rather from information residing on a thumb drive. The company has not revealed whether the information was encrypted, but one can make some assumptions here that the information was not encrypted since the federal loan guarantor is offering 12 months of credit protection to the 3.3 million individuals, representing 5% of the federal student loans (Fox News, 2010). Organizations would not incur that expense if there was no real security breach. As noted in the previous chapter, similar breaches of a portable device occurred in November 2010 when Health Net, Inc., lost an unencrypted hard drive containing Social Security numbers and bank account numbers on 1.5 million people.

The first step in protecting portable media is to ensure that policies are in place as to what can and cannot be copied to flash drives, USB thumb drives, CDs, DVDs, and by whom. Policies in themselves may provide the protections once detected, however, without adequate technical controls, enforcement of the policies may be very difficult at best. Care also must be taken to ensure that information is appropriately classified and segregated for access control to reduce the likelihood that the wrong individuals will have access to the information. Monitoring also needs to be in place to see what information is being copied. When people inside the organization know that monitoring activities are taking place, this can serve as a strong deterrent toward copying information to external media. The copying may not even be malicious, but may increase the risk that the information would be exposed through accidental loss of the drive.

Social Security Numbers Printed on Outside of Envelopes

Issue: Social Security numbers printed on outside of envelopes
Company: CitiGroup
Date: January 2010
Impact: 600,000 CitiGroup customers
Lessons learned: The annual tax documents that were mailed contained the Social Security number on the outside envelope. CitiGroup's communications indicated, "The digits were not identified as a Social Security number, and they were printed at the lower edge of the mailing envelope with other numbers and letters that together resembled a mail routing number." It also stated, "We believe there is little or no risk to our customers. The error has been corrected for all future mailings."

These communications sound almost like a denial that there was a real issue in the public relations announcements, attempting to downplay the fact that Social Security numbers were printed on the envelopes. Was this the result of a genuine mistake? Did CitiGroup use the social security number as part of a series of numbers to control the printing reconciliation process? Was this the idea of one programmer? (Fox Business, 2010) Did this error slip though the peer reviews, and was the design implementation reviewed by information security before rolling this out the door? Or was this result of a quick, subcontract relationship by a small external vendor that was unaware of the security implications? Or was it the result of all of the above?

Printing of Social Security numbers on envelopes is not a new phenomenon. Several state agencies have been guilty of doing the same and in some cases multiple times. For example, the State of Wisconsin repeated the mistake three times in one year, once blaming an external contractor and another time blaming the error on a malfunction of the folding machines permitting the Social Security number to be shown in the envelope window. Obviously a procedure change did not occur by the external contractor to prevent the issue from happening a second time by the same contractor.

People make mistakes and that is a given. However, care must be taken when it comes to critical information, such as identifiers like Social Security numbers, credit card information, driver's license numbers, birth dates, maiden names, and security codes. Most organizations do not have a good handle on where this information resides and where it flows. Security dollars need to be allocated to the highest risk assets to be effective, so why not target these high-value information assets when constructing the security program. In this case, the printing of the Social Security numbers should be traced from the birth (receipt) of the Social Security number, life (storage, printing), to death (no longer needed), and incorporate the appropriate protection and quality assurance strategies to ensure that the information is protected throughout the life cycle.

Valid E-Mail Addresses Exposed

Issue: Issuer of 40 billion e-mails per year is breached
Company: Epsilon
Date: March 2011
Impact: Active e-mail accounts of users of at least 50 major companies disclosed
Lessons learned: Most people have never heard of the company named Epsilon and have not had a prior relationship with them—until this breach was revealed. Epsilon provides e-mail services for many major brands, including Brookstone, Best Buy, Chase, Citi, Capital One, Walgreens, Marriott, and Kroger. Epsilon sends approximately 40 billion e-mails per year for over 2500 clients. The breach at Epsilon provided the active e-mail accounts of customers of these firms, which could be used in future phishing attacks. Not only do the hackers have the valid e-mail account addresses, but now they also have the names of companies where individuals shop, which can lead to clever phishing attacks (Schwartz, 2011).

The companies issued e-mails offering apologies, while also emphatically stating in bold print, "but did not include any customer account or financial information." They also issued further reminders about not revealing personal information in e-mail requests. As in the case of the Sony PlayStation, this breach represents a public relations issue. However, in the Epsilon case the organizations involved simply passed the blame for the breach by stating "we have been informed by Epsilon, a vendor we use to send e-mails …" Fortunately, there was enough foresight to not share customer account and financial information with the e-mail service provider to limit the risk. There is still the risk when engaging a subcontractor that their actions will cause issues for the business. While the full extent of the damage of this may never be known, as it is not clear who accessed the information and what motives they had (was it the work of script kiddies or motivated hackers for subsequent financial gain), these situations illustrate the care that must be taken when subcontracting work to another company. Are they being audited frequently? Are these audits rigorous? What is their process when a security incident occurs? What is the liability of the contracted firm versus the liability of the one contracting? Who determines if credit monitoring must be offered in case of a breach and who pays for it? These items should be discussed and clearly documented well in advance of the breach.

E-mail addresses when compared to transaction-type information, such as credit card information, Social Security numbers, or a health care subscriber ID may be considered to be less of a risk to the organization if disclosed. This breach illustrates that this thinking may be in error, as the knowledge of the e-mail address, combined with the company name, provides the opportunity for hackers to exploit existing account holders through phishing attacks or provide targeted marketing (i.e., phony ads requesting personal account information entry) to obtain account information.

This breach could eclipse the largest breach, which occurred at Heartland Payment Systems where 130 million credit and debit card accounts were impacted, causing Heartland to examine stronger security controls, such as end-to-end encryption, tokenization, and chip technology. Albert Gonzalez was convicted for the Heartland break-in and earned the harshest sentence given to date for this type of crime, 20 years, which resulted in losses exceeding $200 million according to federal prosecutors.

Office Copier Hard Disk Contained Confidential Information

Issue: 409,000 records breached after being left on office copier
Company: Affinity Health Plan
Date: March 2010
Impact: Medical information, Social Security numbers, date of birth released
Lessons learned: Information was left on a company copier that was returned to the leasing company (Rey, 2010). Who knew the copier had a hard drive? Many of the copiers today have the capability to scan and e-mail information, and may have remnants left on the copier. Who has access to this information? How was it configured? Can information from the copier be sent to people outside of the organization, unencrypted? What processes are in place for media sanitization and disposal? What are the procedures to prevent access of the information by the firm servicing the equipment?

The incident illustrates that when new technology is introduced to an organization, the policies need to ensure that information security is involved. This situation could have been avoided if some simple questions about storage and encryption were answered with respect to the copiers. The incident also highlights that information security governance must take a holistic approach to information security and consider information in all forms—written, oral, and electronic—when considering the security controls that may be required.

Advanced Persistent Threat Targets Security Token

Issue: RSA issues letter explaining advanced persistent threat on SecurID tokens
Company: RSA Security
Date: March 2011
Impact: Uneasiness of RSA token security
Lessons learned: Advanced persistent threats (APTs) whereby targets are chosen and a series of ongoing attacks against a specific, targeted organization to achieve a particular objective are on the increase. As opposed to the typical phishing attack whereby millions of potential targets are presented with a phishing e-mail and the hope is that a

small percentage will bite, the advanced persistent attacks attempt to penetrate a particular target over a period of time to gain access to valuable information. In this case, RSA Security's security token was the target. The token generates a random number every 30 to 60 seconds based upon the token ID, time, and a seed value. The algorithm was reverse engineered about 10 years ago, so with the token ID or the seed value, it would be possible to generate the pass code. A pin number also has to be supplied by the end user and the login ID would need to be known, each of which could be obtained through social engineering, thus reducing the strength of this method of authentication. RSA had not yet disclosed what information was accessed through the APT (Kirk, 2011).

Eventually, hackers working to defeat a security control, given enough time and resources, may defeat the control. While it is still unknown as to the impact of the RSA Security breach, it may require that millions of tokens be invalidated and reissued if this is the case. The lesson here is not so much about the viability of the RSA product, but rather that an organization needs to fully understand what software, hardware, and security controls are in place to protect the organization and if there are issues with any of those products. This is not to suggest that an organization discontinues the use of an industry product upon the initial news, especially if there is not a better alternative. However, when these events do occur, it demonstrates that products that were once secure may require some additional controls or require an upgrade or replacement as a result of a breach. This is part of the cost of doing business.

The organization needs to be aware of technology changes and when they become insufficient to protect the information assets. Wired Equivalent Privacy (WEP) was a standard approved in 1999 to protect wireless networks. However, the standard was replaced by the Wi-Fi Protected Access (WPA) standard and WPA2 standards in 2003 and 2004, respectively, after it was determined that the WEP standard was too easily broken into and was no longer sufficient. WEP was one of the vulnerabilities that caused the T.J. Maxx company to be breached. The Payment Card Industry's Data Security Standard (PCI DSS) subsequently required all companies handling credit card data after June 2010 to implement WPA security or better.

Who Will Be Next?

Financial services firms have long understood the need for information security to protect the financial information and provide contingencies for the losses by replacing the funds in the customer accounts and making them whole again. This becomes more difficult in the case of medical information. Once the disclosure has happened and the individual's personal information is disclosed, it is impossible to "put the information back in the bottle." The damage is already done after the disclosure and it is then up to civil penalties to make it right. However, unlike the banking scenario, the confidentiality breach cannot be undone and appear as if it never happened to the consumer.

The disclosures in the preceding examples may or may not result in actual financial damages to the consumer or the company, depending upon to whom the information was provided. In the copier example, the company was able to retrieve some of the hard drives from the leasing company. Had anyone seen the data at the leasing company? If they had, were they the type of individual that would have acted or sold the information? If the disclosure was accidental, odds are that the information would not have fallen into malicious hands unless the attack was initiated in that manner. An organization may misplace a tape, CD, DVD, or USB drive, but unless the whereabouts are clearly known, there is the possibility that it was accidentally discarded in a place that no one would have accessed it (e.g., shredded, thrown out in the garbage). This does not suggest that the follow-on precautions do not need to be observed in investigating the incident, reviewing policies and procedures to reduce the likelihood of the event happening again in the future, and increasing the security controls, but rather that it is possible that no one was harmed by the incident. In today's world where we fear having our identities stolen, organizations need to be on the conservative side of providing the proper assurance after a breach, or the company risks losing the customer base. On the other hand, when an organization thinks that the compromise is the result of a targeted attack (versus an accidental mishandling of information), since the attack is the result of malicious intent, the organization needs to assume that any information disclosed will be used in subsequent activities by the hacker for financial gain.

Unfortunately individuals who have been victims of identity theft may need to spend years to undo the damage done to their credit histories and encounter problems in purchasing new houses, cars, or even applying for credit at the local big-box store. Assuming that each of the individuals affected will tell at least 10 of their friends of the breach, if they know the source of the breach, such as identity theft occurring shortly after the Heartland Payment Systems breach or the Epsilon breach, they may create a loss in revenue for the organizations issuing their credit cards even though they did not directly cause the breach. As noted earlier, the work of the subcontractors is often attributed to the company that hired them. It is doubtful that few people could name the subcontractors that printed viewable social security numbers in the State of Wisconsin example, but surely the State of Wisconsin was viewed as not appropriately managing the process.

So, what organization will be next? Hopefully, lessons can be learned without having to experience them firsthand. It becomes very costly once a breach occurs, not only for the cost of the actual breach in terms of breach notification, credit monitoring, public relations, restoring the infrastructure, and upgrading security controls, but also in legal fees to fend off lawsuits, fines, and increased use of external audits, vulnerability assessments, and penetration testing. After an incident these services are also usually needed very rapidly, and as a result, the costs for the services may be much higher than if the processes were built into and prices negotiated as part of an ongoing information security program.

Every Control Could Result in an Incident

One way to view security controls is, "What could happen if we didn't implement the control?" The answer to this question can be answered by scanning the *USA Today* articles referred to at the beginning of this chapter. A useful exercise would be to construct what the headline would be: "UPSTARTXYZ Company Fails to Protect Millions," "ABCHealth Reveals 500,000 AIDS Patients," or "Local Newspaper buys 123Company Intellectual Property Hard Drive on e-Bay." The information security governance program must focus on the risk of the assets and ensure that the appropriate controls are in place.

Examining the lessons learned on a periodic basis from other companies and subsequently testing the information security policies, results in asking the right questions to examine where there may be new vulnerabilities.

From a cost perspective, reviewing the incidents of other companies is a very cost-effective way to enhance the security governance. What is learned is not only what the incident was, but the press releases also typically indicate what actions the company is planning to provide comfort to the public that the company can again be entrusted with its customers' sensitive information. Information gleaned from these incidents should be regarded as "free research." Someone else has already done their homework after the incident to reduce the risk of the occurrence happening again, and much can be learned from the incident and subsequent resolution.

Suggested Reading

1. National Institute of Standards and Technology (NIST). August 2009. Special Publication 800-53 Rev 3: Recommended security controls for federal information systems and organizations. http://csrc.nist.gov/publications/nistpubs/800-53-Rev3/sp800-53-rev3-final_updated-errata_05-01-2010.pdf
2. IT Governance Institute. 2007. Mapping of NIST SP 800-53 Rev 1 with COBIT 4.1. http://www.itgi.org
3. National Institute of Standards and Technology (NIST). October 2008. An introductory resource guide for implementing the Health Insurance Portability and Accountability Act (HIPAA) Security Rule. http://csrc.nist.gov/publications/nistpubs/800-66-Rev1/SP-800-66-Revision1.pdf
4. Verizon Business. 2011 data breach investigations report. http://verzonbusiness.com
5. Kitten, T. 2011. Sony breach ignites phishing fears. GovInfo Security (April 28). http://www.govinfosecurity.com/articles.php?art_id=3586
6. Jackson, W. 2011. DHS secretary: "Cyberspace is civilian space." Government Computer News (April 27). http://gcn.com/articles/2011/04/27/napolitano-dhs-role-cybersecurity.aspx
7. Rashid, F. Y. 2011. Personal data for 3.5 million Texans exposed on state comptroller server. eWeek.com (April 12). http://www.eweek.com/c/a/Security/Personal-Data-for-35-Million-Texans-Exposed-on-State-Comptroller-Server-196592/
8. Student loan company: Data on 3.3M people stolen. 2010. Foxnews.com (March 26). http://www.foxnews.com/us/2010/03/26/student-loan-company-data-m-people-stolen/

9. Citi apologizes for envelope gaffe. 2010. Foxbusiness.com (February 24). http://www.foxbusiness.com/story/markets/industries/finance/citi-apologizes-social-security-gaffe/
10. Schwartz, M. J. 2011. Epsilon fell to spear-phishing attack. *InformationWeek* (April 11). http://www.informationweek.com/news/security/attacks/229401372
11. Rey, M. 2010. Photocopier fallout: Company notifies 409,000 of data breach. Cbsnews.com (April 26). http://www.cbsnews.com/8301-31727_162-20003449-10391695.html
12. Kirk, J. 2011. After RSA breach, are SecurID tokens in jeopardy? *PC World* (March 18). http://www.pcworld.com/businesscenter/article/222559/after_rsa_breach_are_securid_tokens_in_jeopardy.html

15

17 Ways to Dismantle Information Security Governance Efforts

> Now, what I want is Facts. Teach these boys and girls nothing but Facts. Facts alone are wanted in life. Plant nothing else, and root out everything else.
>
> **Charles Dickens, 1812–1870**

"17 Ways to Dismantle Information Security Governance Efforts." Now that is an odd title for the last chapter in a book that was written to provide insights on ways to successfully provide the proper information security governance for the organization. Why would we want to know how to dismantle information security governance? Why would we want to know how to effectively sink an information security program? After all, when we set out to achieve something, the objective should be to do our best and succeed, right? The answer is simple. Although implementing the guidance provided in the rest of this book will go a long way toward increasing the chances of success, this book cannot possibly cover all the gotchas that will occur during the life cycle of building and maintaining an effective security program.

This chapter provides insights into a few of these gotchas to watch out for, as any one of them has the capability to put the security officer and his or her department in a position where they could lose credibility with their peers and make implementation of the security program difficult at best. Some of these items are covered in more detail in the other chapters, however, it is useful to have a quick list of items to be aware of. This list could be reviewed on a weekly basis, as a checklist or as a quick assessment of activities that need to be performed that may be beyond the daily job of responding to issues, implementing new controls, and managing the information security program. Just as it is prudent to be prepared for incidents that may occur, management should also be prepared for these security management incidents and have a response plan to deal with these situations.

1. Out of Sight, Out of Mind (Lack of Management Visibility)

The security department may address all the information security areas but may lack in having the appropriate management visibility. This could be due to not being high enough in the organizational structure, reporting to an area that does not have much organizational clout, or not taking the right steps to be engaged with the rest of the management team. More often than not, if the security function is not reporting high enough in the management chain, it is usually buried within the information technology (IT) organization. In recent years, the security function has gained visibility due to the plethora of compliance laws and regulations and the instant notoriety of breaches that has gained the attention of many boards of directors.

2. I Can Do It All by Myself

The technical and analytical competence and desire may exist within the information security department, however, there will always be new technologies and new ways of solving problems to consider. It is unrealistic to believe that a company's information security staff can be proficient in all technologies in all platforms. Typically when a new product is introduced, say a vulnerability scanning tool or data loss prevention (DLP) tool, there will need to be external expertise to install, configure, tune, set up the reporting, and provide assistance to interpret the information delivered by the tool. The company's information security department brings its knowledge of the company environment, infrastructure, and requirements to the table. The external vendors can provide knowledge transfer of the product since they are installing and working with the product on a daily basis. Departments purchasing products without purchasing professional installation assistance or subsequent training for their staff are missing an opportunity to enhance the usage of the product and accelerate development of the product's features to meet the business needs.

3. He That Knows Nothing, Doubts Nothing

The security organization should embrace the lifelong learning concept to its fullest by encouraging certifications of the security staff, online webinars, conferences, subscribing to security publications, and purchasing security books in areas they would like to focus on in greater depth. Without this institutional knowledge, it is very easy to accept whatever explanations are provided for not doing something or assuming that the information assets are adequately protected, when they are not. Without the proper knowledge through individual learning the organization may be accepting risks than they should.

4. Honesty Is the Best Policy

Access is compromised and incidents occur even when the best efforts have been applied to managing the security controls. Sometimes there may be gaps in a process due to other higher priority projects, and a termination fails to be processed on time, a system failure renders the security event information management products temporarily unusable, or the network engineer accidently opens a mail relay on a server while applying maintenance. The security department needs to be honest and deal with the issue that has been created to maintain credibility. The organization needs to have multiple defense-in-depth quality assurance and testing processes to be able to detect when critical security processes temporarily fail.

5. Ignorance of the Law Excuses No Man

The organization not only desires that compliance is achieved, but it expects that the security department is recommending controls that satisfy the laws and regulations within the vertical industry in which it operates. The security department should keep abreast of the pertinent current laws and regulations as well as maintain an understanding of what changes to the laws are emerging.

6. Lightning Never Strikes Twice in the Same Place

Lightning never strikes twice in the same place. But, it strikes twice in the same area! In other words, fixing an item on one server in response to a specific audit issue and considering the issue closed is a recipe for disaster. The question should always be asked, "Have I addressed this particular vulnerability wherever the vulnerability may exist?" This includes identifying the current devices that could also have the same vulnerability, ensuring that the vulnerability is not reintroduced (e.g., reinstalling the vulnerability on a desktop/laptop initial image disk because the initial image disk was not upgraded), and providing for future testing of the vulnerability. Lightning will strike, just on a different device if we do not address the vulnerability for all devices. Likewise, if it is noticed that individuals are inadvertently responding to phishing e-mails, odds are that providing training solely to that set of users will not solve the problem for the organization.

7. Live and Learn

Learn from the security mistakes of other companies. Several of these incidents and the types of learning that may be achieved are highlighted in the chapter on security incidents. Failure to learn means that these will become repeatable. Repeating the mistakes takes valuable time away from other resources that could be used to automate more processes and reduce costs. Rather than waiting to experience the same issues that other companies have experienced the hard way, proactively being aware of current news events can cause the organization to implement controls to avoid the same issue at much less cost.

8. Look after Number 1

Each security organization should invest a fair amount of time in determining which information is the most important to project, or the number 1. No organization has unlimited resources and data classification can serve to identify the information that is important to the business, identify the location, and identify the correct ownership.

When determining the risk assessment, the value of the information to the enterprise should be considered.

9. Look before You Leap

Security technology needs to be evaluated for where it fits into the security architecture and the problem that it will solve. Researching external market intelligence companies, such as Gartner, Forrester, and Burton Group, can provide insights as to where these products are positioned and where they stand in relation to other similar products. The long-term costs need to be evaluated. For example, an identity management system may cost 60% of a competing product, however, it may require extensive customization to provide automation of the provisioning process, driving the subsequent cost to two to three times that of a competing product. This can cause the loss of credibility with management, as the project must be extended for multiple phases due to unforeseen customization.

10. Many Hands Make Light Work

The security department is a small but critical piece toward implementing an effective security program. It is important to identify which skills are contained within information security and which skills are resident outside the department. For example, the corporate communications or marketing departments may have individuals who are skilled in putting together online training. This can ease the burden of the security department, as they can deliver the content desired and have the corporate communications department put together the packaging and tracking mechanisms to complete the training. Similarly, the internal audit department can provide expertise and potentially staff to assist with the external audits. The help desk staff could be trained to reset passwords after lockout, or provide first-level security support. Individual security representatives could be established in each department to coordinate access requests or deliver answers to security questions that the team may have. Business managers could be selected as champions for the security efforts in the different offices. In short, the security department can be much more effective by leveraging the capabilities and personnel within the rest of the organization.

11. Practice What You Preach

It is probably obvious that security departments are not above the law in the execution of daily tasks. However, what if the intentions are good but the results end up representing a violation of policy? For example, disabling or bypassing some of the security features to perform an internal penetration test or vulnerability assessment might produce the unintended consequences of opening the environment to viruses or internal and external exploits. Or, suppose an effort to review the strength of passwords across the organization involved the use of a password-cracking tool, revealing the actual passwords to login accounts? In this case, a control that was not to be shared and was to be kept secret by the company users was now revealed to the security team. Suppose those secrets revealed the passwords of executives and they were concerned that the security team or other information technology individuals now had access to their personal data, such as salary information in the human resources system, or their e-mail messages. This could be very detrimental to the security leader's job situation. The password vulnerability scan may also reveal that the executive had not lived up to his or her vocal support of the security program, and had not followed the rules by making an easy to guess password, such as password, spouses name, or favorite sports team.

To avoid this situation from happening, the security leader could discuss the proposed test in advance with the appropriate and responsible executives and obtain their approval before proceeding. This protects the security leader by having obtained the support up front and would avoid embarrassment. It could be argued that the executives are also responsible for complying with the rules, just like everyone else. Although this is true, this is the where judgment must be exercised by asking the question, "What do I expect to gain out of this approach?" If the objective is to embarrass some key executives who are necessary to support the security program, then do not pursue approval from a higher executive first and also proceed while simultaneously preparing the resume. If on the other hand, the objective is to strengthen the password controls within the entire organization, then soliciting the permission up front is a wiser move. Subsequent individual discussions with the executives failing to comply with the rule can then be held after a senior executive has authorized the testing.

12. Prevention Is Better Than Cure

When choosing between preventive, detective, or corrective controls, preventive controls intuitively win out. This is very logical; however, many organizations will spend enormous resources on detection tools or spend much time responding to audit findings with corrective action plans, and less on people, processes, or technology to stop the problem in the first place. For example, policies and training can be put in place to inform end users that they are not to access personal e-mail from work, as this may increase the potential for malware to enter the organization. Monitoring tools for website access can be monitored and reporting of violations can occur as a detective control and subsequently corrective procedure. Viewing this same issue from a preventive viewpoint, the e-mail site could simply be blocked for all company users, with the restriction lifted for those showing justification for the need for using the site.

13. There Is More Than One Way to Skin a Cat

Not performing security according to best practices? Blasphemy! Lower the standards? Ridiculous! Well, not really. Many times there is a tendency of security professionals, most of whom are very detail oriented, to want to dot every i and cross every t on every security control. After all, who doesn't want to implement a best practice in their profession? The reality is that security controls need to incorporate the concept of risk, just as the business makes decisions about new product launches, services to be provided, and markets to go into based upon business risk. There are typically more potential business opportunities than a business can be engaged in at one time without losing focus and spreading itself too thin. The same is true with security initiatives; these must be prioritized to support the business priorities versus being prioritized to meet the implementation of a best practices model, assuming one did exist. Understanding the business context of the security control is essential to being able to appropriately prioritize the initiative.

One could proceed down the ISO 27001 path, the COBIT path, or any other framework, but at some point, if these initiatives did not involve the business areas in their development, this most likely will be met with resistance. This is especially true if the organization is not required to meet the regulation (i.e., as part of an International Organization for Standardization [ISO] certification).

The security department needs to be flexible and work within the confines of the business while providing the appropriate level of information asset protection.

14. When In Rome, Do as the Romans Do

At the end of the day, the business executives own the decision as to how much risk should be accepted by the organization. The security leader has a responsibility to educate the senior executive on what "accepting the risk" means. This requires the security leader to translate the risk into nontechnical, business terms, which communicate that the security area is not acting as a department with the paranoid switch being in the always-on position, but truly understands what the impact and probability of the threat will mean to the business.

If also the security leader has taken the time to explain the risk, and the business executive is willing to accept it, it may still be beneficial to reach this consensus across the business leaders. For example, the human resources business owner of an employee benefits application may be willing to accept the risk of lower authentication standards, but the chief financial officer (CFO) may have a different viewpoint of the exposure. However the risks are articulated, the security leader should have the business leader sign off on the results of the risk assessment related to the situation and formally provide the business justification and authorization to accept the risk. Amazingly, this process tends to make individuals more accountable and less willing to accept the risk. Typically, the only risks that end up being accepted are those risks that would cause major business disruptions or would be too costly to mitigate.

Security leader should not view this scenario as the ability to abdicate the decision to the business leaders. The reality is that security leaders must act as if they own the decision and therefore would perform their due diligence to ensure that the decision has considered all the relevant variables to making the best decision. In the end, security officers must then own the decision as well, and as new information changes the risk profile of the decision, be diligent in ensuring that executives are informed to make a possible change in direction. Taking this approach promotes a business partnership between security officers and executives and has the impact that the next time there is a significant issue, security officers are more likely to be seen as credible in communicating the risks and discerning which ones are more critical.

15. When the Cat's Away, the Mice Will Play

Integrity is doing the right thing when no one is watching. Most individuals inside an organization will strive to do the right thing; others will do the right thing as long as someone's back is not turned. This is why monitoring becomes important and reporting on accountability. If end users are habitually appearing on information security violation reports, then these need to be reported to management for training and corrective action. The individual managers need to be made accountable for their staff and have vested ownership in their success. For example, periodic recertification of the end users access engages managers to ensure that they know what information their staff needs. The managers provide the re-review of the access and attestation that the end users need the access. The managers need to be held responsible for ensuring that their staffs are operating in a secure manner. Most end users are not malicious, but they may try to circumvent security controls when met with pressing deadlines or if they are in disagreement with the security procedures.

16. You Win Some, You Lose Some

Security controls establish barriers to entry and reduce the risk of loss due to disclosure, destruction or loss of information, or the unavailability of information. By implementing the appropriate security policies and procedures, and managing the governance of these implementations, the risk of loss should be minimal. However, the organization must be prepared to handle the losses that do occur, so that the subsequent financial impact is minimal. This requires appropriate logging and monitoring, establishment of computer incident response teams (CIRTs), redundant failover servers if high availability is needed, backup and recovery capabilities (business continuity and disaster recovery planning), off-site processing, and so forth. In other words, effective security governance can greatly reduce the risk, but it cannot eliminate it. This message should also be communicated well before an incident occurs, so that the expectation is not that all of the security investments will completely eliminate the risk, no matter how effective the control may be. DNA testing, for example, is 99.99% accurate; however this assumes that the correct evidence chain of custody was managed throughout the process and documentation was correct.

17. Bad News Travels Fast

When there is a security breach, the incident must be responded to very quickly. This sounds like saying "What goes up must come down." The reality is that in many organizations, the security incident response procedures are outdated, individuals have changed positions, the reporting requirements are unknown, incidents are not clearly defined, or there has not been a major incident in a while, which ensures that the process is being followed and improved on a regular basis. Therefore, sometimes the security leader may be out of the loop in responding to the incident, as the technical staff handles it.

With the lack of documentation and training for incident response, it may be unclear who is actually in charge and responsible for ensuring that the incident is followed up on appropriately. It is important the security leader and his department be viewed as being front and center with respect to the security issue. Sometimes the scope or the potential damage possible by an incident is not immediately known. For example, the loss of a hard drive, memory stick, or a laptop may be inconsequential to an organization if it does not contain financial or protected health information (PHI). However, it may contain these items or the Social Security numbers useful to identity thieves or a business strategy that would be useful to a competitor. The security leader needs to be able to exercise good judgment early in the process to ascertain the potential impact to the business. There will be many times when the security leader will have to rely on the facts provided by the information technology staff, the security department, and the business users to determine the actions required.

The security leader needs to have excellent facilitation, oral communication, and active listening skills to work through a security issue. The ability to remain calm, permit the technical analysis to occur without requesting updates so frequent that the technical staff cannot do the investigation, and the ability to know who within the organization is needed to resolve the problem are key determinants of how quickly and accurately the problem will be resolved.

The corporate communications department should have preestablished procedures for interacting with the media after an incident. Individuals within the company should also be instructed o never talk with the media, as they could provide misleading information that is taken out of context. Consider the 2010 multiple recalls by Toyota to fix a problem with unintended acceleration of the vehicles. Toyota was not only criticized for withholding the initial knowledge that there was a problem, but also had to issue multiple recalls and issued premature statements that the problem was fixed. Security incidents need to be reported soon after the facts confirm that there is a suspected problem, followed by comments to the effect that the company takes the issue very seriously and is working to resolve the problem.

Final Thoughts

As we are in the final chapter of this book, it is only appropriate to repeat the definition of information security governance stated in the first chapter:

> Information Security Governance is a subset of enterprise governance that provides strategic direction, ensures objectives are achieved, manages risk appropriately, uses organizational resources responsibly, and monitors the success or failure of the information security programme.

As we went through this journey together, building rock after rock, we explored what was required to build the information security strategy, gain the support of the executives, understand the risks facing the organization, implement policies to govern the management intentions, utilize control frameworks and standards to provide structure and a roadmap; implement controls to comply with laws and regulations; audit the controls to ensure their constant effectiveness and sufficiency; communicate with all levels of the organization to reinforce the security message; monitor the incidents of others to avoid making the same mistakes; and monitor the effectiveness through tracking, remediation, and reporting mechanisms. Each of the rocks that were added one by one in building the foundation for information security governance were built with a centrally managed information security management structure and supporting information security council with defined visions, missions, goals, and responsibilities.

Information security as a profession offers an ever-changing environment, with new threats, technological advances, and consumers and business process owners demanding more access to information in more places. The governance concepts presented in this book will still be relevant for years to come, even though the specific technology may change. Information security leadership, by management and technical security professionals, is necessary to stay current with the emerging business drivers. Technology is always changing and fades from our memory, such as removing perforated leader strips from continuous-feed paper printouts, calculator watches, using a public phone booth, looking up numbers in a telephone book, watching VCRs or laser discs, using carbon copy paper, or going to an arcade to play video games (Raphael, 2009). While the technology may change, the functionality offered by the previous technology does not go away. We still watch movies, albeit via DVDs; we look up phone numbers on an online search engine or mobile phone application; we still view documents in printed form, produced by higher speed laser or inkjet single-sheet feed printers or scanners. And with worldwide mobile users increasing from 500 mobile subscriptions to over 5 billion from the year 2000 to 2011, and Internet users increasing sevenfold from 250 million to over 2 billion in the same time period (MercoPress, 2011), it is easy to see where the applications and need to have information at our fingertips are headed. Public phone booths, busy signals, and long-distance charges for the most part are a thing of the past with a cell phone and Internet data plan in every pocket. We still communicate—enhanced by video webcams, phone cameras, texting, and voice-to-text conversions. As security professionals, we need to be able to secure the platforms, the communications between them, and protect the data at rest and in transit across whatever mechanism may be storing the information. As we venture into virtualization, cloud computing, smartphones, tablet computing, Web 2.0, continuous security monitoring, tackling advanced persistent threats, or whatever the next security focus is for our organization, the foundation that was built in the preceding chapters will be able to be leveraged to guide the appropriate solution, without having to radically change the underlying governance foundation. This is the true essence of building information security governance to meet the objectives of the organization.

Suggested Reading

1. Two billion Internet users worldwide and mobile phone users increases. 2011. *MercoPress* (January 27). http://en.mercopress.com/2011/01/27/two-billion-internet-users-worldwide-and-mobile-phone-users-increases
2. Raphael, JR. 2009. Obsolete technology: 40 big losers. *PC World* (August 12). http://www.pcworld.com/article/169863-2/obsolete_technology_40_big_losers.html

Index

H

I